Biology

Class 12 CBSE Board

10 Year-wise

(2013-2022) SOLVED PAPERS

Powered with Concept Notes

Corporate Office

DISHA PUBLICATION
45, 2nd Floor, Maharishi Dayanand Marg,
Corner Market, Malviya Nagar, New Delhi - 110017
Tel : 49842349 / 49842350

By:
Rashi Chauhan

Typeset by Disha DTP Team

Write to us at **feedback_disha@aiets.co.in**

CONTENTS

Chapterwise Division of Questions

The table below presents the chapter-wise division of the questions of the 17 papers. So this book can be put to dual usage-yearwise as well as chapter-wise. To find questions of a chapter just follow the question numbers in its row against the 17 papers. This table also depicts the Trend Analysis of 2022-2013 papers.

Chapter Number	Chapter Name	Year of Examination						
		2022		2021	2020		2019	
		Term-I	Term-II	Exam not held in 2021 due to Covid-19 pandemic	All India	Delhi	All India	Delhi
1.	Reproduction in Organisms	—	—		1	1	5	
2.	Sexual Reproduction in Flowering plants	1, 2, 3, 4, 5, 6, 10, 11, 30, 34, 35	—		3, 14, 15	6, 13, 25	6, 13, 25 (OR)	3 & (OR), 2, 13, 27
3.	Human Reproduction	7, 8, 9, 27, 29, 33, 49, 50, 51, 52, 53, 54	—		10, 24, 27(OR)	13(OR), 25(OR)	13, & OR	18, 27(OR)
4.	Reproductive Health	25, 26, 31, 32			27	17	25	12
5.	Principles of Inheritance and Variation	12, 13, 14, 15, 16, 17, 28. 37, 38, 39, 40, 41, 48, 55, 56, 57	—		13, & OR	14, 26	1, 15 & OR, 26	5, 7, 10
6.	Molecular Basis of Inheritance	18, 19, 20, 21, 22, 23, 24, 36, 42, 43, 44, 45, 46, 47, 58, 59, 60	—		2, 12, 26	2, 7, 15, 26 (OR)	2, 16 & OR, 26 (OR)	1, 22 & OR, 25
7.	Evolution	–	–		8, 26(OR)	3, 16	7, 17	15
8.	Human Health and Disease	—	2		5, 7, 9	8, 22, 23	8, & OR	9(OR), 17 & OR, 20
9.	Strategies for Enhancement in Food Production	—	—		4, 11, 20 & OR	4, 9, 18	9, 19	8, 9, 20
10.	Microbes in Human welfare	—	1(OR), 4, 5, 12		4(OR), 6, & OR, 17	4(OR), 9(OR), 21	4, & OR, 18, 20	2, 16
11.	Biotechnology: Principles and Processes	—	8(OR)		18, 19	10, 27(OR)	10, 21	14, 21, 23
12.	Biotechnology and its Application	—	11, 13(OR)		1, 23	19, 27	11, 22	4 & (OR)
13.	Organisms and Populations	—	6, 7		21, 22	5(OR),11, 24	3(OR), 27	6, 10 & OR
14.	Ecosystem	—	—		25	12,20	12, 27(OR)	24, 26
15.	Biodiversity and Conservation	—	3(OR), 9, 10		16	20 (OR)	12 (OR), 23	26 (OR)
16.	Environmental issues	—	—		25(OR)	5	3, 24	
	Total no. of Questions	**60**	**13**		**35**	**35**	**37**	**35**

Chapterwise Division of Questions

Chapter Number	Chapter Name	Year of Examination		
		2018	2017	
		All India	All India	Delhi
1.	Reproduction in Organisms	19	11	
2.	Sexual Reproduction in Flowering plants	26	6,24	6, 11, 24
3.	Human Reproduction	20, 21, 26(OR)	2, 12, 24(OR)	23
4.	Reproductive Health		1	
5.	Principles of Inheritance and Variation	14, 24	13, 25	1, 12
6.	Molecular Basis of Inheritance	2, 10 (OR), 22, 24(OR)	7, 14	7, 13, 26, &OR
7.	Evolution	3, 10, 11	3, 7(OR), 15, 25(OR)	2,14
8.	Human Health and Disease	1, 5, 9	4, 16	8,15 &OR
9.	Strategies for Enhancement in Food Production	8, 15	8, 17	3,16
10.	Microbes in Human welfare	7, 16	9, 18	9,17
11.	Biotechnology: Principles and Processes	17, 18	5, 19, 20	18,19
12.	Biotechnology and its Application	12	21	4,20
13.	Organisms and Populations	25	26	21,25
14.	Ecosystem	25(OR)	26(OR)	22,25(OR)
15.	Biodiversity and Conservation	13	22, & OR	10(OR)
16.	Environmental issues	6, 13 (OR), 23	10, 23	5, 10
	Total no. of Questions	**30**	**31**	**30**

Chapterwise Division of Questions

Chapter Number	Chapter Name	Year of Examination			
		2016		2015	
		All India	Delhi	All India	Delhi
1.	Reproduction in Organisms	1, 6	6	1, 6	7
2.	Sexual Reproduction in Flowering plants	11, 24(OR)	2, 24	11, 24	11, 24
3.	Human Reproduction	24	11, 24(OR)	24(OR)	12, 24 (OR)
4.	Reproductive Health	11(OR), 23	23	23	6
5.	Principles of Inheritance and Variation	12	4, 12, 25	12, 25	1, 13, 25
6.	Molecular Basis of Inheritance	7, 13, 25 & OR	9, 21, 25 (OR)	2, 25 (OR)	2,14,21,25(or)
7.	Evolution	5, 14	1, 13	7, 14	3, 15
8.	Human Health and Disease	8, 15	10, 20	3, 15	4, 16
9.	Strategies for Enhancement in Food Production	2, 16	3, 10 (OR), 14	8, 16	8, 17, 26(OR)
10.	Microbes in Human welfare	9, 17	8, 22	9, 17	9, 18, 22(OR)
11.	Biotechnology: Principles and Processes	3, 18, 19	5, 15	18	5, 19, 20
12.	Biotechnology and its Application	20	16, 18	4, 19, 20	
13.	Organisms and Populations	21, 26	17, 26(OR)	10, 21, 26	10, 26
14.	Ecosystem	22, 26(OR)	19	26(OR)	10 (OR)
15.	Biodiversity and Conservation	10(OR)	7,26		22
16.	Environmental issues	4, 10	19(OR)	5, 22	23
	Total no. of Questions	**31**	**31**	**28**	**31**

Chapterwise Division of Questions

Chapter Number	Chapter Name	Year of Examination			
		2014		2013	
		All India	Delhi	All India	Delhi
1.	Reproduction in Organisms	1	1, 9, 28	1	
2.	Sexual Reproduction in Flowering plants	19 & OR, 28 (OR)	19	9,27,28	1,9
3.	Human Reproduction	9	20, 22, 28 (OR)	19, 28 (OR), 29 (OR)	10, 19, 28
4.	Reproductive Health	20, 28		19 (OR)	28 (OR)
5.	Principles of Inheritance and Variation	2, 4, 10, 11, 12 & OR, 21, 22	10, 11, 21 & OR	20	3, 11, 21, 30
6.	Molecular Basis of Inheritance	29 & OR	11 (OR), 29	4, 21, 29	22
7.	Evolution	27	29 (OR)	11, 22	4, 7
8.	Human Health and Disease	3, 13, 14, 23	3, 8	2, 12, & OR, 30	2, 12, 29
9.	Strategies for Enhancement in Food Production	30, & OR	2, 13, 23, 24, 30	3	5, 23, 29 (OR)
10.	Microbes in Human welfare	8		13, 23	24
11.	Biotechnology: Principles and Processes	6, 15, 16, 25	4, 14	14, 15	6, 13, 15 & OR, 25
12.	Biotechnology and its Application	5	15, 18, 25, 26	16, 24	14
13.	Organisms and Populations	7, 17, 18	6, 16		18
14.	Ecosystem	26	5, 17	5, 6, 18, 25, 26	8, 17, 26
15.	Biodiversity and Conservation		7, 27	8, 17	7
16.	Environmental issues		8	7	16, 26(OR)
	Total no. of Questions	**34**	**34**	**33**	**33**

All India 2022

CBSE Board Solved Paper Term-II

Time Allowed : 2 Hours *Maximum Marks : 35*

General Instructions:

(i) This question paper contains **13** questions. All questions are compulsory.

(ii) This question paper has **three** Sections – Section **A, B** and **C**.

(iii) Section-**A** has **6** questions of **2** marks each, Section-**B** has **6** questions of **3** marks each, and Section-**C** has a case based question of **5** marks.

(iv) There is no overall choice. However, internal choices have been provided in some questions. A candidate has to attempt **only one** of the alternative in such questions.

(v) Wherever necessory, neat and properly labelled diagrams should be drawn.

SECTION - A

1. State the impact of constant mechanical agitation and pumping of air in the aeration tank on the sewage during the biological treatment.

OR

(a) Cattle excreta is important source for producing a domestic fuel. Name the fuel and write its main components.

(b) Write the biological process that is responsible for the production of this fuel.

2. Mention the two types of acquired immune response present in our body. Give one major role of each.

3. The histogram given below representing the data for annual shark harvest in the great barrier reef / coral reed located on the east coast of Queensland, Australia, Study the histogram and answer the questions that follow.

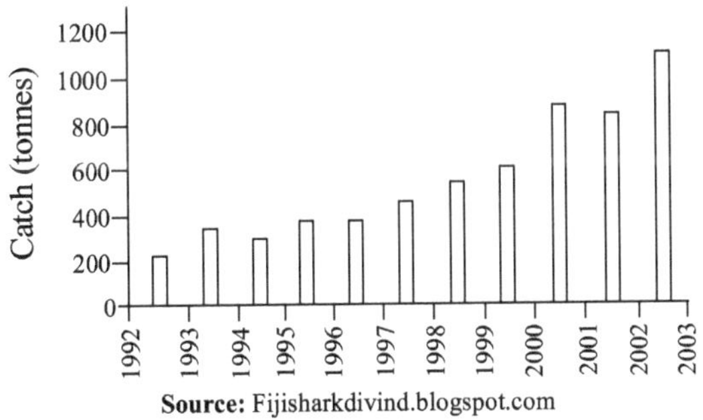

Source: Fijisharkdivind.blogspot.com

(a) Write your interpretation of the data given.

(b) Write the impact on the biodiversity of the area that you can interpret on the basis of given data.

OR

"Stability of community depends upon its species richness." How did David Tilman show this experimentally?

4. Name the source organism (scientific name) that produces statins. Mention its use in medical field and how does it act.

5. (a) Give an example of viral biocontrol agent.

(b) Why are they considered to be desirable when an ecologically sensitive area is being treated?

6. Study the graph given below, showing the population growth curves 'A' and 'B' respectively. Answer the following questions:

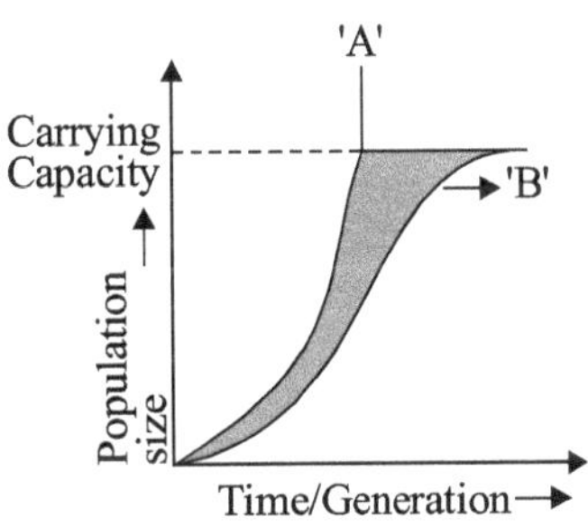

(a) What is 'Carrying Capacity' in respect of Curve 'B' indicative of?

(b) Mention the action of possible natural forces that could have lead to curve 'B'.

SECTION - B

7. (a) What does the equation dN/dt = rN express in terms of population growth?

(b) Write the significance of 'r' in a population survey.

8. (i) State the role of a selectable marker in r-DNA technology.
(ii) Name one such selectable marker which is considered to be useul for *E.coli.*
(iii) Give one reason why is it considered to be a useful marker.

OR

What are plasmids? How are they different from cloning vectors? Give one example each for a viral and a bacterial cloning vector.

9. Explain giving reason the action plan followed by organic farmers that support their key belief "biodiversity furthers health of crop lands."

10. Bio-diversification of life started to occur almost 3 billion years ago. Since then new species have been evolving and then disappearing en masse from earth.
(a) How many episodes of mass extinctions of species have already taken place and which one is in progress in the current era?
(b) How is current episode in progress different from the previous episodes and why? Explain.

11. (i) Name three molecular diagnostic techniques for diagnosis of a disease.
(ii) List three advantages of molecular diagnostic techniques over conventional method of diagnosis.

12. Enumerate the main sources of bio-fertilisers giving one example of each.

SECTION - C

13. To save the crop plant from the attack of various insect pests the biotechnologists have developed many pest resistant plants. One such example is Bt corn plant. In this plant 'cry' genes were introduced which produces cry-proteins in the plant that has toxic effect on the pest (corn borer). Thus saves the corn plant from the attack of the corn borer. An experimental field study was conducted by the scientists to see the efficacy of the Bt corn plant against the attack of corn borers. Three different species of corn borers namely 'A', 'B', 'C' were collected and were independently fed on non Bt corn plants and Bt corn plants separately for the same period. The extent of the damage caused to the leaf area of the plant was observed and noted down. With the help of the observations and data collected the following bar graph was plotted. Study the graph and answer the questions that follow.

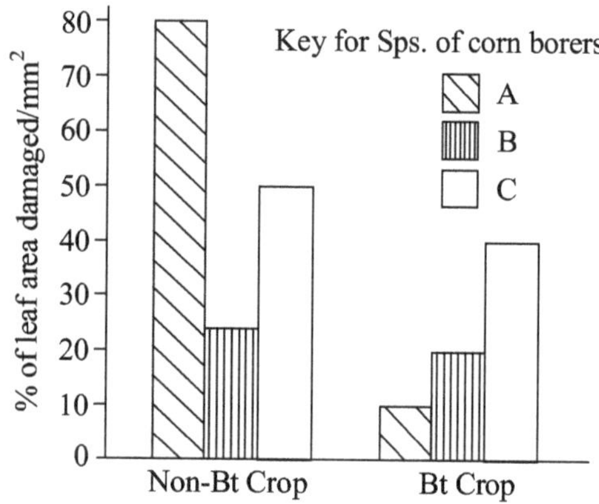

(i) Identify the species of the corn borer that was most successfully controlled by Bt corn plant. Give appropriate reason for your inference.
(ii) Identify the species of the corn borers which shows least impact of toxin produced by Bt genes.
(iii) What would be your advise as a Scientist, to the farmers for growing this particular Bt corn variety in the area which is infested by species-'B' of corn borers?
(iv) Name one Bt gene that encodes protein in corn plants to control corn borers.

OR

A gene was identified in a fungus by a research worker in a lab which was considered to be of a great importance in the field of agriculture. As a student of biotechnolgy, write the steps you would suggest to (i) Isolate this gene of interest from the fungus and (ii) amplify this gene for further experimentation and research.

Solutions

1. The primary effluent is passed into large aeration tanks, where it is constantly agitated mechanically and air is pumped into it. This allows vigorous growth of useful aerobic microbes into flocs (masses of bacteria associated with fungal filaments to form mesh like structures). While growing, these microbes consume the major part of the organic matter in the effluent. This significantly reduces the BOD (biochemical oxygen demand) of the effluent. **[2 Marks]**

OR

(a) The excreta of cattle, commonly called gobar, is rich in these bacteria. Dung can be used for generation of biogas, commonly called **gobar gas.** **[1 Mark]**

(b) Some bacteria, which grow anaerobically, digest the bacteria and the fungi in the sludge. During this digestion, bacteria produce a mixture of gases such as methane, hydrogen sulphide and carbon dioxide. These gases form biogas and can be used as a source of energy as it is inflammable. **[1 Mark]**

Biochemical oxygen demand (BOD):
BOD is defined as the amount of oxygen consumed by bacteria and other micro-organisms while they decompose organic matter under aerobic conditions at a specified temperature.

2. The two type of acquired immune response present in human body are-
(a) Humoral immune response
(b) Cell- mediated immunity **[1 Mark]**
Major roles are:
(i) Humoral immune response protects against extracellular virus and bacteria. **[½ Mark]**
(ii) Cell- mediated immunity protects against virus, fungi and other intracellular bacterial pathogens. **[½ Mark]**

3. (a) The annual catching data of shark is gradually increases and reached upto 1200 tonnes in a year of 2003. **[1 Mark]**
(b) Healthy shark populations may aid the recovery of coral reefs. But if shark populations in a coral reef system are severely reduced due to commercial fishing, herbivorous fish that graze on algae may also decline. Fewer herbivorous fish keep algae growth in check, which in turn, harms coral reefs. **[1 Mark]**

OR

A stable community should not show too much variation in productivity from year to year; it must be either resistant or resilient to occasional disturbances, and it must also be resistant to invasions by alien species. May be these attributes are linked to species richness in a community, but David Tilman's long-term ecosystem experiments using outdoor plots provide some tentative answers. Tilman found that plots with more species showed less year to-year variation in total biomass. He also showed that in his experiments, increased diversity contributed to higher productivity. The rich biodiversity is not only essential for ecosystem health but imperative for the very survival of the human race on this planet. **[2 Marks]**

4. Statins produced by the yeast ***Monascus purpureus.*** **[1 Mark]**
Statins have been commercialised as **blood cholesterol lowering agents**. It acts by competitively inhibiting the enzyme responsible for synthesis of cholesterol. **[1 Mark]**

Statins are a group of medicines that can help lower the level of Law-density lipoprotein (LDL) cholesterol in the blood. LDL cholesterol in often referred to as "bad cholesterol" and statins reduce the production of it inside the liver.

5. (a) **Baculoviruses** is the one of the best example of viral biocontrol agent. **[½ Mark]**
(b) Baculoviruses showed no negative impacts on plants, mammals, birds, fish or non-target insects. This is especially desirable when beneficial insects are being conserved to aid in the overall integrated pest management (IPM) programme, or when an ecologically sensitive area is being treated. **[1½ Marks]**

6. (a) In logistic growth, a population's per capita growth rate gets smaller and smaller as population size approaches a maximum imposed by limited resources in the environment, known as the carrying capacity (K).
$dN/dt = rN(K - N/K)$ **[1 Mark]**
(b)
- Resources for growth for most animal populations are finite and become limiting sooner or later, the logistic growth model is considered a more realistic one.
- The 'fittest' individual will survive and reproduce.
- In nature, a given habitat has enough resources to support a maximum possible number, beyond which no further growth is possible. **[1 Mark]**

7. (a) The equation $dN/dt = rN$ express for Exponential growth. **[1 Mark]**
(b) The r in this equation is called the 'intrinsic rate of natural increase' and is a very important parameter chosen for assessing the impacts of any biotic or abiotic factor on population growth. **[2 Marks]**

8. (i) A selectable marker helps in identifying and eliminating non-transformants and selectively permitting the growth of the transformants. **[1 Mark]**
(ii) The genes encoding resistance to antibiotics such as ampicillin, chloramphenicol, tetracycline or kanamycin, etc., are considered useful selectable markers for E. coli. **[1 Mark]**
(iii) The selectable markers are the gene substances that are injected into the cell so that they can offer resistance to the action of the antibiotics. **[1 Mark]**

OR

Plasmids are autonomously replicating circular extra – chromosomal DNA, present only in prokaryotic organisms. **[1 Mark]**
Plasmids can able to replicate within bacterial cells independent of the control of chromosomal DNA. While cloning vector is a small piece of DNA, taken from any organism into which a foreign DNA fragment can be inserted for cloning purposes. **[1 Mark]**
The example of viral cloning vector is Bacteriophage. **[½ Mark]**
The example of bacterial cloning vector is *E.coli*. **[½ Mark]**

9. Yes, the organic farmer indeed believes that biodiversity furthers health.

- An **organic farmer** depends on composting and using absolutely natural ingredients in conducting his cultivation.
- There is no use of pesticides or chemicals and crop cultivation is done in an all-natural environment.
- Farmer uses biodiversity to counter the problems of cultivation and by doing so he believes that this helps in overall health improvement.
- As no chemical is used and only **natural produce is utilized** this indeed improves the health of all. **[3 Marks]**

Organic farming can be defined as "an integrated farming system that strives for sustainability, the enhancement of soil fertility and biological diversity. It increased species richness by about 30%.

10. (a) During the long period (> 3 billion years) since the origin and diversification of life on earth, there were five episodes of mass extinction of species.
Presently, 12 per cent of all bird species, 23 per cent of all mammal species, 32 per cent of all amphibian species and 31per cent of all gymnosperm species in the world face the threat of extinction. **[1½ Marks]**

(b) The difference is in the rates between the current episode and the previous episode; the current species extinction rates are estimated to be 100 to 1,000 times faster than in the pre-human times and our activities are responsible for the faster rates. Ecologists warn that if the present trends continue, nearly half of all the species on earth might be wiped out within the next 100 years. **[1½ Marks]**

11. (i) Recombinant DNA technology, Polymerase Chain Reaction (PCR) and Enzyme Linked Immuno sorbent Assay (ELISA) are some of the techniques that serve the purpose of early diagnosis. **[1 Mark]**

(ii) Advantages of molecular diagnostic techniques are:

- It is being used to detect mutations in genes in suspected cancer patients too.
- It is a powerful technique to identify many other genetic disorders.
- Infection by a pathogen can be detected by the presence of antigens (proteins, glycoproteins, etc) or by detecting the antibodies synthesised against the pathogen. **[2 Marks]**

12. **Biofertilisers** are organisms that enrich the nutrient quality of the soil.
The main sources of biofertilisers are **bacteria, fungi** and **cyanobacteria.**

(i) The **bacteria** fix atmospheric nitrogen into organic forms, which are used by the plant as a nutrient. Other bacteria can fix atmospheric nitrogen while free-living in the soil (example, Azospirillum and Azotobacter), thus enriching the nitrogen content of the soil. **[1 Mark]**

(ii) The **fungal** symbiont in these associations absorbs phosphorus from soil and passes it to the plant. Plants having such associations show other benefits also, such as resistance to root-borne pathogens, tolerance to salinity and drought, and an overall increase in plant growth and development. **[1 Mark]**

(iii) In paddy fields, **cyanobacteria** serve as an important biofertiliser. Blue-green algae also add organic matter to the soil and increase its fertility. **[1 Mark]**

Biofertilizer can be defined as biological products containing living micro-organisms that, when applied to seed, plant surfaces, or soil, promote growth by several mechanisms such as increasing, the supply of nutrients, increasing root biomass or root area & increasing nutrient uptake capacity of the plant.

13. (i) The species 'A' of the corn borer was most successfully controlled by the Bt corn plant. It is because cry gene is expressed in plants to provide resistance to insects. And show less damage in comparison to species B and C. **[1 Mark]**

(ii) Species B shows very less impact of the Bt gene because the damage rate is almost equal in plant species of non-Bt crop and Bt crop. **[1 Mark]**

(iii) The scientist we must give advice to farmer are –

- When different species of plants are cultivated on the same field, there is a definite distance between crops of the same species. So, it is efficient in attracting pests away from their target host plant.
- To manage pests, the crop rotation farming method also increases the fertility of the soil.
- Organic pesticides allow the farmers to turn agricultural outputs into natural pesticides and do not affect their health or damage the crops. like farmers can use Bacillus thuringiensis (bacteria) on their crops to reduce the effect of insects on the plant. **[2 Marks]**

(iv) The cry gene protein is the Bt gene that encodes protein in corn plants. **[1 Mark]**

OR

(i) **Isolation of the Genetic Material (DNA)**

- To cut the DNA with restriction enzymes, it needs to be in pure form, free from other macro-molecules. Since the DNA is enclosed within the membranes, we have to break the cell open to release DNA along with other macromolecules such as RNA, proteins, polysaccharides and also lipids. This can be achieved by treating the fungi with the enzymes chitinase. **[1½ Marks]**
- The RNA can be removed by treatment with ribonuclease whereas proteins can be removed by treatment with protease. Other molecules can be removed by appropriate treatments and purified DNA ultimately precipitates out after the addition of chilled ethanol. This can be seen as a collection of fine threads in the suspension. **[1½ Marks]**

(ii) **Amplification of Gene of Interest using PCR**

- The enzyme extends the primers using the nucleotides provided in the reaction and the genomic DNA as a template. If the process of replication of DNA is repeated many times, the segment of DNA can be amplified approximately a billion times, i.e., 1 billion copies are made. **[1 Mark]**
- The amplified fragment if desired can now be used to ligate with a vector for further cloning. **[1 Mark]**

Cry gene:
Cry proteins are encoded by cry genes, these proteins are protoxin, produced by bacteria *bacillus thuringiensis.* These bacteria contain proteins in their inactive from, when these inactive protein in ingested by insect, it get activated by the alkaline pH of the gut.

All India 2022

CBSE Board Solved Paper Term-I

Time Allowed : 90 Minutes | *Maximum Marks : 35*

General Instructions:

(i) The questions paper contains three sections : Sectrion **A**, **B** and **C**.
(ii) Section **A** has **24** questions. Attempt any **20** questions.
(iii) Section **B** has **24** questions. Attempt any **20** questions.
(iv) Section **C** has **12** questions. Attempt any **10** questions.
(v) All questions carry equal marks.
(vi) There is no negative marking.

SECTION - A

*This section consists of **24** questions. Attempt any **20** questions from this section. The first **20** questions attempted would be evaluated.*

1. Enclosed within the integuments of a typical anatropous ovule is a diploid mass of cellular tissue known as :
(a) Megaspore mother cell
(b) Nucellus
(c) Synergids
(d) Embryo sac

2. Researchers the world over are trying to transfer apomietic genes to hybrid varieties as hybrid characters in the progeny :
(a) do not segregate
(b) segregate
(c) develop genetic variations
(d) will remain unexpressed

3. The aquatic plant having long and ribbon like pollen grains is :
(a) *Vallisneria*
(b) *Hydrilla*
(c) *Eicchornia*
(d) *Zostera*

4. In a typical dicotyledonous embryo, the portion of embryonal axis above the level of cotyledons is :
(a) Plumule
(b) Coleoptile
(c) Epicotyle
(d) Hypocotyle

5. To overcome incompatible pollinations so as to get desired hybrids, a plant breeder must have the knowledge of ________.
(a) pollen – nucellar interaction
(b) pollen – egg cell interaction
(c) pollen – pistil interaction
(d) pollen – embryo sac interaction

6. Pollen grains retain viability for months in plants belonging to different families given below :
(i) Solanaceae (ii) Leguminosae
(iii) Gramineae (iv) Rosaceae
(v) Liliaceae
The correct option is :
(a) (i), (ii) and (v) (b) (i), (ii) and (iv)
(c) (ii), (iv) and (v) (d) (i), (iii) and (v)

7. Given below is a diagramatic view of the human male reproductive system :

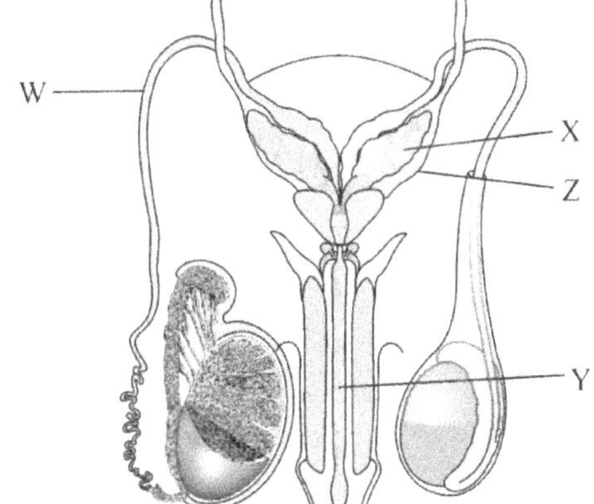

Identify the correct labelling for W, X, Y and Z and choose the correct option from the table below :

	W	X	Y	Z
(a)	Epididymis	Prostrate Gland	Glans Penis	Bulbourethral Gland
(b)	Bulbourethral Gland	Glans Penis	Prostrate Gland	Epididymis
(c)	Vas deferons	Seminal Vesicle	Urethra	Prostrate Gland
(d)	Rete testis	Bulbourethral Gland	Epididymis	Glans Penis

8. During human embryonic development, the heart in the embryo is formed after :
(a) 15 days of pregnancy
(b) 30 days of pregnancy
(c) 45 days of pregnancy
(d) 60 days of pregnancy

9. The uterus opens into the vagina through a narrow :
(a) Ampulla (b) Isthmus
(c) Cervix (d) Infundibulum

10. In the tranverse section of a young anther shown below, identify the correct sequence of wall layers from outside to inside :

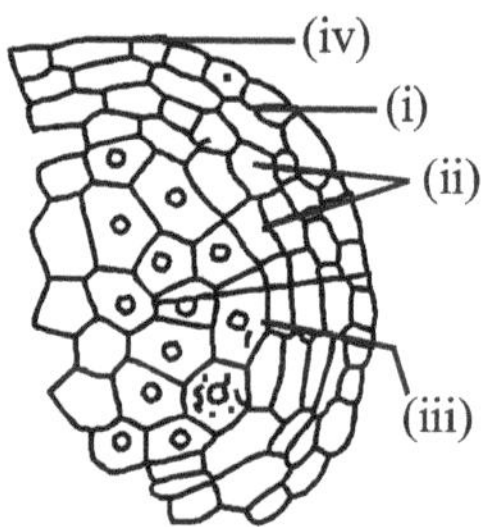

	(i)	(ii)	(iii)	(iv)
(a)	Middle layers	Endothecium	Epidermis	Tapetum
(b)	Tapetum	Middle layers	Endothecium	Epidermis
(c)	Epidermis	Endothecium	Middle layers	Tapetum
(d)	Endothecium	Middle layers	Tapetum	Epidermis

11. Floral reward/s provided by insect pollinated flowers to sustain animal visit is/are :
(a) nectar and fragrance
(b) nectar and pollen grains
(c) pollen grains and fragrance
(d) fragrance and bright colour

12. The cause of Klinefelter's syndrome in humans is :
(a) Absence of Y-chromosome
(b) Absence of X-chromosome
(c) Extra copy of an autosome
(d) Extra copy of an X-chromosome

13. Select the **incorrect** pair :
(a) Polygenic inheritance : Haemophilia
(b) Linkage : *Drosophila*
(c) Incomplete dominance : *Antirrhinum*
(d) Pleiotropy : Phenylketonuria

14. According to Mendel, the nature of the unit factors that control the expression of traits were :
(a) Stable (b) Blending
(c) Stable and discrete (d) Discrete

15. Which of the following animals exhibit male heterogamety ?
(i) Fruit fly (ii) Fowl
(iii) Human (iv) Honey bee
(a) (i) and (iii)
(b) (ii) and (iv)
(c) (ii) and (iii)
(d) (i) and (iv)

16. The probability of all possible genotypes of offsprings in a genetic cross can be obtained with the help of :
(a) Test cross (b) Back cross
(c) Punnett square (d) Linkage cross

17. The number of different types of gametes that would be produced from a parent with genotype AABBCc is :
(a) 1 (b) 2
(c) 3 (d) 4

18. Select the important goals of HGP from the given options :
(i) Store the information for data analysis
(ii) Cloning and amplification of human DNA
(iii) Identify all the genes present in human DNA
(iv) Use of DNA information to trace human history
(a) (i) and (ii) (b) (ii) and (iii)
(c) (i) and (iii) (d) (ii) and (iv)

19. A codon is a 'triplet of bases' was suggested by :
(a) Marshall Nirenberg
(b) Har Gobind Khorana
(c) Georgee Gamow
(d) Francis Crick

20. The correct feature of Double-helical structure of DNA as given by Waston and Crick is :
(a) Right-handed helix, pitch is 3.4 nm
(b) Left-handed helix, pitch is 3.8 nm
(c) Right-handed helix, pitch is 3.8 nm
(d) Left-handed helix, pitch is 3.4 nm

21. Charging of tRNA during translation is necessary for :
(a) Binding of anticodons of tRNA to the respective codons of mRNA
(b) Peptide bond formation between two amino acids
(c) Movement of ribosomes from codon to codon
(d) Binding of ribosomes to the mRNA

22. If *E.* coli were allowed to grow in the culture medium for 80 minutes by Matthew Meselson and Franklin Stabi in their experiments, the proportion of light and hybrid density DNA molecule would have been :
   (a) 87.5% of light density DNA and 12.5% of hybrid density DNA
   (b) 75.0% of light density DNA and 25% of hybrid density DNA.
   (c) 50% of light density DNA and 50% of hybrid density DNA.
   (d) 12.5% of light density DNA and 87.5% of hybrid density DNA.

23. A diagrammatic illustration of the process of transcription by RNA polymerase-II in eukaryote is given below. Choose the most appropriate statement with respect to the fate of the precursor of mRNA transcribed that will be :

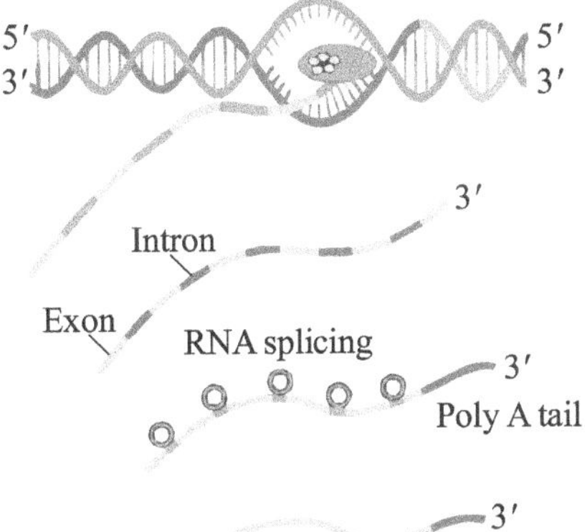

   (a) Translation will take place once the precursor of mRNA leaves the nucleus.
   (b) Translation on mRNA will not take place once the precursor of mRNA leaves the nucleus.
   (c) Translation will take place in the nucleus.
   (d) The precursor of mRNA has to be processed further in next step before being translated.

24. Identify the correct pair of codon with its corresponding pair of amino acid :
   (a) UAA : Leucine (b) UGA : Serine
   (c) AUG : Histidine (d) UUU : Phenylalanine

SECTION - B

*This section consists of **24** questions. Attempt any **20** questions from this section. The first **20** questions attempted should be evaluated.*

***Direction:** Question Nos. **25 to 28** consists of two statements – **Assertion (A)** and **Reason (R)**. Answer these questions selecting the appropriate option given below :*

(a) Both Assertion (A) and Reason (R) are true and Reason (R) is the correct explanation of Assertion (A).
*(b) Both Assertion (A) and Reason (R) are true, but Reason (R) is **not** the correct explanation of Assertion (A).*
(c) Assertion (A) is true, but Reason (R) is false.
(d) Assertion (A) is false, but Reason (R) is true.

25. **Assertion (A) :** Very often persons suffering from Sexually Transmitted Diseases (STD) do not go for timely detection and proper treatment.
   Reason (R) : Absence or less significant symptoms in the early stages of STDs and the social stigma attached to the disease.

26. **Assertion (A) :** Vasectomy is a sterilisation procedure advised for females as a terminal method.
   Reason (R) : In vasectomy, a small part of the vas deferens is removed or tied by blocking gamete transport therefore preventing conception.

27. **Assertion (A) :** Interstitial spaces outside the seminiferous tubule have blood vessels and sertoli cells.
   Reason (R) : Sertoli cells provide nutrition to the germ cells.

28. **Assertion (A) :** Accumulation of phenylalanine in the brain results in metal retardation in Phenylketonuria.
   Reason (R) : The affected person lacks phenylalanine which is therefore not converted to tyrosine.

29. Choose the correct option for the features of functional mammary gland of all female mammals from the statements below :
   (i) Glandular tissue with variable amount of fat.
   (ii) Mammary lobes, 30 – 40 in number called alveoli.
   (iii) Mammary ducts joining to form mammary tubules.
   (iv) Mammary ampulla connected to lactiferous duct.
   (a) (i) and (iii) (b) (ii) and (iii)
   (c) (i) and (iv) (d) (ii) and (iv)

30. Which condition of gynoecium (pistil) is shown the figures (i) and (ii) ?

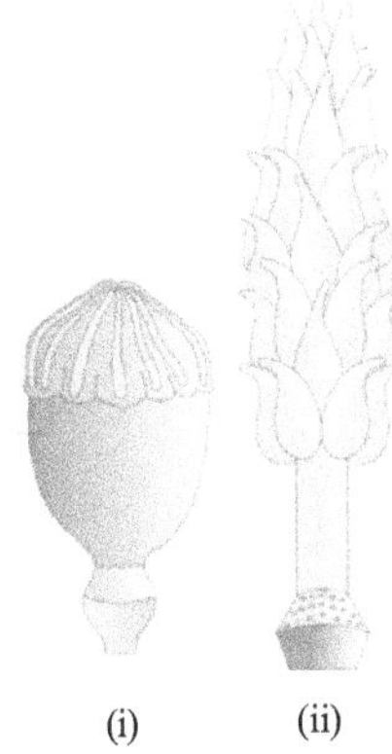

(i) (ii)

   (a) (i) multicarpellary apocarpous, (ii) multicarpellary syncarpous
   (b) (i) multicarpellary syncarpous, (ii) multicarpellary apocarpous
   (c) (i) bicarpellary apocarpous, (ii) bicarpellary syncarpous
   (d) (i) bicarpellary syncarpous, (ii) bicarpellary apocarpous

31. An IUD recommended to promote the cervix hostility to the sperms is

(a) CuT (b) Multiload-375
(c) LNG-20(d) Cu7

32. Identify the disease which is ***not*** a sexually transmitted disease :

(a) Gonnorhoea (b) Syphilis
(c) Amoebiasis (d) Chalamydiasis

33. The nature of meiotic division during oogenesis in a human female is :

(a) equal cell division
(b) suspended cell division
(c) continuous cell division
(d) rapid cell division

34. Choose the correct labellings for the parts X, Y and Z in the given figure of the stages in embryo development in a dicot :

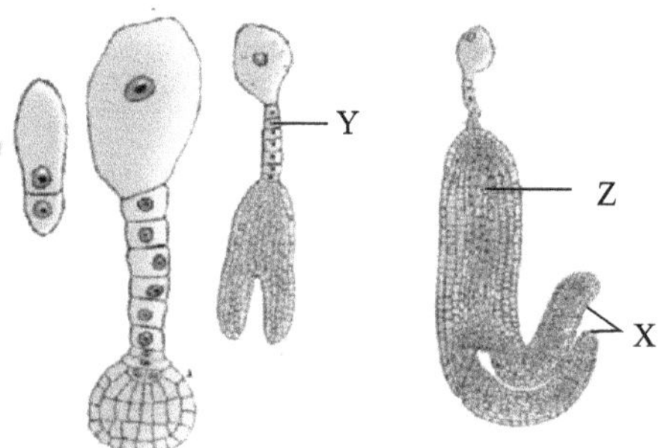

(a) X is suspensor, Y is radicle and Z is cotyledon
(b) X is radicle, Y is cotyledon and Z is suspensor
(c) X is cotyledon, Y is suspensor and Z is radicle
(d) X is zygote, Y is radicle and Z is cotyledon

35. Which of the following outbreeding devices are used by majority of flowering plants to prevent inbreeding depression ?

(i) Pollen release and stigma receptivity are not synchronised.
(ii) Different positions of anther and stigma.
(iii) Production of different types of pollen grains.
(iv) Formation of unisexual flowers along with bisexual flowers.
(v) Preventing self-pollen from fertilising the ovules by inhibiting pollen germination.

(a) (i), (ii) and (v) (b) (ii), (iii) and (v)
(c) (i), (iii) and (v) (d) (iii), (iv) and (v)

36. Histone proteins that help in forming the nucleosomes in the nucleus are rich in basic amino acids such as :

(a) Arginine and tyrosine
(b) Lysine and histidine
(c) Arginine and lysine
(d) Histidine and tryptophan

37. In *Pisum sativum*, the flower position may be axial (allele A) or terminal (allele a). What would be the percentage of the offspring with respect to axial flower position, if a cross is made between parents Aa × aa ?

(a) 25% (b) 50%
(c) 75% (d) 100%

38. In humans rolling of tongue is an autosomal dominant trait (R). In a family both the parents have the trait of rolling tongue but their daughter does not show the trait, whereas the sons have the trait of rolling of tongue.
The genotypes of the family would be :

	Mother	Father	Daughter	Son
(a)	Rr	Rr	rr	rr
(b)	Rr	Rr	rr	RR
(c)	rr	Rr	RR	rr
(d)	RR	rr	Rr	Rr

39. Study the pedigree analysis of human given below and identify the type of inheritance along with an example :

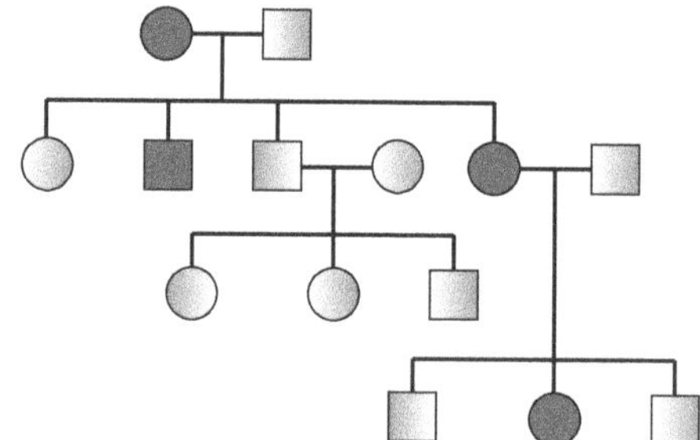

(a) Sex-linked recessive, Haemophilia
(b) Sex-linked dominant, Vitamin D resistant rickets
(c) Autosomal recessive, Sickle-cell anaemia
(d) Autosomal dominant, Myotonic Dystrophy

40. Possibility of the blood groups of the children in a family where the father is heterozygous for blood group 'A' and the mother is heterozygous for blood group 'B', would be :

(a) Blood groups 'A', 'B'
(b) Blood groups 'A', 'B', 'O'
(c) Blood group 'AB', 'O'
(d) Blood groups 'A', 'B', 'AB', 'O'

41. The correct statement with respect to Thalassemia in humans is :

(a) α-Thalassemia is controlled by a single gene HBB.
(b) The gene for α-Thalassemia is located on chromosome-16.
(c) β-Thalassemia is controlled by two closely linked genes HBA-1 and HBA-2.
(d) In β-Thalassemia the production of α-globin chain is affected.

42. A region of coding strand of DNA has the following nucleotide sequence :
5′–TACGCCG–3′
The sequence of bases on mRNA transcribed by this would be :
(a) 5′–UACGCCG–3′
(b) 3′–UACGCCG–3′
(c) 5′–ATGCGGC–3′
(d) 3′–ATGCGGC–3′

43. A DNA molecule is 160 base pairs long. If it has 20% adenine, how many cytosine bases are present in this DNA molecule ?
(a) 48 (b) 64
(c) 96 (d) 192

44. A template strand in a bacterial DNA has the given base sequence: :
5′–AGGTTTAACG–3′
What would be the RNA sequence transcribed from this template strand ?
(a) 5′–CGUUAAACCU–3′
(b) 5′–AGGUUUUUCG–3′
(c) 5′–TCCAAATTGC–3′
(d) 5′–AGGTTTAACG–3′

45. In the presence of allolactose, the lac repressor in the operon of *E. coli* :
(a) binds to the operator
(b) cannot bind to the operator
(c) binds to the promoter
(d) binds to the regulator.

46. Taylor and colleagues performed experiments on _________ using radioactive _________ to prove that the DNA is chromosomes replicate semi-conservastively. (Select the correct option for the blanks)
(a) *Vicia faba*, Uridine
(b) *E. coli*, Uridine
(c) *Vicia faba*, Thymidine
(d) *E. coli*, Thymidine

47. The reactive hydroxyl group in the nucleotide of RNA is :
(a) 5′OH (b) 4′OH
(c) 3′OH (d) 2′OH

48. Given below are the pairs of contrasting traits in *Pisum Sativum* as studied by Mendel. Identify the **incorrect** pair of traits :

	Character	Dominant	Recessive
(a)	Stem height	Tall	Dwarf
(b)	Seed shape	Round	Wrinkled
(c)	Pod colour	Yellow	Green
(d)	Flower position	Axial	Terminal

SECTION - B

*This section consists of one case followed by **6** questions. Besides this **6** more questions are given. Attempt any **10** questions from this section. The first **10** questions attempted would be evaluated.*

Case Study: (Qs. 49-54)

A group of medical students carried out a detailed study on the impact of various factors on the different hormones during the menstrual cycle in a human female. They collected the data with different factors. Given below is the graph plotted from the data collected showing the morning temperature and concentration of hormones FSH, LH, estrogen and progesterone during normal menstrual cycle in a woman.

Temperature Graph

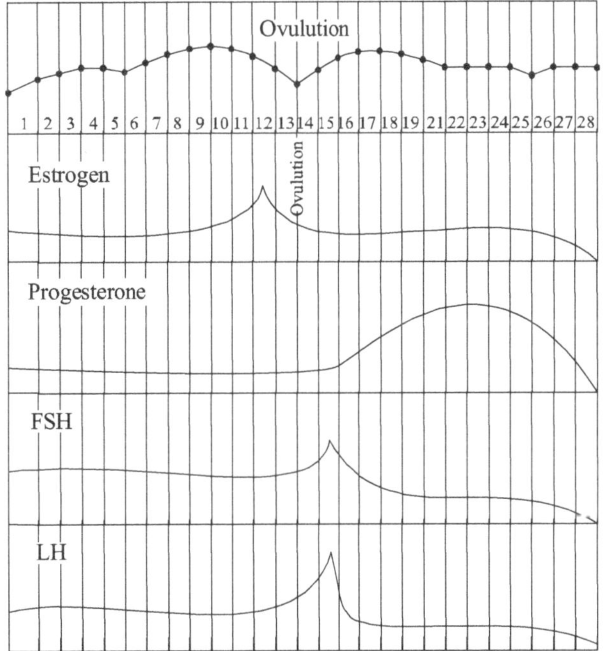

Study the graph and answer the given questions

49. The early morning recording of temperature in the graph during actual and during ovulation respectively are :
(a) low, high
(b) high, low
(c) low, low
(d) high, high

50. The time of ovulation is of importance in cases of :
(i) couples having difficulty in conception.
(ii) to know the safe period for prevention of pregnancy.
(iii) to inhibit the process of ovulation.
(iv) to stimulate ovarian follicular development.
(a) (i) and (iv)
(b) (ii) and (iv)
(c) (i) and (ii)
(d) (iii) and (iv)

51. The increase in the level of progesterone is maximum under the influence of LH during :

(a) Secretory phase
(b) Follicular phase
(c) Menstruation
(d) Proliferative phase

52. Which of the following hormone/hormones is'are showing rapid surge leading to changes in Graafian follicle just before ovulation ?

(a) LH (b) FSH
(c) FSH and Estrogen (d) FSH and LH

53. The human corpus luteum starts regressing _______ days after ovulation. (Identify the correct choice for the blank).

(a) 10 – 11 (b) 14 – 15
(c) 16 – 17 (d) 18 – 20

54. As per the data plotted in the graph, in which period of the menstrual cycle is the chance of fertilisation very high in human female ?

(a) $3^{rd} - 9^{th}$ days
(b) $10^{th} - 17^{th}$ days
(c) $18^{th} - 23^{rd}$ days
(d) $23^{rd} - 28^{th}$ days

55. A plant breeder crossed a pure bred tall plant having white flowers with a pure bred dwarf plant having blue flowers. He obtained 2002 F_1 progeny and found that they are all tall having blue flowers. Upon selfing these F_1 plants he obtained a progeny of 2160 plants. Approximately how many of these are likely to be short having blue flowers ?

(a) 1215 (b) 405
(c) 540 (d) 135

56. Given below is a Karyotype of a human foetus obtained for screening to find any probable genetic disorder :

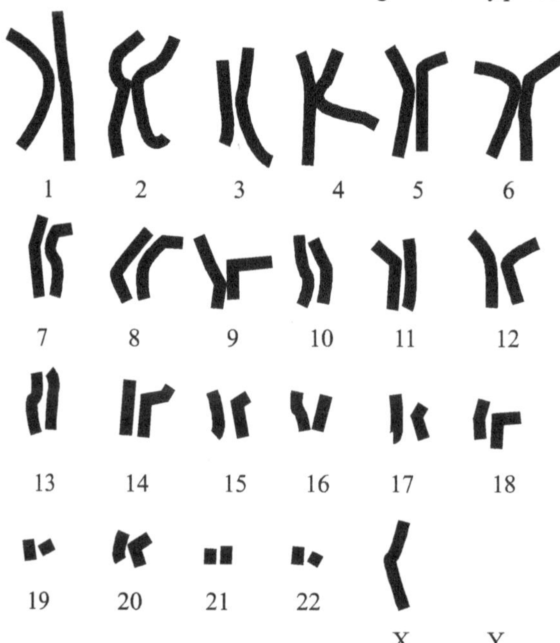

Based on the Karyotype, the chromosomal disorder detected in unborn foetus and the consequent symptoms the child may suffer from are :

(a) Turner's syndrome : Sterile ovaries, short stature
(b) Down's syndrome : Gynaecomastia, overall masculine stature
(c) Turner's syndrone : Small round head, flat back of head
(d) Down's syndrome : Furrowed tongue, short stature.

57. In the dihybrid cross that was conducted by Morgan involving mating between parental generation for genes yellow bodied, white eyed female *Drosophila* and wild type male *Drosophila*, upto F_2 generation is given below :

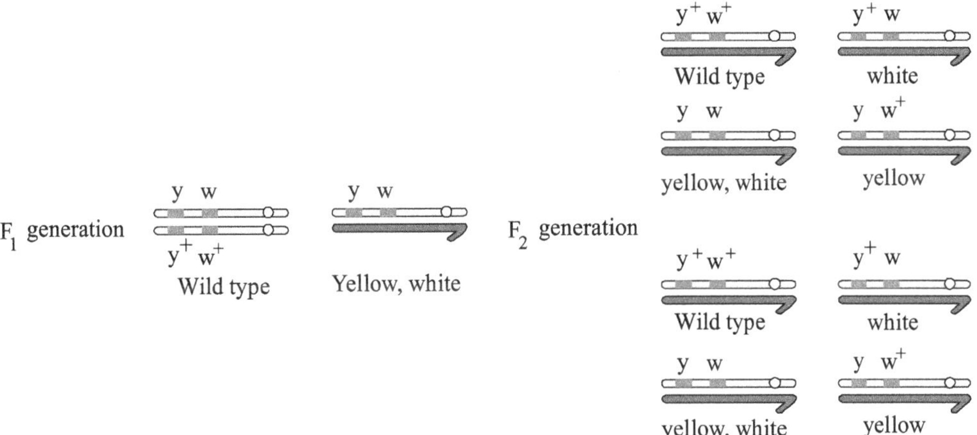

Study the result obtained of the F_2 progeny. Select the correct option from the given choices for the F_2 progeny.

(a) Parental type, 1.3% : Strength of linkage high
(b) Recombinant types, 1.3% : Strength of linkage low
(c) Parental type 98.7% : Strength of linkage high
(d) Recombinant types, 98.7% : Strength of linkage low.

58. Study the given diagrammatic representation of Griffth's experiment to demonstrate transformation in bacteria :

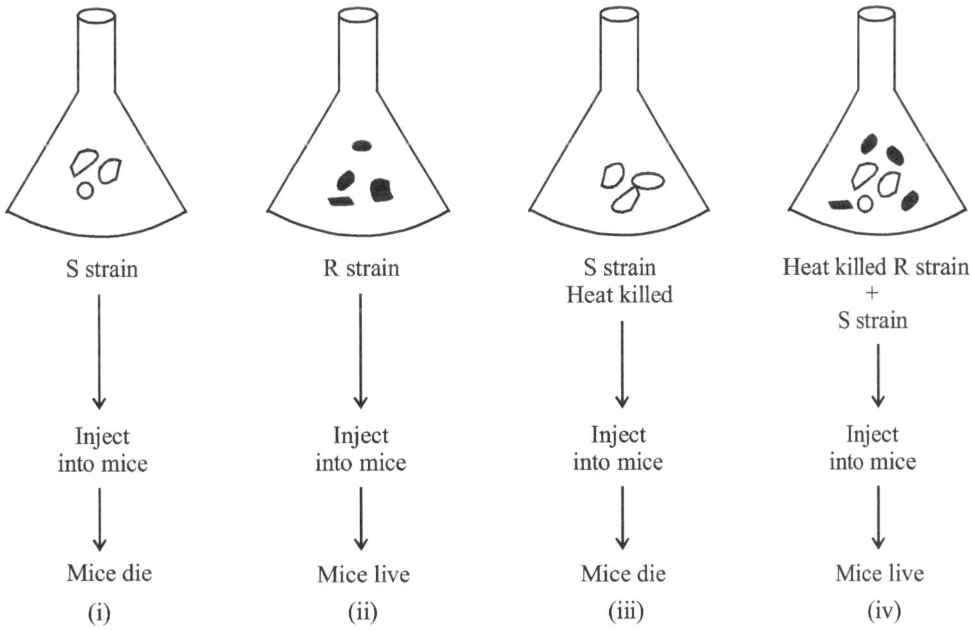

Select the option which is **incorrectly** representing the experiment :

(a) (i) and (iii)
(b) (ii) and (iii)
(c) (iii) and (iv)
(d) (ii) annd (iv)

59. Which one of the following diagram correctly represents DNA replication in eukaryotes ?

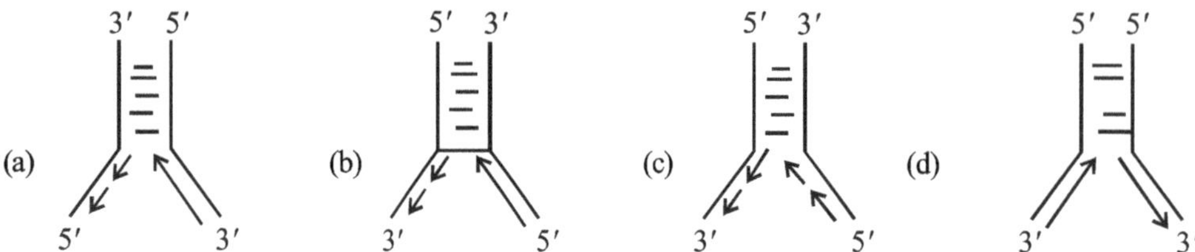

60. In the given figure of translation machinery of eukaryotes, select the correct labellings for (i), (ii), (iii) and (iv) :

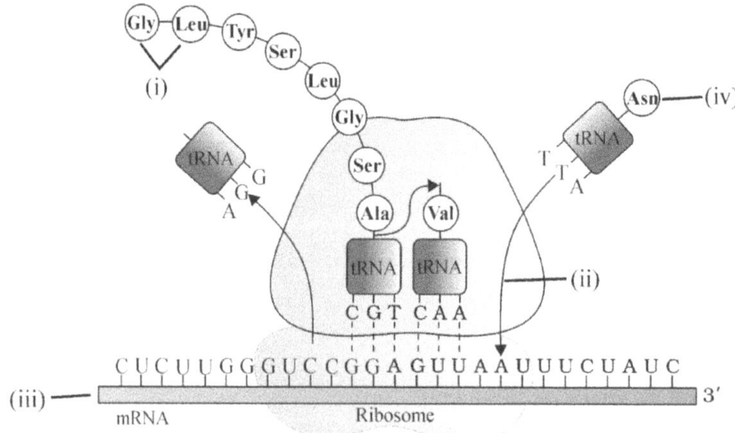

(a) (i) Codon, (ii) Anticodon, (iii) tRNA, (iv) 3′ end of mRNA
(b) (i) Anticodon, (ii) Codon, (iii) 3′ end of mRNA, (iv) 5′ end of mRNA
(c) (i) Polypeptide chain, (ii) Large subunit of ribosome, (iii) 5′ end of mRNA, (iv) tRNA.
(d) (i) Ribozyme, (ii) Polypeptide chain, (iii) tRNA, (iv) 5′ end of tRNA.

Solutions

1. **(b)** Enclosed within the integuments is a mass of cells called the nucellus. Cells of the nucellus have abundant reserve food materials. Located in the nucellus is the embryo sac or female gametophyte.

At the time of fertilization, the nucellus consist of a bulky tissue ventral to the embryo sac and a rather thin layer elsewhere.

2. **(a)** Production of hybrid seeds is costly and hence the cost of hybrid seeds becomes too expensive for the farmers. If these hybrids are made into apomicts, there is no segregation of characters in the hybrid progeny. Then the farmers can keep on using the hybrid seeds to raise new crop year after year and he does not have to buy hybrid seeds every year.
3. **(a)** Zostera is a submerged marine sea grass that releases long, ribbon-like pollen grains underwater. The pollen grains are carried passively by water and ultimately reach female flowers.
4. **(c)** The portion of embryonal axis above the level of cotyledons is the epicotyl, which terminates with the plumule or stem tip.
5. **(c)** To overcome incompatible pollination so us to get a desirable hybrid a plant breeder must have the knowledge of pollen pistil interaction.

Pollination does not guarantee the transfer of right type of pollen C comptabile pollen of some species as the stigma.

6. **(b)** In some members of Rosaceae, Leguminoseae and Solanaceae, they maintain viability of pollen grains for months.
7. **(c)**

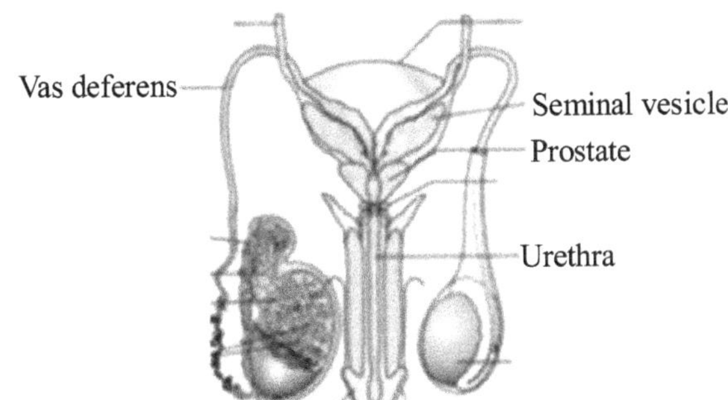

8. **(b)** In human being after one month of pregnancy, the embryo's heart is formed.

The first sign of growing foetus may be noticed by listening to the heart sound carefully through stethoscope.

9. **(c)** The uterus opens into vagina through a narrow **cervix** and the cavity of the cervix is called cervical canal.

The uterus is single and it is also known as womb.

10. **(d)**

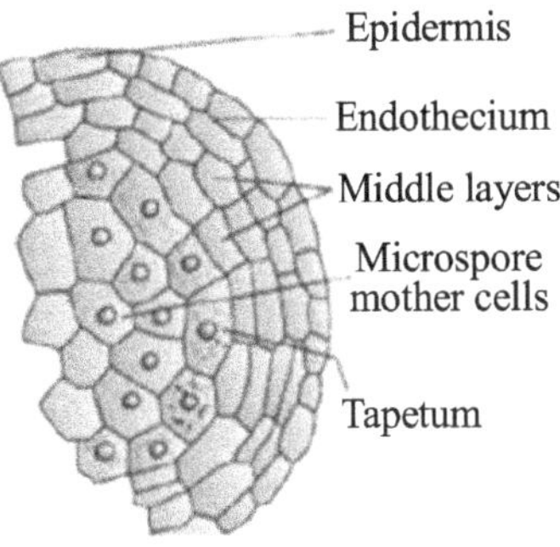

11. **(b)** To sustain animal visits, the flower have to provide rewards to the animals. Nectar and pollen grains are usual floral rewards.
12. **(d)** Klinefelter's Syndrome is a genetic disorder that is also caused due to the presence of an additional copy of the X chromosome resulting in a karyotype of 47, XXY.
13. **(a)** Such trait that controlled by two or more than two genes are thus called polygenic inheritance. Human skin colour is one of the example of this.
14. **(c)** According to Mendel, the natures of unit factor that control the expression of trait were stable and discrete.
15. **(a)** Males produce two different types of gametes, (a) either with or without X chromosome or (b) some gametes with X-chromosome and some with Y-chromosome. Such types of sex determination mechanisms are designated to be an example of male heterogamety.
16. **(c)** Reginald Punnett, an English geneticist, established one of the simplest methods for calculating the mathematical chance of inheriting a given feature. Punnett square became popular as a result of his technique. It's the simplest graphical method for determining all conceivable genotype combinations in children.

Test-cross invalves mating an unknown genotypic individual with a known homozygous recessive.

17. **(d)** Three genes A, B, and C control skin colour in humans with the dominant forms A, B and C responsible for dark skin colour and the recessive forms 'c' for light skin colour. Hence, The type of gametes produced by the parent with genotype AABBCc is 4.

18. **(c)** Some of the important goals of HGP were as follows:
(i) Identify all the approximately 20,000-25,000 genes in human DNA;
(ii) Determine the sequences of the 3 billion chemical base pairs that make up human DNA;
(iii) Store this information in databases;
(iv) Improve tools for data analysis;
(v) Transfer related technologies to other sectors, such as industries;
(vi) Address the ethical, legal, and social issues (ELSI) that may arise from the project.

19. **(c)** **George Gamow** suggested that the genetic code should be made up of a combination of three nucleotides. He proposed that If 20 amino acids are to be coded by 4 bases, then the code should be made up of three nucleotides.

20. **(a)** The two chains are coiled in a right-handed fashion. The pitch of the helix is 3.4 nm and there is roughly 10 bp in each turn.

The structure of DNA is reffered to as a double helix as it resembles a twisted staircase.

21. **(b)** Charging of tRNA during translation process is called amino-acylation of tRNA. When two such charged tRNAs are brought close enough the formation of peptide bond between the corresponding amino acids would be favoured energetically. The presence of a catalyst would enhance the rate of peptide bond formation.

22. **(a)** *E. coli* divides in 20 minutes. So, after 80 minutes there will be 4 generations. In the first generation all the strands will be hybrid (as the heavy isotope will be incorporated in the newly synthesised strand of DNA) i.e the two DNA will be of intermediate nature. In the second generation, 50% the DNA will be light and 50% will be hybrid. In the 3rd generation, 25% will be hybrid and 75% will be light and in the fourth generation 12.5% will be hybrid and 87.5% will be light strand.

23. **(a)** The fully processed hnRNA, now called mRNA, that is transported out of the nucleus for translation.

24. **(d)** The code is nearly universal: for example, from bacteria to human UUU would code for Phenylalanine (phe).

Codon is triplet of bases in the DNA coding far one amino-acid.

25. **(a)** Infected person may often be asymptomatic and hence, may remain undetected for long. Absence or less significant symptoms in the early stages of infection and the social stigma attached to the STIs, deter the infected persons from going for timely detection and proper treatment.

26. **(d)** Sterilisation procedure in the male is called 'vasectomy' and that in the female is called 'tubectomy'. The statement in reason is correct.

27. **(d)** The regions outside the seminiferous tubules called interstitial spaces, contain small blood vessels and interstitial cells or Leydig cells. The statement in reason is correct.

28. **(c)** The affected individual lacks an enzyme that converts the amino acid phenylalanine into tyrosine. As a result of this phenylalanine is accumulated and converted into phenylpyruvic acid and other derivatives. Accumulation of these in brain results in mental retardation.

Un-treated phenylketouria can lead to brain damage, intellectual disabilities, behavioural symptoms or seizures.

29. **(c)** The mammary glands are paired structures (breasts) that contain glandular tissue and a variable amount of fat. The glandular tissue of each breast is divided into 15-20 mammary lobes containing clusters of cells called alveoli. The cells of alveoli secrete milk, which is stored in the cavities (lumens) of alveoli. The alveoli open into mammary tubules. The tubules of each lobe join to form a mammary duct. Several mammary ducts join to form a wider mammary ampulla which is connected to the lactiferous duct.

30. **(b)** The gynoecium may consist more than one pistil is called multicarpellary. When there are more than one, the pistils may be fused together (syncarpous) or may be free (apocarpous).

31. **(c)** The hormone releasing IUDs (Progestasert, LNG-20), make the uterus unsuitable for implantation and the cervix hostile to the sperms.

An IUD is small plastic T-shape device used far birth control.

32. **(c)** Amoebiasis caused by protozoan parasites *Entamoeba histolytica* in large intestine of human. The main source of infection is contaminated drinking water and food.

33. **(b)** In oogenesis, diploid oogonium go through mitosis until one develops into a primary oocyte, which will begin the first meiotic division, but then arrest; it will finish this division as it develops in the follicle, giving rise to a haploid secondary oocyte and a smaller polar body.

34. **(c)**

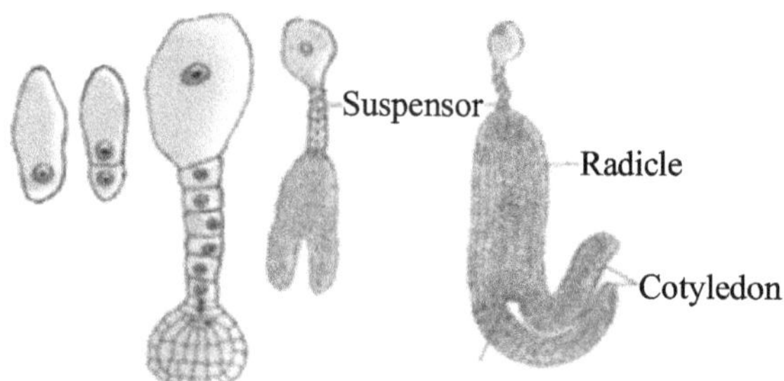

35. **(a)** Flowering plants Continued self-pollination result in inbreeding depression. For this it developed many devices to discourage self-pollination and encourage cross-pollination. In some species, pollen release and stigma receptivity are not synchronised.
In some other species, the anther and stigma are placed at different positions so that the pollen cannot come in contact with the stigma of the same flower.
The third device to prevent inbreeding is self-incompatibility.

Majority of flowering plants hermaphrodite flowers and pollen grain are likely to come in contact with stigma of same flower.

36. (c) Histones are rich in the basic amino acid residues lysine and arginine. Both the amino acid residues carry positive charges in their side chains.

As in this question, only one trait is considered, it is an example of mono-hybrid cross.

37. (b) when cross is occur between axial (Aa) and terminal (aa) then,

Parent Aa (Axial) aa (Terminal)

F1 Gen.

	A	a
a	Aa	a
a	Aa	a

as shown in punnett square the phenotype ratio of Axial flower is 50 % and terminal flower is 50 %.

38. (b) Parent Rr (Mother) × Rr (Father)

F1 gen

	R	r
R	RR	Rr
r	Rr	rr

Mother and father have autosomal dominant traits with Rr and Rr respectively. After crossing between these two traits, the son is born with this autosomal dominant trait RR whereas the daughter is born with the recessive trait rr.

39. (d) Representative pedigree analysis is the example of Autosomal dominant trait Myotonic dystrophy.

40. (d) If the Father is with heterozygous A blood group (I^AI^O) and mother with heterozygous B blood group (I^BI^O) then the progeny of such parents are,

	I^A	I^O
I^B	I^AI^B	I^BI^O
I^O	I^AI^O	I^OI^O

Phenotype blood group of I^AI^B – AB blood group
I^BI^O – B blood group
I^AI^O – A blood group
I^OI^O – O blood group

Therefore, progeny is with blood group A, B, AB, and O.

41. (b) â Thalassemia is controlled by a single gene HBB on chromosome 11 of each parent and occurs due to mutation of one or both the genes.
â Thalassemia, production of â globin chain is affected.
á Thalassemia is controlled by two closely linked genes HBA1 and HBA2 on chromosome 16 of each parent.

42. (a) 5'-TACGCCG–3' Coding strand
3'–ATGCGGC–5' Template strand
Therefore mRNA strand transcribed by template strand is 5'- UACGCCG -3'

43. (a) As per Chargaff rule ratio of Adenine is equal to Thymine and Guanine is equal to Cytosine.
Therefore, if Adenine is of 20 % then Thymine is also 20% whereas Guanine is of 30% then cytosine is also of 30%.
Hence, if DNA molecule with 160 bp then amount of cytosine is 30% of 160 = 48

44. (a) 5'-AGGTTTAACG -3' Template strand
As template strand code from 3' to 5'
Then the strand will become **3'- GCAATTTGGA- 5'**
Therefore the mRNA strand for this template is-
5'- CGUUAAACCU -3'

The RNA sequence is complementary to DNA sequence. RNA have "U" in place of "T".

45. (b) In the presence of allolactose, a binary complex is formed between allolactose and the repressor that makes binding of the repressor to the operator region impossible.

46. (c) The experiments involving use of radioactive thymidine to detect distribution of newly synthesised DNA in the chromosomes was performed on *Vicia faba* (faba beans) by Taylor and colleagues in 1958. The experiments proved that the DNA in chromosomes also replicate semiconservatively.

47. (d) The 2'-OH hydroxyl protons are responsible for differences in conformation, hydration, and thermodynamic stability of RNA and DNA oligonucleotides. Additionally, the 2'-OH group plays a central role in RNA.

The OH group present at 2' of sugar molecule is the difference between DNA and RNA.

48. (c) The dominant pod colour of *Pisum sativum* is green colour while recessive pod colour is yellow in colour.

49. (a) As per graph during menstrual estrogen is low while during ovulation it reach to its higher peak.

The reproductive cycle in female primates is called menstrual cycle.

50. (c) Contraceptive are used to inhibit the ovulation process. Progesterone is important to stimulate ovarian follicular development. Hence only statements i and ii are important for ovulation.

51. (a) The ovulation (ovulatory phase) is followed by the luteal phase during which the remaining parts of the Graafian follicle transform into the corpus luteum. The corpus luteum secretes large amounts of progesterone which is essential for the maintenance of the endometrium. Hence progesterone level is highest during secretory phase.

52. (d) Both LH and FSH attain a peak level in the middle of the cycle (about 14th day). Rapid secretion of LH leading to its maximum level during the mid-cycle called LH surge induces rupture of Graafian follicle and thereby the release of an ovum (ovulation).

53. (c) In human ovulation followed by 14th to 15th day of menstrual cycle. Then corpus luteum starts regressing at 16th -17th days after ovulation.

54. (b) The chances of fertilisation is highest during ovulation period hence, 10th -17th period of the menstrual cycle is the chance of fertilisation.

The chances of fertilization is maximum during the period of ovulation.

55. (b) The cross between pure breed of tall plant with write colour flower (TTbb) with pure breed with short plant and blue flower (ttBB). Then the F_2 progeny will be :
Tall plant with blue flower: 9
Tall plant with white flower: 3
Dwarf plant with blue flower: 3
Dwarf plant with white flower: 1
Therefore, the probability of short plant with blue flower is 3/16 of 2160 = 405

56. (a) Turner's Syndrome is a disorder is caused due to the absence of one of the X chromosomes, i.e., 45 with X0, Such females are sterile as ovaries are rudimentary.

Symptoms of Turner syndrome include short stature, heart defects and certain learning disabilities.

57. (c)

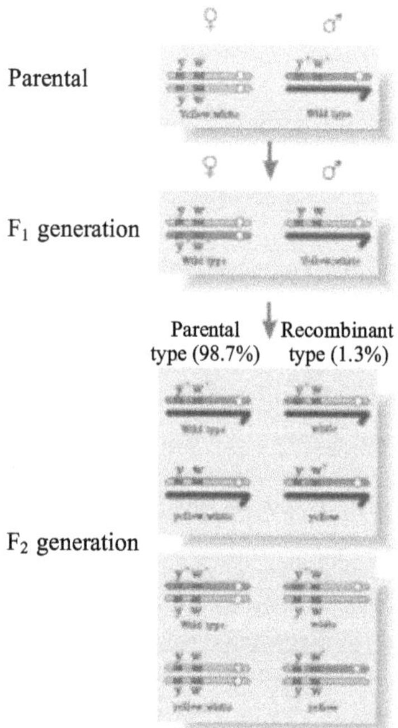

58. (c) Griffith was able to kill bacteria by heating them. He observed that heat-killed S strain bacteria injected into mice did not kill them. When he

S strain (heat-killed) → Inject into mice → Mice live

S strain (heat-killed) + R strain (live) → Inject into mice → Mice die

Note

In 1928, Fredericok Griffith, in a series of experiments with ifreptococcus pneumoniae.

59. (d)

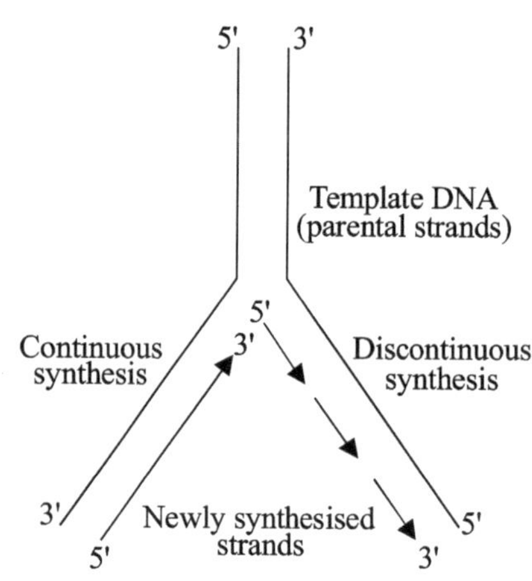

60. (c)

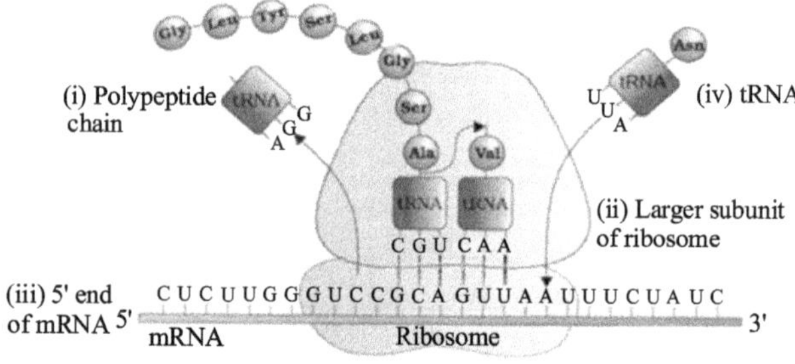

All India 2021-22

CBSE Board Sample Paper Term-II

Time Allowed : 2 Hours | *Maximum Marks : 35*

General Instructions:

(i) All questions are compulsory.

(ii) The question paper has three sections and **13** questions. All questions are compulsory.

(iii) Section–**A** has **6** questions of **2** marks each; Section–**B** has **6** questions of **3** marks each; and Section–**C** has a case-based question of **5** marks.

(iv) There is no overall choice. However, internal choices have been provided in some questions. A student has to attempt only one of the alternatives in such questions.

(v) Wherever necessary, neat and properly labeled diagrams should be drawn.

SECTION - A

1. Humans have innate immunity for protection against pathogens that may enter the gut along with food. What are the two barriers that protect the body from such pathogens?

2. A patient admitted in ICU was diagnosed to have suffered from myocardial infarction. The condition of coronary artery is depicted in the image below. Name two bioactive agents and their mode of action that can improve this condition.

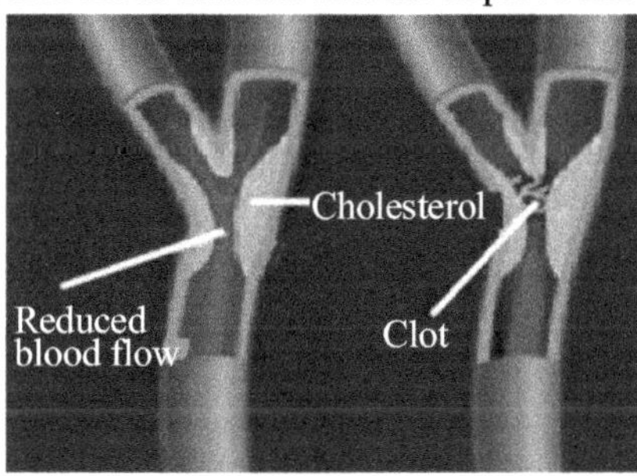

OR

Substantiate by giving two reasons as to why a holistic understanding of the flora and fauna the cropland is required before introducing an appropriate biocontrol method.

3. Identify the compound chemical structure is shown below. State any three of its physical properties.

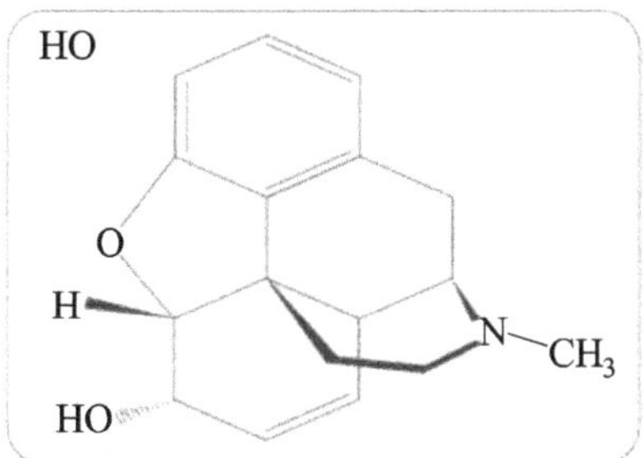

4. Water samples were collected at points A, B and C in a segment of a river near a sugar factory and tested for BOD level. The BOD levels of samples A, B and C were 400 mg/L, 480 mg/L and 8 mg/L respectively. What is this indicative of? Explain why the BOD level gets reduced considerably at the collection point C?

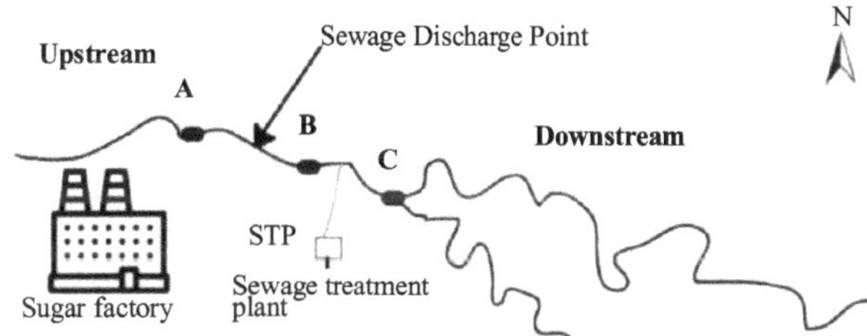

5. An ecologist study an area with population A, thriving on unlimited resources and showing exponential growth, introduced population B and C to the same area. What will be the effect on the growth pattern of the population A, B and C when living together in the same habitat?

6. With the decline in the population of fig species it was noticed that the population of wasp species also started to decline. What is the relationship between the two and what could be the possible reason for decline of wasps?

OR

With the increase in the global temperature, the inhabitants of Antarctica are facing fluctuations in the temperature. Out of the regulators and the conformers, which of the two will have better chances of survival? Give two adaptations that support them to survive in the ambient environment? Give one suitable example.

SECTION - B

7. How do normal cells get transformed into cancerous neoplastic cells? Elaborate giving three examples of inducing agent. OR A person is suffering from a high-grade fever. Which symptoms will help to identify if he/she is suffering from Typhoid, Pneumonia or Malaria?

8. Recognition of an antigenic protein of a pathogen or exposure to a pathogen occurs during many types of immune responses, including active immunity and induced active immunity. Specify the types of responses elicited when human beings get encountered by a pathogen.

9. In a pathological lab, a series of steps were undertaken for finding the gene of interest. Describe the steps, or make a flow chart showing the process of amplification of this gene of interest.

10. (a) 'The Evil Quartet' describes the rates of species extinction due to human activities. Explain how the population of organisms is affected by fragmentation the habitats.
    (b) Introduction of alien species has led to environmental damage and decline of indigenous species. Give any one example of how it has affected the indigenous species?
    (c) Could the extinction of Steller's sea cow and passenger pigeon be saved by man? Give reasons to support your answer.

11. (a) The image shown below is of a sacred grove found in India. Explain how has human involvement helped in the preservation of these biodiversity rich regions.

    (a) Value of Z (regression coefficient) is considered for measuring the species richness of an area. If the value of Z is 0.7 for area A ,and 0.15 for area B, which area has higher species richness and a steeper slope?

12. The image below depicts the result of gel electrophoresis

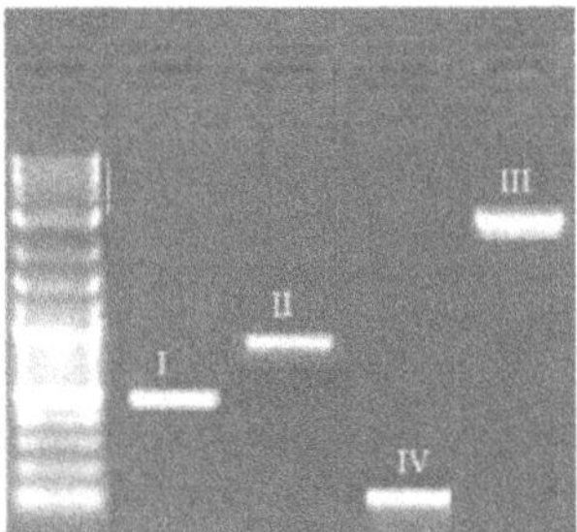

If the ladder represents sequence length upto 3000 base pairs (bp),
(a) Which of the bands (I - IV) correspond to 2500 bp and 100 bp respectively?
(b) Explain the basis of this kind of separation and also mention the significance of this process.

SECTION - C

13. Some restriction enzymes break a phosphodiester bond on both th7e DNA strands, such that only one end of each molecule is cut and these ends have regions of single stranded DNA. BamH1 is one such restriction enzyme which binds at the recognition sequence, 5'-GGATCC- 3'and cleaves these sequences just after the 5'- guanine on each strand.
(a) What is the objective of this action?
(b) Explain how the gene of interest is introduced into a vector.
(c) You are given the DNA shown below.
5'ATTTTGAGGATCCGTAATGTCCT 3'
3'TAAAACTCCTAGGCATTACAGGA 5'
If this DNA was cut with BamHI, how many DNA fragments would you expect? Write the sequence of these double-stranded DNA fragments with their respective polarity.
(d) A gene M was introduced into *E.coli* cloning vector PBR322 at BamH1 site. What will be its impact on the recombinant plamids? Give a possible way by which you could differentiate non recombinant to recombinant plasmids.

OR

GM crops especially Bt crops are known to have higher resistance to pest attacks. To substantiate this an experimental study was conducted in 4 different farmlands growing Bt and non Bt-Cotton crops. The farm lands had the same dimensions, fertility and were under similar climatic conditions. The histogram below shows the usage of pesticides on Bt crops and non-Bt crops in these farm lands.

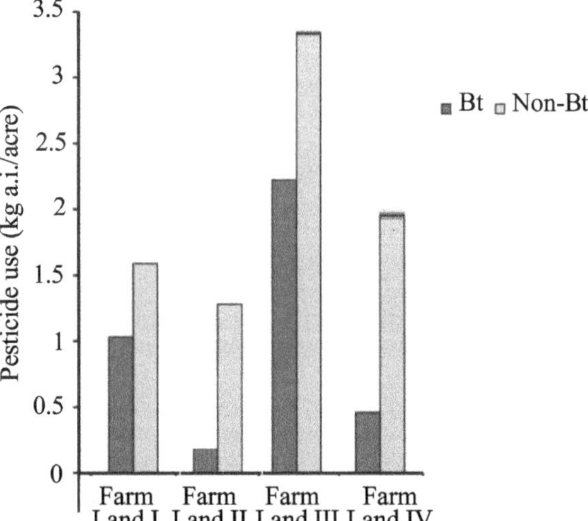

(a) Which of the above 4 farm lands has successfully applied the concepts of Biotechnology to show better management practices and use of agrochemicals? If you had to cultivate, which crop would you prefer (Bt or Non- Bt) and why?
(b) Cotton Bollworms were introduced in another experimental study on the above farm lands wherein no pesticide was used. Explain what effect would a Bt and Non Bt crop have on the pest.

Solutions

1. Microbial pathogens enter the gut of humans along with food:
   - Physical barriers: Mucus coating of the epithelium lining the gastrointestinal tract helps in trapping microbes entering our body. **[1 Mark]**
   - Physiological barriers: Acid in the stomach, saliva in the mouth prevent microbial growth. **[½ + ½ Mark]**

2. Streptokinase (produced by the bacterium Streptococcus) is used as a 'clot buster' for removing clots from the blood vessels of patients who have undergone myocardial infarction. **[1 Mark]**
   Statins (produced by the yeast Monascus purpureus) act as blood-cholesterol lowering agents. **[1 Mark]**

   OR

   Eradication of pests will disrupt predator-prey relationships, where beneficial predatory and parasitic insects which depend upon flora and fauna as food or hosts, may not be able to survive. **[1 Mark]**
   Holistic approach ensures that various life forms that inhabit the field, their life cycles, patterns of feeding and the habitats that they prefer are extensively studied and considered. **[1 Mark]**

3. It is Morphine. **[½ Mark]**
   Physically it appears as a white, odourless, crystalline compound. **[1½Mark]**

4. At collection points A and B, the BOD level is high due to high organic pollution caused by sugar factory and sewage discharge. **[1 Mark]**
   At the collection point C, the water was released after secondary treatment/ biological treatment (where vigorous growth of useful aerobic microbes into flocs consume the major part of the organic matter present in the river water or effluent due to sugar factory and sewage discharge). **[1 Mark]**

5. This interaction will lead to competition between the individuals of population A,B and C for resources. Eventually the 'fittest' individuals will survive and reproduce. **[1 Mark]**
   The resources for growth will become finite and limiting, and population growth will become realistic. **[1 Mark]**

6. The relationship between the plant and pollinator is called mutualism. Fig depends on wasp for pollination, and wasp depends on fig for food and shelter. **[1 Mark]**
   With the decline in population of figs, wasp loses its source of food and shelter. **[1 Mark]**

   OR

   Regulators; Thermoregulation, Osmoregulation Birds/ mammals (any one) **[½ × 4 Marks]**

7. Transformation of normal cells into cancerous neoplastic cells may be induced by following physical, chemical or biological agents causing DNA damage:
   - Ionising radiations like X-rays and gamma rays
   - Non-ionizing radiations like UV.
   - Chemical carcinogens present in tobacco smoke
   - Cellular oncogenes (c-onc) or proto-oncogenes, when activated under certain conditions cause cancer. Viruses with oncogenes can transform normal cells to cancerous cells. **[any 3; 1 × 3 Marks]**

   OR

   If the person has sustained high fever (39° to 40°C), weakness, stomach pain, constipation, headache and loss of appetite, it is Typhoid. **[1 Mark]**
   If the person has fever, chills, cough and headache; and the lips and fingernails turn gray to bluish, it is Pneumonia. **[1 Mark]**
   If the person has chills and high fever recurring every three to four days then, it is Malaria. **[1 Mark]**

8. - When our body encounters an antigenic protein or a pathogen for the first time it produces a response which is of low intensity and our body retains memory of the first encounter. **[1 Mark]**
   - The subsequent encounter with the same pathogen elicits a highly intensified response carried out with the help of two special types of lymphocytes present in our blood, B-lymphocytes, and T-lymphocytes. **[1 Mark]**
   - The B-lymphocytes produce an army of proteins in response to these pathogens into our blood to fight with them. These proteins are called antibodies. The T-cells themselves do not secrete antibodies but help B-cells produce them. **[1 Mark]**

9. The flow chart shows the three steps involved in the process of PCR showing the following
   – Denaturation The DNA strands are treated with a temperature of 940C (Heat) and the strands are separated.
   – Annealing The primers anneal to the complementary strands.
   – Extension The DNA polymerase facilitates the extension of the strands. **[1 × 3 = 3 Marks]**

OR

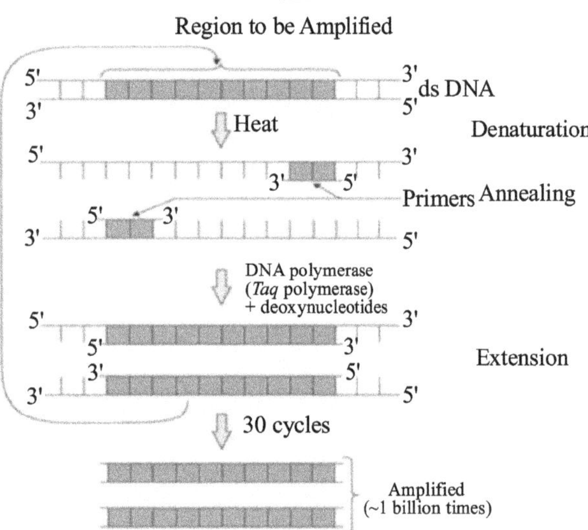

Diagram : Polymerase Chain Reaction

10. (a) When a large habitat is broken into small fragments due to various activities, mammals and birds requiring large territories and certain animals with migratory habitats are badly affected, leading to population decline. **[1 Mark]**

(b)
- Nile perch introduced in Lake Victoria eventually led to the extinction of an ecologically unique assemblage of more than 200 species of cichild fish.
- Parthenium/Lantana/water hyacinth caused environmental damage and threat to our native species
- African catfish-Clarias gariepinus introduced for aquaculture purposes is posing a threat to the indigenous catfishes in our rivers. (Any one) **[1 Mark]**

(c) Yes; Humans have overexploited natural resources for their 'greed' rather than 'need' leading to extinction of these animals. Sustainable harvesting could have prevented extinction of these species. **[1 Mark]**

11. (a) India fs history of religious and cultural traditions emphasized the protection of nature. In many cultures, tracts of forest are set aside, all the trees and wildlife within are venerated and given total protection. Sacred groves in many states are the last refuges for a large number of rare and threatened plants. **[2 Marks]**

(b) Area A will have more species richness and a steeper slope. **[1 Mark]**

12. (a) Band III corresponds to 2500 base pairs, and Band IV corresponds to 100bp. **[½ + ½ Mark]**

(b) The fragments will resolve according to their size. The shorter sequence fragments would move farthest from well as seen in Band IV (100 bp) which is lighter as compared to Band III which is heavier being 2500 base pairs. **[1 Mark]**

The significance of electrophoresis is to purify the DNA fragments for use in constructing recombinant DNA by joining them with cloning vectors. **[1 Mark]**

13. (a) The two different DNA molecules will have compatible ends to recombine. **[½ Mark]**

(b) Restriction enzyme cuts the DNA of the vector and then ligates the gene of interest into the DNA of the vector. **[1 Mark]**

(c) 2 fragments **[½ Mark]**

5'ATTTTGAG 3'5'GATCCGTAATGTCCT 3'
3'TAAAACTCCTAG 5'.3'GCATTACAGGA 5' **[1 Mark]**

(d) BamH1 site will affect tetracycline antibiotic resistance gene, hence the recombinant plasmids will lose tetracycline resistance due to inactivation of the resistance gene. **[1 Mark]**

Recombinants can be selected from non recombinants by plating into a medium containing tetracycline, as the recombinants will not grow in the medium because the tetracycline resistance gene is cut. **[1 Mark]**

OR

(a) Farm Land II. **[½ Mark]**

Bt crop. **[½ Mark]**

Because the use of pesticides is highly reduced for Bt crop // Decrease of pesticide used is also more significant for Bt crop. **[1 Mark]**

(b) In Bt cotton a cry gene has been introduce from bacterium Bacillus thuringiensis (Bt) which causes synthesis of a toxic protein. This protein becomes active in the alkaline gut of bollworm feeding on cotton, punching holes in the lining causing death of the insect. **[2 Marks]**

However; a Non Bt crop will have no effect on the cotton bollworm/ the yield of cotton will decrease / non Bt will succumb to pest attack. **[1 Mark]**

All India 2021-22

CBSE Board Sample Paper Term-I

Time Allowed : 90 Minutes | *Maximum Marks : 35*

General Instructions:

(i) The Question Paper contains three sections.

(ii) Section **A** has **24** questions. Attempt any **20** questions.

(iii) Section **B** has **24** questions. Attempt any **20** questions.

(iv) Section **C** has **12** questions. Attempt any **10** questions.

(v) All questions carry equal marks.

(vi) There is no negative marking.

SECTION - A

This section consists of 24 questions. Attempt any 20 questions from this section. The first attempted 20 questions would be evaluated.

1. The structure of bilobed anther consists of

(a) 2 thecae, 2 sporangia (b) 4 thecae, 4 sporangia

(c) 4 thecae, 2 sporangia (d) 2 thecae, 4 sporangia

2. In the figure of anatropous ovule given below, choose the correct option for the characteristic distribution of cells within the typical embryo sac

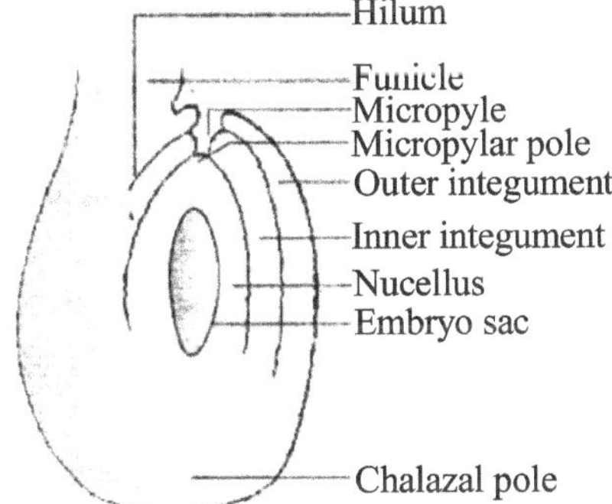

	Number of cells at chalazal end	Number of cells at micropylar end	Number of nuclei left in central cell
A	3	2	3
B	3	3	2
C	2	3	3
D	2	2	4

3. The coconut water from tender coconut is

(a) cellular endosperm.

(b) free nuclear endosperm.

(c) both cellular and nuclear endosperm.

(d) free nuclear embryo.

4. Pollen grains are well preserved as fossils because of presence of

(a) sporopollenin (b) cellulose

(c) lignocellulose (d) pectocellulose

5. Which of the following statements are true related to Seed X and Y?

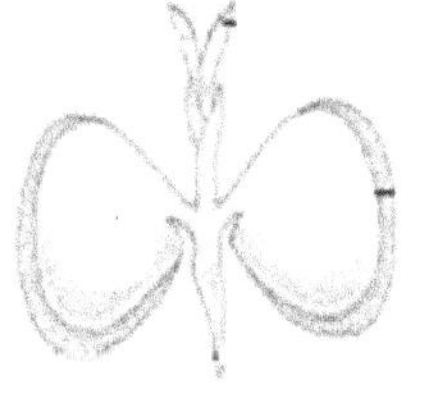

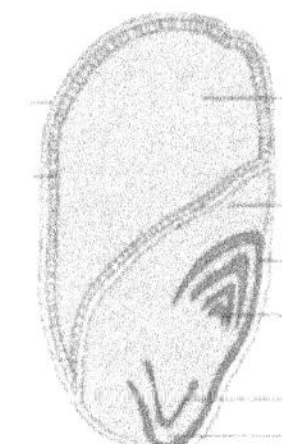

Seed X **Seed Y**

(i) Seed X is dicot and endospermic or albuminous.

(ii) Seed X is dicot and non-endospermic or non-albuminous.

(iii) Seed Y is monocot and endospermic or albuminous.

(iv) Seed Y is monocot and non-endospermic or non-albuminous.

Choose the correct option with the respect to the nature of the seed

(a) (i), (iii) (b) (ii), (iii)

(c) (i), (iv) (d) (ii), (iv)

6. Which of the following statements are correct with respect to hormones secreted by placenta?

(i) Placenta secretes relaxin during later stage of pregnancy.

(ii) Placenta secretes high amount of FSH during pregnancy.

(iii) Placenta secretes relaxin during initial stage of pregnancy.

(iv) Placenta secretes hCG and hPL during pregnancy.

(a) (i) and (iv) (b) (i), (ii) and (iv)

(c) (iii) and (iv) (d) (ii), (iii) and (iv)

7. Figure A shows the front view of the human female reproductive system and Figure B shows the development of a fertilized human egg cell

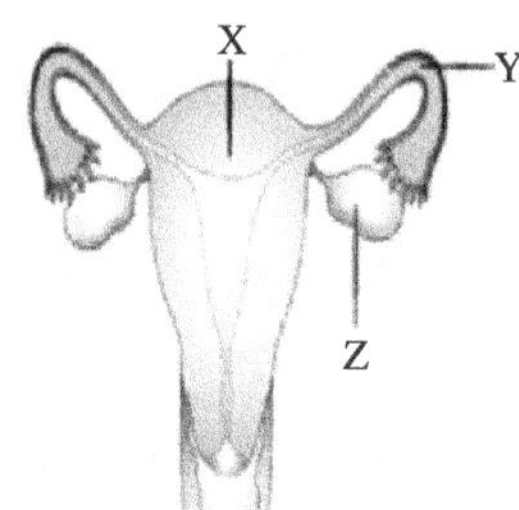

Figure B

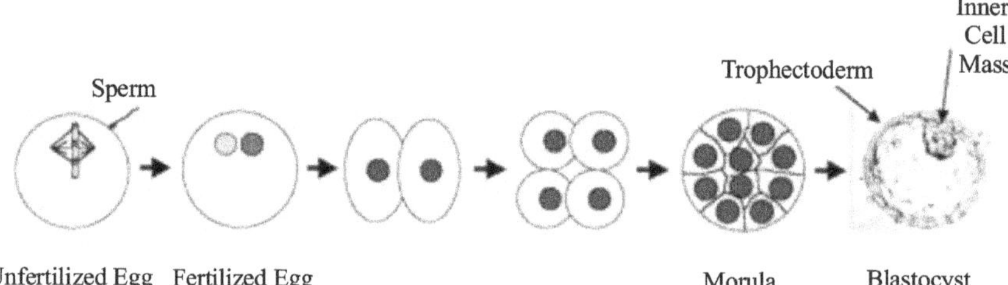

Identify the correct stage of development of human embryo (Figure B) that takes place at the site X, Y and Z respectively in the human female reproductive system (Figure A).

Choose the correct option from the table below:

	X	Y	Z
A	Morula	Fertilized egg	Blastocyst
B	Unfertilized egg	Fertilized egg	Morula
C	Blastocyst	Fertilized egg	Unfertilized egg
D	Fertilized egg	Morula	Blastocyst

8. Penetration of the sperm in the ovum is followed by
(a) formation of first polar body.
(b) completion of meiosis II.
(c) first meiosis.
(d) dissolution of zona pellucida.

9. The correct sequence of hormone secretion from beginning of menstruation is
(a) FSH, progesterone, estrogen.
(b) estrogen, FSH, progesterone.
(c) FSH, estrogen, progesterone.
(d) estrogen, progesterone, FSH.

10. In the dioecious aquatic plant shown, identify the characteristics of the male flowers that reach the female flowers for pollination:

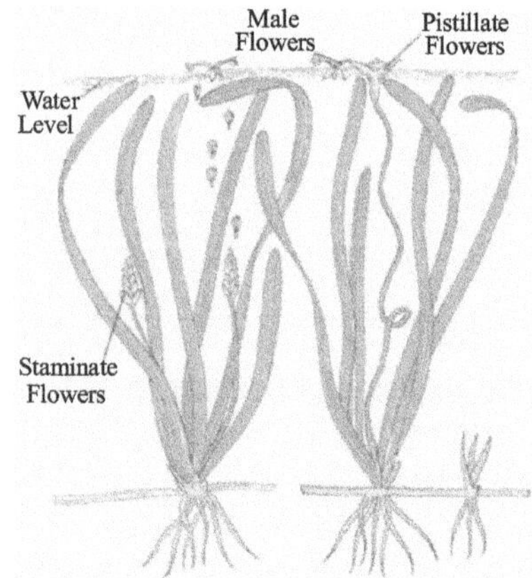

	Size of the flower	Colour of flower	Characteristic feature of pollengrain
A	small	brightly coloured	Light weight and non-sticky
B	large	colourless	large and sticky
C	small	white	small, covered with mucilage
D	large	colourless	non sticky

11. The thalamus contributes to the fruit formation in
(a) banana (b) orange
(c) strawberry (d) guava.

12. How many types of gametes would be produced if the genotype of a parent is AaBB?
(a) 1 (b) 2
(c) 3 (d) 4

13. Which of the following statements indicates parallelism in genes and chromosomes?
(i) They occur in pairs
(ii) They segregate during gamete formation
(iii) They show linkage
(iv) Independent pairs segregate independently
(a) (i) and (iii) (b) (ii) and (iii)
(c) (i), (ii) and (iii) (d) (i), (ii) and (iv)

14. Which of the following amino acid substitution is responsible for causing sickle cell anemia?
(a) Valine is substituted by Glutamic acid in the á globin chain at the sixth position
(b) Valine is substituted by Glutamic acid in the â globin chain at seventh position
(c) Glutamic acid is substituted by Valine in the á globin chain at the sixth position
(d) Glutamic acid is substituted by Valine in the â globin chain at the sixth position

15. In human beings, where genotype AABBCC represents dark skin colour, aabbcc represents light skin colour and AaBbCc represents intermediate skin colour; the pattern of genetic inheritance can be termed as:
(a) Pleiotropy and codominance
(b) Pleiotropy and incomplete dominance
(c) Polygenic and qualitative inheritance
(d) Polygenic and quantitative inheritance

16. Which of the following combination of chromosome numbers represents the correct sex determination pattern in honey bees?
(a) Male 32, Female 16
(b) Male 16, Female 32
(c) Male 31, Female 32
(d) Female 32, Male 31

17. Rajesh and Mahesh have defective haemoglobin due to genetic disorders. Rajesh has too few globin molecules while Mahesh has incorrectly functioning globin molecules. Identify the disorder they are suffering from.

	Rajesh	Mahesh
(a)	Sickle cell anaemia- an autosome linked recessive trait	Thalassemia - an autosome linked dominant trait
(b)	Thalassemia - an autosome linked recessive blood disorder	Sickle cell anaemia - an autosome linked recessive trait
(c)	Sickle cell anaemia - an autosome linked recessive trait	Thalassemia - an autosome linked recessive blood disorder
(d)	Thalassemia - an autosome linked recessive blood disorder	Sickle cell anaemia - an autosome linked dominant trait

18. Which of the following criteria must a molecule fulfil to act as a genetic material?
(i) It should not be able to generate its replica
(ii) It should chemically and structurally be stable
(iii) It should not allow slow mutation
(iv) It should be able to express itself in the form of Mendelian Characters
(a) (i) and (ii)
(b) (ii) and (iii)
(c) (iii) and (iv)
(d) (ii) and (iv)

19. The promoter site and the terminator site for transcription are located at
(a) 3' (downstream) end and 5 Œ (upstream) end, respectively of the transcription unit
(b) 5' (upstream) end and 3 Œ (downstream) end, respectively of the transcription unit
(c) the 5' (upstream) end of the transcription unit
(d) the 3' (downstream) end of the transcription unit

20. Which of the following is correct about mature RNA in eukaryotes?
(a) Exons and introns do not appear in the mature RNA.
(b) Exons appear, but introns do not appear in the mature RNA.
(c) Introns appear, but exons do not appear in the mature RNA.
(d) Both exons and introns appear in the mature RNA.

21. In *E.coli*, the lac operon gets switched on when
(a) lactose is present and it binds to the repressor.
(b) repressor binds to operator.
(c) RNA polymerase binds to the operator.
(d) lactose is present and it binds to RNA polymerase.

22. Oswald Avery, Colin MacLeod and Maclyn McCarty used enzymes to purify biochemicals such as proteins, DNA and RNA from the heat-killed S cells to see which ones could transform live R cells into S cells in Griffith's experiment. They observed that
(a) Proteases and RNases affected transformation.
(b) DNase inhibited transformation.
(c) Proteases and Lipases affected transformation.
(d) RNases inhibited transformation.

23.

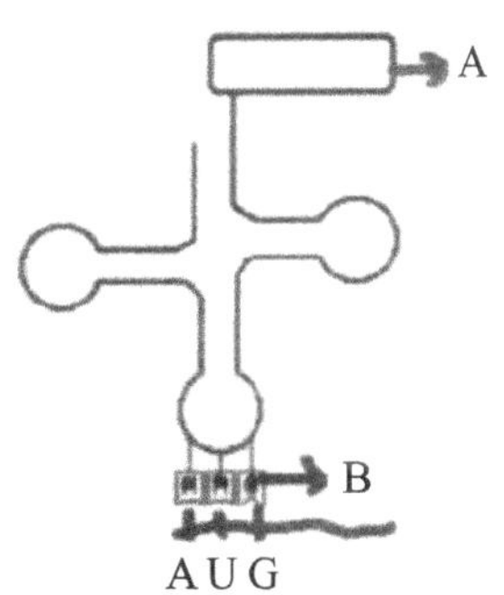

AUG on the mRNA will result in the activation of which of the following RNA having correct combination of amino acids:

	Site A	Site B
(a)	UAC	Methionine
(b)	Methionine	UAC
(c)	Methionine	AUG
(d)	AUG	Methionine

24. Short stretches of DNA used to identify complementary sequence in a sample are called
(a) probes (b) markers
(c) VNTRs (d) primers

SECTION - B

DIRECTION: *This section consists of 24 questions (Sl. No.25 to 48). Attempt any 20 questions from this section. The first attempted 20 questions would be evaluated.*

***Direction:** Question Nos. **25 to 28** consist of two statements Assertion (A) and Reason (R). Answer these questions selecting the appropriate option given below:*

(a) If both Assertion and Reason are True and the Reason is a correct explanation of the Assertion.
(b) If both Assertion and Reason are True but Reason is not a correct explanation of the Assertion.
(c) If the Assertion is True but Reason is False.
(d) If both Assertion and Reason are False.

25. **Assertion:** Lactational amenorrhea is the natural method of contraception.
Reason: It increases the phagocytosis of sperm.

26. **Assertion:** Saheli, an oral contraceptive for females, contains a steroidal preparation.
Reason: It is a "once a week" pill with very few side effects.

27. **Assertion:** Parturition is induced by a complex neuro endocrine meachanism.
Reason: At the end of gestation period, the maternal pituitary releases prolactin which causes uterine contractions.

28. **Assertion:** When the two genes in a dihybrid cross are situated on the same chromosome, the proportion of parental gene combinations is much higher than nonparental type.
Reason: Higher parental gene combinations can be attributed to crossing over between two genes.

29. Concentration of which of the following substances will decrease in the maternal blood as it flows from embryo to placenta through the umbilical cord?

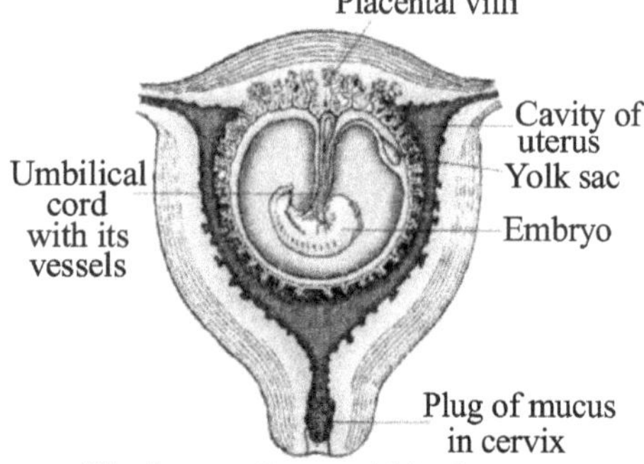

The human foetus within the uterus

(i)	Oxygen	(ii)	Amino Acids
(iii)	Carbon dioxide	(iv)	Urea
(a)	(i) and (ii)	(b)	(ii) and (iv)
(c)	(iii) and (iv)	(d)	(i) and (iv)

30. In a fertilized ovule, n, 2n and 3n conditions occur respectively in
(a) antipodal, zygote and endosperm
(b) zygote, nucellus and endosperm
(c) endosperm, nucellus and zygote.
(d) antipodals, synergids and integusments

31. A botanist studying Viola (common pansy) noticed that one of the two flower types withered and developed no further due to some unfavorable condition, but the other flower type on the same plant survived and it resulted in an assured seed set. Which of the following will be correct?
(a) The flower type which survived is Cleistogamous and it always exhibits autogamy
(b) The flower type which survived is Chasmogamous and it always exhibits geitonogamy.
(c) The flower type which survived is Cleistogamous and it exhibits both autogamy and geitonogamy.
(d) The flower type which survived is Chasmogamous and it never exhibits autogamy.

32. During parturition, a pregnant woman is having prolonged labour pains and child birth has to be fastened. It is advisable to administer a hormone that can
(a) increase the metabolic rate.
(b) release glucose in the blood.
(c) stimulate the ovary.
(d) activate smooth muscles.

33. A female undergoing IVF treatment has blocked fallopian tubes. The technique by which the embryo with more than 8 blastomeres will be transferred into the female for further development is
(a) ZIFT (b) GIFT
(c) IUT (d) AI

34. The mode of action of the copper ions in an IUD is to
(a) increase the movement of sperms.
(b) decrease the movement of the sperms.
(c) make the uterus unsuitable for implantation.
(d) make the cervix hostile to the sperms.

35. To produce 400 seeds, the number of meiotic divisions required will be
(a) 400 (b) 200
(c) 500 (d) 800

36. A cross is made between tall pea plants having green pods and dwarf pea plants having yellow pods. In the F2 generation, out of 80 plants how many are likely to be tall plants?
(a) 15 (b) 20
(c) 45 (d) 60

37. In Antirrhinum, RR is phenotypically red flowers, rr is white and Rr is pink. Select the correct phenotypic ratio in F1 generation when a cross is performed between RR X Rr:
(a) 1 red: 2 Pink: 1 white (b) 2 Pink: 1 white
(c) 2 Red: 2 Pink (d) All Pink

38. What would be the genotype of the parents if the offspring have the phenotypes in 1:1 proportion?
(a) Aa X Aa (b) AA X AA
(c) Aa X AA (d) Aa x aa

39. What is the pattern of inheritance in the above pedigree chart?

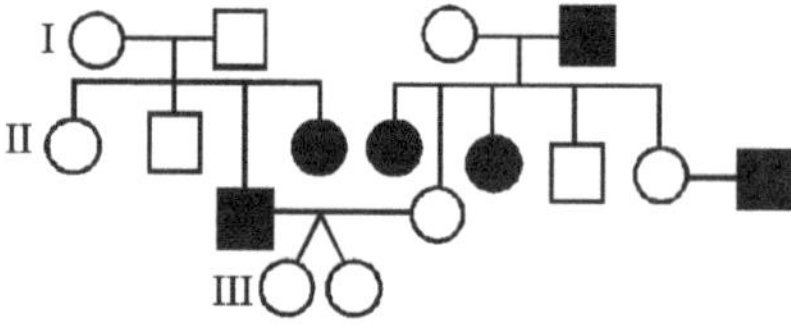

(a) Autosomal dominant (b) Autosomal recessive
(c) Sex -linked dominant (d) Sex -linked recessive

40. A couple has two daughters. What is the probability that the third child will also be a female?
(a) 25% (b) 50%
(c) 75% D. 100%

41. Genotypic ratio of 1:2:1 is obtained in a cross between
(a) AB X AB (b) Ab X Ab
(c) Ab X ab (d) ab X ab

42. Total number of nucleotide sequences of DNA that codes for a hormone is 1530. The proportion of different bases in the sequence is found to be Adenine = 34%, Guanine = 19%, Cytosine = 23%, Thymine = 19%.
Applying Chargaff's rule, what conclusion can be drawn?
(a) It is a double stranded circular DNA.
(b) It is a single stranded DNA.
(c) It is a double stranded linear DNA.
(d) It is a single stranded DNA coiled on Histones.

43. A stretch of an euchromatin has 200 nucleosomes. How many bp will there be in the stretch and what would be the length of the typical euchromatin?
(a) 20,000 bp and $13,000 - 10^{-9}$ m
(b) 10,000 bp and $10,000 - 10^{-9}$ m
(c) 40,000 bp and $13,600 \times 10^{-9}$ m
(d) 40,000 bp and $13,900 \times 10^{-9}$ m

44. Observe structures A and B given below. Which of the following statements are correct?

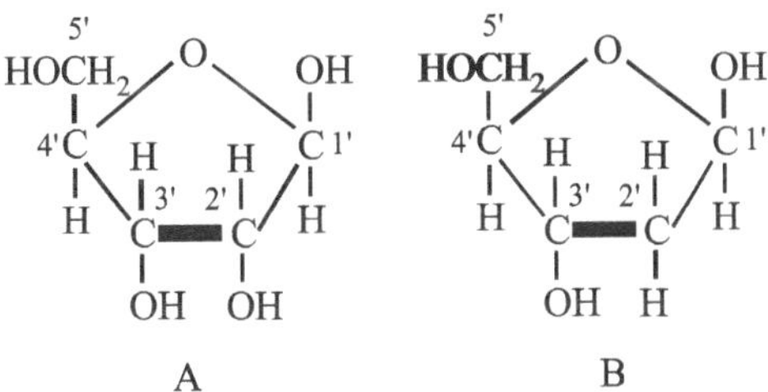

(a) A is having 2'-OH group which makes it less reactive and structurally stable, whereas B is having 2'-H group which makes it more reactive and unstable.
(b) A is having 2'-OH group which makes it more reactive and structurally unstable, whereas B is having 2'-H group which makes it less reactive and structurally stable.
(c) A and B both have -OH groups which make it more reactive and structurally stable.
(d) A and B both are having -OH groups which make it less reactive and structurally stable

45. If Meselson and Stahl's experiment is continued for sixth generations in bacteria, the ratio of Heavy strands 15N/15N : Hybrid15N/14N : light 14N/14N containing DNA in the sixth generation would be
(a) 1:1:1 (b) 0:1:7
(c) 0:1:15 (d) 0:1:31

46. Two important RNA processing events lead to specialized end sequences in most human mRNAs: ____(i)____ at the 5' end, and ____(ii)____ at the 3' end. At the 5' end the most distinctive specialized end nucleotide, ____(iii)____ is added and a sequence of about 200 (iv) is added to the 3' end.
(a) (i) Initiator codon (ii) Promotor (iii) Terminator codon (iv) Release factors
(b) (i) Promotor (ii) Elongation (iii) Regulation (iv) Termination.
(c) (i) Capping (ii) Polyadenylation (iii) mGppp (iv) Poly(A).
(d) (i) Repressor (ii) Co repressor (iii) Operon (iv) sRelease factors

47. What are minisatellites?
(a) 10-40 bp sized small sequences within the genes
(b) Short coding repetitive region on the eukaryotic genome
(c) Short non-coding repetitive sequence forming large portion of eukaryotic genome
(d) Regions of coding strands of the DNA

48. There was a mix-up at the hospital after a fire accident in the nursery division. Which of these children belong to the parents?

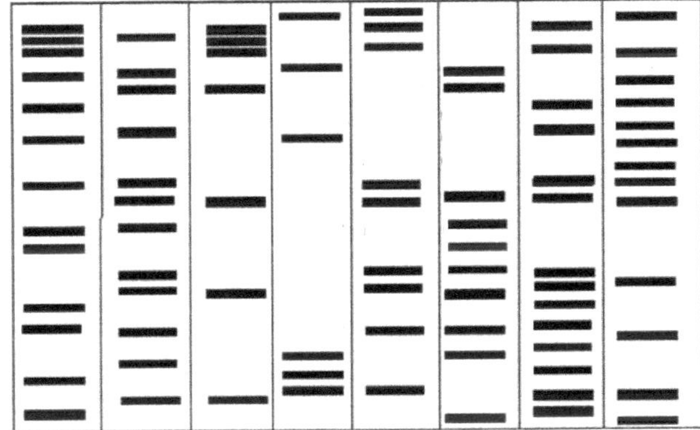

(a) All of the children (b) Children 2, 3 & 6
(c) Children 1 & 3 (d) Children 2 & 4

SECTION - B

DIRECTION: *This section consists of one case followed by 6 questions linked to this case (Q.No.49 to 54). Besides this, 6 more questions are given. Attempt any 10 questions in this section. The first attempted 10 questions would be evaluated.*

Case: ***To answer the questions, study the graphs below for Subject 1 and 2 showing different levels of certain hormones.***

Subject - 1

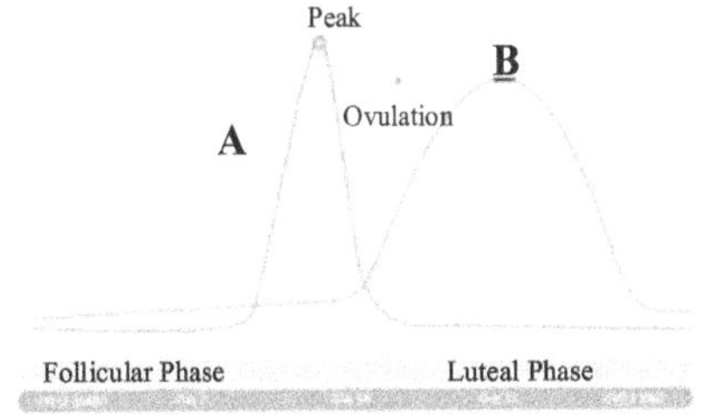

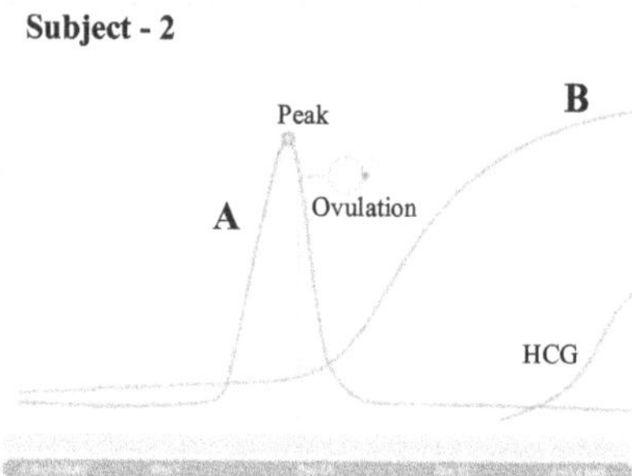

49. The peak observed in Subject 1 and 2 is due to
   (a) estrogen
   (b) progesterone
   (c) luteinizing hormone
   (d) follicle stimulating hormone

50. Subject 2 has higher level of hormone B, which is
   (a) estrogen
   (b) progesterone
   (c) luteinizing hormone
   (d) follicle stimulating hormone

51. If the peak of Hormone A does not appear in the study for Subject 1, which of the following statement is true?
   (a) Peak of Hormone B will be observed at a higher point in the graph
   (b) Peak of Hormone B will be observed at a point lower than what is given in the graph
   (c) There will be no observed data for Hormone B
   (d) The graph for Hormone B will be a sharp rise followed by a plateau

52. Which structure in the ovary will remain functional in subject 2?
   (a) Corpus Luteum (b) Tertiary follicle
   (c) Graafian follicle (d) Primary follicle

53. For subject 2 it is observed that the peak for hormone B has reached the plateau stage. After approximately how much time will the curve for hormone B descend?
   (a) 28 days (b) 42 days
   (c) 180 days (d) 280 days

54. Which of the following statements is true about the subjects?
   (a) Subject 1 is pregnant
   (b) Subject 2 is pregnant
   (c) Both subject 1 and 2 are pregnant
   (d) Both subject 1 and 2 are not pregnant

55. The gene that controls the ABO blood group system in human beings has three alleles - I^A, I^B and i. A child has blood group O. His father has blood group A and mother has blood group B. Genotypes of other off springs can be:
   (i) I^BI^B (ii) I^Ai
   (iii) I^Bi (iv) I^AI^B
   (v) ii
   (a) (i), (ii), (iii), (v)
   (b) (ii), (iii), (iv), (v)
   (c) (iii),(iv), (v)
   (d) (iv), (iii), (i)

56. Placed below is a karyotype of a human being.

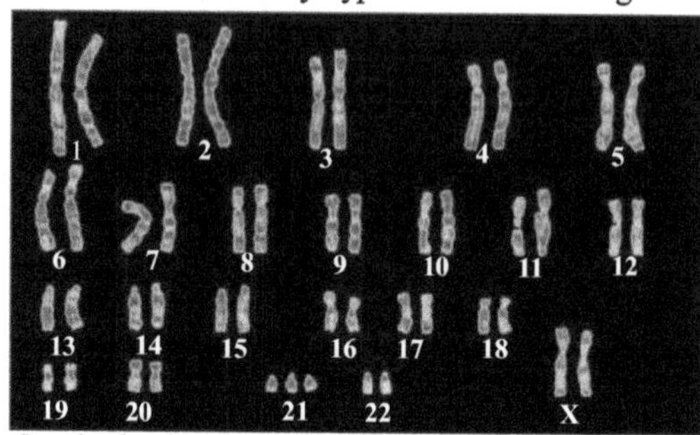

On the basis of this karyotype, which of the following conclusions can be drawn:
   (a) Normal human female
   (b) Person is suffering from Colour Blindness
   (c) Affected individual is a female with Down's syndrome
   (d) Affected individual is a female with Turner's syndrome

57. Given below is a dihybrid cross performed on Drosophila.

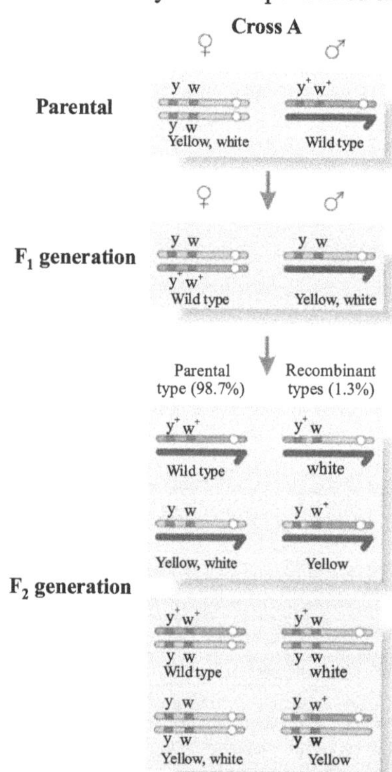

Which of the following conclusions can be drawn on the basis of this cross?

When yellow bodied (y), white eyed (w) Drosophila females were hybridized with brown bodied (y+), red eyed males (w+) and F1 progenies were intercrossed, F2 generation would have shown the following ratio:
   (a) 1:2:1 because of linkage of genes
   (b) 9:3:3:1 because of recombination of genes
   (c) Deviation from 9:3:3:1 ratio because of segregation of genes
   (d) Deviation from 9:3:3:1 ratio because of linkage of genes

58. Which cellular process is shown below?

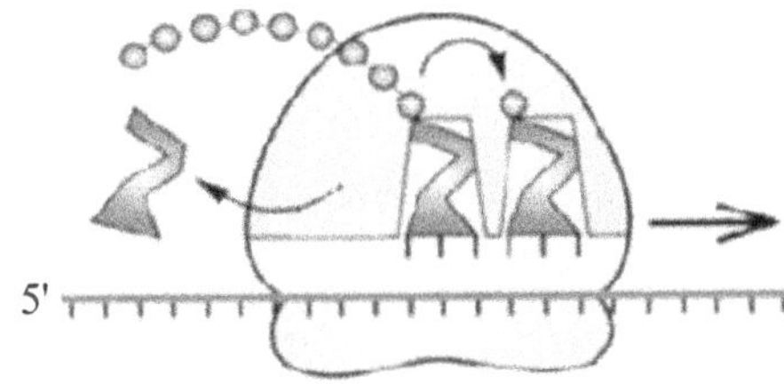

(a) DNA Replication
(b) Translation - Initiation
(c) Translation - Elongation
(d) Translation – Termination

59. Origin of replication of DNA in E. coli is shown below, Identify the labelled parts (i), (ii), (iii) and (iv)

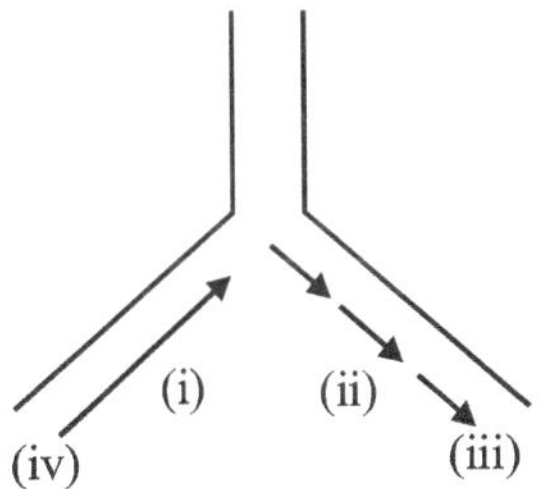

(a) (i)- discontinuous synthesis , (ii)- continuous synthesis (iii) 3' end (iv) 5'end
(b) (i)- continuous synthesis , (ii)- discontinuous synthesis (iii) 5' end (iv) 3'end
(c) (i)- discontinuous synthesis, (ii)- continuous synthesis (iii) 5' end (iv) 3'end
(d) (i)- continuous synthesis , (ii)- discontinuous synthesis (iii) 3' end (iv) 5'end

60. Transcription unit is represented in the diagram given below. Identify site (i), factor (ii) and Enzyme (iii) responsible for carrying out the process.

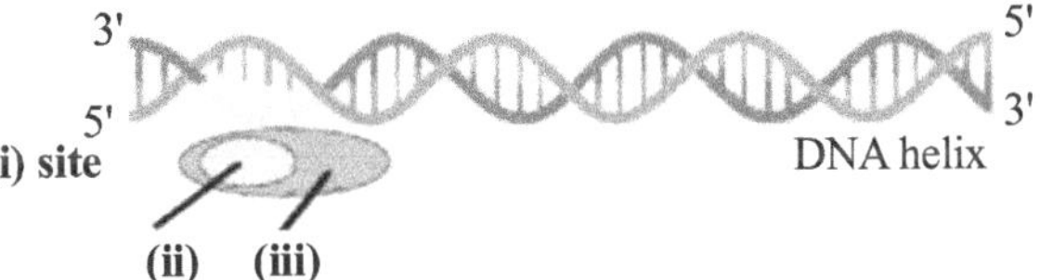

(a) (i) Promoter Site, (ii) Rho factor (iii) RNA polymerase
(b) (i) Terminator Site, (ii) Sigma factor (iii) RNA polymerase
(c) (i) Promoter Site, (ii) Sigma factor (iii) RNA polymerase
(d) (i) Promoter Site, (ii) Sigma factor (iii) DNA polymerase

Solutions

1. **(b)** 2 thecae, 4 sporangia
2. **(b)** 3, 3, 2
   3 in chalazar end 3 in the micropolar end and 2 nuclei in the center.
3. **(b)** Free nuclear endosperm
4. **(a)** sporopollenin
5. **(b)** (ii), (iii)
6. **(a)** (i) and (iv)
7. **(c)** blastocyst, Fertilized egg, Unfertilized egg
8. **(b)** completion of meiosis II
9. **(c)** FSH, estrogen,progesterone
10. **(c)** small, White, Small, covered with mucilage
11. **(c)** strawberry
12. **(b)** 2
13. **(d)** (i), (ii) and (iv)
14. **(d)** Glutamic acid is substituted by Valine in β chain at the sixth position
15. **(d)** Polygenic and quantitative inheritance
16. **(b)** Male 16, Female 32
17. **(b)**

Rajesh	Mahesh
Thalassemia - an autosome linked recessive blood disorder	Sickle cell anaemia - an autosome linked recessive trait

18. **(d)** (ii) and (iv)
19. **(b)** 5' (upstream) end and 3' (downstream) end, respectively of the transcription unit
20. **(b)** exons appear but introns do not appear in the mature RNA
21. **(a)** lactose is present, and it binds to the repressor
22. **(b)** DNase inhibited transformation
23. **(b)** Methionine – UAC
24. **(a)** Probes
25. **(c)** A is true but R is false
26. **(d)** A is False but R is true
27. **(c)** A is true but R is False
28. **(c)** A is true but R is false
29. **(a)** (i) and (ii)
30. **(a)** antipodal, zygote and endosperm
31. **(a)** The flower type which survived is Cleistogamous and it will always exhibit autogamy
32. **(d)** activate smooth muscles
33. **(b)** GIFT
34. **(b)** decrease the movement of the sperms
35. **(c)** 500
36. **(d)** 60
   Out of $9:3:3:1 = 16$
   $9 + 3$ will be tall.
   Therefore, $12/16 \times 80 = 60$
37. **(c)** 2 Red : 2 Pink
38. **(d)** Aa × aa
39. **(b)** Autosomal recessive
40. **(b)** 50%
41. **(b)** Ab × Ab
42. **(b)** It is a single stranded DNA
43. **(c)** 40,000 bp and $13{,}600 \times 10^{-9}$ m
44. **(b)** A is having 2'-OH group which makes it more reactive and structurally unstable whereas B is having 2'-H group which makes it less reactive and structurally stable
45. **(d)** 0 : 1 : 31
46. **(c)** (i) Capping (ii) Polyadenylation (iii) $^{m}G_{ppp.}$ (iv) Poly(A).
47. **(c)** Short non-coding repetitive sequence forming large portion of eukaryotic genome
48. **(c)** A. Children 1 & 3
49. **(c)** luteinizing hormone
50. **(b)** Progesterone
51. **(c)** There will be no observed data for Hormone B
52. **(a)** Corpus Luteum
53. **(d)** 280 days
54. **(b)** Subject 2 is pregnant
55. **(b)** (ii), (iii), (iv), (v)
56. **(c)** Affected individual is a female with Down's syndrome
57. **(d)** Deviation from 9:3:3:1 ratio because of linkage of genes
58. **(c)** Translation- Elongation
59. **(d)** (i)- continuous synthesis , (ii)- discontinuous synthesis (iii) 3' end (iv) 5' end
60. **(c)** (i) Promotor Site, (ii) Sigma factor (iii) RNA polymerase

All India 2020

CBSE Board Solved Paper

Time Allowed : 3 Hours *Maximum Marks : 70*

General Instructions:

Read the following instructions very carefully and strictly follow them:

(i) Question paper comprises **five** sections – **A, B, C, D** and **E**.

(ii) There are **27** questions in the question paper. All questions are compulsory.

(iii) Section **A** - Questions no. **1** to **5** are multiple choice questions, carrying **1** mark each.

(iv) Section **B** – Questions no. **6** to **12** are short-answer questions type-**I,** carrying **2** marks each.

(v) Section **C** – Questions no. **13** to **21** are short-answer questions type-**II,** carrying **3** marks each.

(vi) Section **D** – Questions no. **22** to **24** are short-answer questions type-**III,** carrying **3** marks each.

(vii) Section **E** – Questions no. **25** to **27** are long-answer questions, carrying **5** marks each.

(viii) Answer should be brief and to the point.

(ix) There is no overall choice in the question paper. However, an internal choice has been provided in **two** questions of **1** mark, **one** question of **2** marks, **two** questions of **3** marks and **three** questions of **5** marks. Only **one** of the choices in such questions have to be attempted.

(x) The diagrams drawn should be neat, proportionate and properly labelled, wherever necessary.

(xi) In addition to this, separate instructions are given with each section and question, wherever necessary.

SECTION - A

1. ' 'Cry' protein' coded by gene Cry IAb controls

(a) Cotton bollworm

(b) Corn borer

(c) Tobacco budworm

(d) Mosquito

2. Meselson and Stahl carried out centrifugation in $CsCl_2$ density gradient to separate:

(a) DNA from RNA

(b) DNA from protein

(c) the normal DNA from $^{15}N - DNA$

(d) DNA from tRNA

3. Self-pollination is fully ensured if

(a) the flower is bisexual

(b) the style is longer than the filament

(c) the flower is cleistogamous

(d) the time of pistil and anther maturity is different

OR

Zoozpores are the reproductive units to carry asexual reproduction in

(a) Chlamydomonas (b) Spirogyra

(c) Yeast (d) Rhizopus

4. Micropropagation can be achieved by

(a) self-pollination

(b) asexual reproduction

(c) tissue culture

(d) vegetative propagation

OR

The microbes commonly used in kitchens are

(a) Lactobacillus and Yeast

(b) Penicillium and Yeast

(c) Microspora and E. coli

(d) Rhizopus and Lactobacillus

5. The main barrier that prevents the entry of micro-organisms into our body is
   (a) Antibodies
   (b) Macrophages
   (c) Monocytes
   (d) Skin

SECTION - B

6. Name the genus of bacolovirus that acts as a biological control agent in spite of being a pathogen. Justify by giving three reasons that make it an excellent for the job.

OR

"Micro-organisms play an important role for the biological treatment of sewage." Justify.

7. It is often observed that the chances of a person suffering from measles in his or her lifetime are low if he or she has suffered from the disease in their early childhood. Justify the statement.

8. Wings of birds and wings of butterflies contribute to locomotion. Explain the type of evolution such organs are a result of.

9. Name and mention the events that occur in the cells when HIV gets into blood after gaining entry into the human body.

10. List the four different human male accessory ducts.

11. State what is out-crossing type of breeding. Mention on what type of cattle this practiced.

12. Given below is one of the strands of a DNA segment:

$$3' \xrightarrow{TACGTACGTACGTACG} G'$$

   (a) Write its complementary strand.
   (b) Write a possible RNA strand that can be transcribed form the above DNA molecule formed.

SECTION - C

13. Generally it is observed that human males suffer from hemophilia more than that of human females who rarely suffer from it. Explain giving reason.

OR

F_1 progeny of pea plant bearing violet flowers and snapdragon plant bearing red flowers were selfed to produce their respective F_2 progeny. Compare the phenotypes, the genotypes and the pattern of inheritance of their respective F_2 progeny.

14. For a layman, both apple and banana are fruits. But a biology student categorises fruits as true fruits, false fruits and parthenocarpic fruits. Justify.

15. Draw a schematic transverse section of a mature anther of an angiosperm. Label tis epidermis, middle layers, tapetum, endothecium, sporogenous tissue and the connective.

16. Alien species invasion has been a threat to biodiversity. Justify with the help of a suitable example. List any other three causes responsible for such a loss.

17. Explain the changes that milk undergoes when suitable starter/inoculum is added to it. How does the end product formed prove to be beneficial for human health?

18. Explain the three steps carried out in the formation of recombinant DNA using the enzyme EcoRI.

19. In an E. coli cloning vector pBR 322, state the role of the following genes:
   (a) ori gene
   (b) Antibiotic resistance gene
   (c) rop gene

20. Study the table given below and identify a, b, c, d, e and f:

Crops	Variety	Resistance to disease
A	Pusa sadabahar	B
C	d	White rust
E	Himgiri	f

OR

What is plant breeding? Explain the two steps involved in classical plant breeding.

21. Study the population growth curve given below and answer the questions that follow:

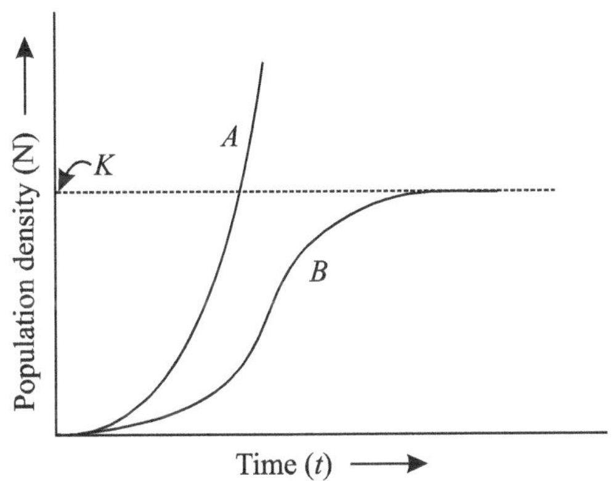

(a) Identify 'A' and 'B' shown in the graph.
(b) When and why do such curves occur in a population?

SECTION - D

22. Study the age pyramid 'A', 'B' and 'C' of the human population given below and answer the questions that follow:

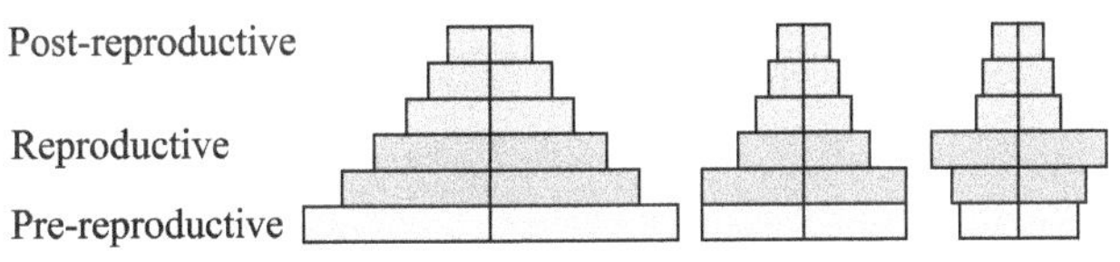

(a) Identify pyramid 'B' and 'C'.

(b) Write the basis on which the above pyramids are plotted.

23. Insulin in the human body is secreted by pancreas as prohormone/proinsulin. The schematic polypeptide structure of proinsulin is given below. This proinsulin needs to undergo processing before it becomes functional in the body. Answer the questions that follow:

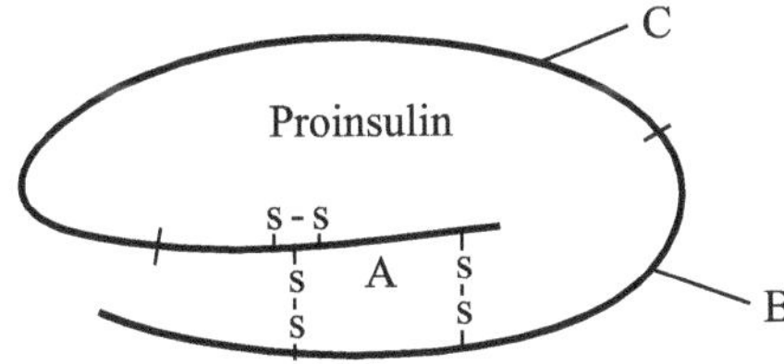

(a) State the change the proinsulin undergoes at the time of its processing to become functional.

(b) Name the technique the American company Eli Lilly used for the commercial production of human insulin.

(c) How are the two polypeptides of a functional insulin chemically held together?

24. The cytological observations made in a number of insects led to the development of the concept of genetic/chromosomal basis of sex-determination mechanism. Honey bee is an interesting example to study the mechanism of sex-determination. Study the schematic cross between the male and the female honey bees given below and answer the questions that follow:

Parent Female honey bee 32 chromosomes
Male honey bee
A
B
Gametes
Gametes
Fertilisation
C
Offspring Male honey bee
Female honey bee 32 chromosomes

(a) Identify the cell divisions 'A" and 'B' that lead to gamete formation in female and male honey bees respectively.

(b) Name the process 'C' that leads to the development of male honey bee (drone).

SECTION - E

25. Describe the model of phosphorus cycle in the terrestrial ecosystem.

OR

Describe the DDT biomagnification occurring in an aquatic food chain. State the negative effects the process has on the organisms at the last trophic level of the food chain.

26. (a) Write the features that a biomolecule must fulfil to be able to act as a genetic material.

(b) DNA and RNA are both genetic materials. Which one of the two is more stable and why?

OR

(a) Explain Hardy-Weinberg Principle on the basis of the algebraic equation $p^2 + 2pq + q^2 = 1$.

(b) How do gene migration and genetic drift affect this genetic equilibrium?

27. (a) IVF is a very popular method these days that is helping childless couples to bear a child. Describe the different steps that are carried out in this technique.

(b) Would you consider Gamete Intrafallopian Transfer (GIFT) as an IVF? Give a reason in support of your answer.

OR

(a) Draw a sectional view of a human ovary and label primary follicle, tertiary follicle, Graafian follicle and corpus luteum in it.

(b) Name the gonadotropins and explain their role in oogenesis and the release of ova.

Solutions

SECTION - A

1. (b) The *Bt* toxin genes were isolated from *Bacillus thuringiensis.* The toxin which is coded by a gene called cry. The 'Cry' protein encoded by gene *Cry IAb* controls corn borer. **(1 Mark)**

2. (c) The Meselson and Stahl carried out of centrifugation in $CsCl_2$ density gradient for separation the normal DNA from ^{15}N DNA. The normal DNA was extracted from the culture one generation after the transfer ^{15}N to ^{14}N medium which has hybrid or intermediate density. **(1 Mark)**

3. (c) The process of self-pollination is fully insured if the flower is cleistogamous. The clesitogamous flowers are the type of flower which does not open at all. In such flowers, the anther and stigma lie close to each other and when the anthers dehisce in the flower buds, and then the pollen grains come in contact with the stigma results in self-pollination. **(1 Mark)**

Note

Cleistogamous flowers are autogamous flowers as there are no such chances of cross-pollination.

OR

(a) *Chlamydomonas* is an aquatic and unicellular organism. The *Chlamydomans* reproduce asexually by zoospores. Zoospores are flagellated asexual spores and they are formed during the night time under favourable condition. **(1 Mark)**

4. (c) The method of micropropagation involves the production of thousands of plants by tissue culture. The plants grown by micropropagation are identical to their original plant and are called somaclones. **(1 Mark)**

OR

(a) The microbes that are commonly used in kitchens are *Lactobacillus* and *Yeast (Saccharomyces cerevisiae).* The bacteria *Lactobacillus* and other Lactic acid bacteria (LAB) are used for conversion of milk into curd. As, *Lactobacillus* and other Lactic acid bacteria (LAB) are grow in milk and these bacteria produce acids which helps in the coagulation of milk and partially digest the milk proteins. While the yeast is used for fermentation and in baking and bread making. **(1 Mark)**

5. (d) The main barrier that prevents the entry of microorganisms into our body is skin. Skin on human body serves as the main physical barrier that prevents the entry of the microorganisms. **(1 Mark)**

SECTION - B

6. Baculoviruses are the pathogens which attack insects and other arthropods and are used as a biological control agents. Baculoviruses belongs to the genus *Nucleopolyhedrovirus.* These viruses are used as an excellent source for species-specific, narrow specturum insecticidal applications. They are not harmful for plants, mammals, birds, fishes and on target insects. **(2 Marks)**

OR

Secondary treatment of sewage is also called biological treatment because it involves biological organisms such as aerobic and anaerobic microbes and fungi for digestion of organic waste.

In this, the primary effluent is passed into the large aeration tanks and is constantly agitated mechanically. In this, air is pumped and this allows the vigorous growth of useful aerobic microorganisms into flocs. These microbes consume the maximum part of the organic matter in the effluent. This significantly reduces the biochemical oxygen demand (BOD) of the effluent. The sewage water is treated till the BOD is reduced. ` **(2 Marks)**

Note

***Flocs** are the masses of bacteria associated with fungal filaments to form a mesh like structures. **BOD** refers to the amount of oxygen consumed if all the organic matter in one litre of water were oxidised by bacteria.*

7. During the initial stage of infection, memory cells are generated in the body. The memory cells create information about the pathogen that causes measles in the human body for the first time and produce antibodies for them. During the second stage of measles infection, the memory cells are activated that are formed during first encounter. These memory cells produce an antibody against the antigen that cause measles and kills the virus that causes measles. **(2 Marks)**

Acquired immunity is pathogen specific and is characterised by memory. This means that our body when it encounters a pathogen for the first time produces a response called primary response which is of low intensity.

8. The wings of butterfly and wings of birds are look alike but are not anatomically similar structures but they perform similar functions. Such organs are called analogous organs. Analogous organs are the results of convergent evolution. **(2 Marks)**

9. Replication of viral RNA genome takes place in the cells when the HIV gets into the blood after gaining entry into the human body. The RNA genome of the HIV virus tends to replicate with the help of an enzyme of reverse transcriptase. The viral DNA gets incorporated into host cell's DNA and directs the infected cells to form virus particles. **(2 Marks)**

Infected all can survive while viruses are being replicated and released.

10. The human male sex accessory ducts are rete testis, vasa efferentia, vas deferens and epididymis.

    Rete testis: The seminiferous tubules of the testis open into the vasa efferentia through rete testis.

    Vasa efferentia: It leaves the testis and opens into the epididymis which is located along the posterior surface of each testis.

    Epididymis: This leads to vas deferns which ascends to the abdomen and loops over the urinary bladder. The epididymis receives a duct from seminal vesicle that opens into urethra as the ejaculatory duct. **(2 Marks)**

All the male sex accessory ducts plays an important role in the storage and transportation of the sperms from the testis to the outside via urethra.

11. **Outcrossing:** This type of mating occurs between the animals of the same breed but have no common ancestors on either side of their pedigree up to 4-6 generations. The offspring produced by such mating is called out-cross. This method is considered as the best breeding method for animals that are below average in milk production, growth rate in beef cattle and so on. **(2 Marks)**

Outcrossing helps to overcome the inbreeding depression.

12. (a) The complementary strand formed is: **(1 Mark)**

    Given strand-

    3'-TACGTACGTACGTACG-5'

    Complementary strand-

    5'-ATGCATGCATGCATGC-3'.

    (b) The RNA strand that can be transcribed from the given DNA segments 3'-TACGTACGTACGTACG-5' is 5'-AUGCAUGCAUGCAUGC-3'. **(1 Mark)**

SECTION - C

13. Hemophilia is a recessive X-linked genetic disorder. Hemophilia is more common among males than females because males only inherit one X-chromosome. Humans have 22 pairs of autosomal chromosomes and one pair of sex chromosome. There are 46 chromosomes in humans. Females have XX chromosome while males have X and Y chromosome. So, male offspring inherit X-chromosome from their mother and Y-chromosome from their father. Males only have one X-chromosome and if the X-chromosome and this is the reason that males are suffering from haemophilia as the X-chromosome carries mutation. While in females, as they have two X chromosomes, and this is a recessive disorder so females are carrier of this disease and can pass this disorder to male offsprings. **(3 Marks)**

Hemophilia is caused because of the absence of blood clotting factor VIII (Hemophilia-A) and IX (haemophilia-B).

OR

The pattern of inheritance is Incomplete dominance in which the none of the two alleles are dominant over each other. So, when both the alleles are present together intermediate or new phenotypes are formed. Intermediate formed is intermediate between the independent expressions of two alleles.

The phenotypic ratio and genotypic ratio such as 1:2:1 are same in case of incomplete dominance. **(3 Marks)**

14. Fruits that are matured ovaries of flowers are called true fruits and false fruits are develop only from the ovary. Fruits formed as a result of fertilization, while some species of fruits that are develop without fertilisation and such fruits are called parthenocarpic fruits. Banana is a parthenocarpy and seedless fruit. **(3 Marks)**

15. Diagrammatic representation of mature anther:

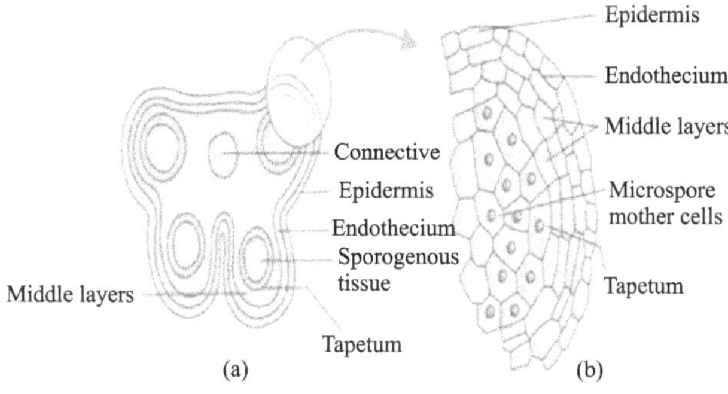

A typical angiosperm anther is bilobed with each lobe having two theca such as they are dithecous. **(3 Marks)**

16. Alien species are introduced and cause decline or extinction of indigenous species. When the Nile perch introduced into Lake Victoria in east Africa results in the extinction of an ecologically unique assemblage of more than 200 species of cichlid fish in the lake. Other invasive species are carrot grass *(Parthenium), Lantana* and water hyacinth *(Eicchornia)*. Introduction of African catfish *Clarias gariepinus* for purpose of aquaculture causes threat to the indigenous catfishes in the rivers. **(3 Marks)**

17. LAB (lactic acid bacteria) and *Lactobacillus* are commonly grow in milk and helps in the conversion of milk into curd. It produces acid that helps in coagulation and partial digestion of milk proteins. LAB also plays essential role in checking disease causing microbes. A small amount of curd is added to the fresh milk that serves as an inoculum. The inoculum contains millions of LAB, and LAB at suitable temperature tends to multiply results in the conversion of milk into curd. LAB also improves the nutritional quality by increasing vitamin B_{12}. **(3 Marks)**

18. The steps involved in the formation of recombinant DNA by the action of restriction endonuclease enzymes EcoRI:

- EcoRI cuts the DNA between the nitrogenous bases G and A only when the sequence GAATTC is present in the DNA.
- The restriction endonuclease enzyme cuts both the DNA strands such as vector DNA and foreign DNA at the same site.
- Then, the DNA fragments are joined at sticky ends and recombinant DNA is produced. **(3 Marks)**

Diagrammatic representation of steps involved in the formation of recombinant DNA by action of restriction endonuclease enzyme EcoRI.

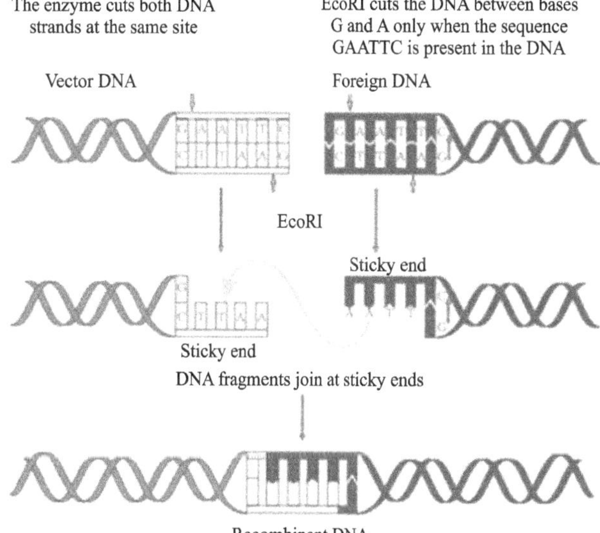

19. (a) ori gene: It is origin of replication. A gene sequence that initiates the process of replication. It controls the copy number of linked DNA. **(1 Mark)**

(b) Antibiotic resistance gene: Some genes encoding resistance to antibiotics such as ampicillin, chloramphenicol, tetracycline or kanamycin are considered as useful selectable markers for *E.coli.* The normal *E.coli* cells that does not carry resistance against any of these antibiotics. Antibiotic resistance gene helps in the selection of transformants.

(1 Mark)

(c) rop gene: The rop gene present in pBR322 cloning vectors codes for the protein which is involves in the replication of plasmid. **(1 Mark)**

20.

Crops	Variety	Resistance to disease
Chilli	*Pusa sadabahar*	*Chilly mosaic virus, leaf curl and Tobacco mosaic virus*
Brassica	*Pusa swarnim*	White rust
Wheat	*Himgiri*	*Leaf and stripe rust and hill bunt*

(3 Marks)

OR

Plant breeding is defined as the manipulation of plant species for the formation of desired plant species. The desired plants produced by plant breeding are better for cultivation, provide better yields and are disease resistant.

The steps involved in the classical plant breeding are:

- Hybridisation of pure lines
- Artificial selection for the production of plants having desired characters for higher yield or development of resistance against diseases. **(3 Marks)**

21. (a) **A** in the given graph is $\frac{dN}{dt} = rN$ that indicates exponential growth and **B** in the given graph is $dN = rN\frac{(K-N)}{K}$ that indicates logistic growth.

(b) The exponential growth occurs when the resources such as food and space are available unlimited. While the logistic growth occurs when the resources are limited and there is competition between the individuals in a given habitat. So, only the 'fittest' individual will survive and reproduce. **(3 Marks)**

SECTION - D

22. (a) The pyramid **B** is stable while pyramid **C** is declining. **(1 Mark)**

(b) Age pyramid is defined as a way for representing the age-sex structure of a population. There are three types of age distribution pyramids such as expanding, stable and declining. A population is composed of individuals of different age groups.

In a stable or Bell-shaped age pyramid the number of pre-reproductive and reproductive individuals is almost equal. If the post-reproductive individuals are comparatively fewer then the population size remains stable as it is neither growing nor diminishing.

The declining or urn-shaped age pyramid indicates the number of reproductive individuals is higher than that of number of pre-reproductive individuals. The declining age pyramid indicates declining growth. **(2 Marks)**

The structure of age pyramids for human population emphasis on providing food to population, development of proper health care facilities and so on.

23. The various steps involved in the production of artificial insulin are as follows: **(1 Mark)**

- The artificial insulin consists of two short polypeptide chains such as chain A and chain B.
- These two short polypeptide chains are linked together by disulphide bond.
- In mammals such as humans, insulin is synthesised as a prohormone that contains an extra stretch called the **C peptide.**
- This **C peptide** is not present in mature insulin and is removed during maturation into insulin.
- The proinsulin is cleaved in order to remove extra stretch called C-peptide for the formation of mature insulin that contains only two chains such as A-chain and B-chain which is joined together by disulphide bond.

(b) The technique used by American company Eli Lilly is recombinant DNA technology for the formation of recombinant insulin. **(1 Mark)**

(c) Insulin is composed of two peptide chains such as A-chain and B-chain. The A-chain is consists of 21 amino acids and B-chain is consists of 30 amino acids. The two chains are joined together by disulphide bonds for the formation of human insulin. **(1 Mark)**

24. (a) **'A'** Female honeybees are diploid so, the process of meiosis takes place for the gamete formation in female honeybees. While **'B'** male honeybees are haploid so, mitosis takes place for the gamete formation in male honeybees. **(1½ Marks)**

(b) Honeybees are classified into three categories such as queen, drone and workers. So, the male honey bees are called drones. The male honey bees or drones are developed from the unfertilized female eggs and this phenomenon is called arrhenotoky. Arrhenotoky is a type of parthenogenesis in which unfertilized eggs are develop into males. **(1½ Marks)**

SECTION - E

25. Phosphorus is a major constituent of all biological membranes such as nucleic acids and cellular energy transfer systems. Animals also require a large amount of phosphorus to make shells, bones and teeth. Naturally phosphorus is found in rocks in the form of phosphates. Plants absorb phosphorus through roots from soil when the rocks are weathered, minute amount of phosphates that is dissolved in soil solution. So, the herbivores and other animals obtain phosphorus from plants. Whereas the waste products and the dead organisms are decomposed by phosphate-solubilising bacteria releasing phosphorus.

Diagrammatic representation of Phosphorus cycle:

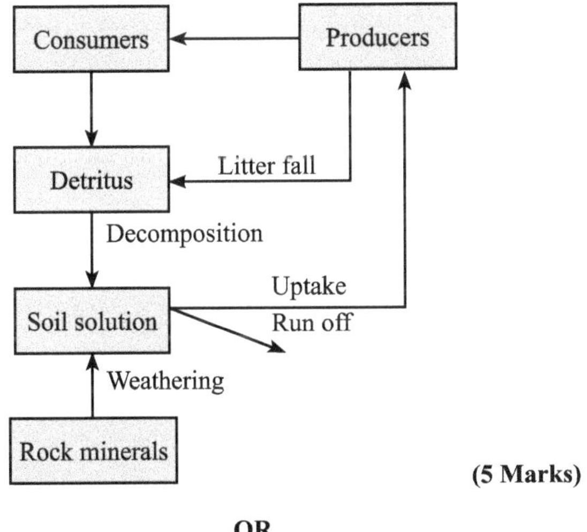

(5 Marks)

OR

Biomagnification is the process of increase in the concentration of the toxicant at successive trophic levels. Biomagnification takes place in the aquatic food chain. This process takes places because a toxic substance such as mercury and DDT is accumulated by an organism that cannot be metabolised and excreted and tends to passed on to the next higher trophic levels. The concentration of DDT is increased at successive trophic level by biomagnifications and it can be 25ppm in fish-eating birds through biomagnifications. High concentrations of DDT results in calcium metabolism disturbance in the birds. It causes thinning of eggshells and their premature breaking that eventually causes decline in their bird populations.

(5 Marks)

26. (a) The features that biomolecules must fulfil as a genetic material are as follows: **(3 Marks)**

- Ability to replicate means a biomolecule should have an ability to generate replica.
- Stability means a biomolecule should be chemically and structurally stable.
- Mutation means a biomolecule should provide a scope for slow changes which is required for evolution.
- Expression means a biomolecule should be able to express itself in the form of 'Mendelian characters'.

(b) DNA is more stable because of the presence of thymine that provides extra stability to the DNA. **(2 Marks)**

OR

(a) The algebraic equation $p^2 + q^2 + 2pq = 1$ is a binomial expansion of $(p + q)^2$. This algebraic equation represents the Hardy-Weinberg's principle that is used to calculate the genetic variation of a population at equilibrium. The Hardy-Weinberg principle states that the allele frequencies in a population are stable and which is remains constant from one generation to another generation.

So, p represents the frequency of allele A, q represents the frequency of allele a, p^2 represents the frequency of AA (homozygous) individuals in a population. Whereas q^2 represents the frequency of aa and 2pq represents the frequency of Aa (heterozygous) individuals. It also indicates that the sum of all the allelic frequencies is equal to one. **(3 Marks)**

(b) Gene migration refers to the movement of the alleles from one population to another that result in inbreeding between the members of the two population. So, the removal of alleles from one population or addition of alleles into another population is called gene migration. While genetic drift which is also called 'Swell Wright Effect'. Genetic drift is random in allele frequencies. It results in elimination of alleles or fixation of the other alleles in the population. **(2 Marks)**

27. (a) The technique suggested to the couples who are not able to conceive is IVF (In vitro fertilisation).

This method involves embryo transfer. In this method, ova from the wife or donor female and sperms from the husband or donor male are collected. The ova and sperm are induced to form zygote under stimulated conditions in the laboratory. **(2 Marks)**

IVF is the method of fertilization that takes place outside the body in almost the conditions similar to that of body. This technique is also called test tube programme.

(b) ZIFT (Zygote Intra Fallopian Transfer) is an assisted reproductive technology. The doctor suggests **ZIFT (Zygote intra fallopian transfer)** to those couples who are not able to bear a child. In this procedure, the sperm is collected either from the husband or donor and an ovum is collected from wife or donor. Then sperm and ova are induced to form zygote under controlled conditions in the laboratory. Then the zygote or early embryos upto 8 blastomeres stages are then transferred into the fallopian tube of the female for further development. **(3 Marks)**

ART (Assisted reproductive technology) *involves the treatments and procedures for those couples that are not able to bear child.*

OR

(a) **Diagrammatic representation of sectional view of human ovary: (3 Marks)**

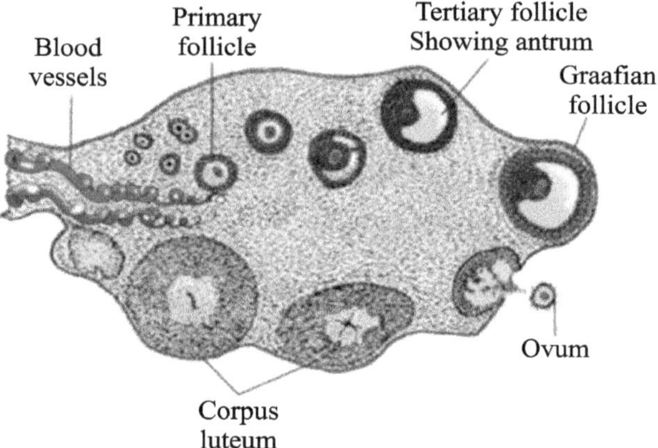

(b) The gonadotropin hormones are luteinizing hormones and follicle stimulating hormones that are secreted by the anterior lobe of the pituitary gland. As, these hormones stimulates ovaries in females and plays an essential role in the process of reproduction. FSH stimulates egg formation in females and LH alongwith FSH helps in the process of ovulation and also prepares the uterus for pregnancy. Whereas estrogen hormone is secreted by the ovaries that induces and also maintains secondary sexual characteristics in females.

(2 Marks)

Delhi 2020

CBSE Board Solved Paper

Time Allowed : 3 Hours ***Maximum Marks : 70***

General Instructions:

(i) Question paper comprises **five** sections – **A, B, C, D** and **E**.

(ii) There are **27** questions in the question paper. **All** questions are compulsory.

(iii) Section **A** question number **1** to **5** are multiple choice questions, carrying **one** mark each.

(iv) Section **B** question number **6** to **12** are short answer questions type-**I**, carrying **two** marks each.

(v) Section **C** question number **13** to **21** are short answer questions type-**II**, carrying **three** marks each.

(vi) Section **D** question number **22** to **24** are short answer questions type-**III**, carrying **three** marks each.

(vii) Section **E** question number **25** to **27** are long answer questions, carrying **five** marks each.

(viii) Answer should be brief and to the point also the above word limit be adhered to as far as possible.

(ix) There is no overall choice in the question paper. However, an internal choice has been provided in **two** questions of **1** mark, **one** question of **2** marks, **two** questions of **3** marks and **three** questions of **5** marks questions. Only **one** of the choices in such questions have to be attempted.

(x) The diagram drawn should be neat proportionate and properly labelled, wherever necessary.

(xi) In addition to this, separate instructions are given with each section and question, wherever necessary.

SECTION - A

1. Which one of the following part of the plant when put into the soil is likely to produce new offspring?

(a) Part of an internode

(b) A stem cutting with a node

(c) Part of a primary root

(d) A flower

2. In a bacterium when RNA-polymerase binds to the promoter on a transcription unit during transcription, it

(a) terminates the process

(b) helps remove introns

(c) initiates the process

(d) inactivates the exons

3. The hypothesis that "Life originated from pre-existing non-living organic molecules was proposed by

(a) Oparin and Haldane (b) Louis Pasteur

(c) S.L. Miller (d) Hugo de Vries

4. Mating of a superior male of a breed of a cattle to a superior female of another breed is called

(a) in breeding (b) out crossing

(c) out breeding (d) cross breeding

OR

Large-holes in 'Swiss-Cheese' are due to

(a) Propionibacterium sharmanii

(b) Saccharomyces cerevisae

(c) Penicillium chrysogenum

(d) Acetobacter aceti

5. Increased concentration of DDT in fish-eating birds is due to

(a) eutrophication (b) bio-magnification

(c) cultural eutrophication (d) accelerated eutrophication

OR

Species-Area relationship is represented on a log scale as

(a) hyperbola (b) rectangular hyperbola

(c) linear (d) inverted

SECTION - B

6. State two advantages of an apomictic seed to a farmer.

7. Explain when is a genetic code said to be

(a) Degenerate (b) Universal

8. Differentiate between opioids and cannabinoids on the basis of their

(a) specific receptor site in human body.

(b) mode of action in human body.

9. (a) Name the two techniques employed to meet the increasing demand of fish in the world.

(b) Name any two fresh water fishes.

OR

Describe the contributions of Alexander Fleming, Ernest Chain and Howard Florey in the field of microbiology.

10. All cloning vectors do have a 'selectable marker'. Describe its role in recombinant DNA-technology.

11. Mention how have plants developed mechanical and chemical defence against herbivores to protect themselves with the help of one example of each.

12. Name and explain the processes earthworm and bacteria carry on detritus.

SECTION - C

13. Explain three different modes of pollination that can occur in a chasmogamous flower.

OR

Explain the formation of placenta after implantation in a human female.

14. State Mendel's law of dominance. How did he deduce the law? Explain with the help of a suitable example.

15. What are 'SNPs'? Where are they located in a human cell? State any two ways the discovery of SNPs can be of importance to humans.

16. (a) State what does the study of Fossils indicate.

(b) Rearrange the following group of plants according to their evolution from Palaeozoic to Cenozoic periods:

Rhynia; Arborescent Lycopods; Conifers; Dicotytedon.

17. (a) Explain the mode of action of Cu^{++} releasing IUDs as a good contraceptive. How is hormone releasing IUD different from it?

(b) Why is 'Saheli' a preferred contraceptive by women (any two reasons)?

18. (a) Explain why bee-hives are setup on the farms for some of our crop-species. Name any two such crop species.

(b) List any three important steps to be kept in mind for successful bee keeping.

19. Why GMOs are so called? List the different ways in which GMO plants have benefitted and have become useful to humans.

20. Differentiate between "Pioneer-species"; "Climax-community" and "Seres".

OR

Explain any three ways other than zoological parks, botanical gardens and wildlife safaries, by which threatened species of plants and animals are being conserved 'ex situ'.

21. Explain 'Integrated organic' farming as successfully practiced by Ramesh C. Dagar, a farmer in Sonepat (Haryana).

SECTION - D

22. Study the diagram showing the entry of HIV into the human body and the processes that are followed:

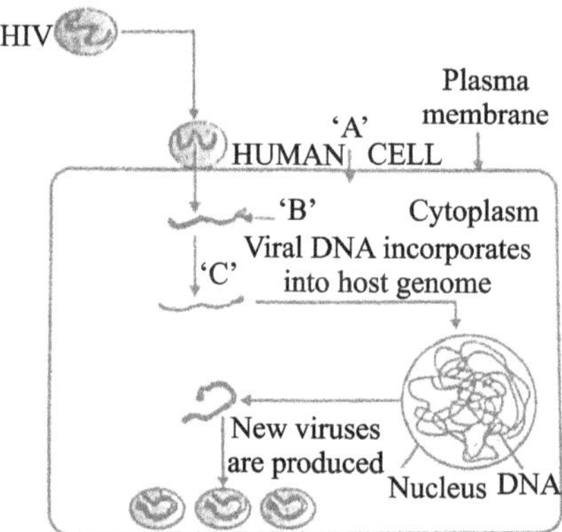

(a) Name the human cell 'A' HIV enters into.

(b) Mention the genetic material 'B' HIV releases into the cell.

(c) Identify enzyme 'C'.

23. Following a road accident four injured persons were brought to a nearby clinic. The doctor immediately injected them with tetanus antitoxin.

(a) What is tetanus antitoxin?

(b) Why were the injured immediately injected with this antitoxin?

(c) Name the kind of immunity this injection provided.

24. "The population of a metro city experiences fluctuations in its population density over a period of time."

(a) When does the population in a metro city tend to increase?

(b) When does the population in metro city tend to decline?

(c) If 'N' is the population density at the time 't', write the population density at the time 't + 1'.

SECTION - E

25. (a) Describe the process of megasporogenesis, in an angiosperm.

(b) Draw a diagram of mature embryo sac of angiosperm, label its any six parts.

OR

(a) Where and how in the testes process of spermatogenesis occur in humans.

(b) Draw diagram of human sperm and label four parts.

26. (a) Why did T.H. Morgon select Drosophila melanogaster for his experiments?

(b) How did he disprove Mendelian dihybrid F_2 phenotypic ratio of 9 : 3 : 3 : 1? Explain giving reasons.

OR

(a) List any four major goals of Human Genome project.

(b) Write any four ways the knowledge from HGP is of significance for humans.

(c) Expand BAC and mention its importance.

27. (a) Name the insect that attacks cotton crops and causes log of damage to the crop. How has Bt cotton plants overcome this problem and saved the crop? Explain.

(b) Write the role of gene Cry IAb.

OR

(a) Explain the different steps carried out in Polymerase Chain Reaction, and the specific roles of the enzymes used.

(b) Mention application of PCR in the field of

(i) Biotechnology

(ii) Diagnostics

Solutions

SECTION - A

1. (b) Stem cuttings with leaf node when buried in soil tend to produce new offspring with new roots usually at the node. This process is called vegetative propagation in which plants parts like leaves, stem and roots are used to produce a new plant. **(1 Mark)**

2. (c) When the RNA polymerase in bacteria get binds with the promoter in order to initiates the process of transcription. Promoter is a sequence of DNA that provides a binding site for RNA polymerase enzyme. It is located towards 5'-end (upstream) of a structure gene. **(1 Mark)**

3. (a) "Life originated from pre-existing non-living organic molecules (RNA, protein and so on)" was proposed by Oparin and Haldane. He also stated that the formation of life was preceded by chemical evolution such as the formation of diverse organic molecules from inorganic constituents. The conditions on earth were-high temperature, volcanic storms, reducing atmosphere containing CH_4, NH_3 and so on. **(1 Mark)**

4. (d) Mating of a superior of a breed of cattle to a superior female of another breed is called cross-breeding. This breeding method allows the desirable qualities of two different breeds to be mated. The progeny hybrid animals are then used for commercial production. For example: *Hisardale* is a new breed of sheep developed in Punjab by crossing Bikaneri ewes and Marino rams. **(1 Mark)**

OR

(a) The large holes in the 'Swiss-cheese' are due to the production of a large amount of carbon dioxide by bacterium *Propionibacteriumsharmanii.* **(1 Mark)**

5. (b) The increased concentration of DDT in fish-eating birds is due to biomagnifications. Biomagnifications refers to the increase in concentration of the toxicant at successive trophic levels. This takes place because a toxic substance is accumulated by an organism that cannot be metabolised or excreted. **(1 Mark)**

OR

(b) The species-Area relationship is represented on a log scale as rectangular hyperbola. Alexander von Humboldt observed that within a region species richness increased with increased explored area but only upto a limit. On a logarithm scale, the relationship is a straight line described by the equation: **(1 Mark)**

$\log S = \log C + Z \log A$

where S = species richness

A = Area

Z = slope of the line (regression coefficient)

C = Y-intercept

SECTION - B

6. Apomixis is a form of asexual reproduction that mimics sexual reproduction. As some species of plants such as *Asteraceae* and grasses have evolved special mechanism in order to produce seeds without fertilisation.

Advantage of Apomixis:

Apomixis reduces the cost of hybrid production and helps plant breeders to produce new varieties of seeds more quickly and more cheaply. **(2 Marks)**

7. (a) **Degenerate:** Code is said to be degenerate as some amino acids are coded by more than one codon.

(b) **Universal:** The code is said to be universal as a genetic code is same in all organisms. For example: from bacteria to human UUU would code for Phenylalanine (Phe).

(2 Marks)

Codon is set of the three nucleotides that codes for a single amino acid. As genetic codon is triplet in nature and there are 64 codons. Out of which, 61 codons codes for amino acid and 3 are stop codons.

8. **Difference between opioids and cannabinoids:**

Categories	Opioids	Cannabinoids
Specific receptor site in human body	Opioid receptors present in the central nervous system and gastrointestinal tract of human beings.	Cannabinoid receptors present in the brain.
Mode of action in human body	Opioids such as heroin act a depressant and slow down body functions.	Cannabinoids such as marijuana, hashish, charas and ganja effects on cardiovascular system of the body.

(2 Marks)

Opioids are the drugs that are obtained from the latex of poppy plant called Papaversomniferum. Whereas cannabinoids are the group of chemicals that are naturally obtained from the inflorescences of the plant Cannabis sativa.

9. (a) To meet the increasing demands on fisheries different techniques such as aquaculture and pisciculture techniques are employed to increase production. By using these two techniques, both fresh-water and marine fish production will increases. **(1 Mark)**

(b) Example of fresh water fishes are *Catla, Rohu* and common carp. **(1 Mark)**

OR

Alexander Fleming while working on *Staphylococci* bacteria observed that a mould growing in one of his unwashed culture plates around which *Staphylococci* could not grow. During this, he found that it was due to a chemical produced by the mould and he named it as Penicillin after the *Penicillium notatum.* Ernest Chain and Howards Florey give its full potential to prove it as an effective antibiotic. This antibiotic was used for treatment of American soldiers that wounded in World War II. Fleming, Chain and Florey were awarded the Nobel Prize in 1945 for this discovery.

(2 Marks)

10. The use of selectable marker in Recombinant DNA helps in the identification and elimination of non-transformants. It selectively permitting the growth of the transformants.

Transformation refers to the process through which a piece of DNA is introduced in a host bacterium and the genes encoding resistance to antibiotics such as ampicillin, chloramphenicol, tetracycline or kanamycin are considered as useful selectable marker for *E.coli.* **(2 Marks)**

11. Unlike animals, plants cannot move away from their predators. So they developed a variety of mechanical and chemical defences against herbivores. Herbivores are predator. Some plants such as *Acacia* and *Cactus* develop specific structures like thorns for defence. Many plants produce and store chemicals that make herbivore sick when they are eaten as they inhibit feeding and digestion. This chemical also disrupts its reproduction or even kills it.

For example: A weed called *Calotropis* growing in abandoned fields produces a highly poisonous cardiac glycosides that causes cardiac arrest in herbivores.

(2 Marks)

12. Decomposition is a process in which the Earthworm and bacteria carry on detritus. Detritus is composed of dead remains of plants such as leave, bark, flowers and dead remains of animals involves fecal matter. All these material serves as a raw material for decomposition.

Detritivores such as earthworm breakdown detritus into smaller particles and this process is called fragmentation. Then, by the process of leaching, the water soluble inorganic nutrients go down into the soil horizon and get precipitated as unavailable salts. Bacterial and fungal enzymes degrade detritus into simpler inorganic substances by the process called as catabolism. During the process of decomposition, humifiation and mineralisation also occurs. **(2 Marks)**

Humification *involves the process of accumulation of dark coloured amorphous substance that is highly resistant to microbial action. Whereas humus is further degraded by some microbes and release of inorganic nutrients occurs and this process is called* ***mineralisation****.*

SECTION - C

13. The three types of pollination that takes place in a chasmogamous flower are as follows:

(a) Autogamy: In this type, the process of pollination is achieved within the same flower. It involves the transfer of pollen grains from the anther to the stigma of the same flower. Chasmogamous flowers are type of flowers that are similar to the flowers of other species with exposed anthers and stigma.

In chasmogamous flowers, the anthers and stigma lie close to each other. When anther dehisces in the flower buds, the pollen grain comes in contact with the stigma to effect pollination.

(b) Geitonogamy: It involves the transfer of pollen grains from the anther to the stigma of another flower of the same plant. It is functionally a type of cross-pollination that involves pollinating agents. But genetically it is similar to autogamy so the pollen grains come from the same plant.

(c) Xenogamy: It involves the transfer of pollen grains from anther to stigma of a different plant. This is the only type of pollination in which pollination brings genetically different types of pollen grains to the stigma. **(3 Marks)**

Pollination refers to the process of transfer of pollen grains (shed from the anther) to the stigma of a pistil.

OR

After implantation of foetus, a finger-like projections appears on the trophoblast called chorionic villi that is surrounded by the uterine tissue and maternal blood. The chorionic villi and uterine tissue become interdigitated with each other and they jointly give rise to a structural and functional unit between developing embryo as well as maternal body called as placenta. **(3 Marks)**

Placenta helps to facilitate the supply of oxygen and nutrients to the developing embryo and also responsible for the removal of carbon dioxide as well as other excretory waste produced by the embryo.

14. Mendal's law of dominance states that characters are controlled by discrete unit called factors. They occur in pair. In a dissimilar pair of factors one member of the pair dominates (dominant) over the other (recessive).

This law is used to explain the expression of only one of the parental characters in a monohybrid cross in the F1 generation. The expression of both alleles in the F2 generation. He also explained the proportion of 3:1 obtained at the F2 generation.

Diagrammatic Representation of an Example of Mendel's law of Dominance:

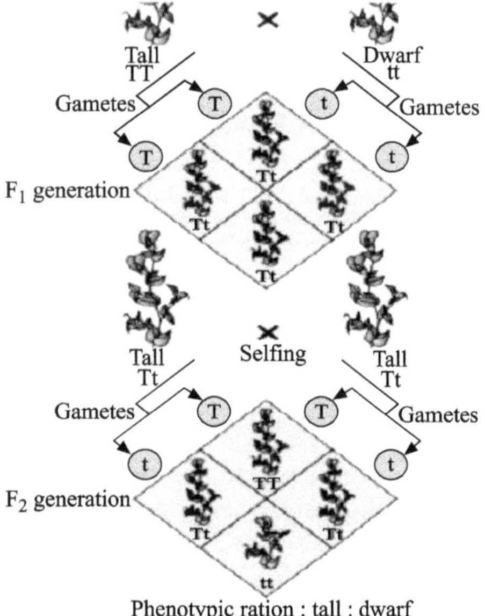

(3 Marks)

15. **SNPs** are single nucleotide polymorphism that occurs in humans. These are the most common form of genetic variation among people. Each SNPs represents a difference in a single nucleotide sequence of DNA. SNPs are located in a DNA between the genes such as promoters, exons, introns or 5' and 3' untranslated regions. Basically they are located within a gene or in a regulatory region near a gene.

They act as biological markers that helps scientist to locate the genes that are associated with diseases. It helps to measure the genetic variations among individuals.

(3 Marks)

16. The study of fossils is considered as the important evidence for evolution because it represents that the life on the earth was once different from the life that is found on earth today. The study of fossils is important because it helps to determine and study the physical structure of extinct organisms. With the help of fossils, one can determine that how long life has existed on earth and how the different plants as well as animals are evolved and are related to each other. **(2 Marks)**

Fossils are the dead remains impression or trace of an animal on plant of are preserved in Earth's rust from a past geological age.

(b) **Paleozoic** – Rhynia

Arborescent Lycopods

Mesozoic – Conifers

Dicotyledons **(1 Mark)**

17. (a) IUDs are Intra Uterine Devices (IUDs) increases phagocytosis of sperms within the uterus and the copper ions are released suppress sperm mortality and the fertilising capacity of sperms.

Example of copper releasing IUDs are cuT, cu7, Multiload 375.

The hormone releasing IUDs make the uterus unsuitable for implantation and the cervix hostile to the sperms. IUDs are ideal contraceptives for the females who want to delay pregnancy.

Example of hormone releasing IUDs is Progestasert, LNG-20. **(2 Marks)**

IUDs is one of most widely accepted methods of contraception in India.

(b) Saheli-The new oral contraceptive pill for the females that contains a non-steroidal preparation. It is a 'once a week' pill with very few side effects and high contraceptive value. They inhibit ovulation and implantation as well as alter the quality of cervical mucus to prevent or retard the entry of sperms.

(1 Mark)

18. (a) Bee-keeping or apiculture is the maintenance of hives of honeybees for the production of honey. Handling and collection of honey and of beeswax. Bees are the pollinators of many of our crop species such as sunflower, *Brassica,* apple and pear. Keeping the beehives in crop fields during flowering period increases pollination efficiency and improves the yield-beneficial both from the point of view of crop yield and honey yield.

(2 Marks)

(b) The following points are important for successful bee-keeping:

- Knowledge of the nature and habits of bees,
- Selection of selection location for keeping of beehives
- Catching and hiving of Swarms or group of bees,
- Management of beehives during different seasons.

(1 Mark)

19. **GMOs** are Genetically Modified Organisms that are produced by alteration in genes of plants, bacteria, fungi and animals. GM plants are useful in many ways such as:

- Genetic modification made crops more tolerant to abiotic stresses such as cold, drought, salt and heat.
- It also reduces the reliance of chemical pesticides such as pest-resistant crops
- It helps to reduce post-harvest losses.
- It also increases the efficiency of mineral usage by plants
- GM enhanced nutritional value of foods such as vitamin A enriched rice. **(3 Marks)**

20. Difference between pioneer species, ecological succession and sere are as follows:

Pioneer species	Ecological succession	Sere
(i) The species that invade a bare area are called pioneer species.	(i) The gradual and predictable change in the species composition of a given area is called ecological succession.	(i) The entire sequences of communities that successively change in a given area are called sere.

(3 Marks)

OR

Except from zoological parks, wildlife sanctuaries and botanical gardens, ex-situ conservation also involves a method for preservation of endangered or extinct species such as by

Cryopreservation: Gametes (sperms, eggs, tissues and embryo) of several endangered plants and animal species can be preserved by methods involves cryopreservation (–196°C). It can be fertilized in vitro followed by propagation through tissue culture methods.

Seeds of different genetic strains of commercially important plants are also kept for longer period in seed banks.

(3 Marks)

21. Integrated organic farming is a cyclical, zero-waste procedure in which the waste products from one process are cycled in as nutrients for other processes. This allows the maximum utilisation of resources and increases the efficiency of production. Ramesh Chandra Dagar, a farmer in Sonipat, Haryana is practising this farming. He involves bee-keeping, dairy management, water-harvesting, composting and agriculture in a chain of processes that support each other and also allow an extremely economical as well as sustainable venture.

In this type of farming, there is no need to use chemical fertilisers for crops such as cattle excreta (cow dung) are used as manure. Crop waste is also used to create compost that can be used as a natural fertiliser or can be used to generate natural gas for satisfying the energy needs of the farms. **(3 Marks)**

SECTION - D

22. (i) The human cell 'A' is animal cell in which HIV virus enters.

(ii) Viral RNA is introduced into the cell.

(iii) Viral DNA is produced by reverse transcriptase enzyme and then the viral DNA is incorporates into the host genome. **(3 Marks)**

23. (i) Antitoxins are the preparation containing antibodies to the toxins. Tetanus antitoxins is preparation that contains antibodies that kill *Clostridium tetnani.* A causal organisms of tetanus.

(ii) Tetanus antitoxin is administered to an injured person to neutralize the effect of toxin produced by *Clostridium tetani.*

(iii) Tetanus antitoxin provides a short-term passive immunity to injured person. As it contains preformed antibodies against *Clostridium tetani* and produces a quick immune response in the patients. **(3 Marks)**

24. (a) The size of a population changing with time and it depends on various factors such as availability of food, predation pressure, weather conditions. So the size of population in a metro city tends to increase when all the conditions are favourable. The size of population in a particular habitat fluctuates because of four basic processes such as natality, mortality, immigration and emigration. Out of which **Natality** (refers to the number of births during a given period of time in a population) and **Immigration** (refers to the number of individuals of the same species that have come into the habitat from somewhere else in a specific time period) tends to increase the population size in a given locality.

(1 Mark)

(b) **Mortality** (refers to the number of deaths in the population during a given period) and **Emigration** (refers to the number of individuals of a population who left the habitat and gone somewhere else during the time period) tends to decreases the population.

(1 Mark)

(c) If N is the population density at time t, then its density at time t + 1 is:

$N_{t+1} = N_t + [(B + I) - (D + E)]$

Where B = Natality

I = Immigration

E = Emigration

D = Mortality **(1 Mark)**

SECTION - E

25. (a) The process of formation of megaspores from the megaspore mother cell is called megasporogenesis. The megaspore mother cell undergoes the process of meiosis and forms a four haploid tetrad megaspores. The chalazal megaspore remains functional whereas the other 3 will degenerate. So, the functional megaspore is the first cell of the female gametophyte. The cell enlarges and undergoes three free nuclear mitotic divisions.

So the first meiotic division produces two nucleate embryo sac and two nuclei shift to the two ends and again gets divide and forms four nucleate. In this way, eight nucleate structures is formed. One nucleus from each side moves to the middles and they are called polar nuclei. Then the remaining three nuclei form cells at the two ends, 3-celled egg apparatus at the micropylar end and three antipodal cells at the chalazal end.

(3 Marks)

(b) **Diagrammatic Representation of mature embryo sac in angiosperm:**

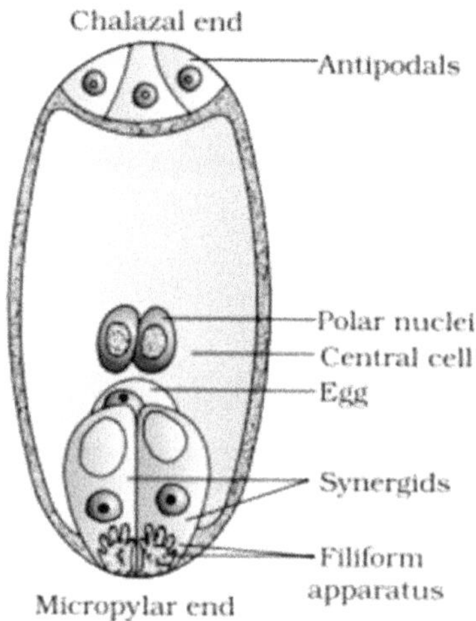

(2 Marks)

OR

(a) In the testis, the immature male germ cells or spermatogonia produce sperms by spermatogenesis that begins at puberty. The spermatogonia present on the inside wall of seminiferous tubules get multiply by mitotic division and increases in numbers. Each spermatogonium is diploid in nature as it contains 46 chromosomes.

Some of the spermatogonia are called primary spermatocytes that periodically undergo meiosis. A primary spermatocyte completes the first meiotic division results in the formation of two equal, haploid cells called secondary spermatocytes that contains only 23 chromosomes each.

The secondary spermatocytes undergo the second meiotic division to produce four equal, haploid spermatids. The spermatids are then transformed into spermatozoa or sperms by the process called spermiogenesis. After spermiogenesis, sperm heads become embedded in the sertoli cells and then are finally released from the seminiferous tubules by the process called spermiation. **(3 Marks)**

(b) **Diagrammatic Representation of human sperm:**

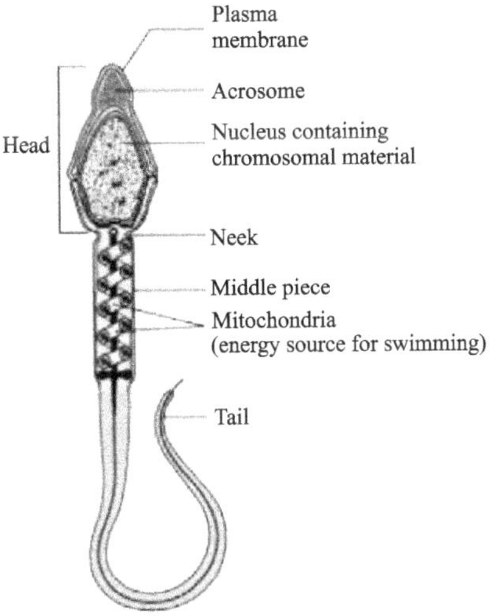

(2 Marks)

26. (a) T.H Morgan selected *Drosophila melanogaster* for his experiments because he found that fruit flies are suitable for studies as they could be easily grown on simple synthetic medium in the laboratory.

- They tend to complete their life cycle in about two weeks and a single mating could produce a large number of progeny flies.
- Sexes are clearly differentiated between male and female flies.
- They exhibit several types of hereditary variations that can be observed with low power microscope.

(2 Marks)

(b) Morgan carried out many dihybrid crosses in *Drosophilla* to study the genes that were sex-linked. These crosses were similar to the dihybrid cross performed by Mendel in peas. He hybridised yellow-bodied, white-eyed females to brown-bodied, red-eyed males and intercrossed their F1 progent.

Then he observed that the two genes did not segregate independently to each other and the F2 ration deviated very significantly from the 9:3:3:1 ratio.

He observed that the genes were located on the X-chromosome and they saw quickly that when the two genes in a dihybrid cross were situated on the same chromosome, the proportion of parental gene combinations were much higher than the non-parental type. According to Morgan, this is because of physical association or linkage of the two genes and coined the term linkage. It used to describe this physical association of genes on a chromosome and is called recombination. It is term used to describe the generation of non-parental gene combinations.

(3 Marks)

OR

(a) The important goals of Human Genome Project are as follows:

- Identify all the approximately 20,000-25000 genes in human DNA.
- Determine the sequences of the 3 billion chemical base pairs that make up human DNA.
- Store this information in databases
- Improve tools for data analysis. **(2 Marks)**

(b) The four ways by which HGP is significant for humans are as follows:

- Repeated sequences make up very portions of the human genome.
- Repetitive sequences are stretches of DNA sequences that are repeated several times sometimes hundred to thousand times.
- Scientist have identified about 1.4 million locations where single base DNA differences called SNPS or single nucleotide polymorphism occur in humans.
- The human genome contains 3164.7 million nucleotide bases. **(2 Marks)**

(c) **BAC** is bacterial artificial chromosomes. BAC is a vector that is used for transforming DNA and cloning in bacteria especially in *E.coli.* **(1 Mark)**

27. (a) Cotton bollworms are the insect that attacks and destroy the cotton crops. Some strains of *Bacillus thuringiensis* produces proteins that kill insects that the cotton crops. They forms protein crystals during a particular phase of their growth. These crystals contain a toxic called insecticidal protein.

This protein exists in an inactive form but once it is ingested by the insect, this protein is converted into an active form of toxin because of alkaline pH of the gut. It tends to solubilise the crystals. Then the activated toxin binds to the surface of midgut epithelial cells and creates pores that cause cell swelling as well as lysis and eventually results in the death of the insect.

(4 Marks)

(b) The gene *cryIAb* controls the growth of cotton corn borer. **(1 Mark)**

OR

(a) With the help of recombinant DNA technology called Polymerase Chain Reaction technique (PCR) multiple copies of gene of interest are obtained in *Vitro*. A single PCR amplification cycle involves three steps which are as follows:

(i) **Denaturation:** This is the first step of PCR, in which the target DNA is heated at high temperature such 94-96°C. It facilitates the separation of two strands of DNA. Each separated strand of DNA acts as a template for synthesis of DNA.

(ii) **Annealing:** This is the second step of PCR, in which two oligonucleotide primers are used to hybridize each single stranded template DNA. The sequence of primers is complementary to 3′ end of the template DNA strand.

This step of PCR occurs at low temperature 40-60°C than denaturation. The annealing temperature depends upon the length and sequence of the primers.

(iii) **Extension:** This is third and last step of PCR, in which enzyme *Taq* DNA polymerase synthesizes the DNA between the primers. This step also requires dNTPS and Mg2++. The optimum temperature for extension is 72°C. **(3 Marks)**

Diagrammatic representation of PCR cycle:

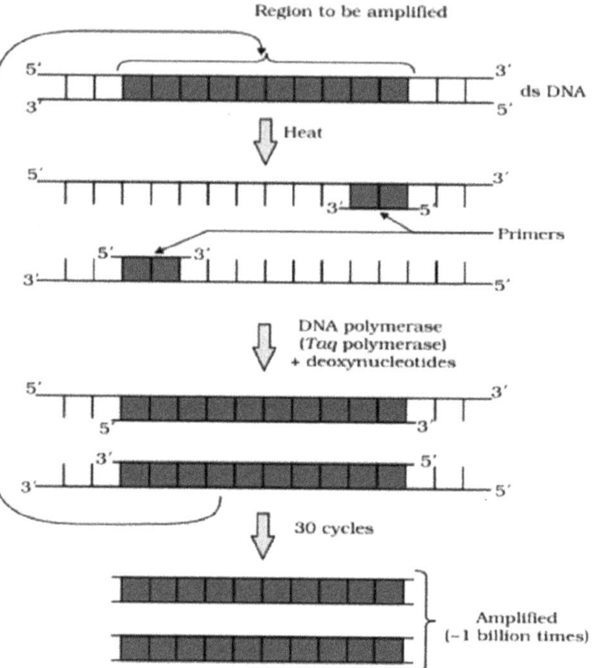

(b) (i) **Application of PCR in the field of biotechnology:** Polymerase Chain Reaction is a widely used method in the field of biotechnology as it helps in amplification billions of copies of desired DNA sequence from small sample of DNA.

(ii) **Application of PCR in the field of diagnostic:** Now days, PCR can be used in molecular diagnostic and biochemical analyses. Even with the help of small sequence of DNA, the genotypes can be determined. PCR helps in diagnosis of genetic disorder. **(2 Marks)**

Enzyme used in PCR is a DNA polymerase such as Taq polymerase. This enzyme is stable at high temperature as it is isolated from thermostable bacteria Thermusaquaticus.

All India 2019

CBSE Board Solved Paper

Time Allowed : 3 Hours | ***Maximum Marks : 70***

General Instructions:

(i) There are total **27** questions and four sections in the question paper. All questions are compulsory.

(ii) Section **A** contains questions number **1** to **5**, very short answer type questions of **one** mark each.

(iii) Section **B** contains questions number **6** to **12**, short answer type-I questions of **two** marks each.

(iv) Section **C** contains questions number **13** to **24**, short answer type-II questions of **three** marks each.

(v) Section **D** contains question number **25** to **27**, long answer type questions of **five** marks each.

(vi) There is no overall choice in the question paper, however, an internal choice is provided in **two** questions of **one** mark, **two** questions of **two** marks, **four** questions of **three** marks and all the **three** questions of **five** marks. In these questions, an examinee is to attempt any **one** of the **two** given alternatives.

(vii) Wherever necessary, the diagram drawn should be neat and properly labelled.

SECTION - A

1. British geneticist R.C. Punnett developed a graphical representation of a genetic cross called "Punnett Square". Mention the possible result this representation predicts of the genetic cross carried.

2. State the two principal outcomes of the experiments conducted by Louis Pasteur on origin of life.

3. Name the layer of the atmosphere that is associated with 'good ozone'.

OR

Mention the term used to describe a population interaction between an orchid growing on a forest tree.

4. What are 'flocs', formed during secondary treatment of sewage ?

OR

Write any two places where methanogens can be found.

5. At what stage does the meiosis occur in an organism exhibiting haploidic life cycle and mention the fate of the products thus produced.

SECTION - B

6. You are conducting artificial hybridization on papaya and potato. Which one of them would require the step of emasculation and why ? However for both you will use the process of bagging. Justify giving one reason.

7. How would the gene flow or genetic drift affect the population in which either of them happen to take place ?

8. Differentiate between the roles of B-lymphocytes and T-lymphocytes in generating immune responses.

OR

Principle of vaccination is based on the property of "memory" of the immune system.

Taking one suitable example, justify the statement.

9. Explain the relevance of "Totipotency" and "Somaclones" in raising healthy banana plants from virus infected banana plants.

10. How is a continuous culture system maintained in bioreactors and why ?

11. List any four ways by which GMO's have been useful for enhanced crop output.

12. Mention four significant services that a healthy forest ecosystem provide.

OR

Substantiate with the help of one example that in an ecosystem mutualists (i) tend to co-evolve and (ii) are also one of the major causes of biodiversity loss.

SECTION - C

13. Pollen banks are playing a very important role in promoting plant breeding programme the world over. How are pollens preserved in the pollen banks ? Explain. How are such banks benefiting our farmer ? Write any two ways.

14. Draw a labelled diagram to show interrelationship of four accessory ducts in a human male reproductive system.

OR

Draw a sectional view of the human ovary showing the different stages of developing follicles, corpus luteum and ovulation.

15. Compare in any three ways the chromosomal theory of inheritance as proposed by Sutton and Bovery with that of experimental results on pea plant presented by Mendel.

OR

(a) Explain linkage and recombination as put forth by T.H. Morgan based on his observations with *Drosophila melanogaster* crossing experiment.

(b) Write the basis on which Alfred Sturtevant explained gene mapping.

16. Explain the mechanism of DNA replication with the help of a replication fork. What role does the enzyme DNA-ligase play in a DNA replication fork ?

OR

Construct and label a transcription unit from which the RNA segment given below has been transcribed. Write the complete name of the enzyme that transcribed this RNA.

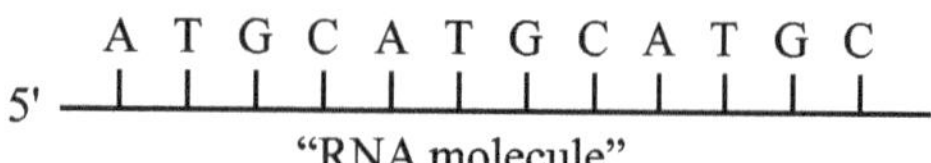

"RNA molecule"

17. (a) Write two differences between *Homo erectus* and *Homo habilis.*

(b) Rearrange the following from early to late geologic periods :

Carboniferous, Silurian, Jurassic.

18. Name the group of bacteria involved in setting milk into curd. Explain the process they carry in doing so. Write another beneficial role of such bacteria.

19. Bee keeping practice is a good income generating industry. Write the different points to be kept in mind for successful bee keeping. Write the scientific name of the most common Indian species used for the purpose.

20. (a) Match the microbes listed under Column-A with the products mentioned under Column-B.

Column – A	**Column – B**
(H) *Penicillium notatum*	(i) Statin
(I) *Trichoderma polysporum*	(ii) ethanol
(J) *Monascus purpurea*	(iii) antibiotic
(K) *Saccharomyces cerevisiae*	(iv) Cyclosporin-A

(b) Why does 'Swiss Cheese' develop large holes ?

21. Describe the formation of recombinant DNA by the action of EcoRI.

OR

Describe the process of amplification of "gene of interest" using PCR technique.

22. Two children, A and B aged 4 and 5 years respectively visited a hospital with a similar genetic disorder. The girl A was provided enzyme-replacement therapy and was advised to revisit periodically for further treatment. The girl, B was, however, given a therapy that did not require revisit for further treatment.

(a) Name the ailments the two girls were suffering from ?

(b) Why did the treatment provided to girl A required repeated visits ?

(c) How was the girl B cured permanently ?

23. List six advantages of "ex-situ" approach to conservation of biodiversity.

24. While on a visit to a pond in the city-neighbourhood, the visitors were delighted to find large expanse of water covered with colourful algal mass.

(a) As a student of biology, do you agree with their delight ? Give reasons in support of your answer.

(b) Explain the cause of such algal growth.

SECTION - D

25. (a) Explain one application of each one of the following :

(A) Amniocentesis

(B) Lactational amenorrhea

(C) ZIFT

(b) Prepare a poster for the school programme depicting the objectives of : "Reproductive and Child Health Care Programme".

OR

(a) Explain any two ways by which apomictic seed can develop.

(b) List one advantage and one disadvantage of a apomictic crop.

(c) Why do farmers find production of hybrid seeds costly ?

26. Differentiate between incomplete dominance and co-dominance. Substantiate your answer with one example of each.

OR

(a) Write the contributions of the following scientists in deciphering the genetic code. Georce Gamow ; Hargobind Khorana ; Marshall Nirenberg ; Severo Ochoa

(b) State the importance of a Genetic code in protein biosynthesis.

27. (a) What is "population" according to you as a biology student ?

(b) "The size of a population for any species is not a static parameter." Justify the statement with specific reference to fluctuations in the population density of a region in a given period of time.

OR

(a) What is hydrarch succession ?

(b) Compare the pioneer species and climax communities of hydrarch and xerarch succession respectively.

(c) List the factors upon which the type of invading pioneer species depend in secondary hydrarch succession. Why is the rate of this succession faster than that of primary succession ?

Solutions

SECTION - A

1. The Punnett square helps in understanding the production of gametes by the parents, and formation of the zygotes in F_1 and F_2 generation. The Punnett square is a graphical representation for the calculation of probability of all the possible genotypes of offsprings in a genetic cross. **(1 Mark)**

The Punnett square was developed by a British geneticist, Reginald C. Punnett. Phenotypes refer to the observable characteristics of organisms that involve appearance, development and behaviour of organisms. Genotypes refer to the genetic constitution of organisms.

2. The two principle outcomes of the experiments conducted by Louis Pasteur on origin of life are as follows: **(1 Mark)**
   - He showed that in pre-sterilised flasks, life did not come from killed yeast.
   - Whereas in another flask open to air, new living organisms arose from 'killed yeast'.
3. Stratosphere is also called as 'good' ozone and is found in the upper part of the atmosphere. **(1 Mark)**

The stratosphere acts as a shield for absorbing ultraviolet radiation from the sun.

OR

The term used to describe a population interaction between an orchids growing on a forest tree is called commensalism. Commensalism is a biological interaction between two organisms in which one organism gets benefits from others while the other organism is neither benefited nor harmed.

An orchid growing on the branch of a forest tree is an epiphyte (plants that are growing on other plants). In this biological interaction, the orchid gets support, more sunlight for photosynthesis and nutrients from the mango tree. Whereas mango tree remains unaffected. **(1 Mark)**

4. The secondary treatment plant allows the vigorous growth of useful microbes into **flocs. Flocs** are the masses of bacteria associated with fungal filaments to form mesh like structures. They are formed when the primary effluent is passed into large aeration tanks where it is constantly agitated mechanically and then air is pumped into it. **(1 Mark)**

OR

Methanogens are commonly found in the guts of animals, hydrothermal vents, wetlands and deep layers of marine sediments.

5. The haploidic stage is a multi-cellular and a diploid stage. It is a single celled stage in which meiosis take place during zygote formation at the time of fertilization. **(1 Mark)**

SECTION - B

6. Potato require emasculation because it has bisexual flower whereas papaya would require only bagging for artificial hybridisation as papaya has unisexual flowers. After pollinating with the desired pollen grain it is required to bag the plant in order to prevent the plant from pollination by undesirable pollen grains. **(2 Marks)**

The process of removal of anthers from the flower bud before the dehiscence of anther by a pair of forceps is called ***Emasculation.*** *The emasculated flower is covered with a bag of suitable size which is made up of butter paper in order to prevent from contamination of stigma with unwanted pollen and this process is called* ***bagging.***

7. If gene migration occurs multiple times then it is known as gene flow. The Hardy-Weinberg law states that the gene pool remains constant. Gene flow is the transfer of genetic information from one population to another. If the same change takes place by chance then it is called genetic drift. When migration of a section of population to another place and population occurs, gene frequencies change in the original as well as in the new population. New genes or alleles are added to the new population and are lost from old population. There would be a gene flow if this gene migration happens multiple times. If the same change occurs by chance, then it is called genetic drift. **(2 Marks)**

Gene pool refers to the total number of genes and their alleles in a population.

8.

B-lymphocytes	T-lymphocytes
(i) The B-lymphocytes produces an army of proteins in response to pathogen into the blood and these proteins are called antibodies.	(i) The T-lymphocytes do not secrete any antibodies but help B-cells to produce antibodies.
(ii) The response produced by B-lymphocytes is also called as **humoral immune response.**	(ii) The response produced by T-lymphocytes is also called as **Cell-mediated immune response.**
(iii) B-cells mature in the bone marrow	(iii) T-cells mature in the Thymus.

(2 Marks)

Both B-lymphocytes and T-lymphocytes are formed in the bone marrow.

OR

In case of polio vaccination, an antigenic protein preparation of pathogen is introduced into the body which is inactivated or weakened form. The antibodies produced in the body against polio antigens would neutralise the pathogenic agents which responsible for causing polio. The vaccines also generate memory B-and T-cells which recognises the pathogen on subsequent exposure and encounter the pathogen by the production of antibodies. **(2 Marks)**

9. Totipotency is the capacity to generate a whole plant from any cell or explants whereas somaclones are formed by micropropagation and the plants produced are genetically identical to their original plant from which they were grown. In the virus infected banana plant, the meristem (apical or axillary) is free from virus and one can remove the meristem and grow it In-vitro to obtain virus free banana plant. **(2 Marks)**

10. A continuous culture system is maintained in a bioreactor by continuously and regularly feeding with culture medium steadily and by providing optimum growth conditions such as pH, temperature, vitamins, salts, oxygen. The used medium is drained out from one side of the bioreactor and the fresh medium is added from the other side. Continuous culture system is maintained in bioreactors in order to maintain the cells in their physiologically most active log/ exponentially phase. This type of culturing method produces a large biomass results in higher yield of the desired protein. **(2 Marks)**

11. The four ways by which GMO's have been useful for enhanced crop output are as follows:

- GMOs made crop more tolerant to abiotic stress such as cold, drought, salt and heat.
- It reduces dependency on chemical pesticides such as pest-resistant crops.
- It helped in the reduction post harvest losses.
- GMOs increases the efficiency of mineral usage by plants and this helps in the prevention of early exhaustion of fertility of soil.
- GMOs also enhance nutritional value of food such as vitamin 'A' enriched rice. **(2 Marks)**

12. Ecosystems are communities formed by the interaction between living (plants, animals, microbes) and non-living components (air, water, mineral soil) of the environment. The benefits are known as ecosystem services. A healthy forest ecosystem contains all the biotic and abiotic components of the environment.

The four significant services provided by healthy forest ecosystems are:

- Ecological functions such as carbon storage, nutrient cycling, water and air purification, as well as the maintenance of wildlife habitat.
- Maintenance of biodiversity.
- Provides goods such as timber, food, fuel and bioproducts.
- Social and cultural benefits such as recreation, traditional resource uses and spirituality. **(2 Marks)**

OR

(i) In nature, mutualists often co-evolve such as in Mediterranean orchid *Ophrys*. *Ophrys* employs sexual deceit to get pollinated by a species of bee. One petal of flower resemble to female bee. If female bee changes its colour pattern ever slightly the success of pollination will be reduced unless orchid flower co-evolves to maintain resemblance with female bee. **(1 Mark)**

(ii) Co-extinction is one of the 'Evil Quartet' in which organisms with obligatory relationship like plant pollinator mutualism will result in extinction of one partner if other is eliminated in nature. **(1 Mark)**

SECTION - C

13. Pollen grains are preserved in a pollen bank in liquid nitrogen at temperature -196° C and this process are called cryopreservation. Pollen grains in plants are used for transferring haploid male genetic material from the anther to the stigma of another flower in case of cross-pollination. The pollen grains are preserved to introduce the desired characters into hybrid varieties of plant. Pollen banks are used to store pollen grains for a short as well as a very long period of time in viable conditions. These pollen grains can be used in various crop breeding programs, biochemical and physicochemical studies. The very important application of pollen bank is to preserve the biodiversity in the form of preservation of the value of genetic resources.

The pollen grains can be stored by two methods such as:

The pollen grains can be stored by two methods:

(i) **Short term storage of pollen grain:** It involves the storage of pollen grains under low temperature and low humidity, and storage in an organic solvent (the simple method by which pollen grains are dried over silica and stored in organic solvents and maintained in the refrigerator or deep freezer)

(ii) **Long term storage of pollen:** It involves the storage of pollen grains in freeze or vacuum-dried conditions [in which pollen grains are stored at subzero temperature (–60 degrees C to –80 degrees C)] and cryopreservation (pollen grains are dried by using a 'Pollen Drier' containing air of 20 degrees C and 20–40 % humidity to bring their water content below a threshold level and stored in liquid nitrogen (–196 degrees C)). This method is very effective for storage of pollen grains of a number of species, including cereals, even for over 10 years).

The pollens preserved in pollen banks are benefitting farmers in the following two ways:

- By using these pollens the plants that are facing extinction can be reproduced.
- Pollen grains can be later used in plant breeding programs.
- By conserving agricultural biodiversity. **(3 Marks)**

14. The internal organs of the male reproductive system are called accessory organs. They include the vas deferens, seminal vesicles, prostate gland, and bulbourethral glands.

Diagrammatic representation of interrelationship of four accessory ducts in a human male reproductive system:

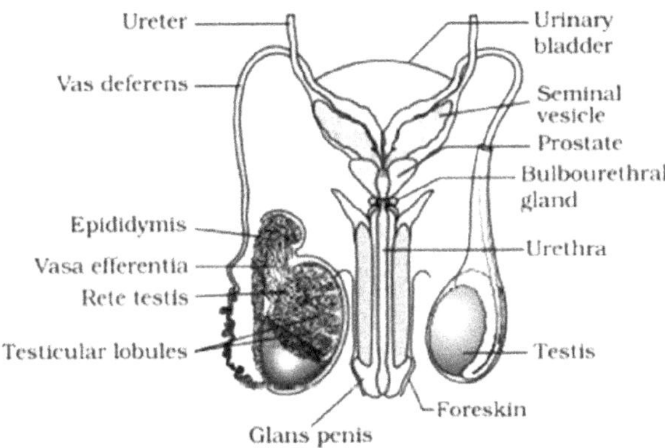

(3 Marks)

OR

Diagrammatic representation of human ovary showing the different stages of developing follicles, corpus luteum and ovulation:

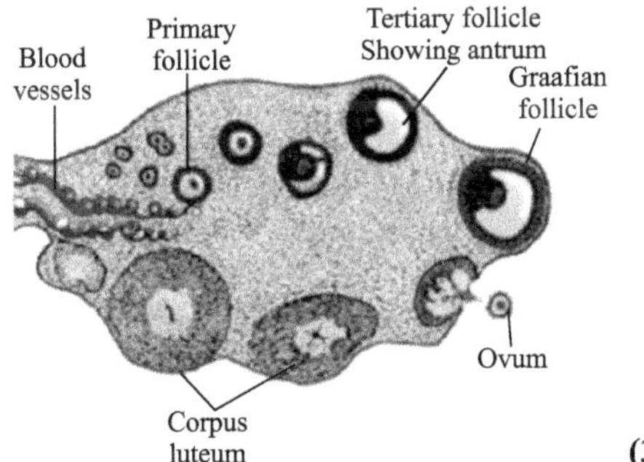

(3 Marks)

15. The chromosomal theory of inheritance given by Sutton and Boveri and experimental results presented by Mendel can be compared in the following ways:

(i) In a diploid organism, the factors (genes) and chromosomes occur in pairs.

(ii) Both chromosomes as well as genes segregate at the time of gamete formation such that only one of each pair is transmitted to a gamete. So, a gamete contains only one chromosome of a type and only one of the two alleles of a trait.

(iii) Each pair of chromosome and gene segregates independent of another pair.

(iv) The paired condition of both chromosomes as well as Mendelian factors is restored during fertilisation.

(3 Marks)

The chromosomal theory of inheritance was proposed by Sutton and Boveri states that the genes are located at specific loci on the chromosome that segregate and assort independently during the process of meiosis and then recombine at the time of fertilization in the zygote.

OR

(a) T.H. Morgan studied X-linked genes in *Drosophila* and observed that when the two genes in a dihybrid cross were situated on the same chromosome, the proportion of parental gene combinations is much higher than the non-parental type. He attributed this due to the physical association or linkage of the two genes on a chromosome and coined the term linkage and the term recombination describes the generation of non-parental gene combinations.

(b) Alfred Sturtevant used the frequency of recombination between gene pairs on the same chromosome as a measure of distance between them and mapped their position on the chromosome. **(3 Marks)**

Genes present on the same chromosome are separated during meiosis and the new combination of the gene could be formed and this phenomenon is called recombination of the gene. They are attached to one another like beads on a string in a linear organisation. The distance between the linked genes indicates the strength of linkage.

16. DNA replication is semiconservative. The replication occurs at origin of replication within a small opening of DNA helix called as 'replication fork'. It requires helicase, topoisomerase, single strand binding proteins, DNA-dependent DNA polymerase for polymerisation of deoxyribonucleotides, deoxyribonucleotides as substrate and source of energy for polymerisation reaction, primase for the synthesis of RNA primer, and DNA ligase to join DNA fragments.

The various steps of DNA replication are as follows:

(i) Helicase unwinds the double helix by breaking the hydrogen bonds between complementary base pairs, while single strand binding proteins helps to stabilize the single strands prevent them from rejoining. The enzyme topoisomerase enzyme releases tension generated due to unwinding and super coiling at the end of DNA opposite to the replication fork.

(ii) The DNA-dependent DNA polymerases cannot initiate the process of replication on their own. So, primase enzyme forms short sequences of RNA called primers that provide a starting point for elongation.

(iii) DNA polymerase catalyses polymerisation only in one direction i.e. 5'→ 3' so on one strand (the template with polarity 3' 5') the replication is continuous while on other (the template with polarity 5' 3'), it is discontinuous. These discontinuously synthesised fragments are called 'Okazaki fragments'. Okazaki fragments are later joined by enzyme DNA ligase.

Diagrammatic representation of replication fork:

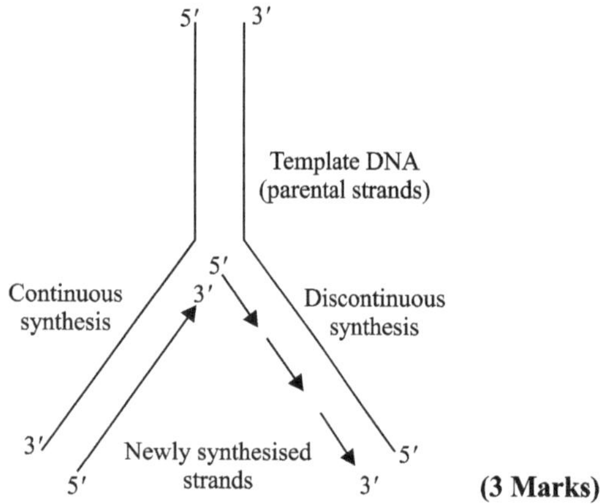

(3 Marks)

DNA (Deoxyribonucleic acid) is a biological process the formation of two identical copies of DNA from parent DNA.

OR

The process of copying genetic information from one strand of DNA into RNA is called transcription. The enzyme catalyse the polymerisation only in one direction that is 5'→3', the strand that has polarity 3'→5' acts as a template and is called template strand. Whereas the other strand is called coding strand and has polarity 3'→5'. The promoter is located towards 5'-end (upstream) of the structural gene. Promoter provides binding site for RNA polymerase. Terminator is located towards 3'-end (downstream) of the coding strand and terminates the process of transcription. For the given RNA, the transcription unit will be:

Diagrammatic representation of transcription unit:

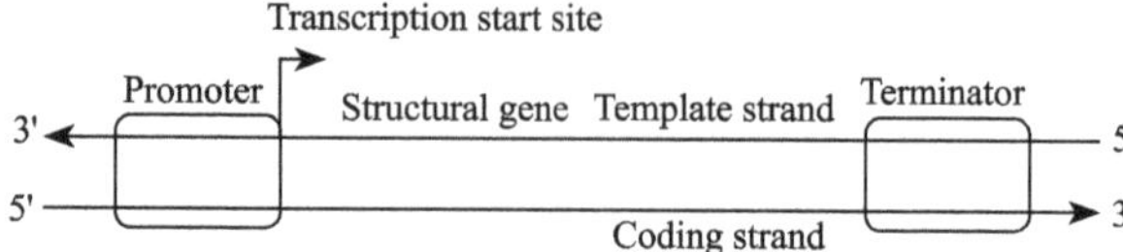

DNA dependent RNA polymerase enzyme is required for the process of transcription. **(3 Marks)**

The mRNA molecule have uracil (U) in place of thymine (T).

17. Difference between *Homo erectus* and *Homo habilis.*

S. No.	Character	*Homo erectus*	*Homo habilis*
(i)	**Brain capacity**	900 cc	650–800 cc
(ii)	**Eating habit**	They probably ate meat	They probably did not eat meat

(b) The correct sequence from early to late geological period is: Silurian period Carboniferous period and Jurassic period. **(3 Marks)**

18. Lactic acid bacteria (LAB) are involved in setting milk into the curd.

Process of curd formation from milk: Milk is converted into curd by the process of fermentation. Milk consists of globular proteins called casein. The curd forms because of the chemical reaction between the lactic acid bacteria and casein. During fermentation, the bacteria use enzymes to produce energy (ATP) from lactose. Under suitable condition, these bacteria multiply and produce acids which coagulate and partially digest the milk proteins and change the milk into curd. Lactobacilli bacteria present in curd multiply in milk and convert the lactose sugar into lactic acid.

Beneficial role played by lactic acid bacteria are:

(i) they are used in food fermentation.

(ii) also found in the human stomach where these bacteria prevent the growth of certain disease-causing microbes.

(iii) improve lactose digestion and increases the content of vitamin B_{12} in curd.

(iv) play a role in preventing and treating diarrhoea and act on the immune system, helping the body to resist and fight infection. **(3 Marks)**

19. Apiculture (also called bee keeping) is a process of rearing and management of honey bees for commercial production of bee wax, honey and royal jelly. The rearing of bees can be done in the area with plantation such as orchards, farms, etc., where sufficient pollen and nectar are available. Such places are called apiary sites.

The following points should be kept in mind for beekeeping:

(i) Since pollen and nectar are available only in the flowering season so seasonal management is very important. This season is known as honey flow season. In this season the pollination efficiency as well as honey production, both get increased. The nectar collected by the bees is passed through the pre-oral cavity and tongue to ripen it. Honey is then deposited in the cells. Hence, more space for storage of honey should be provided during this season.

(ii) During the summer season, adequate shade and water should be provided by artificial constructions or by keeping the beehives under the trees. Proper ventilation, sugar syrup and pollen supplements should also be provided as a food source.

(iii) During winter season, disease-free colonies should be maintained. The hives should be provided with new queens.

(iv) During the rainy season, dampness should be avoided and since bees cannot go out to collect pollen and nectar, sugar syrup should be provided as food.

(v) One should wear protective clothing and gloves while handling the honey bees and collecting honey. Smokers are also used by the bee-keepers to keep them calm while handling them.

Apis indica (Indian bee) is the most common species of bee reared in India. The other important species that can also be reared are *Apis mellifera* (Italian bee), *Apis dorsata* (rock bee) and *Apis florea* (little bee). **(3 Marks)**

20. (i)

Column A	Column B	Correct Options
(H) *Penicillium notatum*	(i) Statin	**(H) – (iii)**
(I) *Trichoderma polysporum*	(ii) ethanol	**(I) – (iv)**
(J) *Monascus purpurae*	(iii) antibiotic	**(J) – (i)**
(K) *Saccharomyces cerevisae*	(iv) cyclosporin-A	**(K) – (ii)**

(ii) The development of large holes in 'Swiss cheese' is because of the production of large amount of carbon dioxide by the bacterium *Propionibacterium-sharmanii.* **(3 Marks)**

21. The various steps involved in the formation of recombinant DNA by the action of *Eco*RI are as follows:

- Both vector DNA and foreign DNA is cut with *Eco*RI.
- Both DNAs will possess smaller fragments with overhanging stretches called sticky ends on each strand.
- After digestion, both vector DNA and foreign DNA are mixed and allowed to join together with the help of DNA ligase enzyme. This results in the formation of recombinant DNA molecules.

Diagrammatic representation of steps involved in the formation of recombinant DNA by action of restriction endonuclease enzyme-EcoRI:

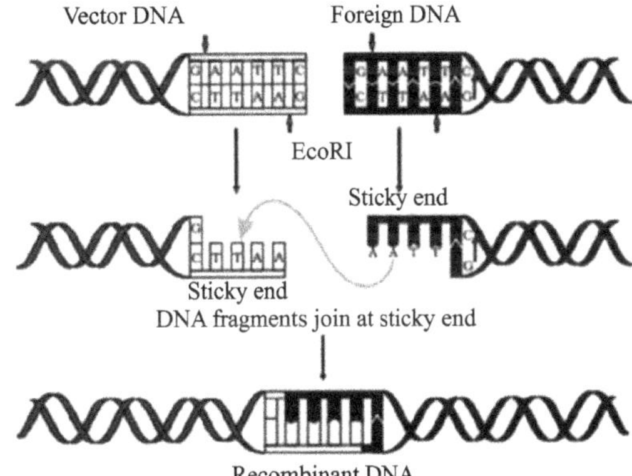

(3 Marks)

OR

With the help of recombinant DNA technology called Polymerase Chain Reaction technique (PCR) multiple copies of the 'gene of interest' are obtained in *Vitro.* A single PCR amplification cycle involves three steps which are as follows:

(a) **Denaturation:** This is the first step of PCR, in which the target DNA is heated at high temperature such as 94-96°C. It facilitates the separation of two strands of DNA. Each separated strand of DNA acts as a template for synthesis of DNA.

(b) **Annealing:** This is the second step of PCR, in which two oligonucleotide primers are used to hybridize each single-stranded template DNA. The sequence of primers is complementary to 3' end of the template DNA strand.

This step of PCR occurs at low temperature 40-60°C than denaturation. The annealing temperature depends upon the length and sequence of the primers.

(c) **Extension:** This is the third and the last step of PCR, in which enzyme *Taq*DNA polymerase synthesizes the DNA between the primers. This step also requires dNTPs and Mg2++. The optimum temperature for an extension is 72°C.

Diagrammatic representation of steps involved in PCR:

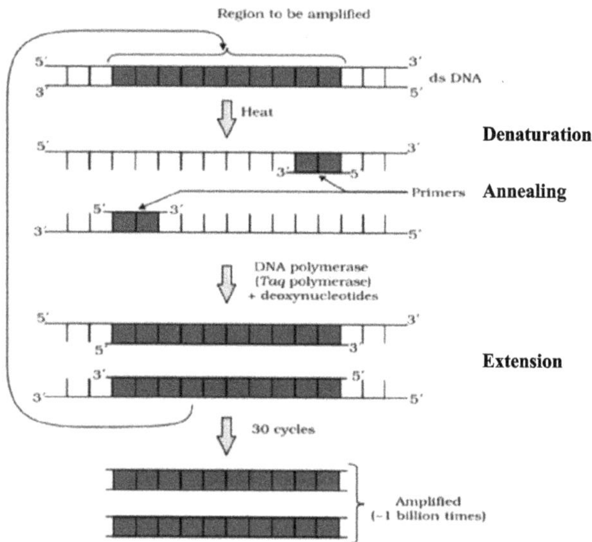

(3 Marks)

Enzyme used in PCR is a DNA polymerase such as Taq polymerase. This enzyme is stable at high temperature as it is isolated from thermostable bacteria Thermus aquaticus.

22. (a) The two girls are suffering from a genetic disorder resulting in adenosine deaminase (ADA) deficiency due to deletion of its gene that codes for adenosine deaminase enzyme **(1 Mark)**

(b) Girl A was treated by enzyme replacement therapy, in which functional ADA is given to the patient by injection. This technique is not completely curative as it requires repeated infusion. **(1 Mark)**

(c) Girl B was treated using gene therapy where the gene isolate from marrow cells producing ADA was introduced into cells at an early embryonic stage in order to provide permanent cure. **(1 Mark)**

ADA deficiency is caused because of the deletion of the gene that codes for adenosine deaminase enzyme. Severe combined Immunodeficiency disorder (SCID) is caused because of the defect in gene which codes for adenosine deaminase enzyme.

23. *Ex-situ* ('off site') conservation is a set of conservation techniques involving the transfer of a target species away from its native habitat to a place of safety, such as a zoological garden, botanical garden or seed bank. *Ex-situ* techniques include: seed storage, captive breeding, slow-growth storage, DNA storage.

Advantages of ex-situ conservation

(i) Organisms are completely protected from predation and poaching.

(ii) To preserve gametes of threatened species in viable condition through cryopreservation.

(iii) To grow plants with recalcitrant seeds in orchards where all possible varieties are maintained.

(iv) To conserve seeds of commercially important plants in seed banks. Genetic diversity of the population can be measured

(v) To save endangered or threatened plant that needs urgent measure to save it from extinction in botanical gardens.

(vi) To propagate threatened plants via tissue culture.

(3 Marks)

Ex-situ conservation is a conservation technique that involves the conservation of selected rare or endangered plants and animal species in places outside their natural environment or homes. It involves offsite collection and gene banks.

24. (a) As a student of biology, I disagree to the delight of visitors to find large expense of water covered with colorful algal mass because algal mass is the cause of deterioration of water quality (decline in dissolved oxygen) leading to death of fish and other aquatic organisms. Some bloom-forming algae are extremely also toxic to human beings and animals.

(b) The cause of algal growth is because of excessive growth of planktonic (free-floating) algae, called an algal bloom due to the addition of large amounts of nutrients (nitrogen and phosphorous) in water bodies through human activities such as agricultural runoff, excessive use of fertilisers, industrial effluents, sewage treatment and soil erosion. **(3 Marks)**

SECTION - D

25. (a)

(A) Amniocentesis: This is also called amniotic fluid test as it is used for the detection of chromosomal abnormalities in the developing foetus. This test is done after the 16 weeks of pregnancy. In this, a small quantity of sample is taken from the amniotic sac and DNA is examined for genetic abnormalities.

(B) Lactational amenorrhea: It is a type of natural contraceptive method is characterized by absence of menstruation. In this method, the ovulation and menstrual cycle do not occur during the period of intense lactation followed by parturition.

(C) **ZIFT (Zygote Intra-fallopian Transfer):** It is an assisted reproductive technology. In this method, ova is collected from the female (wife/ donor) and sperms from the male (husband/ donor). Both the ova and sperms are induced to form zygote in the laboratory. The zygote is allowed to form 8 blastomeres stage and is transferred into fallopian tube of female.

(3 Marks)

(b) **Poster presentation on "Reproductive and Child Health Care Programme"**

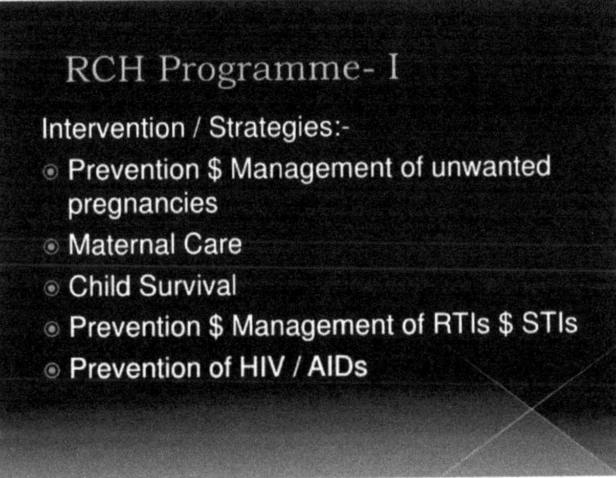

(2 Marks)

The goal of "Reproductive and child Health Care programme" is to provide facilities and support for building up a reproductively healthy society.

OR

(a) The different ways by which apomictic seeds are developed involved:

(i) Formation of diploid egg as embryo without undergoing reduction division or fertilization for example: *Asteraceae.*

(ii) In several citrus fruits and mango varieties, nuclear cells surrounding the embryo sac start dividing and project into the embryo sac. It gets further developed into the embryos. **(2 Marks)**

(b) **Advantages of apomictic crop:** Apomixis reduces the cost of the hybrid production so that new varieties of seeds are produced more quickly and at a cheaper rate.

Disadvantages of apomictic crop:

Apomictic seeds reduce the genetic diversity because of a lack of variations. **(1 Mark)**

(c) Hybrid seeds are produced by cross-pollination of plants and in order to produce desirable hybrid character, plant breeders and scientists are trying thousands of combination to produce such hybrids. So hybrid seeds are produced every years and it requires a lots of scientific research for the production of such hybrid seeds. It is expensive and hence the cost of hybrid becomes too expensive for the farmers.

(2 Marks)

26. The difference between incomplete and co-dominance are as follows:

Incomplete dominance	Codominance
(i) It is a phenomena in which none of the alleles of a gene is dominant over each other and a new phenotype is formed. The new phenotype is intermediate between the independent expression of two alleles.	(i) Codominance is a phenomena in which both the alleles of a gene expresses themselves independently in a heterozygote.
(ii) New phenotypes are always formed as a result of incomplete dominance.	(ii) In case of codominance, no new phenotype is formed.
(iii) Examples are snapdragon and mirabilis jalapa	(iii) Examples are Roan character in cattles and blood grouping in humans.

(5 Marks)

OR

(a) **George gamow:** He worked on radioactive decay that affects the nucleus of atomon a stellar nucleosynthesis and star formation.

Hargobind Khorana: He synthesized copolymers of nucleotides such as UGUGUGUG. They observed that they have stimulated the formation of polypeptides having alternatively similar amino acid sequence such as cysteine-valine-cysteine.

Marshall Nirenberg: He discovered the first "triplet"-a sequence of three bases of DNA that codes for one of the twenty amino acids which serves as the building blocks of the proteins.

Severo Ochoa: He investigated how DNA and RNA are formed as well as which enzymes control this process. He discovered polynucleotide phosphorylase enzyme which helps in polymerization of ribonucleotides in template independent manner.

(3 Marks)

(b) Genetic code is the biochemical basis of heredity consisting of codons in DNA and RNA that determine the specific amino acid sequence in proteins and appear to be uniform for nearly all known forms of life.

Importance of genetic code in protein biosynthesis:

- Genetic code is important because it provides information encoded in genetic material (DNA or RNA sequences) to be translated into proteins (amino acid sequences) by living cells.
- All organisms on Earth utilise proteins in chemical reactions to facilitate physiological functions.
- Differences in genetic code result in coding of different proteins, and it leads to cause genetic variations in organisms. **(2 Marks)**

27. (a) Population is the number of people or animals of the same group or species, living in a particular geographical area, and have the capability of interbreeding. **(2 Marks)**

(b) The size of a population for any species is not a static parameter because it keeps changing with time, depending on various factors including food availability, predation, pressure and adverse weather. The density of a population in a given area during a period fluctuates due to changes in four basic processes two of which are natality and immigrationcontribute to an increase in population density and two are mortality and emigration to a decrease.

(i) **Natality:** Number of births during a given period in the population that are added to the initial density.

(ii) **Mortality:** Number of deaths in the population during a given period.

(iii) **Immigration:** Number of individuals of the same species that have come into the habitat from elsewhere during given time period.

(iv) **Emigration:** Number of individuals of the population who had left the habitat and gone elsewhere during given time period. **(3 Marks)**

OR

(a) **Hydrarch succession** occurs in the wetter areas and the successional series progress from hydric to the mesic conditions. **(1 Mark)**

(b) Comparison of pioneer species and climax communities of hydrarch and xerarch succession:

Characteristics	Hydrarch succession	Xerarch succession
Pioneer species	Pioneer communities are small phytoplanktons for example: Diatoms.	Pioneer communities are usually lichens. For example: Lichens secretes acids to dissolve rocks and also helps in weathering as well as in soil formation.
Climax communities	Climax community would be a forest, the water body is converted into land with time. It also results in mesic conditions.	The climax community would be a forest. Xerarch succession results in mesic conditions.

(1 Mark)

The species that invade a bare rocks are called ***pioneer species*** *and* ***Climax community*** *involves the changes that lead finally to a community which is in near equilibrium with the environment.*

(c) Factors on which invading pioneer species depend in a secondary hydrarch succession are as follows:

Condition of soil, presence of seeds or propagules in the environment, and availability of water

Secondary succession is the ecological succession that occurs after the initial succession has been disrupted and some plants and animals still exist. Rate of secondary hydrarch succession is faster than that of primary succession because of the following reasons:

(i) Some soil and nutrients were already present due to which climax reaches more quickly. So there is no need for pioneer species to colonize the land nor does decomposition need to occur to create a layer of topsoil.

(ii) Seeds, roots and underground vegetative organs of plants may still survive in the soil.

Delhi 2019

CBSE Board Solved Paper

Time Allowed : 3 Hours ***Maximum Marks : 70***

General Instructions:

(i) There are total **27** questions and four sections in the question paper. All questions are compulsory.
(ii) Section **A** contains questions number **1** to **5**, very short answer type questions of **one** mark each.
(iii) Section **B** contains questions number **6** to **12**, short answer type-I questions of **two** marks each.
(iv) Section **C** contains questions number **13** to **24**, short answer type-II questions of **three** marks each.
(v) Section **D** contains question number **25** to **27**, long answer type questions of **five** marks each.
(vi) There is no overall choice in the question paper, however, an internal choice is provided in **two** questions of **one** mark, **two** questions of **two** marks, **four** questions of **three** marks and all the **three** questions of **five** marks. In these questions, an examinee is to attempt any **one** of the **two** given alternatives.
(vii) Wherever necessary, the diagram drawn should be neat and properly labelled.

SECTION - A

1. What do 'X' and 'Y' represent in the transcription unit of the DNA molecule shown?

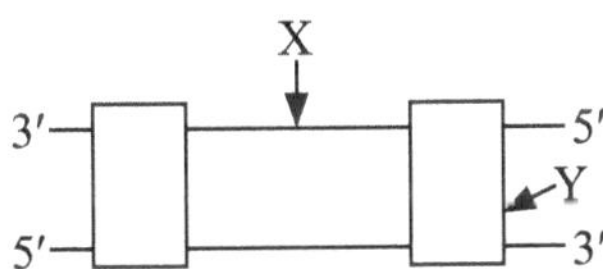

2. How are the members of genus Glomus useful to organic farmers?

3. The diploid number of chromosomes in an angiospermic plant is 16. What will be the number of chromosomes in its endosperm and antipodal cells?

OR

State the reason why pollen grains lose their viability when the tapetum in the anther is malfunctioning.

4. Biotechnologic techniques can help to diagnose the pathogen much before the symptoms of the disease appear in the patient. Suggest any two such techniques.

OR

Mention the form in which inactive protein toxin is produced by *Bacillus thuringiensis*. How does it get activated in the pest body to kill it?

5. Name the disorder in humans with the following karyotype:

(a) 22 pairs of autosomes + XO

(b) 22 pairs of autosomes + 21st chromosome + XY

SECTION - B

6. Humans are categorised as "regulators". Explain how they maintain a constant normal body temperature.

7. You are given a tall pea plant and asked to find its genotype. How would you find its genotype? Explain.

8. Scientists are trying to solve the issues of malnutrition and hunger by using microbes. By taking one suitable example, explain how they have been able to help.

9. MOET is a programme for herd improvement. Write the steps in correct sequence that are carried in the programme.

OR

Why is tobacco smoking associated with rise in blood pressure and emphysema? Explain.

10. **(a)** How will you measure population density of fish in a lake?

(b) In a pond there are 100 frogs. 20 more were born in a year. Calculate the birth rate of this population.

OR

Draw a "stable" human age pyramid. Comment on the population growth rate that is depicted by it.

SECTION - C

11. What is cryopreservation? Mention how it is used in conservation of biodiversity.

12. How can childless couples be helped by the followed assisted reproductive technologies:

    (a) GIFT

    (b) Cytoplasmic Sperm Injection

13. Draw a diagram of LS of Maize grain and label its any six parts.

14. Study the figure of vector pBR322 given below:

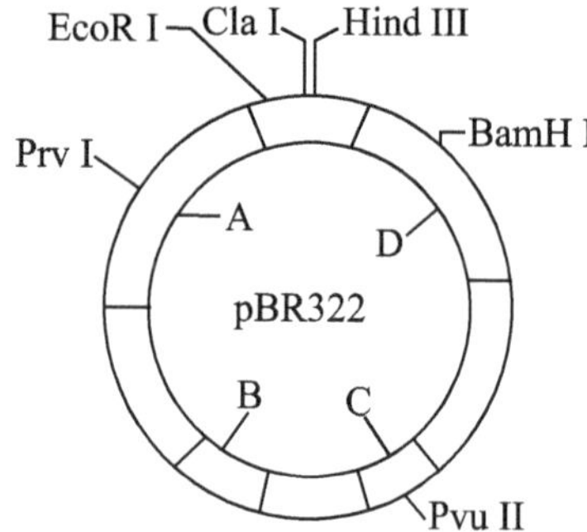

Identify A, B, C and D and explain their roles in cloning a vector.

15. Compare the mechanism of evolution as put forth by Charles Darwin and de Vries.

16. **(a)** A patient had suffered myocardial infarction and clots were found in his blood vessels. Name a 'clot buster' that can be used to dissolve the clots and the micro-organism from which it is obtained.

    (b) A woman had just undergone a kidney transplant. A bioactive molecular drug is administered to oppose kidney rejection by the body. What is the bioactive molecule? Name the microbe from which this is extracted.

    (c) What do doctors prescribe to lower the blood cholesterol level in patients with high blood cholesterol? Name the source organism from which this drug can be obtained.

17. Give reasons for the following:

    (a) Antibody mediated immunity is called humoral immunity.

    (b) How is a child protected from a disease for which he/she is vaccinated?

    (c) Name the type of cells the AIDS virus enters after getting into the human body.

OR

(a) Identify the nos. (i) to (iv) in the following table:

	Name of disease	**Causative organism**	**Symptoms**
w	Penumonia	*Streptococcus*	(i)
x	Typhoid	(ii)	High fever, weakness, headache, stomach pain
y	(iii)	Rhinoviruses	Nasal congestion and discharge, sore throat, cough, headache
z	Ascariasis	*Ascaris*	(iv)

(b) Which one of the above mentioned diseases are transmitted through mechanical carriers?

18. Draw a diagram of the sectional view of a human seminiferous tubule and label any six of its parts.

19. A woman with 'O blood group' marries a man with 'AB blood group'. Work out the cross to show all the possible phenotypes and genotypes of the progeny with respect to blood groups. Explain the pattern of inheritance observed in this cross.

20. **(a)** What is the breeding of crops for enhancing their nutritional value called? Why is the need felt for enhancing the nutritional value of the crops?

    (b) Rice, wheat and maize are the most commonly used food grains the world over. How have these grains improved in their nutritional value in comparison to their conventional varieties?

OR

(a) Write the scientific names of the source plants from where opioids and canabinoids are extracted.

(b) Write their receptor sites in the human body. How do these drugs affect the human beings?

21. Write by taking a suitable example, the convention followed for naming the restriction enzymes.

22. Hershey and Chase carried out their experiment under three steps:

    (a) Infection, (b) Blending, and (c) Centrifugation. Explain each one of these steps that helped them to prove that DNA is the hereditary material.

OR

(a) Why does DNA replication occur within a replication fork and not in its entire length simultaneously?

(b) "DNA replication is continuous and discontinuous on the two strands within the replication fork." Give reasons.

SECTION - D

23. Restriction endonucleases have played a very significant role in rDNA technology. Explain the roles of EcoRI and DNA ligase in formation of recombinant DNA.

SECTION - E

24. Describe the phosphorus cycle in an ecosystem.

25. **(a)** Describe the experiment conducted by F. Griffith in 1928 with *Streptococcus pneumoniae* and write the conclusions he arrived at.

(b) State the contribution of Avery. MacLeod and McCarty in providing biochemical nature to the results as obtained by Griffith.

26. **(a)** State what is an ecological succession.

(b) Write one similarity and one difference between hydarch and xerarch successions.

(c) Explain the mechanism of co-evolution as seen in orchid *Ophrys* and bee.

OR

(a) List any two ways the biodiversity loss affects any region.

(b) Explain any two causes the biodiversity loss affects any region.

27. **(a)** Draw the embryo sac of a flowering plant and label the following:

(i) Central cell (ii) Chalazal and (iii) Synergids

(b) Name the cell and explain the process it undergoes to develop into an embryo sac.

(c) Explain the development of endosperm in coconut.

OR

Write the duration and the events that occur in the ovary and the uterus during folicular and luteal phases of the menstural cycle in humans. How do pituitary and ovarian hormones influence these two phases?

Solutions

SECTION - A

1. The 'X' and 'Y' in the given figure represents template strand and terminator region. **(1 Mark)**

   Template strand: The strand that has polarity 3' → 5' acts as a template strand.

   Terminator region: The terminator region is located towards 3'-end (downstream) of the coding strand and it terminates the process of transcription.

Template strand (3' → 5') is the strand used by DNA dependent RNA polymerase to attach complementary bases during the process of replication or transcription.

2. *Glomus* forms mycorrhiza. It is symbiotic association between the fungi and root nodules of leguminous plants. They absorbs phosphorus from the soil and transport it to the plants. **(1 Mark)**

3. The diploid number of chromosomes in an angiosperm plant (2n) = 16. **(1 Mark)**

   The haploid number (n) will be = 8

   Endosperm of an angiosperm is triploid (3n), so the number of chromosome present in endosperm 3n = 8 × 3 = 24.

   Whereas antipodal cells are haploid (n) in nature. So, the number of chromosome in antipodal cells will be =8

   OR

   Tapetum provides nourishment to the developing pollen grain. When the tapetum in anther is malfunctioning the pollen grain will not get enough nourishment and also loses its viability. **(1 Mark)**

4. **PCR (Polymerase Chain Reaction)** is molecular biology technique that is used for the early diagnosis of symptoms of diseases. It focuses on the actual segment of DNA of its own interest and from a segment of DNA, the genotypes can be determined. In this way, genetic disorders can be diagnosed and detected. This technique is used for the detection of HIV and cancer. **(½ Mark)**

DNA polymerase used in PCR is Taq DNA polymerase which is isolated from a bacterium. Thermus aquaticus. This bacterium is found in hot springs and hydrothermal vents. The Taq Polymerase remains active at high temperature during denaturation.

   Gel electrophoresis is a molecular biology technique and is also used for the early diagnosis of symptoms of diseases. In this technique, DNA sequences are separated according to their size. **(½ Mark)**

5. (i) 22 pairs of autosome + XO occurs in case of turner syndrome. The total number of chromosomes is 45 with XO. Females with turner syndrome are sterile as their ovaries are rudimentary. Such females also lack other secondary sexual characters. **(½ Mark)**

   (ii) 22 pairs of autosomes +21st chromosome+ XY occurs in Klinefelter's syndrome. It is a genetic disorder that is caused due to the presence of an additional copy X-chromosome results in 47 + XXY chromosome. Such males have overall masculine development but they have feminine development such as breast development. Such males are sterile. **(½ Mark)**

SECTION - B

6. **Regulators:** Regulators are those organisms that are able to maintain homeostasis according to external environment. They have ability to maintain their constant body temperature and osmotic concentration. For example: Birds and mammals.

   Regulators during winters when the outside the temperature is less than body temperature, the body start shivering. Shivering is a way to maintain the internal body as this practice produces heat. **(2 Marks)**

The tendency to maintain a stable, relatively constant internal environment is called homeostasis.

7. A test cross is used to determine the genotype of pea plant. In this a tall plant is crossed with dwarf plant. In the F1 generation, all the progeny obtained are tall. So the genotype of the tall plant is TT. In the F2 generation, 50% tall plants and 50% dwarf plants are obtained and the genotype of the tall plant is Tt. **(2 Marks)**

   Diagrammatic Representation of Test cross:

	Male			**Female**
Parents	TT	X		tt
Gametes	(T) (T)	X		(t) (t)
F_1 generation	Tt	Tt	Tt	Tt
	Male			**Female**
Parents	Tt		X	tt
Gametes	(T) (t)		X	(t) (t)
F_2 generation	Tt	Tt	tt	tt

8. Scientist are trying to solve the issues related to malnutrition and hunger by using microbes by using a technique called Single Cell Protein (SCP). In this, microbes such as *Spirulina* are grown on an industrial scale as good source of protein. *Spirulina* can be grown on materials like waste water from potato processing plants that contains starch, straw, molasses, animal manure and even sewage in order to produce a food that contains large quantities of protein, minerals, fats,

carbohydrate and vitamins. This technique also reduces environmental pollution. **(2 Marks)**

9. **MOET** is Multiple Ovulation Embryo Transfer Technology is one such programme for herd improvement. The following steps are involved in this method:
   - A cow is administered with hormone such as FSH (follicle stimulating hormone) to induce follicular maturation and super ovulation instead of one egg that is produced normally per cycle.
   - In this process, they produce 6-8 eggs.
   - Then the animal is either mated with an elite bull or artificially insemination.
   - The fertilised eggs are then at 8-32 celled stage.
   - The 8-32 egg cell stage are recovered non-surgically and transferred to surrogate mother.
   - This genetic mother is then available for another round of super ovulation. **(2 Marks)**

This technology is used for cattle, sheep, rabbits, buffaloes, mares and so on. In this technique, high milk yielding breeds of females and high quality meat yielding bulls have been bred successfully in order to increase the herd size in shorter time.

OR

Tobacco contains nicotine that tends to stimulate the release of adrenaline and non-adrenaline. It increases the blood pressure and heart rate. Smoking increases carbon monoxide content in the blood and reduces the concentration of haem-bound oxygen in the blood. It leads to cause oxygen deficiency in the body. Emphysema is caused because of the over-inflammation of the alveolar sacs that impairs gaseous exchange in the lungs. **(2 Marks)**

10. **(a)** The population density of a fishes in a lake is determined by the fish caught per trap. Population density refers to the measure to determine the number of individuals of a species in a particular unit area. The relative densities are used to determine the population size in a specific area. **(1 Mark)**

(b) To calculate the birth rate of population

$$= \frac{\text{Number of births}}{\text{Total population}} \times 100$$

The birth rate of a frog population $= \frac{20}{120} \times 100$

$= 16.66$ per year

(1 Mark)

OR

In a stable or Bell-shaped age pyramid the number of pre-reproductive and reproductive individuals is almost equal. If the post-reproductive individuals are comparatively fewer than the population size remains stable as it is neither growing nor diminishing.

Age pyramid is defined as a way for representing the age-sex structure of population.

Diagrammatic Representation of Stable Age pyramid:

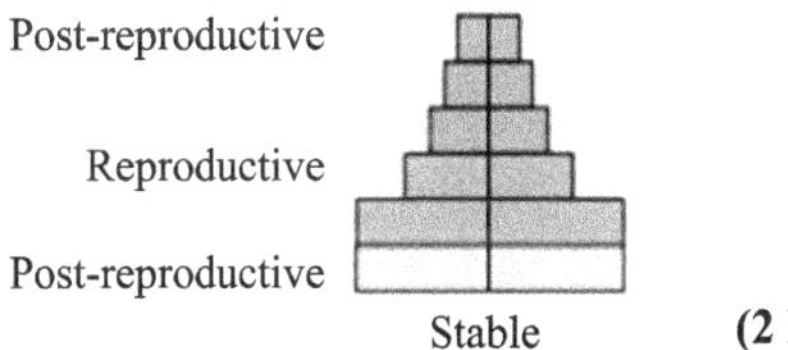

(2 Marks)

11. **Cryopreservation:** It is a method used for the preservation of cells and tissue structures in an extremely cold temperature such as at -196°C in a liquid nitrogen. It inhibits metabolism in cells.

Cryopreservation of biodiversity in a following ways: The gametes of endangered plants and animals are kept viable by preserving them at a very low temperature (–196°C) in a liquid nitrogen. **(2 Marks)**

12. **(a)** **GIFT (Gamete Intra Fallopian Transfer):** It is an in vitro fertilisation technique that involves the transfer of ovum collected from a donor into the fallopian tube of another female who is unable to produce eggs. This technique also provide suitable environment for fertilisation and further development. **(1 Mark)**

(b) **Cytoplasmic sperm injection:** It is another specialised in vitro technique in which an embyo is formed in a laboratory in which a sperm is directly injected into the ovum. **(1 Mark)**

Assisted Reproductive Technology (ARTs) is used for the treatment of infertility. This technology involves the mating of egg and sperm outside of the body (Invitro) under sterilized condition.

SECTION - C

13. **Diagrammatic Representation of L.S of Maize grain:**

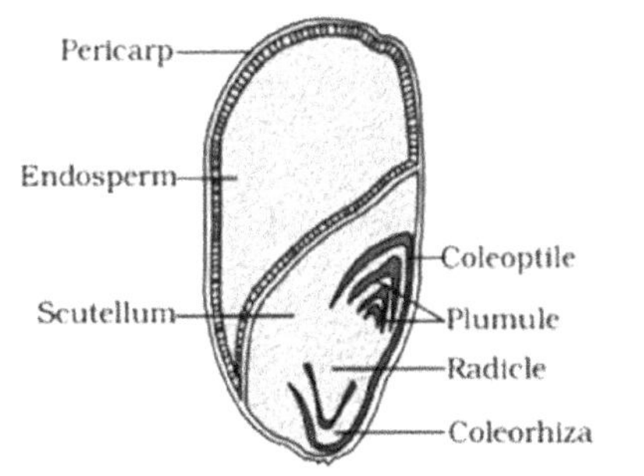

(3 Marks)

14. In the given figure, A is ampicillin resistance gene, B is origin of replication, C is repressor of primer, D is tetracycline resistance gene.

(a) **Ampicillin resistance gene (amp^R):** It acts as a selectable marker that provides resistance against ampicillin antibiotic.

(b) **ori:** It is origin of replication. A sequence that initiates the process of replication. It controls the copy number of linked DNA.

(c) **rop (repressor of primer):** This site is responsible for the restricting the plasmid copy number.

(d) **tet^R:** It is tetracyclin resistance gene that acts as a selectable marker which provides resistance against tetracyclin antibiotic. **(3Marks)**

15. The Darwin's theory of evolution is based on **Natural selection.** According to Darwin's, variation results in evolution. Variations are inheritable and were small as well as directional. Natural selection favours survival of the fittest one as nature selects individuals that are fit and able to adapt as well as survive in changing environment.

The theory of Hugo deVaries is based on mutation. He believed that large differences occurs suddenly in a population. He also said that mutation results in evolution. According to Hugo deVaries mutation are random and directionless. Mutation leads to cause speciation and hence is called as **saltation or single step large mutation.** **(3 Marks)**

16. (a) Streptokinase is used as clot buster for patients suffering from myocardial infraction. It is produced from bacterium *Streptococcus.* **(1 Mark)**

(b) Cyclosporin A is a bioactive molecule that is used as an immunosuppressive agent in organ-transplant patients. It is produced by a fungus *Trichoderma polysporum.* **(1 Mark)**

(c) Statins is a blood-cholesterol lowering agents produced by yeast *Monascus purpureus.* It competitively inhibits the enzyme that is responsible for the synthesis of cholesterol. **(1 Mark)**

17. (a) Antibodies are also called immunoglobulins that are produced by B-lymphocytes in the blood and produces immune response. This type of immune response is called humoral immune response. **(1 Mark)**

(b) Vaccination is based on the memory of the immune system. Vaccination involves the preparation of inactivated or weakened pathogens or a preparation of antigenic proteins of pathogen in the host body. The antibodies produced in the body against these antigens neutralise the pathogenic agents during actual infections. **(1 Mark)**

(c) The AIDS virus after entering into the body get enters into the macrophages. Then the AIDS virus enters into the helper-T cells. **(1 Mark)**

OR

(a) **(i)** Fever, chills, cough, cold and headache. In severe cases, the lips and fingernails may turn grey to bluish in color.

(ii) *Salmonella typhi*

(iii) Common cold

(iv) Internal bleeding, muscular pain, fever, anaemia and blockage of intestinal passage. **(2 Marks)**

(b) None of the above mentioned diseases are transmitted through mechanical carriers. **(1 Mark)**

18. Diagrammatic Representation of seminiferous tubules:

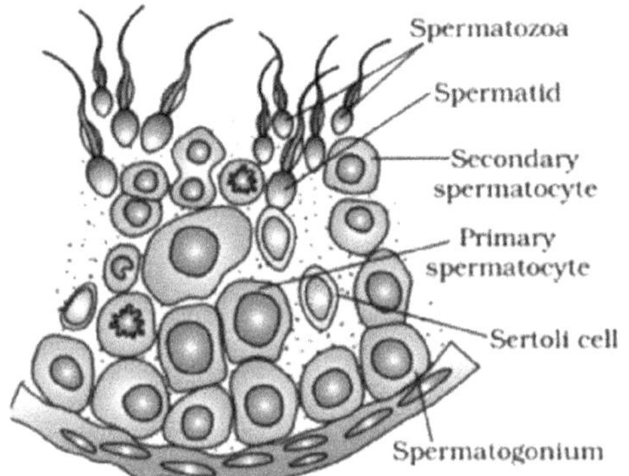

(3 Marks)

The seminiferous tubules is lined on its inside by two types of cells called male germ cells that undergo meiotic divisions results in sperm formation. Whereas Sertoli cells provide nourishment to the germ cells.

19. The inheritance of ABO blood grouping in humans is an example of Co-dominance and multiple alleles. ABO blood grouping in human beings are controlled by I gene. The plasma membrane of the red blood cells has sugar polymers that are found on the surface of RBCs and is controlled by this gene.

Diagrammatic representation of a Cross:

Parents	Father	X	Mother	
	I^AI^B	X	ii	
Gametes	I^A I^B	X	i i	
F_1 genration	I^Ai	I^Ai	I^Bi	I^Bi

The above cross represents that in F1 generation blood A and B are dominant over blood O group. So, the children's have 50 % chances of getting A and B blood group. **(3 Marks)**

Co-dominance is a type of inheritance in which the alleles of a gene pair in a heterozygote are independently expressed themselves. Multiple alleles refer to the more than three alternative forms of allele of a gene.

20. (a) Biofortification is a technique used by farmers for increasing the nutrient content in the breeding crops. This breeding technique involves breeding crops with higher levels of vitamins and minerals or higher protein as well as healthier fats in order to improve public health.

Biofortification involves following objectives for improving nutritional quality of crops such as:

- Increasing protein content and quality
- Oil content and quality
- Vitamin content and
- Micronutrient and mineral content. **(1 Mark)**

(b) Biofortification is a boon for crops such as maize, wheat and rice. As the maize hybrids contains twice the amount of the amino acids lysine and tryptophan as compared to existing maize hybrid.

Wheat variety such as Atlas 66, contains a high protein content and it has been used as a donor for improving cultivated wheat. Iron-fortified rice variety is also developed that contains five times iron than commonly used varieties of rice.

Several vegetables are also rich in Vitamins and minerals for example carrot enriched in vitamin A, spinach, pumpkin, vitamin C enriched bitter gourd, *bathua*, mustard, tomato. Iron and calcium enriched spinach and *bathua*, protein enriched beans such as broad, lablab, French and garden peas. **(2 Marks)**

All the biofortified vegetables are developed by Indian Agricultural Research Institute.

OR

(a) Opioids are the drugs that are obtained from the latex of poppy plant called *Papaver somniferum*. Whereas cannabinoids are the group of chemicals that are naturally obtained from the inflorescences of the plant *Cannabis sativa*. **(1 Mark)**

(b) Opioids are the drugs that get bids with the specific opioid receptors present in the central nervous system and gastrointestinal tract of human beings. Opioids such as heroin acts a depressant and slows down body functions.

Cannabinoids are a group of chemicals that interact with cannabinoid receptors present in the brain. Cannabinoids such as marijuana, hashish, charas and ganja effects on cardiovascular system of the body. **(2 Marks)**

21. The convention for naming these enzymes is the first letter of the name that comes from the genes and the second two letters come from the species of the prokaryotic cell from which they were isolated for *e.g.*, EcoRI comes from *Escherichia coli* RY13.

In EcoRI, in this the letter 'R' is derived from the name of strain. Roman numbers following the names indicate the order in which the enzymes were isolated from that strain of bacteria. **(3 Marks)**

22. To proof that DNA is the genetic material an experiment was performed by Alfred Hershey and Martha Chase in 1952. They worked with viruses that infect bacteria called bacteriophage.

Following steps are involved in Hershey and Chase experiment:

(a) Infection

- They grow viruses on a different medium containing radioactive phosphorus and radioactive sulphur.
- Viruses grown in the presence of radioactive phosphorus contained radioactive DNA but not protein because DNA contains phosphorus but is absent in protein.
- Whereas virus grown in a medium containing radioactive sulphur contained radioactive protein but not radioactive DNA because sulphur is absent in DNA.
- Radioactive phages were allowed to attach to *E.coli* bacteria.

(b) Blending:

- As the infection proceeded, the viral coats were removed from the bacteria by agitating them in a blender.

(c) Centrifugation:

- Then the virus particles were separated from the bacteria by spinning them in a centrifuge.
- So the bacteria that infected with viruses that contain radioactive DNA were radioactive.
- This indicates that DNA was the material that can be passed from the virus to bacteria.
- Bacteria that were infected with viruses that contain radioactive proteins were not radioactive.
- This indicates that proteins did not enter the bacteria from the viruses.
- Hence, it is proved that DNA is the genetic material that is passed from virus to bacteria.

(3 Marks)

Diagrammatic representation of Hershey and Chase experiment:

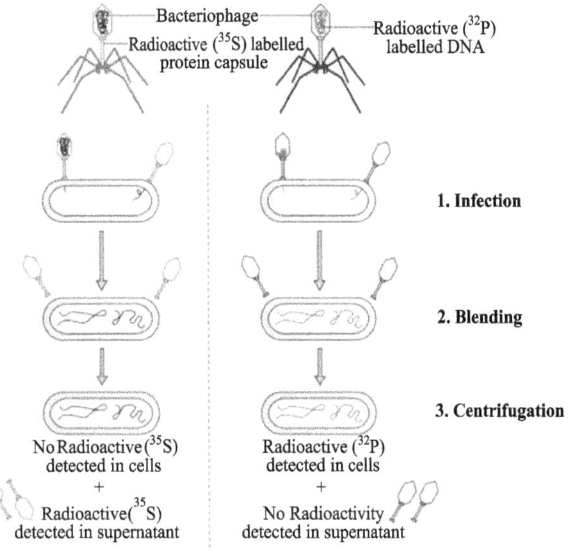

OR

(a) DNA is a large and double helical molecule. The process of DNA replication occurs only in small region of DNA not in its entire length in one time. As large amount of energy is required for opening a whole double helical DNA. **(1 Mark)**

DNA is more stable than RNA due to absence of 2^1 – OH group and presence of thymine in place of uracil in DNA.

(b) In DNA replication, DNA-dependent DNA polymerase is involved in the process of DNA replication. This enzyme catalyses the polymerisation of deoxynucleotides in $5' \rightarrow 3'$ direction, this is called lagging strand of the DNA and replication is discontinuous whereas when the replication takes place in $3' \rightarrow 5'$, this strand is called leading strand and replication is continuous. **(2 Marks)**

The discontinuously synthesised strand of the fragments are joined together by DNA ligase enzyme and such fragments are called OKAZAKI fragments.

SECTION - D

23. In Recombinant DNA technology, EcoRI cuts the DNA between bases G and A only when the sequences GAATTC is present in the DNA. It acts as a molecular scissors that serves as tool for DNA at specific palindromic sites at specific points.

DNA ligase enzyme is also called molecular gum as it is involved in joining the two segments of DNA by creating phosphodiester bond between the two fragments of DNA. **(4 Marks)**

A recombinant DNA molecule is formed from the segments of two or more different DNA molecules.

SECTION - E

24. Phosphorus is a major constituent of all biological membranes such as nucleic acids and cellular energy transfer systems. Animals also require a large amount of phosphorus to make shells, bones and teeth. Naturally phosphorus is found in rocks in the form of phosphates. Plants absorb phosphorus through roots from soil when the rocks are weathered, minute amount of phosphates that is dissolved in soil solution. So, the herbivores and other animals obtain phosphorus from plants. Whereas the waste products and the dead organisms are decomposed by phosphate-solubilising bacteria releasing phosphorus.

Diagrammatic representation of Phosphorus cycle:

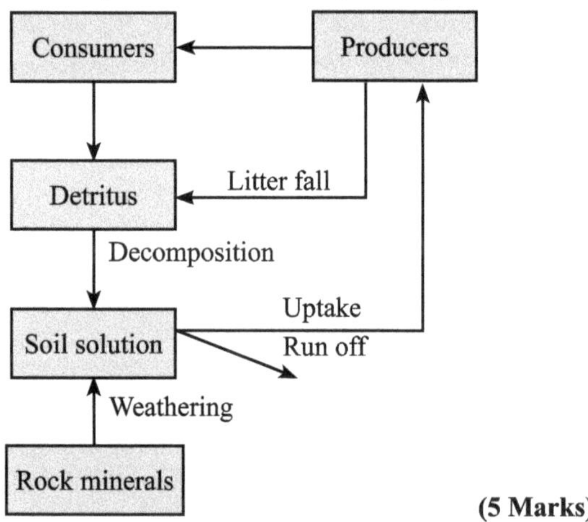

(5 Marks)

25. (a) The transforming principle was proposed by Frederick Griffith in 1928. He performed his experiment with *Streptococcus pneumonia* a bacteria which is responsible for pneumonia.

The following steps are involved in his experiment:

- When *Streptococcus pneumonia* bacteria are grown on a culture plate, some bacteria produces smooth shiny colonies (s) whereas other produce rough colonies (R).
- It is because the S strain bacteria have a mucous polysaccharide coating whereas the R strain bacteria lack this coating.
- When the mice infected with the S strain or virulent strain, the mice die because of pneumonia infection.

- When the mice infected with the R strain do not develop pneumonia.
- Then, Griffith was able to kill bacteria by heating. He observed that heat-killed S strain bacteria injected into mice did not kill them.
- When he injected a mixture of heat-killed S and live R bacteria, the mice died. He recovered living S bacteria from the dead mice.

After this experiment, he concluded that the R strain bacterium has been transformed by the heat-killed S strain bacteria. As some 'transforming principle' was transferred from the heat-killed S strain and enabled the R strain to synthesise a smooth polysaccharide coating and become virulent. This is because of the transfer of the genetic material. **(3 Marks)**

(b) The biochemical characterisation of Transforming principle was determined by Oswald Avery, Colin Macleod and Maclyn McCarty. Prior it was thought that the genetic material was protein.

The following steps are involved in his experiment:

- They purified biochemicals such as proteins, DNA and RNA from the heat-killed S cells to determine which one could transform live R cells into S cells.
- They discovered that DNA alone from S bacteria caused R bacteria to become transformed.
- They also discovered that protein-digesting enzymes such as proteases and RNA-digesting enzymes such as RNases did not affect the transformation.
- Hence, it was proved that the transforming substance was not protein and RNA.
- Digestion with DNase did inhibit transformation and the DNA caused the transformation.
- So, they concluded that DNA is the hereditary material. **(2 Marks)**

26. (a) Ecological succession is defined as the gradual and fairly predictable change in the species composition of a given area. During this process, some species colonies in an area and their populations become more numerous, while populations of other species decline and even disappear. **(1 Mark)**

(b) Difference between Hydrarch succession and Xerarch succession:

Hydrarch succession	Xerarch succession
(i) It takes place in wetter areas.	**(i)** It takes place in the dry areas.
(ii) The successional series progress from hydric to mesic conditons.	**(ii)** The successional series progress from xeric to mesic conditions.

Similarities between hydrarch succession and Xerarch succession:

Both the hydrarch and xerach succession conditions leads to medium water conditions (mesic)- neither too dry (xeric) nor too wet (hydric). **(2 Marks)**

(c) Mediterranean orchid *Ophyrs* employs 'sexual deceit' to get pollination done by species of bees. In this, one petal of its flower bears an uncanny resemblance to the female of the bee in size, colour and markings. The male bee is attracted to what is perceives as a female, then 'pseudocopulates' with the flower, and during that process is dusted with pollen from the flower. When this same bee 'pseudocopulates' with another flower, it transfers pollen to it and thus pollinates the flower. This example represents the phenomena of co-evolution. In this case, if the female bee's colour patterns change even slightly for any reason during evolution, the process of pollination success will be reduced unless the orchid flower co-evolves in order to maintain the resemblance of its petal to the female bee. **(2 Marks)**

OR

(a) Loss of biodiversity in a region may lead to cause following effects such as:

- Decline in plant production,
- Lowered resistance to environmental perturbations such as drought and,
- Increased variability in certain ecosystem processes such as plant productivity, water use and pest and disease cycles. **(2 Marks)**

(b) The causes of biodiversity losses are as follows:

(i) Habitat loss and fragmentation: This is the most important cause of extinction of plants and animals species. Habitat loss comes from tropical rain forests. The Amazon rain forest as it is also called the 'lungs of the planet' harbour millions of species is being cut and cleared for cultivating soya beans or for conversion to grasslands for raising beef cattle. Population also leads to cause degradation of many habitats and threatens the survival of many species. Large habitats are broken into small fragments due to various human activities, mammals and birds require large territories and certain animals with migratory habits are badly affected results in population declines.

(ii) Over-exploitation: Humans are always depended on nature for food and shelter but their need turns into 'greed' and it leads to over-exploitation of natural resources. Many species become extinct in the last decades such as Steller's sea cow, passenger pigeon because of overexploitation by humans. **(3 Marks)**

27. (a) **Diagrammatic representation of embryo sac:**

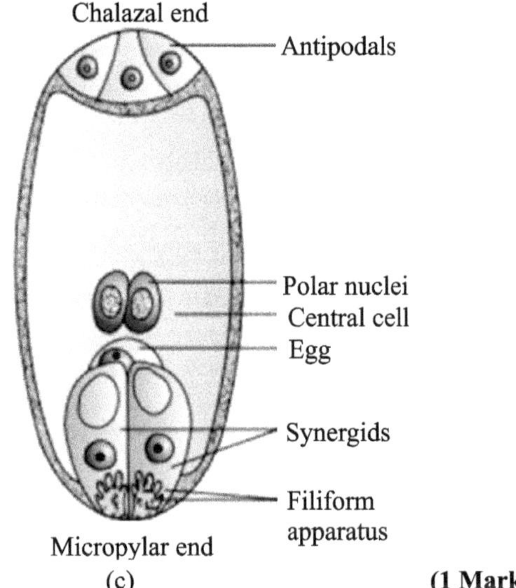

(c) **(1 Mark)**

(b) The process of formation of megaspores from the megaspore mother cell is called megasporogenesis. The megaspore mother cell undergoes the process of meiosis and forms a four haploid tetrad megaspores. The chalazal megaspore remains functional whereas the other 3 will degenerate. So, the functional megaspore is the first cell of the female gametophyte. The cell enlarges and undergoes three free nuclear mitotic divisions.

So the first meiotic division produces two nucleate embryo sac and two nuclei shift to the two ends and again gets divide and forms four nucleate. In this way, eight nucleate structures is formed. One nucleus from each side moves to the middles and they are called polar nuclei. Then the remaining three nuclei form cells at the two ends, 3-celled egg apparatus at the micropylar end and three antipodal cells at the chalazal end. **(3 Marks)**

(c) The Primary Endosperm Nucleus (PEN) is triploid (3n) in nature that undergoes nuclear divisions and give rise to free nuclear endosperm. This free nuclear endosperm is a coconut water whereas its white kernel is the cellular endosperm that is formed when it undergoes cytokinesis. **(1 Mark)**

OR

The menstrual phase is followed by **follicular phase** and during this phase the primary follicles in the ovary grow to become a fully mature Graafian follicle. Then simultaneously the endometrium of uterus regenerates through proliferation. Such changes in the ovary and uterus are induced by changes in the levels of pituitary and ovarian hormones. The secretion of gonadotropins such as luteinizing hormone and follicle stimulating hormone levels gradually increases during follicular phase.

This stimulates follicular development as well as secretion of estrogens hormone by the growing follicles. Both LH and FSH attain a peak level in the middle of cycle that is about 14th day. The rapid secretion of LH surge induces rupture of Graafian follicle and then induces the release of ovum results in ovulation.

The process of ovulation is followed by luteal phase. During this phase, the remaining parts of the Graafian follicle transforms as the corpus luteum. It secretes a large amount of progesterone hormone that is essential for the maintenance of the endometrium.

As, endometrium is necessary for the process of implantation of fertilised ovum and other events during pregnancy.

If the process of fertilisation does not take place, the corpus luteum degenerates results in the disintegration of the endometrium leading to menstruation. This marks a beginning of new cycle.

A decrease in level of ovarian hormone results in the constriction of arteries that lead to cause shredding of uterine lining and menstruation. The deficit in gonadotropins removes the negative feedback on the hypothalamus and menstrual cycle again begins with the GnRH release.

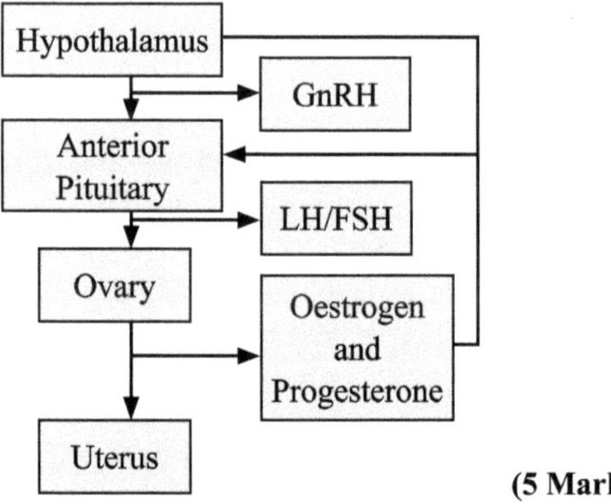

(5 Marks)

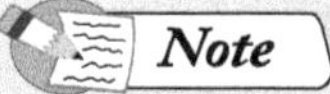

In human females, menstruation is repeated at an average interval of about 28/29 days and the cycle of events starting from one menstruation till the next one is called the ***menstrual cycle.***

All India 2018

CBSE Board Solved Paper

Time Allowed : 3 Hours ***Maximum Marks : 70***

General Instructions:

(i) There are a total of **26** questions and five sections in the question paper. All questions are compulsory.

(ii) **Section A** contains question number **1 to 5**, Very Short Answer type questions of **one mark** each.

(iii) **Section B** contains question number **6 to 10**, Short Answer type **I** questions of **two marks** each.

(iv) **Section C** contains question number **11 to 22**, Short Answer type **II** questions of **three marks** each.

(v) **Section D** contains question number **23**, Value Based Question of **four marks.**

(vi) **Section E** contains question number **24 to 26**, Long Answer type questions of **five marks** each.

(vii) There is no overall choice in the question paper, however, an internal choice is provided in **one** question of **two** marks, **one** question of **three** marks and all **three** questions of **five** marks. An examinee is to attempt any **one** of the questions out of the **two** given in the question paper with the same question number.

SECTION - A

1. How do cytokine barriers provide innate immunity in humans?

2. Write the dual purpose served by Deoxyribonucleoside triphosphates in polymerisation.

3. Write the names of the following :

(a) A 15 my a primate that was ape-like

(b) A 2 my a primate that lived in East African grasslands

4. Mention the chemical change that proinsulin undergoes, to be able to act as mature insulin.

5. Name two diseases whose spread can be controlled by the eradication of *Aedes* mosquitoes.

SECTION - B

6. How did a citizen group called Friends of Arcata Marsh, Arcata, California, USA, help to improve water quality of the marshland using Integrated Waste Water Treatment ? Explain in four steps.

7. Your advice is sought to improve the nitrogen content of the soil to be used for cultivation of a non-leguminous terrestrial crop.

(a) Recommend two microbes that can enrich the soil with nitrogen.

(b) Why do leguminous crops not require such enrichment of the soil?

8. You have obtained a high yielding variety of tomato. Name and explain the procedure that ensures retention of the desired characteristics repeatedly in large populations of future generations of the tomato crop.

9. (a) Name the source plant of heroin drug. How is it obtained from plant?

(b) Write the effects of heroin on the human body?

10. With the help of an algebraic equation, how did Hardy-Weinberg explain that in a given population the frequency of occurrence of alleles of a gene is supposed to remain the same through generations?

OR

Although a prokaryotic cell has no defined nucleus, yet DNA is not scattered throughout the cell. Explain.

SECTION - C

11. (a) Differentiate between analogous and homologous structures.

(b) Select and write analogous structures from the list given below:

(i) Wings of butterfly and birds

(ii) Vertebrate hearts

(iii) Tendrils of *Bougainvillea* and *Cucurbita*

(iv) Tubers of sweet potato and potato

12. How has the use of *Agrobacterium* as vectors helped in controlling *Meloidegyne incognita* infestation in tobacco plants ? Explain in correct sequence.

13. (a) "India has greater ecosystem diversity than Norway." Do you agree with the statement ? Give reasons in support of your answer.

(b) Write the difference between genetic biodiversity and species biodiversity that exists at all the levels of biological organisation.

OR

Explain the effect on the characteristics of a river when urban sewage is discharged into it.

14. Explain the mechanism of 'sex determination' in birds. How does it differ from that of human beings?

15. Explain out-breeding, out-crossing and cross-breeding husbandry.

16. (a) Organic farmers prefer biological control of diseases and pests to the use of chemicals for the same purpose. Justify.

(b) Give an example of a bacterium, a fungus and an insect that are used as biocontrol agents.

17. (a) How has the development of bioreactor in biotechnology?

(b) Name the most commonly used bioreactor and describe its working.

18. Explain the roles of the following with the help of an example each in recombinant DNA technology.

(a) Restriction Enzymes

(b) Plasmids

19. Differentiate between Parthenocarpy and Parthenogenesis. Give one example of each.

20. Medically it is advised to all young mothers that breastfeeding is the best for their newborn babies. Do you agree? Give reasons in support of your answer.

21. Draw a diagram of a mature human sperm. Label any three parts and write their functions.

22. (a) Expand VNTR and describe its role in DNA fingerprinting.

(b) List any two applications of DNA fingerprinting technique.

SECTION - D

23. Looking at the deteriorating air quality because of air pollution in many cities of the country, the citizens are very much worried and concerned about their health. The doctors have declared health emergency in the cities where the air quality is very severely poor.

(a) Mention any two major causes of air pollution.

(b) Write any two harmful effects of air pollution to plants and humans.

(c) As a captain of your school Eco-club, suggest any two programmes you would plan to organize in the school so as to bring awareness among the students on how to check air pollution in and around the school.

SECTION - E

24. (a) Write the scientific name of the organism Thomas Hunt Morgan and his colleagues worked with for their experiments. Explain the correlation between linkage and recombination with respect to genes as studied by them.

(b) How did Sturtevant explain gene mapping while working with Morgan ?

OR

(a) State the 'Central dogma' as proposed by Francis Crick. Are there any exceptions to it ? Support your answer with a reason and an example.

(b) Explain how the biochemical characterization (nature) of "Transforming Principle' was determined, which was not defined from Griffith's experiments.

25. (a) Following are the responses of different animals to various abiotic factors. Describe each one with the help of an example.

(i) Regulate
(ii) Conform
(iii) Migrate
(iv) Suspend

(b) If 8 individuals in a population of 80 butterflies die in a week, calculate the death rate of population of butterflies during that period.

OR

(a) What is a trophic level in an ecosystem? What is 'standing crop' with reference to it?

(b) Explain the role of the 'first trophic level' in an ecosystem.

(c) How is the detritus food chain connected with the grazing food chain in a natural ecosystem?

26. (a) Describe any two devices in a flowering plant which prevent both autogamy and geitonogamy.

(b) Explain the events upto double fertilization after the pollen tube enters one of the synergids in an ovule of an angiosperm.

OR

(a) Explain menstrual cycle in human females.

(b) How can the scientific understanding of the menstrual cycle of human females help as a contraceptive measure?

Solutions

SECTION - A

1. Cytokines play a vital role in the innate immune response by means of direct mechanisms which inhibit viral replication by secreting interferon. Interferons are the proteins secreted by viral-infected cells that provide protection to the non-infected cells from further viral infections. **(1 Mark)**

2. Deoxyribonucleoside triphosphates (DTPs) serves as substrates i.e. nucleotides during replication and also supply energy for polymerisation reaction by breaking of high energy terminal phosphates bond. **(1 Mark)**

DNA replication is the process by which a double stranded DNA molecule is copied to produce two identical DNA molecules. DNA replication takes place in the cytoplasm of prokaryotes and in the nucleus of eukaryotes.

3. (a) The names of a 15 mya primate that was ape-like is *Dryopithecus*.

   (b) The name of a 2 mya primate that lived in East African grasslands is *Australopithecus*. **(1 Mark)**

4. Mature functional protein is produced by the processing or pro-hormone insulin which contains an extra peptide called C-peptide or connecting peptide. This C-peptide is removed during the maturation of proinsulin, and A & B chains are linked by disulphide linkage. **(1 Mark)**

An American company Elilily in 1983 prepared two DNA sequences corresponds to A and B, chains of human insulin and introduced them in plasmids of E.coli to produce insullin chains.

5. The two diseases whose spread can be controlled by the eradication of *Aedes* mosquitoes are chikungunya and dengue. **(1 Mark)**

SECTION - B

6. A citizen group called Friends of the Arcata Marsh (FOAM), Arcata, California, USA, helps to improve water quality of the marshland using Integrated Waste Water Treatment by following ways:

   (a) The conventional sedimentation, filtering and chlorine treatments are given. After this stage, lots of dangerous pollutants like dissolved heavy metals still remain.

   (b) To combat this, an innovative approach was taken and the biologists developed a series of six connected marshes over 60 hectares of marshland.

   (c) Appropriate plants, algae, fungi and bacteria were seeded into this area, which neutralise, absorb and assimilate the pollutants. Hence, as the water flows through the marshes, it gets purified naturally.

   (d) The marshes also constitute a sanctuary, with a high level of biodiversity in the form of fishes, animals and birds. **(2 Marks)**

7. (a) *Azospirillum, Azotobacter, Anabaena, Oscillatoria,* etc.

   (b) Leguminous plants have symbiotic association with *Rhizobium* bacteria which traps N_2 which is present in atmosphere and provides it to the plant, and in turn gets food and shelter. **(2 Marks)**

8. Micropropogation (type of vegetative propogation) ensures retention of the desired characteristics repeatedly in large populations of future generations of the tomato crop. A small part of plant called explant, is excised and grown under sterile condition in special nutrient medium to obtain such plants that would be genetically identical to the original plants. **(2 Marks)**

The method of producing thousands of plants through tissue culture from a single explants is called micropropagation.

9. (a) *Papaver somniferum* is the source plant for heroin drug. This is obtained by the acetylation of morphine, which is extracted from the latex of poppy plant.

   (b) Heroin is a depressant and used to slow down body functions. **(2 Marks)**

Heroin is a opioids. Opioids are the drugs, which bind to specific opioids receptors that are present in central nervous system and gastrointestinal trait.

10. In a given population, one can find out the frequency of occurrence of alleles of a gene or a locus. This frequency is supposed to remain fixed and even remain the same through generations. Hardy-Weinberg principle stated it using algebraic equations.

This principle states that the allele frequencies in a population are stable and is constant from generation to generation. The gene pool (total genes and their alleles in a population) remains a constant. This is called genetic equilibrium. Sum total of all the allelic frequencies is 1. Individual frequencies, for example, can be named p, q, etc. In a diploid, p and q represents the frequency of allele A and allele a. The frequency of AA individuals in a population is simply p^2.

This is simply stated in another ways, i.e., the probability that an allele A with a frequency of p appear on both the chromosomes of a diploid individual is simply the product of the probabilities, i.e., p^2. Similarly of aa is q^2, of Aa 2pq.

Hence, $p^2 + 2pq + q^2 = 1$. This is a binomial expansion of $(p + q)^2$. When frequency measured, differs from expected values, the difference (direction) indicates the extent of evolutionary change. Disturbance in genetic equilibrium, or Hardy-Weinberg equilibrium, i.e., change of frequency of alleles in a population would then be interpreted as resulting in evolution.

OR

In prokaryotes, the DNA (negatively charged) is scattered in the cytoplasm means that it is naked and is not covered by any membrane. The prokaryotes use an arrangement that helps to pack genetic material tightly into a specific region, positively charged protein hold it in large loops known as nucleoid because prokaryote does not have a well defined nucleus. So, the DNA is not scattered but present in the form of membrane less structure called nucleoid. This nucleoid floats in the cytoplasm and can be found anywhere in the cytoplasm. Also the DNA in form of single chromosomes is attached to mesosome at a point.

SECTION - C

11. (a) **Difference between homologous and analogous organs:**

Homologous organ	Analogous organ
(i) Homology is based on divergent evolution.	(i) Analogy is based on convergent evolution.
(ii) In homology, the structures are evolved from the same origin and have common ancestors but they have different functions.	(ii) In analogy, the structures are evolved from different origin and have different ancestors but have similar functions.
Eg. Wings of birds and forelimbs of human.	Eg. Wings of birds and wings insects.

(b) These are the analogous structure from the given list:

(i) Wings of butterfly and birds.

(ii) Tubers of sweet potato and potato. **(3 Marks)**

12. A nematode *Meloidegyne incognita* infects the roots of tobacco plants and causes a great reduction in yield. A novel strategy was adopted to prevent this infestation which was based on the process of RNA inteference (RNAi). Using *Agrobacterium* vectors, nematode-specific genes were introduced into the host plants. The introduction of DNA was such that it produced both sense and anti-sense RNA in the host cells. These two RNA's being complementary to each other formed a double stranded (dsRNA) that initiated RNAi and thus, silenced specific mRNA of the nematode. The consequence was that the parasite could not survive in a transgenic host expressing specific interfering RNA. The transgenic plant therefore got itself protected from the parasite. **(3 Marks)**

13. (a) Yes, India has greater ecosystem diversity than Norway as India has deserts, rain forests, mangroves, coral reefs, wetlands, estuaries, and alpine meadows.

Ecosystem diversity refers to the variations in ecosystems within a geographical location and its overall impact on existance of human population in an environment.

(b) **Genetic diversity:**

(i) It is the total number of genetic characteristics in the genetic makeup of a species.

(ii) A single species might show high diversity at the genetic level (E.g. Man : Chinese, Indian, American, African etc.). India has more than 50,000 genetically different strains of rice, and 1,000 varieties of mango.

(iii) It allows species to adapt to changing environments. This diversity aims to ensure that some species survive drastic changes and thus carry on desirable genes.

Species diversity:

(i) It is the ratio of one species population over total number of organisms across all species in the given biome. 'Zero' would be infinite diversity, and 'one' represents only one species present.

(ii) It is a measure of the diversity within an ecological community that incorporates both species richness (the number of species in a community) and the evenness of species.

(iii) For example, the Western Ghats have greater amphibian species diversity than the Eastern Ghats. There are more than 2, 00,000 species in India of which several are confined to India (endemic).

The genetic variation shown by the medicinal plant Rouwolfia vomitoria growing in different Himalayan ranges have potency and concentration of the active chemical (reserpine) that the plant produces.

OR

Accelerated eutrophication is caused by the nutrient enrichment of lake due to passage of sewage, agricultural & industrial wastes into them. These wastes are rich in nitrates & phosphates which over-stimulate the growth of algae (algal bloom) & other plants, causing unsightly scum and unpleasant odours, and robbing the water of dissolved oxygen vital to other aquatic life. This along with decomposition of dead aquatic plants & animals deplete the water's dissolved oxygen content & a lake can literally choke to death in escalated method. **(3 Marks)**

14. In birds, sex determination is of ZW - ZZ type.

In this type the males are homogametic and have ZZ sex chromosomes, and females are heterogametic with ZW pair of sex chromosomes. **(3 Marks)**

Parents :	Male	X	Female
	ZZ		ZW
Gametes:	(Z)(Z)		(Z)(W)
F_1:	ZW		ZZ
	Female		Male

whereas, in human beings, the chromosomal mechanism of sex determination is of XX - XY type. The human male is heterogametic and have XY sex chromosomes and human female is homogametic with XX sex chromosomes.

15. Out-breeding : Out-breeding is the breeding of the unrelated animals, which may be between individuals of the same breed but having no common ancestors for 4-6 generations (out-breeding) or between different breeds (cross-breeding) or different species (inter-specific hybridization).

Out-crossing: This is the practice of mating of animals within the same breed, but having no common ancestors on either side of their pedigree up to 4-6 generations. The offspring of such a mating is known as an outcross. It is the best breeding method for animals that are below average in productivity in milk production, growth rate in beef cattle, etc. A single outcross often helps to overcome inbreeding depression.

Cross-breeding: In this method, superior males of one breed are mated with superior females of another breed. Cross - breeding allows the desirable qualities of two different breeds to be combined. The progeny hybrid animals may themselves be used for commercial production. Alternatively, they may be subjected to some form of inbreeding and selection to develop new stable breeds that may be superior to the existing breeds. Many new animal breeds have been developed by this approach. *Hisardale* is a new breed of sheep developed in Punjab by crossing *Bikaneri ewes* and *Marino rams*. **(3 Marks)**

16. (a) Biological pest control has important advantages compared to chemical pest control, such as being safer for humans and the environment. Chemical methods often kills both useful and harmful life forms indiscriminately. Eradication of the creatures that are often described as pests in not only possible, but also undesirable, for without them the beneficial predatory and parasitic insects which depend upon them as food or hosts would not be able to survive.

(b) Bacterium, a fungus and an insect that are used as biocontrol agents are:

Insects = Ladybird and Dragonflies.

Bacteria = *Bacillus thuringiensis*.

Fungus = *Trichoderma* **(3 Marks)**

17. (a) Small volume cultures cannot yield appreciable quantities of products. In order to produce in large quantities, bioreactor are developed in which, large volumes (100 - 1000 litres) of culture can be processed. Thus, bioreactors can be thought of as vessels in which raw materials are biologically converted into specific products, individual enzymes, etc., using microbial plant, animal or human cells.

Bioreactor is defined as a vessel that carries out a biological reaction and is used to culture aerobic cells for conducting cellular or enzymatic immobilization.

(b) The most commonly used bioreactors are of stirring type. A stirred - tank reactors is usually cylindrical or with a curved base to facilitate the mixing of the reactor contents. The stirrer facilitates even mixing and oxygen availability throughout the bioreactor. The bioreactor has an agitator system, an oxygen delivery system and a foam control system, a temperature control system. pH control system and sampling ports so that small volumes of the culture can be withdrawn periodically. **(3 Marks)**

18. (a) **Restriction enzymes :**

(i) Restriction enzymes belongs to class of enzymes nucleases which breaks nucleic acids by cleaving their phosphodiester bonds.

(ii) Since restriction endonucleases cuts DNA at specific recognition site, they are used to cut the donor DNA to isolate the desired gene.

(iii) The desired gene has sticky ends which can be easily ligated to cloning vector which was cut by same restriction enzymes having complementary sticky ends to form recombinant DNA.

(iv) An example is EcoRI which is obtained from E.coli bacteria "R" strain which cuts DNA at specific palindromic recognition site.

Pallindromes are the group of letters that form the same words when read both forward and backward for e.g. MALAYALAM.

(b) Plasmids :

(i) Plasmids are autonomous, extra chromosomal circular double stranded DNA of bacteria.

(ii) They are small and self-replicating, and they are used as cloning vectors in genetic engineering.

(iii) Some plasmids have antibiotic resistance genes which can be used as marker genes to identify recombinant plasmids from non-recombinant ones.

(iv) The plasmids are cut and ligated with desired genes and transformed into host cell for amplification to obtain the desired products.

(v) An example of artificial modified plasmids is pBR322 or pUC. **(3 Marks)**

19. Parthenogenesis and parthenocarpy are two such processes that results in fruits and individuals from unfertilized ovules or eggs prior to fertilization.

In most plants, flowers need to be pollinated and fertilized to produce fruits. However, some plants can produce fruits before fertilization or without fertilization.

Parthenocarpy is the process which produces fruits from unfertilized ovules in plants. Unfertilized ovules develop into fruits prior to fertilization. These fruits do not contain seeds. E.g. banana and grapes.

Parthenogenesis is a type of reproduction commonly shown in organisms mainly by some invertebrates and lower plants. It can be described as a process in which unfertilized ovum develops into an individual (virgin birth) without fertilization. Therefore, it can be considered as a method of asexual reproduction.

The key difference between parthenogenesis and parthenocarpy is, parthenogenesis is shown by animals and plants while parthenocarpy is shown only by plants. Parthenogenesis is seen in organism like rotifers, honeybees and even some lizards and birds (turkey).

20. Yes, I do agree with the fact that breastfeeding is the best for newborn babies. Mammary glands of the female undergo differentiation during preganancy and starts producing milk. The milk produced during the initial few days and lactation is called colostrum which contains IgAantibodies. It helps in developing resistance for newborn baby by providing innate immunity to the developing infant. It helps the baby fight to against viruses and bacteria. Thus breast milk is packed with disease-fighting substances that protect the baby from illness. It also naturally contains many of the vitamins and minerals that a required by newborn. **(3 Marks)**

21. **Acrosome :** It is a cap like structure, filled with hydrolytic enzymes that help in the fertilisation of the ovum.

Middle piece : Possesses numerous mitochondria, which produces energy for the movement of tail and facilitate the movement of tail that facilitates sperm motality essential for fertilization.

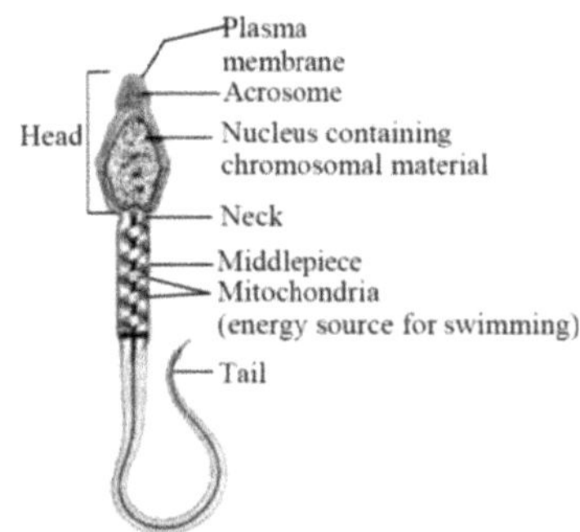

Tail : Facilitate sperm motility essential for fertilisation.

The seminal plasma is rich in fructose, calcium and certain enzymes and seminal plasma alongwith sperms constitute the semen. The secretions of bulbourethral glands also helps in the lubrication of the penis.

22. (a) VNTR stands for "Variable Number of Tandem Repeats". The VNTR belongs to a class of satellite DNA referred to as mini-satellite. A small DNA sequence is arranged tandemly in many copy numbers. The copy number varies from chromosome to chromosome in an individual. The numbers of repeat show very high degree of polymorphism. As a result the size of VNTR varies in size from 0.1 to 20 kb. Consequently, after hybridization with VNTR probe, the autoradiogram gives many bands of differing sizes. These bands give characteristic pattern for an individual DNA which is used to identify individuals.

(b) Since DNA from every tissue (such as blood, hair - follicle, skin, bone, saliva, sperm etc.), from an individual show the same degree of polymorphism, they become very useful identification tool in forensic applications to identify criminals. Further, as the polymorphisms are inheritable from parents to children, DNA fingerprinting is the basic of paternity testing, in case of disputes. **(3 Marks)**

SECTION - D

23. (a) Causes of air pollution are:

(i) Industrial effluents

(ii) Smoke released from vehicles.

(iii) Burning of fossil fuels

(iv) Smoke stacks of thermal power plants.

(b) Harmful effects of air pollution.

(i) It affects respiratory system of animals as well as human beings.

(ii) It also reduces growth and yield of crops & cause premature death of plants.

(c) (i) To boost public transport i.e. buses & using CNG instead of diesel.

(ii) Planting more trees to reduce pollution.

(3 Marks)

Motor vehicles are equipped with catalytic converter should use unleaded petrol because lead in the petrol inactivates the catalyst.

SECTION - E

24. (a) *Drosophila melanogaster* : Morgan carried out several dihybrid crosses in *Drosophila* to study gens that were sex-lined. Morgan and his group knew that the genes were located on the X chromosome and saw quickly that when the two genes in a dihybrid cross were situated on the same chromosome, the proportion of parental gene combinations were much higher than the non-parental type. Morgan attributed this due to the physical association or linkage of the two genes and coined the term linkage to describe this physical association of genes on a chromosome and the term recombination to describe the generation of non- parental gene combination. Morgan and his group also found that even when genes were grouped on the same chromosome, some genes were very tightly linked (showed very low recombination) while others were loosely linked.

Morgans student Alfred Sturtevant used the frequency of recombination between gene pairs on the same chromosome as a measure of the distance between genes and 'mapped' their position on the chromosome.

Genetic maps are extensively used as a starting point in the sequencing of whole genomes.

(b) Alfred Sturtevant expressed the frequency of recombination between gene pairs present on the same chromosome as the distance between those genes. He then mapped the positions of the genes on the chromosome. Today, gene maps are used as a starting point in the genome sequencing.

OR

Francis Crick proposed the central dogma, which states that the genetic information flows from DNA to RNA and then to protein.

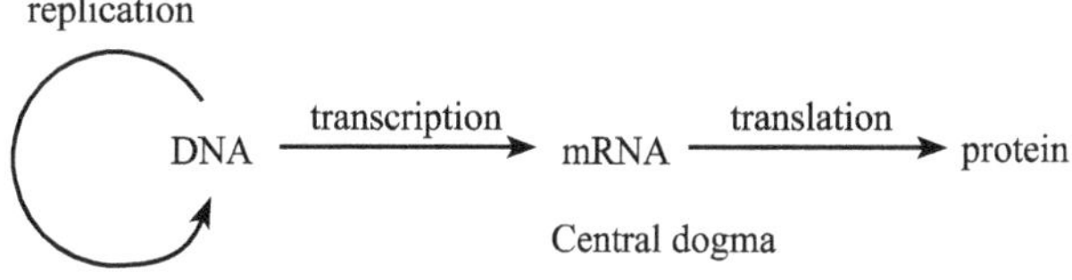

Central dogma

There are few exceptions to this as observed in the case of some viruses (retrovirus). In retro virus, DNA is synthesized from RNA with the help of reverse transcriptase which is known as reverse transcription.

Transforming Principle : In 1928, Frederick Griffith, in a series of experiments with Streptococcus pneumoniae (bacterium responsible for pneumonia), witnessed a transformation in the bacteria. During the cource of his experiment, a living organism (bacteria) had changed in physical form. He concluded that the R strain bacteria had somehow been tranformed by the heat - killed S strain bacteria. Some 'transforming principle', transferred from the heat - killed S strain, had enabled the R strain to synthesise a smooth polysaccharide coat and become virulent. This must be due to the transfer of the genetic material. However, the biochemical nature of genetic material was not defined from his experiments. Oswald Avery, Colin MacLeod and Maclyn McCarty worked to determine the biochemical nature of 'tranforming principle' in Griffith's experiment. They purified biochemicals (proteins , DNA, RNA, etc.) from the heat - killed S cells to see which ones could transform live R cells into S cells. They discoveredf that DNA alone from S bacteria caused R bacteria to become transformed. They also discovered that protein - digesting enzymes (proteases) and RNA - digesting enzymes (RNases) did not affect transformation, so the transforming substance was not a protein or RNA. Digestion with DNase did inhibit transformation, suggesting that the DNA caused the transformation. They concluded that DNA is the hereditary material, but not all biologist were convinced. **(3 Marks)**

25. (a) (i) **Regulate:** Some organisms are able to maintain homeostatis by regulating their body temperatures. The mechanisms used by most mammals to regulate their body temperature are similar to what we humans use. For example: Body temperature remains constant at 37°C. In summer, when outside temperature is more than our body temperature, we sweat profusely and when the temperature is much lower than 37°C, we shiver thus body temperature remains constant. E.g. Birds and mammals.

(ii) **Conform:** Many animals, cannot maintain a constant internal environment. Their body temperature changes with the ambient temperature. These are conformers. Heat loss or heat gain is a function of surface area. Since small animals have a larger surface area relative to their volume, they tend to lose body heat very fast when it is cold outside. Eg. Shrews and humming birds.

(iii) **Migrate:** The organism can move away temporarly from the stressful habitat to a more hospitable area & return when stressful period is over. Eg: Every winter, the famous Keolado National Park in Bharatpur host thousands of migratory birds coming from Siberia & other northern regions.

(iv) **Suspend:** In animals, if migration is not possible, they might avoid the stress by escaping in time. Eg: (1) Bears go into hibernation during winter.

(2) Fishes go into aestvation to avoid summer related problems heat & dessication.

(3) Under unfavourable conditions many zooplankton species in lakes and ponds are known to enter *diapause*, a stage of suspended development.

(b) **Death Rate :** Number of deaths per 1000 individuals of a population.
Death Rate = 8/80 = 0.1

OR

(a) **Tropic level :** Organisms occupy a place in the natural surroundings or in a community according to their feeding relationship with other organisms. Based on the source of their nutrition or food, organisms occupy a specific place in the food chain and this is known as trophic level. Each trophic level has a certain mass of living material at a particular time and this is called as

Standing crop: It is measured as the mass of living organisms (biomass) or the number in a unit area.

(b) **First trophic level** is formed by producers. This is the basic unit. These organisms can live without feeding on any another level. The only thing that these organisms need to survive is sunlight and water which they can turn into energy themselves. All other trophic levels depend on this level for energy.

(c) GFC is Grazing Food Chain : It is depicted as below :
Producers Primary consumers Secondary consumers
DFC is Detritus Food Chain : It begins with dead organic matter. It is made up of decomposers which

are heterotrophic organisms like fungi, bacteria etc. GFC is the major conduct for energy flow. DFC may be connected with GFC at some levels : Some of the organisms of DFC are prey to the GFC animals.

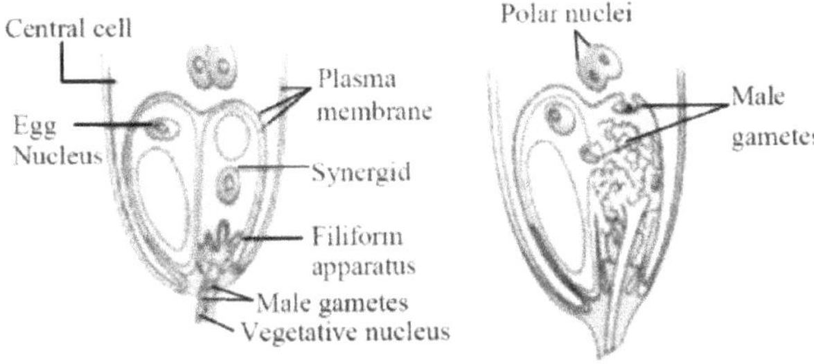

These natural inter connection of food chains forms food web.

Food chain refers to the a linear network of links in a food web which represents the flow of energy from one trophic level to another.

26. (a) **Autogamy :** Transfer of pollen grains from anther to the stigma of same flower. It is a type of self-pollination.

Geitonogamy : Transfer of pollen grains from anther to the stigma of another flower of same plant. Two devices that prevent both autogamy and geitonogamy are :

(i) **Self - incompatibility :** This is a genetic mechanism & prevents self-pollen from fertilising the ovules by inhibiting pollen germination or pollen tube growth in the pistil.

(ii) **Dioecious plants :** Male and female flowers are present on different plants, that is each plant is either male or female.

Geitonogamy is functionally cross-pollination that involves a pollinating agent, genetically it is similar to autogamy since the pollen grains come from the same plant.

(b) The events seen after the pollen tube enters one of the synergids in an ovule are as follows :

(i) Pollen tube, after reaching the ovary, enters the ovule through the micropyle and thus enters one of the synergids through filiform apparatus.

(ii) After entering one of synergids, the pollen tube releases the two male gametes into the cytoplasm of the synergid.

(iii) One of the male gametes move towads the egg cell and fuses with its nucleus thus results in formation of zygote (diploid cell). This is Syngamy.

(iv) The other male gamete move towards the two polar nuclei located in the central cell and fuses to form triploid primary endosperm nucleus (PEN). This involves fusion of three haploid nuclei & hence termed as triple fusion.

(v) Two types of fusions, syngamy & triple fusion takes place in an embryosac and hence the phenomenon is termed as double fertilisation.

(vi) After fertilisation, PEN becomes the primary endosperm cell (PEC) & develops into endosperm while zygote develops into an embyo.

OR

(a) **Menstrual Cycle :**

(i) The reproductive cycle in the female primates (e.g. monkeys, apes and humans) is called menstrual cycle.

(ii) The first menstruation begins at puberty and is called **menarche.**

(iii) In human females, menstruation is repeated at an average interval of about 28/29 days and the cycle of events starting from one menstruation till the next one is **menstrual cycle.**

(iv) **The phases of menstrual cycle are as follows:**
Menstrual phase : It lasts for 3-5 days. The menstrual flow results due to breakdown of endometrial lining of the uterus and its blood vessels which forms liquid that comes out through vagina. Menstruation only occurs if the released ovum is not fertilised.

Follicular phase : It lasts for 8-10 days. During this phase, the primary follicles in the ovary grow to become a fully mature Grafian follicle and simultaneously the endometrium of uterus regerates through proliferation. The secretion of LH and FSH increases gradually.

Ovulatory phase : It lasts for 1 day. There is release of ovum.

Luteal phase : It lasts for 13 days. There is LH surge. These induces the remaining parts of Grafian follicle to tranform as corpus luteum and its secretes progesterone for maintenance of the endometriun.

(v) If fertilisation occurs, endomentrium starts preparing for implantation. In the absence of fertilisation, corpus luteum degenerate.

In human beings, menstrual cycles ceases around 50 years of age and is termed as menopause. Cyclic menstruation is an indicator of normal reproductive phase and extends between menarche and menopause.

(b) Scientific understanding of menstrual cycle of human females are very important as a contraceptive measures. It helps in following ways :

(i) Safe period (Rhythm method)

A week before and a week after menstrual bleeding is considered as safe period for sexual intercourse. The idea is based on following facts :

(ii) Ovulation occurs on 14th day of cycle and ovum survives for about 2 days.

(iii) Sperms remain alive for about 3 days.

This method reduces the chances of pregenancy by about 80%.

(iv) Pills used by females are also dependent on menstrual cycle. The pills have to be taken daily for a period of 21 days starting preferably within first five days of menstrual cycle. It is repeated again after period of 7 days. These inhibit ovulation and implantation as well as alter the quality of cervical mucus to prevent/retard entry of sperms.

All India 2017

CBSE Board Solved Paper

Time Allowed : 3 Hours | *Maximum Marks : 70*

General Instructions:

(i) All questions are compulsory.

(ii) Question number **1** to **5** are very short answer questions and carry **1** mark each.

(iii) Question number **6** to **10** are short answer questions and carry **2** marks each.

(iv) Question number **11** to **22** are also short answer questions and carry **3** marks each.

(v) Question number **23** is a value based question and carry **4** marks.

(vi) Question number **24** to **26** are long answer questions and carry **5** marks each.

(vii) Use log tables, if necessary. Use of calculator is not allowed.

SECTION - A

1. Our government has intentionally imposed strict conditions for M.T.P. in our country. Justify giving a reason.

2. State the fate of a pair of autosomes during gamete formation.

3. What role does an individual organism play as per Darwin's theory of natural selection ?

4. Suggest a method to ensure an anamnestic response in humans.

5. What is biopiracy?

SECTION - B

6. A mature embryo-sac in a flowering plant may possess 7-cells, but 8-nuclei. Explain with the help of diagram only.

7. Describe the structure of a nucleosome.

OR

Mention the evolutionary significance of the following organisms :

(a) Shrews (b) Lobefins

(c) Homo habilis (d) Homo erectus

8. In an agricultural field there is a prevalence of the following organisms and crop diseases which are affecting the crop yield badly :

(a) Write rust (b) Leaf and stripe rust

(c) *Black rot* (d) *Jassids*

Recommend the varieties of crops the farmers should grow to get rid of the existing problem and thus improve the crop yield.

9. How does the application of the fungal genus, Glomus, to the agriculutural farm increase the farm output?

10. Plenty of algal bloom is observed in a pond in your locality.

(a) Write what has caused this bloom and how does it affect the quality of water

(b) Suggest a preventive measure.

SECTION - C

11. (a) List the three states the annuals and biennial angiosperms have to pass through during their life cycle.

(b) List and describe any two vegetative propagules in flowering plants.

12. Draw a labelled diagrammatic sectional view of a human seminiferous tubule.

13. During a medical investigation, an infant was found to possess an extra chromosome-21. Describe the symptoms the child is likely to develop later in the life.

14. A number of passengers were severely burnt beyond recognition during a train accident. Name and describe a modern technique that can help hand over the dead to their relatives.

15. $p^2 + 2pq + q^2 = 1$, Explain this algebraic equation on the basis of Hardy Weinberg's principle.

16. (a) What precaution(s) would you recommend to a patient requiring repeated blood transfusion?

(b) If the advise is not followed by the patient, there is an apprehension that the patient might contract a disease that would destroy the immune system of his/ her body.

Explain with the help of schematic diagram only how the immune system would get affected and destroyed.

17. (a) What is inbreeding depression?

(b) Explain the importance of "selection" during inbreeding in cattle.

18. Describe how do 'flocs' and 'activated sludge' help in Sewage Treatment.

19. Explain the role(s) of the following in Biotechnology.

(a) Restriction endonuclease

(b) Gel - electrophoresis

(c) Selectable markers in pBR322

20. Write the steps you would suggest to the undertaken to obtain a foreign-gene-product.

21. Why do lepidopterans die when they feed on Bt cotton plant? Explain how does it happen.

22. "In-situ' Conversation can help endrangered/threatened species. Justify the statement.

OR

Name and describe any three causes of bio-diversity losses.

SECTION - D

23. Public all over India is very much concerned about the deteriorating air quality in large parts of North India. Alarmed by this situation the Resident's Welfare Association of your locality organized an awareness programme entitled "Bury not burn". They invited you, being a biology student to participate.

(a) How would you justify your arguments that promote burying and discourage burning? (Give two reasons)

(b) With the help of flow charts, one for each practice depict the chain of events that follow.

SECTION - E

24. Read the following statement and answer the questions that follow :

"A guava fruit has 200 viable seeds".

(a) What are viable seeds?

(b) Write the total number of :

(i) Pollen grains

(ii) Gametes in producing 200 viable guava seeds.

(c) Prepare a flow-chart to depict the post-pollination events leading to viable-seed production in a flowering plant.

OR

(a) Arrange the following hormones in sequence of their secretion in a pregnant woman.

(b) Mention their source and the function they perform: hCG, LH, FSH, Relaxin

25. State and explain the "Law of independent assortment" in a typical Mendelian dihybrid cross.

OR

(a) How do the observations made during moth collection in pre and post industrialized era in England support evolution by Natural Selection?

(b) Explain the phenomenon that is well represented by Darwin's finches other than natural selection.

26. (a) What is an age-pyramid?

(b) Name three representative kinds of age-pyramids for human population and list the characteristics for each one of them.

OR

Discuss the role of healthy ecosystem services as a prerequisite for a wide range of economic, environmental and aesthetic goods and services.

Solutions

SECTION - A

1. Our government has imposed strict conditions for M.T.P. to avoid its misuse. Such restrictions are very important to prevent sex determination before birth of a child and illegal female foeticides in our country. MTP are considered relatively safe during the first trimester, *i.e.*, upto 12 weeks of pregnancy. **(1 Mark)**

MTP stands for medical termination of pregnancy is defined as the intentional or voluntary termination of pregnancy before full term. It is done to got rid of unwanted pregnancies failure of the controuptius used during coitus or rapes.

2. The homologous pair of autosomes will separate from each other and will move to different gametes during gamete formation. **(1 Mark)**
3. As per Darwin's theory of natural selection, an individual organism in a population is responsible for passing on the variation and favourable mutations to the next generations by taking part in a successful event of sexual reproduction. **(1 Mark)**
4. Anamestic response is the secondary immune response which is produced when the body encounters the same antigen which is entered previously in the body. As the body recognises the pathogen, immune system starts producing antibodies against the foreign antigens for subsequent encounter and this response is very intense. **(1 Mark)**
5. Biopiracy is the term used to refer to the use of bio-resources by multinational companies and organisations without proper authorisation from the countries and people concerned without compensatory payment. For example, basmati is a type of fragrant rice variety grown in India. But some US based companies crossed this Indian basmati rice with their local variety and produced Texmati - a new American fragrant rice variety and used it commercially. **(1 Mark)**

SECTION - B

6. A mature embryo sac in a flowering plant possess 7 cells, but have 8 nuclei. This can be understood with the help of diagram given below:

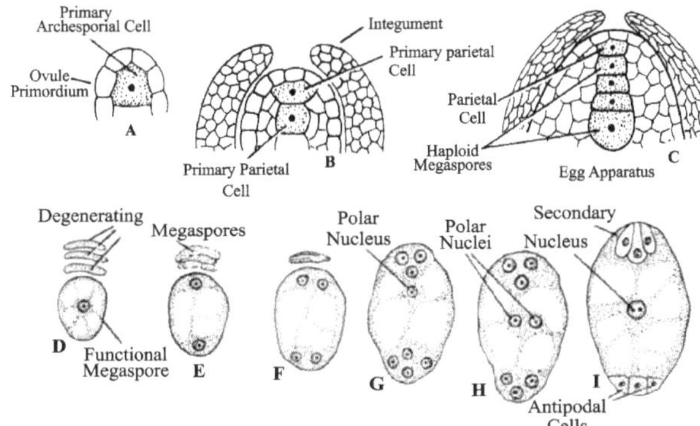

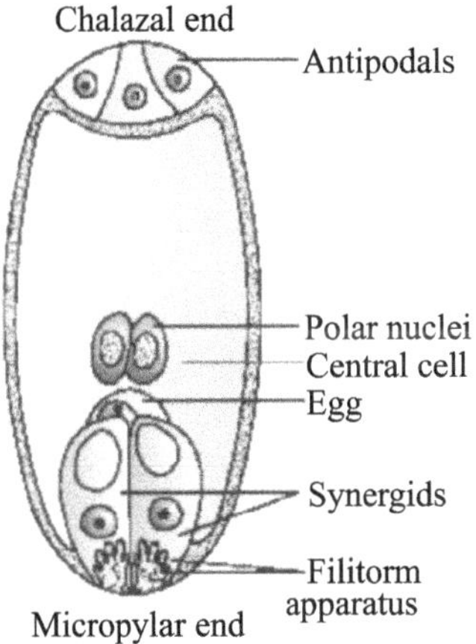

Fig.: Development of embryo sac **(2 Marks)**

7. DNA is organized into bead structure called nucleosome. There is a set of positively charged, basic proteins called histones, which are rich in basic amino acids – lysine and arginine. They have positively charged side chains. Histones organize into unit of 8 molecules called histone octamer. Negatively charged DNA is wrapped around this positively charged octamer to form nucleosome. One histone octamer has 8 histones. One nucleosome (DNA + histone octamer) attaches to other nucleosome with the help of linker DNA associated with H1 protein. **(2 Marks)**

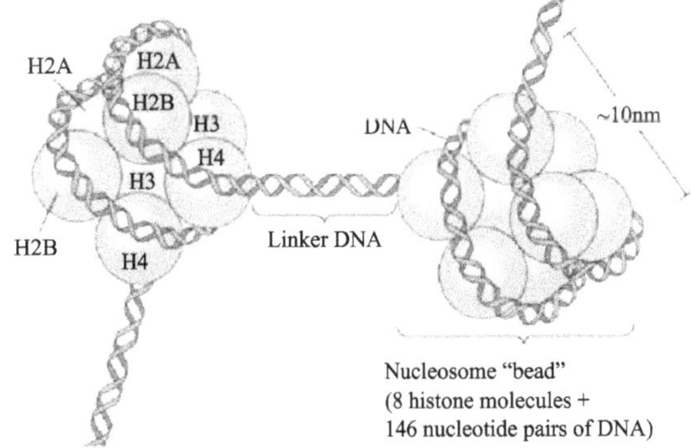

Fig.: Nucleosome structure

A typical nucleosome contains 200 bp of DNA helix. Nucleosome forms chromatin in the form of bead on string. Chromatin condense/super coil at metaphase stage to form chromosomes. Packaging of chromatin to chromosomes occurs with the help of additional set of proteins called NHC (non-histone chromosomal) proteins. **(2 Marks)**

*In a nucleus, some of the region of **chromatin** are loosely packed (and stains light) and are referred to as **euchromatin**. The chromatin that is more densely packed and stains dark are called **heterochromatin***

OR

(a) Shrews were the first mammals. These were the long-tailed insectivorous, squirrel-like creatures, which gave rise to the primitive primates, namely lemurs and tarsiers in the beginning of the tertiary period (Palaeocene epoch).

(b) The discovery of Coelacanth (lobefins) first amphibians is significant as they prove that amphibian have evolved from fish-like organisms. Lobefins were the ancestors of modern day frogs and salamanders.

(c) *Homo habilis* were the first human-like primate who lived in Africa about 2 million years ago. Their brain capacities were between 650- 800cc and they had bipedal locomotion, moved erect and probably didn't eat meat.

(d) *Homo erectus* were the next primates evolved from *Homo habilis* about 1.5 mya. They had a large brain capacities around 900cc and they had an erect posture. They probably ate meat. **(2 Marks)**

8.

S. No.	Crop Disease/ Organism	Resis tant Crop Variety
A	White rust	*Pusa Swarnim*
B	Leaf and stripe rust	*Himgiri*
C	Black rot	*Pusa Shubhra*
D	Jassids	*Pusa Sem 2*

Normal varieties of crops are prone to infection by various pathogens result in poor growth of crops. To get rid of existing problems, the farmers should grow improved hybrid varieties as these are resistance to fungi, bacteria and viral diseases. **(2 Marks)**

9. *Glomus* belongs to the genus fungi that are found in symbiotic relationship with the roots of the seed plants (mycorrhiza). Phosphorus is absorbed by the fungi from the soil and passed into the plants and in return derives sugar from the plant cell for survival. Thus the application of the fungal genus, *Glomus*, to the agricultural farm increases the farm output due to increased phosphorus availability to the crops. **(2 Marks)**

10. (a) Cause - Algal blooms are caused due to the excessive nutrients present in the water bodies. This high availability of nutrients like phosphorus and nitrogen is causes by the chemicals present in fertilisers that get dissolved in the soil and eventually get washed away to the water bodies.

Affect - These algal blooms may shade out plants that would normally live lower in the water column result in a loss of biodiversity. Eutrophication can also result in the development of hypoxic conditions. This oxygen deficiency may cause the death of aquatic organisms. They ultimately degrade the quality of water.

(1 Mark)

***Eutrophication** is the natural aging of the lake by biological enrichment of its water.*

(b) Farmers in areas that are affected by algal blooms need to find alternative ways to fertilize the soil like using manures and techniques such as vermicomposting. Also, people must use cleaning agents and detergents that are biodegradable and that do not contain phosphates. To further reduce the amount of nutrients that are causing an overgrowth of algae in lakes and streams, strict laws need to be created that regulate the dumping of waste water. **(1 Mark)**

SECTION - C

11. (a) Vegetative, reproductive and senescent phases are the phases associated with annual and biennial plants.

(1 Mark)

(b) Roots and leaves are two vegetative parts of the plants which can be used for vegetative propogation. Root propagule include the propagation of a new plant through its fleshy roots, such as in the case of sweet potato and dahlia. **(1 Mark)**

Vegetative propagation through leaves includes case of Bryophyllum. Adventitious buds arising from notches present at margins of leaves helps Bryophyllum1 to propagate vegetatively. When these buds are shed and fall on ground, they grow to form new plants.

(1 Mark)

12. **Diagrammatic sectional view of a seminiferous tubule (enlarged)**

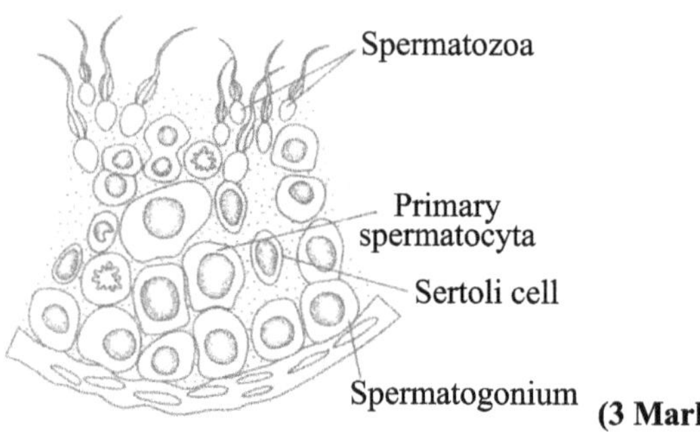

(3 Marks)

Seminiferous tubules is lined by two types of cells such as sertoli cells and male germ cells. The male germ cells undergo meiotic divisions in sperm formation whereas sertoli cells provide nutrition to the germ cells.

13. Down's syndrome is a genetic disorder caused due to the presence of an additional copy of chromosome number 21 (trisomy of 21). The affected individual will have:

(i) short statured with small round head

(ii) furrowed tongue

(iii) partially open mouth

(iv) Simian crease is prominent in the middle of the palm and b road palm

(v) retarded physical, psychomotor and mental development

(vi) IQ is less than 25. **(3 Marks)**

Down's syndrome was first described by Langdon Down in 1866.

14. The technique that will help the authorities to establish the identity of the dead is known as DNA fingerprinting. Basis of DNA Fingerprinting - DNA fingerprinting is a method for comparing the DNA sequences of any two individuals. 99.9% of the base sequences in all human beings are identical. It is the remaining 0.1% that makes every individual unique. In this, certain specific regions called repetitive DNA sequences that are different in every individual, that are used for comparative study. This repetitive DNA is separated from the bulk DNA as different peaks during density gradient centrifugation in which, bulk DNA forms major peak and the other small peaks are referred to as **satellite DNA**. These sequences show high degree of polymorphism and form the basis of DNA fingerprinting.

Methodology of DNA fingerprinting- The DNA fingerprinting technique involves following steps

(i) Extraction –DNA is extracted from cells in a centrifuge

(ii) Amplification - Many copies of extracted DNA are made by polymerase chain reaction.

(iii) Restriction Digestion – DNA is cut into fragments with enzymes into precise sequences.

(iv) Separation of DNA sequences – The cut DNA fragments are passed though electrophoresis set up containing agarose gel and the separated fragments can be seen under UV radiation.

(v) Southern Blotting- The separated sequences are transferred onto a nylon membrane.

(vi) Hybridisation- The nylon membrane is immersed in a bath and radioactive labelled VNTR probes are added.

(vii) Autoradiography- The membrane is pressed onto an X-ray film and dark bands develop the probe sites which resemble bar codes.

After autoradiography, different bands are obtained which are characteristics of an individual. The presence of similarities between the casualties and their relatives determines their relatedness on the basis of which the dead bodies can be handed over to their respective relatives.

(3 Marks)

The VNTR belongs to a class of satellite DNA referred to as mini-satellite. A small DNA sequence which is arranged tandenly in many copy numbers the copy number varies from chromosome to chromosome in an individual.

15. Hardy weinberg's principle states that allele frequencies are stable and is constant from one generation to other generation. The gene pool remains constant called genetic equilibrium. Sum total of all the allele frequencies is one. Suppose there are two alleles '*A*' and '*a*' in a population. Their frequencies are p and q, respectively. The frequency of *AA* individual in a population is P^2. It can be explained that the probability that an allele A with a frequency of p appear on both the chromosomes of a diploid individual is simply the product of the probabilities, *i.e.*, p^2. In the same way, the frequency *aa* is q^2 and for *Aa* is pq.

$p^2 + 2pq + q^2 = 1$

where, p^2 represents frequency of homozygous dominant genotype,

$2pq$ represents the frequency of the heterozygous genotype and represents the frequency of homozygous recessive.

In population genetics studies, the Hardy-Weinberg equation can be used to measure whether the observed genotype frequencies in a population differ from the frequencies predicted by the equation. If there is any difference in the frequencies, it indicates the extent of evolutionary change. **(3 Marks)**

16. (a) If a patient requires repeated blood transfusion, he must ensure that the donor's blood has been screened for HIV and other pathogens before transfusion.

(1 Mark)

(b) If this advice is not being followed by the patient he might contract AIDS (Acquired Immunodeficiency Syndrome). AIDS is a serious health problem in which the immune system of the patient gets weakened greatly. It is caused by a virus named HIV (Human Immunodeficiency Virus). It is a retrovirus, which attacks the helper T-cells of the body and greatly reduce their number. These helper T-cells are responsible for stimulating the antibody production by B-cells Thus, reduction in their number results in the loss of natural defence of our body. HIV can attack and replicate inside the host cell by using reverse transcription method, which is shown below:

Diagrammatic Representation of replication of reterovirus:-

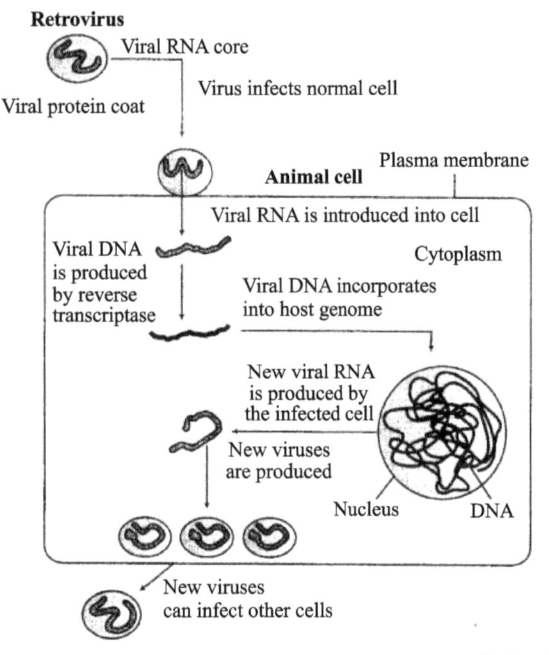

(2 Marks)

Infected cell can survive while viruses are being replicated and released.

17. (a) Inbreeding refers to the mating of more closely related individuals within the same breed for 4-6 generations. This results in the reduction in the fertility and productivity of an organism. This is called inbreeding depression. **(1 Mark)**

(b) Inbreeding is done to evolve a pureline and to express desirable superior genes in any animal. To carry out this, superior males and superior females are selected for mating which contain those desirable charcteristics. In case of cattle, a superior female is a cow or buffalo that produces more milk per lactation and a superior male is the bull which gives rise to superior progeny as compared to those of other males. The improvement in traits occur due to homozygosity. The harmful recessive genes which have come together due to homozygosity are eliminated through selection.

(2 Marks)

18. During sewage treatment the bacteria naturally present in sewage helps in the process. After primary treatment the effluent is passed into large aeration tanks where vigorous growth of useful aerobic microbes form flocs. Flocs are masses of bacteria associated with fungal filaments to form mesh like structures. These microbes consume major part of the organic matter in the effluent reducing biochemical oxygen demand of the effluent. After this effluent is passed into a settling tank where these flocs are allowed to sediment and called activated sludge. This is passed to anaerobic sludge digesters where other kinds of anaerobic bacteria digest the bacteria and fungi of sludge. During this digestion the bacteria produces a mixture of gases like methane, hydrogen sulphide, carbon dioxide forming biogas which is used as a fuel. **(3 Marks)**

19. (a) **Restriction endonuclease -** These are molecular scissors or biological scissors that recognizes and cuts double stranded DNA at specific points. They are used in biotechnology to form recombinant molecules which are composed of DNA from different sources. To insert a foreign DNA into an intact DNA, it must be cut from its source and the intact DNA also must be cut open. Both these processes are carried by using the same restriction endonucleases. **(1 Mark)**

(b) **Gel electrophoresis** is a molecular biology technique which is used for the separation of DNA fragments. DNA fragments are produced by cutting with restriction.

DNA fragments are negatively charged molecules they can be separated by forcing them to move towards the anode under an electric field through a medium/matrix. The smaller, the fragment size, the farther it moves.

(1 Mark)

Ethidium bromide is an intercalating agent which is used to visualise the separated DNA fragments followed by exposure to UV ratiation.

(c) pBR322 has two antibiotic resistance genes, one for ampicillin and other one for tetracycline. Antibiotic resistance serves as selectable marker. If the foreign DNA is ligated at the site of tetracycline resistance gene in pBR322 vector, the recombinant plasmid will lose tetracycline resistance due to insertion of foreign DNA but can still be selected out from non-recombinants by plating the transformants on ampicillin containing medium. The transformants growing on ampicillin containing medium are then transferred on a medium containing tetracycline. The recombinants will grow in ampicillin containing medium but not on the tetracycline-containing medium. However the non-recombinants will grow on both. Thus by using antibiotic resistant genes as selectable markers, we can differentiate between recombinants and non-recombinants. **(1 Mark)**

Insertional inactivation results in the of B-galaitosidase enzyme. The presence of a chromogenic substrate gives blue coloured colonies if the plasmid in bacteria does not have an inert. Presence of insert results into insertional inactivation of the B- galactosidase and colonies do not produce any colour and are identified as recombinant colonies.

20. Recombinant DNA technology allows DNA to be produced via artificial means. The procedure has been used to change DNA in living organisms and may have even more practical uses in the future. Recombinant DNA technology works by taking DNA from two different sources and combining that DNA into a single molecule.

To obtain rDNA steps involved are:

(a) The DNA fragment containing the gene sequence to be cloned (also known as ('insert') is isolated.

(b) Insertion of these DNA fragments into a host cell using a 'vector' (carrier DNA molecule).

(c) The rDNA molecules are generated when the vector self replicates in the host cell.

(d) Transfer of the rDNA molecules into an appropriate host cell.

(e) Selection of the host cells carrying the rDNA molecule using a marker.

(f) Replication of the cells carrying rDNA molecules to get a genetically identical cells population or clone. **(3 Marks)**

21. *Bt* cotton is an insect resistant plant which resist attack of Lepidopterans insects. The plant *Bt* toxin gene cause death of insect larvae by causing cell lysis and swelling of epithelium of midgut. *Bt* toxin is biologically produced by bacterium called *Bacillus thuringiensis (Bt)*. This toxin is insecticidal protein crystal (cry proteins) produced in bacteria (inactive form in bacteria) during a particular phase of growth. Inactive protein (protoxin) is converted into active form of toxin due to alkaline pH of gut of insect which solubilize crystals. The activated toxin binds to surface of midgut epithelial cell and creates pores that cause cell swelling and lysis and eventually death of the insect. **(3 Marks)**

Genes cry IAc and cry II AB control the cotton bollworm while cry IAb controls corn barer.

22. In situ Conservation

- It is the conservation and protection of biodiversity in natural habitat. Population is conserved in surroundings, where they have developed their distinctive features.

  Example: National parks, biosphere reserves, wildlife sanctuaries, etc.

- It also includes the introducion of plants and animal species back into agriculural, horticultural and animal husbandry practices so that they are cultivated/ reproduced and reused by the farmers.
- It also maintains genetic diversity of crop plants/ flowers by saving seeds for next planting season.
- Biodiversity is permanently protected.
- Facilitates scientific research of the site.
- It may be possible to improve the ecological integrity of the area and restore it if it has been damaged by poaching etc. **(3 Marks)**

OR

Three causes of biodiversity losses are:

1. **Habitat destruction-** It is considered as the primary cause of biodiversity loss. It leads to the extinction or decrease in the number of animals living in that particular habitat. Urbanisation, industrialization, clearing forest for agriculture, filling wetlands, caused extinction of endemic species.
2. **Alien species invasion-** Non-native species introduced for economic and other uses, invaded and drive away the local species. Exotic/alien species have proved harmful to both aquatic and terrestrial ecosystem.

The Nile Perch introduced into lakevictoria in east Africa led eventually to the extinction of an ecologically unique assemblage of more than 200 species of cichild fish in the lake. Illegal introduction of the African catfish Clarias gariephinus for aquaculture purposes in posing a threat to the indigenous catfishes in our rivers.

3. **Over exploitation of natural resources-** Over-exploitation of resources has been one of the major contributor to this. Due to increasing human population, resource demands have increased which has resulted into exploitation of already present resources and development of various forms of energy resources. Development of these energy sources modifies natural habitat and accelerates loss of biodiversity. **(3 Marks)**

SECTION - D

23. (a) Following arguments can be put to promote burying and discourage burning:

(i) Burning wastes result in generation of various gases like Co_2 and oxides of nitrogen and sulphur. These gases are very harmful to environment and cause various environmental issues like global warming, acid rain, etc.

(ii) The gases released during burning have various health hazards also, like nausea, headache, respiratory diseases, etc. **(2 Marks)**

(b) Before burying of wastes, following set of events must be followed:

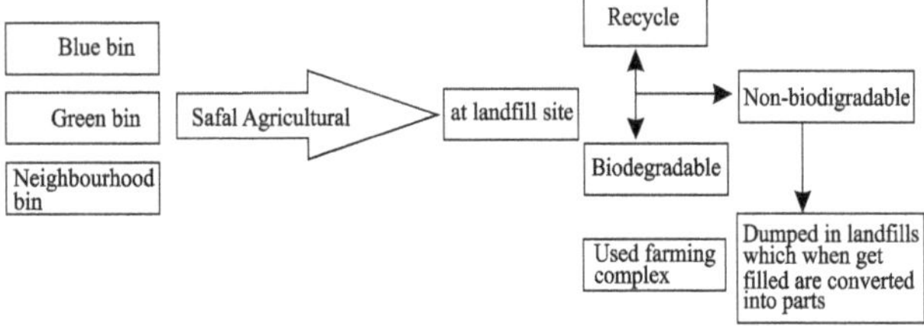

(2 Marks)

SECTION - E

24. (a) Those seeds that carry a living embryo and are capable of germinating into a seedling under appropriate conditions are termed as viable seeds. **(1 Mark)**

(b) (i) Number of pollen grams required to form 200 seeds will be 200 only as each pollen grain carries to generative cells or male gametes and only one of the two are involved in zygote formation.

(ii) In total 400 gamete cells are required for production of 200 viable zygotes leading to formation of 200 guava seeds. **(2 Marks)**

(c) **Flow chart depicting the post pollination events:**

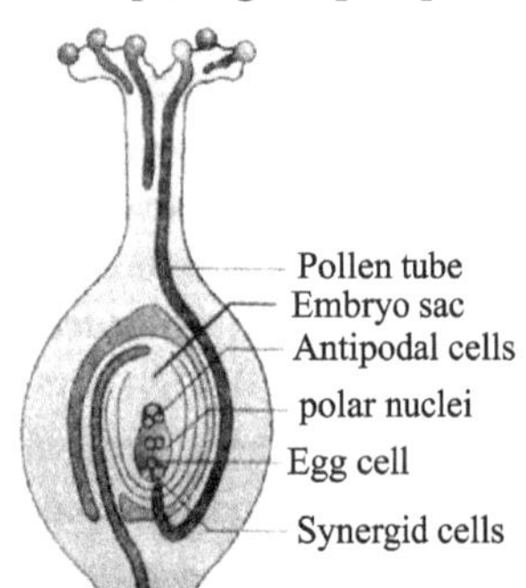

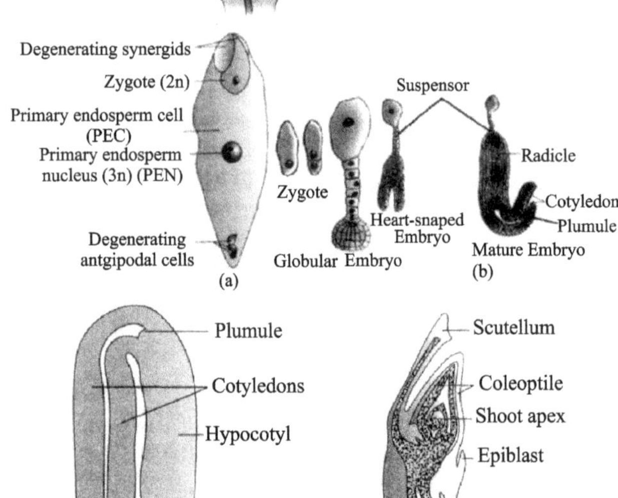

(2 Marks)

OR

(a) The sequence of secretion of the given hormones in a pregnant woman is as follows:

(i) FSH (Follicle Stimulating Hormone)

(ii) LH (Luteinizing Hormone)

(iii) hCG (Human Chromic Gonado tropin)

(iv) Relaxin **(2 Marks)**

(b)

Hormone	**Source**	**Functions**
FSH	Anterior pituitary lobe	Stimulates the growth of ovarian follicles and maturation of primary oocytes
LH	Anterior pituitary lobe	Induces ovulation and maintains corpus luteum
hCG	Chorionic cells of placenta	Maintains the corpus luteum and stimulates the secretion of proges-terone
Relaxin	Ovary	Helps during child birth by relaxing the pelvic muscles as well as mus-cles of the cervix.

(3 Marks)

25. The law of independent assortment that "when two pairs of traits are combined in a hybrid segregation of one pair of chardeters is independent of other pair of characters". This law was proposed by Mendel based on the results of dihybrid crosses, where inheritance of two traits were considered simultaneously. Independent assortment is not applicable for the genes located on the same chromosomes i.e. linked genes. The following cross between a pure-breeding plant with yellow, round seeds and another pure breeding plant with green, wrinkled seeds, can be taken as an example to explain this law.

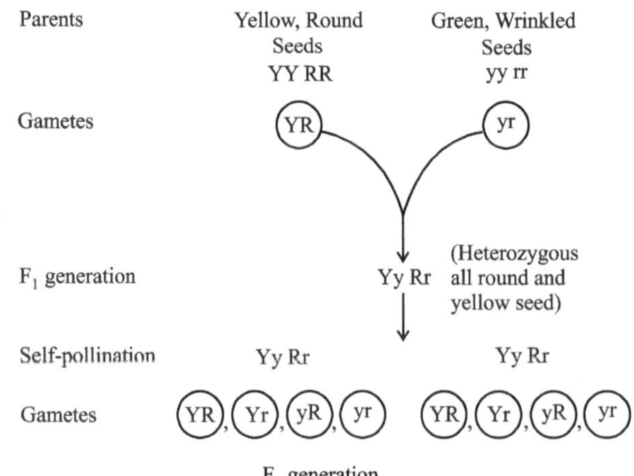

	YR	Yr	yR	yr
YR	YY RR (yellow, round)	YY Rr (yellow, round)	Yy RR (yellow, round)	Yy Rr (yellow, round)
Yr	YY Rr (yellow, round)	YY rr (yellow, wrinkled)	Yy Rr (yellow, round)	Yy rr (yellow, wrinkled)
yR	Yy RR (yellow, round)	Yy Rr (yellow, round)	yy RR (green, round)	yy Rr (green, round)
yr	Yy Rr (yellow, round)	Yy rr (yellow, wrinkled)	yy Rr (green, round)	yy rr (green, wrinkled)

The Phenotypic ratio is : 9 : 3 : 3 : 1

9 round yellow : 3 round green : 3 wrinkled yellow : 1 wrinkled green

Wrinkled yellow and round green are recombinants.

Round yellow and wrinkled green are parental combinations.

The genotypic ratio is :

YY RR	:	YY Rr	:	Yy RR	:	Yy Rr	:	YY rr
1	:	2	:	2	:	4	:	1
Yy rr	:	yy RR	:	yy Rr	:	yy rr		
2	:	1	:	2	:	1		

In this cross, the factors for colour of seeds and those for shape of seeds have segregated independently and each gamete has one factor for each of these two traits.

(5 Marks)

OR

25. (a) **Industrial mechanism** is an example of the natural selection of a particular form of an organism in an environment which has changed due to the ill effects of pollution created by industrial activities. *Biston betularia* is commonly called peppered moth because of the presence of black dots on creamy–white body. These moths during 1850, were mostly gray (*Biston betularia typica*) and during day time used to rest on tree-trunks which had lichens grown on them. They resembled with the background and could not be detected by their predators, mainly birds. During industrial revolution in England, the coal was burnt and the soot got deposited on the tree-trunk. Moreover, sulphur dioxide killed lichens. In such polluted areas all the moths of white coloured now could be spotted by birds. A few black individuals which had mutant gene were selected by nature. Such individuals got more chances of reproduction and the white moth were reduced in number.

After about 100 years (by 1950), more than 90% of the individuals had become black, 'Melanic form' (*Biston betularia carbonaria*). Here biologists could see the evolution occurring before their eyes. This evolution from white to black (Melanic) forms was not due to mutation but due to selection of pre-existing mutant allele by nature (Natural selection). Now, when electricity is being used in industries, the number of white moths is again increasing. This also indicates that industrial pollution has not eliminated the genes responsible for light colour of the moth. The above hypothesis was also tested by Dr. H. B. D. Kettlewell after releasing equal number of dark and light moths.

(2½ Marks)

(b) 'Darwin's Finches' illustrated adaptive radiation. In this, the species, all deriving from a common ancestor, have overtime successfully adapted to their environment via natural selection. Previously, the finches occupied the South American mainland, but somehow managed to occupy the Galapagos islands, over 600 miles away. They occupied an ecological niche with little competition. As the population began to flourish in these advantageous conditions, intraspecific competition became a factor, and resources on the islands were squeezed and could not sustain the population of the finches for long. Due to the mechanisms of natural selection, and changes in the gene pool, the finches became more adapted to the environment. As competition grew, the finches managed to find new ecological niches, that would present less competition and allow them and their genome to be continued. Thus the finches adapted to take advantage of the various food sources available on the island, which were being used by other species. Over the long term, the original finch species may have disappeared, but by diversifying, would stand a better chance of survival. All in all, the finches had adapted to their environment via natural selection, which in turn, has allowed the species to survive in the longer term, the prime directive of any species. **(2½ Marks)**

26. (a) An age pyramid is a graphical representation of the distribution of various age groups within a population of a region forming the shape of a pyramid when the population (percent individual of a given age or age group) is growing. **(2 Marks)**

(b) For human population, the age pyramid shows age distribution of males and females in a combined diagram. These age groups are pre-reproductive, reproductive and post-reproductive. The shape of the pyramids reflects the growth status of the population, Three types of pyramids namely, pyramid with broad base, bell shaped and an urnlike structure indicate rapidly growing population, stable population and a declining population respectively. **(3 Marks)**

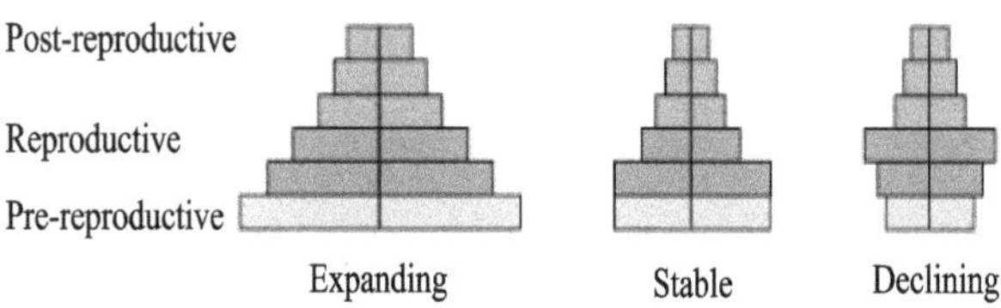

OR

Human beings benefit from a multitude of resources and processes that are supplied by natural ecosystem. Collectively, these benefits are known as ecosystem services, for example, healthy forest ecosystems purify air and water, migrate droughts and floods, cycle nutrients, generate fertile soils, provide wildlife habitat, maintain biodiversity, pollinate crops, provide storage site for carbon and also provide aesthetic, cultural and spiritual values. Services can be subdivided into 5 categories -

(i) Provisioning : Such as the production of food and water.

(ii) Regulating : Such as the control of climate and disease.

(iii) Supporting : Such as nutrients cycle and crop pollination.

(iv) Cultural : Such as spiritual and recreational benefits.

(v) Preserving : Which includes guarding against uncertainty through the maintenance of diversity. **(5 Marks)**

Delhi 2017

CBSE Board Solved Paper

Time Allowed : 3 Hours | *Maximum Marks : 70*

General Instructions:

(i) There are a total of **26** questions and **five** sections in the question paper. All questions are compulsory.

(ii) Section **A** contains questions number **1** to **5**, very short-answer type questions of **1** mark each.

(iii) Section **B** contains questions number **6** to **10**, short-answer type **I** questions of **2** marks each.

(iv) Section **C** contains questions number **11** to **22**, short-answer type **II** questions of **3** marks each.

(v) Section **D** contains question number **23**, value based question of **4** marks.

(vi) Section **E** contains questions number **24** to **26**, long-answer type questions of **5** marks each.

(vii) There is no overall choice in the question paper, however, an internal choice is provided in **one** question of **2** marks, **one** question of **3** marks and all the **three** questions of **5** marks. In these questions, an examinee is toattempt any **one** of the **two** given alternatives.

SECTION - A

1. Name the type of cross that would help to find the genotype of a pea plant bearing violet flowers.

2. State two postulates of Oparin and Haldane with reference to origin of life.

3. A herd of cattle is showing reduced fertility and productivity. Provide one reason and one suggestion to overcome this problem.

4. What are Cry genes ? In which organism are they present ?

5. An electrostatic precipitator in a thermal power plant is not able to generate high voltage of several thousands. Write the ecological implication because of it.

SECTION - B

6. A pollen grain in angiosperm at the time of dehiscence from an anther could be 2-celled or 3-celled. Explain. How are the cells placed within the pollen grain when shed at a 2-celled stage ?

7. Differentiate between the genetic codes given below :

(a) Unambiguous and Universal

(b) Degenerate and Initiator

8. Mention one application for each of the following :

(a) Passive immunization

(b) Antihistamine

(c) Colostrum

(d) Cytokinin-barrier

9. Name the microbes that help production of the following products commercially :

(a) Statin (b) Citric acid

(c) Penicillin (d) Butyric acid

10. List four benefits to human life by eliminating the use of CFCs.

OR

Suggest two practices giving one example of each, that help protect rare or threatened species.

SECTION - C

11. (a) Can a plant flowering in Mumbai be pollinated by pollen grains of the same species growing in New Delhi ? Provide explanations to your answer.

(b) Draw the diagram of a pistil where pollination has successfully occurred. Label the parts involved in reaching the male gametes to its desired destination.

12. Both Haemophilia and Thalassemia are blood related disorders in humans. Write their causes and the difference between the two. Name the category of genetic disorder they both come under.

13. (a) List the two methodologies which were involved in human genome project. Mention how they were used.

(b) Expand 'YAC' and mention what was it used for.

14. Write the characteristics of *Ramapithecus*, *Dryopithecus* and Neanderthal man.

15. Name a human disease, its causal organism, symptoms (any three) and vector, spread by intake of water and food contaminated by human faecal matter.

OR

(a) Why is there a fear amongst the guardians that their adolescent wards may get trapped in drug/alcohol abuse?

(b) Explain 'addiction' and 'dependence' in respect of drug/alcohol abuse in youth.

16. (a) Write the desirable characters a farmer looks for in his sugarcane crop.

(b) How did plant breeding techniques help north Indian farmers to develop cane with desired characters ?

17. Secondary treatment of the sewage is also called Biological treatment. Justify this statement and explain the process.

18. (a) Explain the significance of 'palindromic nucleotide sequence' in the formation of recombinant DNA.

(b) Write the use of restriction endonuclease in the above process.

19. Describe the roles of heat, primers and the bacterium *Thermus aquaticus* in the process of PCR.

20. Explain the various steps involved in the production of artificial insulin.

21. (a) "Organisms may be conformers or regulators." Explain this statement and give one example of each.

(b) Why are there more conformers than regulators in the animal world ?

22. Describe the inter-relationship between productivity, gross primary productivity and net productivity.

SECTION - D

23. It is commonly observed that parents feel embarrassed to discuss freely with their adolescent children about sexuality and reproduction. The result of this parental inhibition is that the children go astray sometimes.

(a) Explain the reasons that you feel are behind such embarrassment amongst some parents to freely discuss such issues with their growing children.

(b) By taking one example of a local plant and animal, how would you help these parents to overcome such inhibitions about reproduction and sexuality ?

SECTION - E

24. (a) When a seed of an orange is squeezed, many embryos, instead of one are observed. Explain how it is possible.

(b) Are these embryos genetically similar or different ? Comment.

OR

(a) Explain the following phases in the menstrual cycle of a human female :

(i) Menstrual phase (ii) Follicular phase

(iii) Luteal phase

(b) A proper understanding of menstrual cycle can help immensely in family planning. Do you agree with the statement? Provide reasons for your answer.

25. (a) Compare, giving reasons, the J-shaped and S-shaped models of population growth of a species.

(b) Explain "fitness of a species" as mentioned by Darwin.

OR

(a) What is an ecological pyramid ? Compare the pyramids of energy, biomass and numbers.

(b) Write any two limitations of ecological pyramids.

26. (a) Describe the structure and function of a t-RNA molecule. Why is it referred to as an adapter molecule?

(b) Explain the process of splicing of hn-RNA in a eukaryotic cell.

OR

Write the different components of a *lac*-operon in *E.coli.* Explain its expression while in an 'open' state.

Solutions

SECTION - A

1. Test cross is used for the determination of genotype of pea plant bearing violet flowers. **(1 Mark)**

Test cross helps the students to determine whether the genotype of the plant is heterozygous dominant (Ww) or homozygous dominant (WW).

2. Oparin and Haldane proposed that the first form of life could have been evolved from pre-existing non-living organic molecules such as RNA, protein and so on.

   They also state that the formation of life was preceded by chemical evolution such as the formation of diverse organic molecules from inorganic constituents.

   The conditions on the earth for survival were high temperature, volcanic storms and reducing atmosphere contains CH4, NH3 and so on. **(1 Mark)**

3. Reduced fertility and productivity in a herd of cattle is because of inbreeding depression. Inbreeding depression occurs because of inbreeding. This problem can be overcome by mating of selected animals with the unrelated superior animals of the same breed. This helps to restore the fertility and productivity. **(1 Mark)**

Inbreeding refers to the mating of more closely related individuals within the same breed for 4-6 generations.

4. *Cry* genes are present in bacterium *Bacillus thuriengiensis*. It codes for toxin called Bt toxin. The proteins encoded by the genes *cryI*Ac and *cryII*Ab control the cotton bollworms whereas *cryI*Ab controls corn borer. **(1 Mark)**

The Bt toxin protein exist as inactive protoxins but once an insect ingest the inactive toxin, it is converted into an active form of toxin due to the alkaline pH of the gut which solubilise the crystals. The activated toxin binds to the surface of midgut epithelial cells and create pores that causes cell swelling and lysis and eventually cause death of the insects.

5. An electrostatic precipitator will not able to remove particulate matter present in the exhaust of thermal power plants and because of this dust particles will be released into the air. This results in air pollution. **(1 Mark)**

SECTION - B

6. In many angiosperms, pollen grains are released in 2-celled stage while in other plant species, the generative cells are dividing into 2-male gametes and they will form 3-celled stage. When the pollen grain is shed at 2-celled stage then it has two unequal cells such as a bigger vegetative cell and smaller generative cell. **(2 Marks)**

7. (a) Difference between unambiguous and universal:

Unambiguous	Universal
Unambiguous means code is specific as one codon codes for only one amino acid.	**Universal** means codon is same in all organisms.

(b) Difference between degenerate and initiator:

Degenerate	Initiator
Degenerate means when an amino acid is coded by more than one codon.	**AUG** is an initiator codon as it initiates the process of translation and codes for amino acid methionine.

(2 Marks)

In prokaryotes, GUG acts as a initiation codon and codes for amino acid Valine.

8. (a) **Passive immunization:** When readymade antibiotics are introduced into the body, then it is called passive immunization. Passive immunization provides quick immune response in the body.

   (b) **Anti-histamines:** Anti-histamines are the chemicals that are given against allergic reactions.

   (c) **Colostrum:** Colostrum is the yellow fluid produced during the initial days of lactation. It is rich in antibodies IgA. It provides innate immunity to the new baby.

   (d) **Cytokinin barrier:** It involves interferons. Virus-infected cells secrete proteins called **interferons** that protect non-infected cells from further viral infections.

(2 Marks)

9. (a) **Statin:** It is produced by yeast called as *Monascus purpureus*. It is used for blood-cholesterol lowering agents.

   (b) **Citric acid:** It is produced by fungus *Aspergillus niger*.

   (c) **Penicillin:** Penicillin is an antibiotic that is produced by bacteria called *Penicllium notatum*.

   (d) **Butyric acid:** It is produced by a bacterium called *Clostridium butylicum*. **(2 Marks)**

10. CFCs (Chlorofluorocarbons) are responsible for affecting the human life. As the chlorinated molecules from CFCs releases leads to cause pollution and ozone layer depletion. Reduction in the use of CFCs helps in following ways:

- It helps in the prevention of ozone layer depletion.
- It also helps in reduction of greenhouse effect.
- It also reduced El Nino effect or odd climatic changes.
- Reduction in CFCs will also help in the prevention of snow blindness and inflammation of cornea.

CFCs are widely released into the atmosphere from refrigerators and is discharged in the lower part of atmosphere. Then it move upwards and reach atmosphere. Chlorine atoms are releasing into the atmosphere by the action of UV rays. It results in the ozone depletion.

OR

Practices that help to prevent rare or threatened species are as follows:

(i) **Ex-situ conservation:** In this, the rare or threatened plants and animal species are taken out from their natural habitat and place them in special area where they can be protected and given special care.

(ii) **Cryopreservation:** Gametes (sperms, eggs, tissues and embryo) of several endangered plants and animal species can be preserved by methods involves cryopreservation (-196°C). It can be fertilized in Invitro followed by propagation through tissue culture methods.

(iii) **In-situ conservation:** This approach involves conservation and protection of entire ecosystem, in order to protect its biodiversity at the levels. As if we save forest then we save the tiger. **(2 Marks)**

Ecologically unique and biodiversity-rich regions in India are legally protected as biosphere reserves, national parks and sanctuaries.

SECTION - C

11. (a) Yes, it can be only possible by means of artificial hybridisation in which a pollen grain of one flower is artificially introduced on the stigma of another flower. But it does not involve self-incompatibility of flowers.

- In this, one flower is emasculated and bagged.
- After some time, the bag is removed and then desired pollen grains are introduced on its stigma.

Emasculation refers to the removal of anthers from the floral bud before the anther dehiscence by using a pair of forceps. Whereas bagging refers to the covering of emasculated flower with a bag made of butter paper in order to prevent contamination of stigma with unwanted pollen.

(b) **Diagrammatic representation of pistil:**

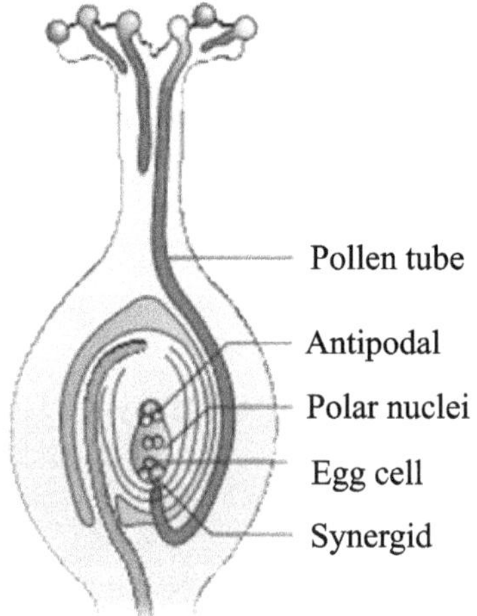

(3 Marks)

12.

Category	Haemophilia	Thalassemia
Cause	It is caused due to the absence of blood clotting factor VIII and IX.	It is caused due to the mutation or deletion of gene that controls the formation of globin chain of haemoglobin.
Difference	Blood clotting is affected.	This results in anaemia.
Type of genetic disorder	Sex-linked recessive genetic disorder	Autosomal recessive disorder.

(3 Marks)

Both haemophilia and thalassemia are Mendelian disorder.

13. (a) Human Genome Project was also called mega project that has approximately 3×10^9 bp. Human Genome Project involves two major approaches such as ESTs and Sequence Annotation and The two approaches are ESTs and Sequence Annotation.

- **Expressed sequence Tags:** This approach aims identifying all the genes that expressed as RNA.
- **Sequence Annotations:** This approach involves sequencing of the entire set of genome either coding or non-coding sequences or later assigning different region with functions.

(b) **YAC** stands for Yeast Artificial Chromosome. It is used as cloning vectors for cloning DNA fragments in suitable host to carry out the process of DNA sequencing.

(3 Marks)

14.

Characteristics of *Ramapithecus*	Characteristics of *Dryopithecus*	Characteristics of Neanderthal man
Ramapithecus walked like gorillas and chimpanzees.	*Dryopithecus* has hairy arms and legs of same length.	Nenderthal man has brain capacity of 1400cc
They had dental structure more similar to man.	They walked like gorillas, chimpanzees, and apes.	They hide in order to protect their bodies and also buried their dead ones.

(3 Marks)

15. The infectious disease that is caused because of the intake of contaminated food and water by human faecal matter is Amoebic dysentery or Amoebiasis.

This disease is caused by a protozoa *Entamoeba histolytica.*

Its symptoms involve constipation, abdominal pain and cramps, stools with excess mucous and blood clots. Houseflies act as carrier for the transmission of parasites from faeces of infected person to food and water.

(3 Marks)

OR

(a) The adolescent's wards may get trapped in drug/ alcohol abuse involves following reasons:

- Peer pressure
- Curiosity and need to try for adventure, excitement and experiment.
- To escape from stress, frustration and depression.
- To overcome hardships of life.
- Unstable or unsupportive family structure.

(1½ Marks)

(b) **Addiction:** Addiction is defined as the psychological attachment to certain effects such as Euphoria or temporary feeling of well-being.

Dependence: Dependence is defined as the tendency of the body to show withdrawal syndrome or appearance of symptoms because of regular doses of drug or alcohol abuse is abruptly discontinued.

(1½ Marks)

16. (a) The desirable characteristics a farmer wants to see in his sugarcane crop are:

- Higher yielding capacity
- Thicker stem
- Higher sugar content
- Ability to grow in North India. **(1½ Marks)**

(b) North Indian farmers developed sugarcane with desired characters by crossing two varieties of sugarcane such as *Saccharum barberi* that was originally grown in North India. It had low sugar content and yield. While *Saccharum officinarum* was originally grown in South India and had thicker stems and higher sugar content. When these two species of sugarcane were successfully crossed desirable qualities such as higher yielding capacity, thicker stems, higher sugar content and ability to grow in the sugar cane areas of North India.

(1½ Marks)

17. Secondary treatment of sewage is also called biological treatment because it involves biological organisms such as aerobic and anaerobic microbes and fungi for digestion of organic waste.

In this, the primary effluent is passed into the large aeration tanks and is constantly agitated mechanically. In this air is pumped and this allows the vigorous growth of useful aerobic microorganisms into **flocs.** These microbes consume the maximum part of the organic matter in the effluent. This significantly reduces the biochemical oxygen demand (BOD) of the effluent. The sewage water is treated till the BOD is reduced. **(3 Marks)**

***Flocs** are the masses of bacteria associated with fungal filaments to form a mesh like structures. BOD refers to the amount of oxygen consumed if all the organic matter in one litre of water were oxidised by bacteria.*

18. (a) The palindromic sequences are the groups of letters that form the same word that is when both read forward and backward. For e.g "MALAYALAM". Palindrome where the same word is read in both directions, the palindrome in DNA is a sequence of base pairs that reads the same on the two strands when orientation of reading is kept the same.

For example: The following sequences read the same on the two strands in 5'→3' direction. The same sequence read in the 3'→5' direction.

5'-----GAATTC----3'

3'----CTTAAG----5' **(1½ Marks)**

(b) On finding the palindrome, the endonuclease binds to the DNA. It cuts the opposite strands of DNA, but between the same bases on both the strands and form 'Sticky-ends'. This 'sticky ends' facilitates the action of enzyme DNA ligase and also helps in the formation of recombinant DNA. **(1½ Marks)**

19. Role of heat in PCR:

Heat helps in the denaturation process in PCR. In this process, the dsDNA is heated in this process at very high temperature (94-96°C) results in the separation of two strands of DNA into single strands.

Role of primers in PCR:

Primers are the short synthetic single stranded DNA fragments that are complementary to DNA sequences that flank the target region of the DNA.

DNA polymerase enzyme extends the primers by using the nucleotides provided in the reaction and the genomic DNA as template. It helps in the extension of new chain.

Role of Bacterium *Thermus aquaticus:*

The bacteria *Thermus aquaticus is* thermostable bacteria. An enzyme Taq DNA polymerase is isolated from these thermostable bacteria. This enzyme remains active during high temperature during denaturation of double stranded DNA. **(3 Marks)**

20. The various steps involved in the production of artificial insulin are as follows:

- The artificial insulin consists of two short polypeptide chains such as chain A and chain B.
- These two short polypeptide chains are linked together by disulphide bond.
- In mammals such as humans, insulin is synthesised as a prohormone that contains an extra stretch called the **C peptide**.
- This **C peptide** is not present in mature insulin and is removed during maturation into insulin.
- The two DNA sequences corresponding to A and B polypeptide chains of human insulin were prepared and these were introduced into *E.coli* in order to produce A and B chains separately, and these chains were extracted and then combined by creating disulphide bonds.

Diagrammatic representation of artificial insulin:

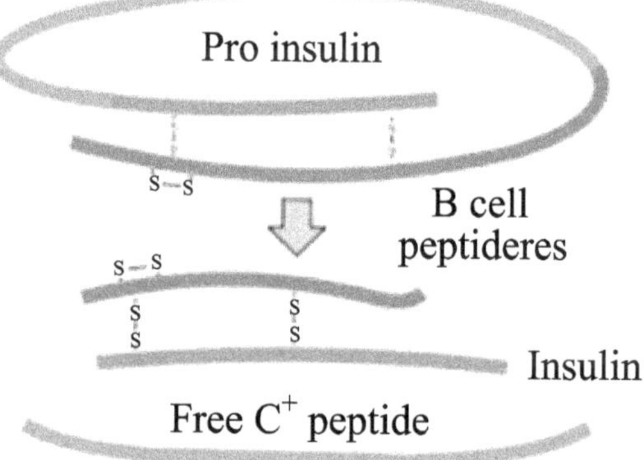

(3 Marks)

21. (a) **Conformers:** Conformers are those organisms that are not able to maintain a constant internal body temperature with the external environmental conditions. They change body temperature and osmotic concentration with the changing external environmental. For example: all plants and fishes.

Regulators: Regulators are those organisms that are able to maintain homeostasis is according to external environment. They have ability to maintain their constant body temperature and osmotic concentration. For example: Birds and mammals. **(2 Marks)**

(b) There are more conformers than regulators in the animal world because they lack the ability to maintain the constant internal body temperature with the changing external environment. **(1 Mark)**

22. Productivity: Productivity is defined as the rate of biomass production.

Gross primary productivity: Gross primary productivity is defined as the rate of organic matter production during photosynthesis.

Net primary productivity: Net primary productivity involves the gross-productivity minus respiratory losses (R).

So, NPP = GPP-R

As per their definitions, all the terms are interrelated to each other. **(3 Marks)**

SECTION - D

23. (a) The important reasons that parents feel embarrassed to discuss freely with their adolescent children about sexuality and reproduction are illiteracy, conservative attitude, myths and misconceptions among parents. They feel shy to discuss such issues with their children freely. But it is responsibility of every parent to give right information to their children about sexuality, reproduction, adolescence changes and sexual practices so that their children will never be misleaded.

(2 Marks)

(b) An example of male honey bee and orchid *Ophrys* flower represents the sexual attraction phenomena in which the honey bee is attracted towards the *Ophrys* flower. The Mediterranean orchid *Ophrys* employs 'sexual deceit' to get pollination done by a species of one petal of its flower bears an uncanny resemblance to the female of the bee in size, colour and markings. The male bee is attracted to what it perceives as a female, 'Pseudo-copulates' with the flower, and during that process is dusted with pollen from the flower. When this same bee 'Pseudo-copulates' with another flower, it transfers pollen to it and thus pollinates the flower. So, it is a natural phenomenon and similarly parents should openly talk about such matter with their children. **(2 Marks)**

SECTION - E

24. (a) The occurrence of more than one embryo in a seed in oranges is because of polyembryony. In orange, the nucellar cells, synergids and integument cells are developed into a number of embryos of different sizes. For Example: citrus. **(2½ Marks)**

Sometimes the formation of more than one egg in an embryo sac can lead to polyembryony.

(b) Parental characters are maintained in the embryos formed as a result of polyembryony and hence they are genetically similar. As, in this process there is no segregation of characters in the progeny. **(2½ Marks)**

OR

(a) The menstrual cycle involves following phases such as:

(i) **Menstrual phase:** This phase takes place when released ovum is not fertilised. This phase occurs within the first 3rd-5th days of cycle where menstrual flow occurs because of the breakdown of endometrial lining of the uterus.

(ii) **Follicular phase:** This phase occurs within the 5th-14th day of the cycle where the primary follicles grow to become a fully mature Graafian follicle, endometrium of uterus regenerates and Graafian follicle ruptures to release ova as ovulation occurs on 14th day.

(iii) **Luteal phase:** This phase occurs within the 15th -28th day. In this phase, the remaining parts of the Graafian follicle transform into Corpus luteum and secretion of progesterone occurs that is essential for the maintenance of endometrium.

(4 Marks)

(b) Yes, I agree with the statement that taking appropriate precautions between 10th -17th day of menstrual cycle when the chances of fertilisation are high.

(1 Mark)

25. (a) The difference between J shaped-growth curve and S shaped-growth curve are as follows:

J shaped-growth curve	S shaped-growth curve
(i) In this type of growth curve, the resources are unlimited.	In this type of growth curve, the resources are limited.
(ii) In J shaped-growth curve, growth is exponential.	In S shaped-growth curve, growth is logistic.
(iii) Because of the availability of unlimited resources, all individuals will survive and reproduce.	This type of curve favours the survival and reproduction of the fittest one.
(iv) Growth equation for J shaped-shaped curve is $dN/dt = R_n$	Growth equation for S shaped-curve is $dN/dT = rN$

(3 Marks)

(b) According to Darwin, "Fitness of a species" means a specific species is reproductively fit. When the availability of resources are limited, competition takes place between the species and it only favours the survival of the fittest one who reproduce to leave more progeny. **(2 Marks)**

OR

Ecological pyramid is defined as the relationship between producers and consumers in an ecosystem that can be graphically represented in the form of a pyramid.

Different types of ecological pyramids are as follows:

(i) **Pyramid of number:** It is defined as the relationship between producers and consumers in an ecosystem that can be presented in the form of a pyramid in terms of number.

Diagrammatic Representation of Pyramid of number:

Trophic level **Number of individuals**

TC Tertiary consumer 3

SC (Secondary consumer) 3,54,000

PC (Primary consumer) 708,000

PP (Primary producer) 5,842,000

(ii) **Pyramid of biomass:** It is defined as the relationship between producers and consumers in an ecosystem that can be represented in the form of a pyramid in terms of biomass. It can be upright or inverted.

Diagrammatic Representation of Pyramid of Biomass:

Trophic level **Dry weight (kg m^{-2})**

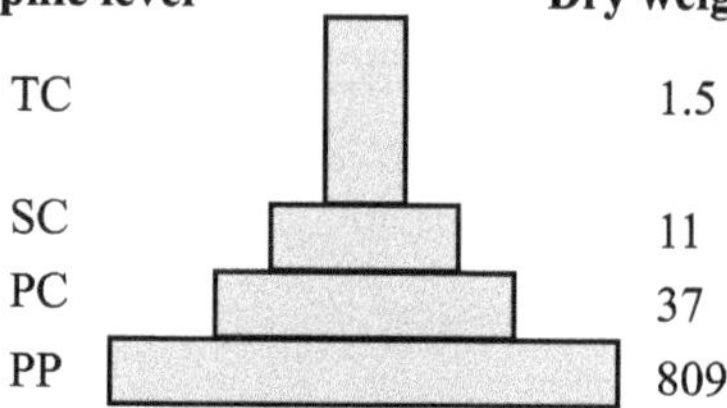

(iii) **Pyramid of energy:** It is defined as the relationship between producer and consumers in an ecosystem that can be represented in the form of pyramid in terms of flow of energy. It is always upright as the energy is lost as heat at each step.

Diagrammatic Representation of Pyramid of energy:

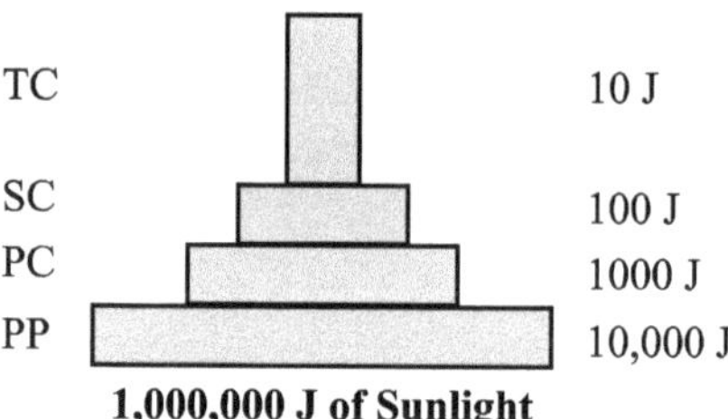

(3 Marks)

(b) The limitations of ecological pyramids are as follows:

- It levels takes into account the same species belonging to two or more trophic levels.
- Ecological pyramids assume a simple food chain that never existed in nature. **(2 Marks)**

26. (a) **Structure of t-RNA:**

- The structure of t-RNA looks like a clover-leaf but its 3-D structure is inverted L-shaped
- It has an anticodon loop that has bases complementary to the code.
- It also contains amino acid acceptor end to which it gets bind with an amino acids.
- They are specific for each amino acid.
- The T-loop of t-RNA helps in binding to ribosome.
- D-loop help in binding of amino acyl synthetase.
- It also contains a variable loop.

Diagrammatic Representation of structure of t-RNA:

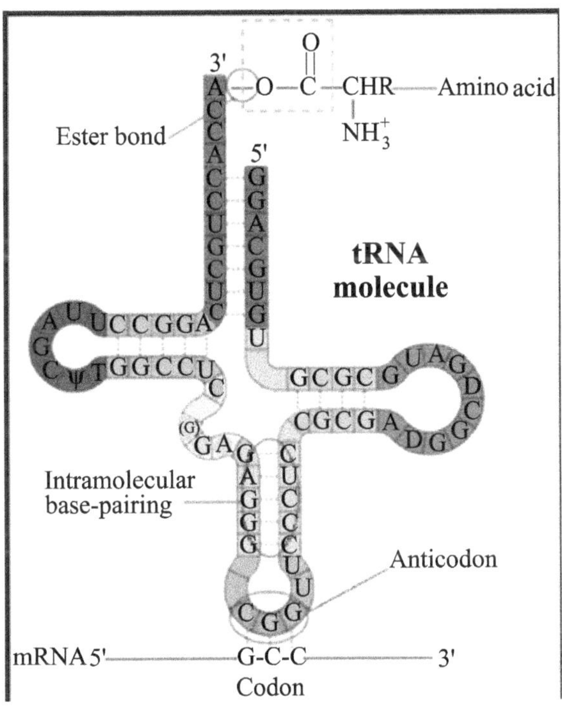

Function of t-RNA:

- It has anticodon loop that has bases complementary to the code.
- It also contains an amino acid acceptor end to which it gets binds with amino acid.
- t-RNA are specific for each amino.
- It is an adaptor molecule because it reads the code and on the another hand it binds with the specific amino acid.

(3 Marks)

(b) The primary transcript contains both coding and non-coding sequences called as exon and introns. So, the non-coding sequences or introns are removed by the process of splicing and exons are joined together in a specific manner. Primary transcript after splicing is called hnRNA. It undergoes two additional processes called capping and tailing. In capping, an unusual nucleotide called methyl guanosine triphosphate is added to the 5'-end of hnRNA whereas in tailing, adenylate residues contains 200-300 bp are added at the 3'-end in a template independent manner. The fully processed hnRNA or primary transcript is called mRNA which is further transported into the nucleus for the process of translation. **(2 Marks)**

OR

Lac operon was proposed by Jacob and Monad in 1961. It contains following components such as:

(i) **Structural gene:** There are three types of structural genes that codes for different enzymes and facilitates the process of transcription in the presence of inducer (lactose).

- The **z gene** codes for enzyme beta-galactosidase that regulates the switching on and is responsible for the hydrolysis of disaccharide, lactose into its monomeric unit's glucose.
- **y gene** codes for enzyme permease that increases the permeability of the cell to beta-galactosides.
- **a gene** codes for enzyme transacetylase.

(ii) **Promoter:** It is the sequence of DNA at which the RNA polymerase enzyme get binds and initiates the process of transcription.

(iii) **Operator:** It is sequence of DNA that is adjacent to promoter.

(iv) **Regulator gene:** A gene that codes for repressor protein and binds with the operator and because of it operon is switched "off".

(v) **Inducer:** Lactose is inducer that helps in switching "on" of operon.

Lactose acts as the substrate for enzyme beta-galactosidase. This enzyme regulates the switching on and off the operon because of this it is termed as inducer. So, in the absence of glucose (carbon source), if lactose is added in the growth medium of the bacteria. The lactose is transported into the cells by the action of permease enzyme that increases permeability of the cell to beta-galactosides.

Lactose induces the operon in following manner:

- In a lac operon, the repressor protein is synthesised from the *i gene*.
- This repressor protein gets bind with the operator region of the operon and prevents RNA polymerase enzyme from transcribing the operon.

- In the absence of lactose, the repressor gene produces repressor protein and get binds with the operator gene. It prevents the RNA polymerase enzyme to get binds with the operon.

Diagrammatic Representation of lac operon in the absence of lactose:

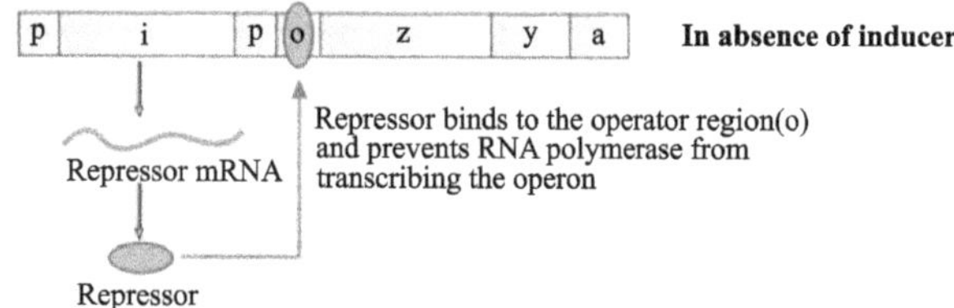

- In the presence of lactose as an inducer, the repressor protein is inactivated. It allows RNA polymerase enzyme to activate the promoter and initiates the process of transcription by structural genes.

Diagrammatic Representation of lac operon in the presence of inducer:

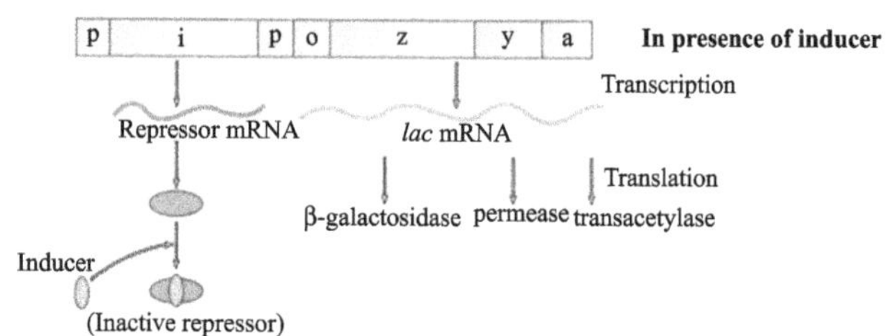

(5 Marks)

All India 2016
CBSE Board Solved Paper

Time Allowed : 3 Hours | ***Maximum Marks : 70***

General Instructions:

(i) There are a total of **26** questions and five sections in the question paper. **All** questions are **compulsory**.
(ii) Section **A** contains questions number **1** to **5**, very-short answer type questions of **1** mark each.
(iii) Section **B** contains questions number **6** to **10**, short-answer type **I** questions of **2** marks each.
(iv) Section **C** contains questions number **11** to **22**, short-answer type **II** questions of **3** marks each.
(v) Section **D** contains question number **23**, value based question of **4** marks.
(vi) Section **E** contains questions number **24** to **26**, long-answer type questions of **5** marks each.
(vii) There is no overall choice in the question paper, however, an internal choice is provided in **one** question of **2** marks, **one** question of **3** marks and all the **three** questions of **5** marks. In these questions, an examinee is to attempt any **one** of the **two** given alternatives.

SECTION - A

1. A male honeybee has 16 chromosomes whereas its female has 32 chromosomes. Give one reason.

2. Mention the role of genetic mother in MOET.

3. What is biopiracy

4. Mention two advantages for preferring CNG over diesel as an automobile fuel.

5. Write the probable differences in eating habits of (*Homo habilis*) and (*Homo erectus*).

SECTION - B

6. A single pea plant in your kitchen garden produces pods with viable seeds, but the individual papaya plant does not. Explain.

7. Following are the features of genetic codes. What does each one indicate? Stop codon; Unambiguous codon; Degenerate docon; Universal codon

8. Suggest four important steps to produce a disease resistant plant through conventional plant breeding technology.

9. Name a genus of baculovirus. Why are they considered good biocontrol agents?

10. Explain the relationship between CFC's and ozone in the stratosphere.

OR

Why are sacred grooves highly protected?

SECTION - C

11. (a) Name the organic material exine of the pollen grain is made up of. How is this material advantageous to pollen grain?

(b) Still it is observed that it does not form a continuous layer around the pollen grain. Give reason.

(c) How are 'pollen banks useful?

OR

(a) Mention the problems that are taken care of by Reproduction and Child Health Care Programme.

(b) What is amniocentesis and why there is a statutory ban on it?

12. What is a test cross? How can it decipher the heterozygosity of a plant?

13. (a) What do 'Y' and 'B' stand for in 'YAC' and 'BAC' used in Human Genome Project (HGP). Mention their role in the project.

(b) Write the percentage of the total human genome that codes for proteins and the percentage of discovered genes whose functions are known as observed during HGP.

(c) Expand 'SNPs' identified by scientists in HGP.

14. Differentiate between homology and analogy. Give one example of each.

15. (a) It is generally observed that the children who had suffered from chicken-pox in their childhood may not contract the same disease in their adulthood. Explain giving reasons, the basis of such an immunity in an individual. Name this kind of immunity.
(b) What are interferons? Mention their role.

16. (a) Write the two limitations of traditional breeding technique that led to promotion of micro propagation
(b) Mention two advantages of micro propagation
(c) give two examples where it is commercially adopted.

17. (a) How do organic farmers control pests? Give two examples.
(b) State the difference in their approach from that of conventional pest control methods.

18. (a) Name the selectable markers in the cloning vector pBR322? Mention the role they play.
(b) Why is the coding sequence of an enzyme β galactosidase a preferred selectable marker in comparison to the one named above?

19. (a) Why must a cell be made 'competent' in biotechnology experiments? How does calcium ion help in doing so?
(b) State the role of 'biolistic gun' in biotechnology experiments.

20. Explain enzyme-replacement therapy to treat adenosine deaminase deficiency. Mention two disadvantages of this procedure.

21. Name and explain the type of interaction that exists in mycorrhizae and between cattle egret and cattle.

22. Differentiate between primary and secondary succession. Provide one example of each.

SECTION - D

23. A large number of married couples the world over are childless. It is shocking to know that in India the female partner is often blamed for the couple being childless.
(a) Why in your opinion the female partner is often blamed for such situations in India? Mention any two values that you as a biology student can promote to check this social evil.
(b) State any two reasons responsible for the cause of infertility.
(c) Suggest a technique that can help the couple to have a child where the problem is with male partner

SECTION - E

24. (a) Explain the menstrual phase in a human female. State the levels of ovarian and pituitary hormones during this phase.
(b) Why is follicular phase in the menstrual cycle also referred as proliferative phase? Explain.
(c) Explain the events that occur in a graafian follicle at the time of ovulation and thereafter.
(d) Draw a graafian follicle and label antrum and secondary oocyte.

OR

(a) As a senior biology student you have been asked to demonstrate to the students of secondary level in your school, the prodedure(s) that shall ensure crosspollination in a hermaphrodite flower. List the different steps that you would suggest and provide reasons for each one of them.
(b) Draw a diagram of a section of a megasporangium of an angiosperm and label funiculus, micropyle, embryosac and nucellus.

25. Describe Meselson and Stahl's experiment that was carried in 1958 on E. Coli. Write the conclusion they arrived after the experiment.

OR

(a) Describe the process of transcription in bacteria.
(b) Explain the processing the hnRNA needs to undergo before becoming functional mRNA eukaryotes.

26. (a) Name the two growth models that represent population growth and draw the respective growth curves they represent.
(b) State the basis for the difference in the shape of these curves.
(c) Which one of the curves represent the human population growth at present? Do you think such a curve is sustainable? Give reason in support of your answer.

OR

(a) Taking an example of a small pond, explain how the four components of an ecosystem function as a unit.
(b) Name the type of food chain that exists in pond.

Solutions

SECTION - A

1. Male honeybees are formed by the process of parthenogenesis which involves development from unfertilized eggs. The unfertilised eggs carry only half number of chromosome such as 16 chromosomes (haploid). While female honeybees are developed from unfertilized eggs and has 32 chromosomes. **(1 Mark)**

2. **MOET** is Multiple Ovulation Embryo Transfer Technology. This programme is started for herd improvement. The genetic mother is available for another round of super ovulation. **(1 Mark)**

The genetic mother or cow is administered with FSH (follicle stimulating hormone) in order to induce follicular maturation and super ovulation.

3. Biopiracy is defined as the use of bio-resources by multinational companies and other organisations without proper authorisation from the countries and people concerned without compensatory payment. **(1 Mark)**

4. The CNG is better than diesel because:
   - CNG burns most efficiently than petrol and diesel in the automobiles and very little amount of it is left unburnt.
   - CNG is cheaper than petrol or diesel. **(1 Mark)**

CNG is compressed Natural Gas and LPG is Liquified Petroleum Gas.

5. Difference between eating habits of *Homohabilis* and *Homo erectus* are as follows:

Characteristics	*Homo habilis*	*Homo erectus*
Eating habits	They did not eat meat.	They ate meat.

(1 Mark)

The brain capacities of Homo habilis were in between 600-800 cc while Homo erectus had larger brain capacities around 900 cc.

SECTION - B

6. The pea plant is monoecious as the male and female gametes are found on the same plant. So, self pollination takes place in such plants results in the production of seeds. Whereas the papaya plant is dioecious as male and female gametes are found located on the different plants. So, cross pollination takes place in such plants results in no seed formation. **(2 Marks)**

7. **Stop codon:** There are 64 codons out of which 61 codons codes for 20 amino acids and three are stop codon that terminates the process of protein synthesis (translation). Stop codons are UAA, UGA and UAG.

   Unambiguous codon: One codon codes only for one amino acid and hence is called unambiguous and specific.

   Degenerate codon: The codon is read in mRNA in a contiguous fashion as there are no punctuations.

   Universal codon: The code is nearly universal. For example: from bacteria to human UUU would code for phenylalanine (Phe) amino acid. **(2 Marks)**

Codons are three nucleotide DNA or RNA sequences those codes for specific amino acid for the process of translation.

8. The four important steps involved in the production of disease resistant plant through conventional plant breeding technology are:

   (i) **Collection of variability:** The entire collection of either plants or seeds having all diverse alleles for all genes in a given crop is called **germplasm.**

   (ii) **Evaluation and selection of parents:** The germplasm is evaluated for the identification of plants having desirable combination of characters.

   (iii) **Cross hybridisation among the selected parents:** The desired characters are combined from two different plants (parents). For example: high protein quality of one parent may required to be combined with disease resistance from another parents.

(iv) **Selection and testing of superior recombinants:** This step involves the selection among the progeny of the hybrids, those plants that have the desired character combination. The selection process is crucial to the success of the breeding objective and also requires careful scientific evaluation of the progeny. **(2 Marks)**

9. Baculoviruses are the pathogen that attack insects and other arthropods. The baculoviruses are used as a biological control agent. They belong the genus *Nucleopolyhedrovirus.* These viruses are excellent candidates for species-specific, narrow spectrum insecticidal applications. **(2 Marks)**

10. CFCs are widely used as a refrigerants and can be discharged in the lower part of the atmosphere that move upward and reach stratosphere. In stratosphere, UV rays act on them releasing Cl atoms. Cl degrades ozone releasing molecular oxygen with these atoms acting merely as catalysts, Cl atoms are not consumed in the reaction. When CFCs are added to the stratosphere, they have permanent and continuing affects on Ozone levels results in ozone layer depletion in the strastophere. **(2 Marks)**

Ozone layer depletion is marked over the Antartic region results in the formation of a large area of thinned ozone layer which is commonly called as the ozone hole.

OR

The scared grooves are largely protected because they have large number of rare and threatened plants species. They are also protected because of the cultural and religious values of the communities. The scared grooves are found in Khasi and Jaintia Hills in Meghalaya, Aravalli Hills of Rajasthan, Western Ghat regions of Karnataka and Maharashtra and the Sarguja, Chanda and Bastar areas of Madhya Pradesh. **(2 Marks)**

SECTION - C

11. (i) The hard outer layer of the pollen grain is called the exine which is made up of sporopollenin. Sporopollenin is one of the most resistant organic material as it tolerate high temperatures and strong acids as well as alkali. It cannot be degraded by enzymatic degradation.

(ii) The sporopollenin is not continuous because the exine of the pollen grain has prominent apertures called **germ pores** where the sporopollenin is absent.

(iii) The pollen grain of a large number of species are stored for many years in liquid nitrogen at -196°C. The stored pollen grains are used as pollen banks and can be used in crop breeding programmes. **(3 Marks)**

OR

(a) The "Reproductive and Child Health care (RCH) programmes" create awareness among people about the various reproduction related aspects and also providing facilities as well as support for building up a reproductively healthy society as the major goals of this programmes.

(b) **Amniocentesis** is a foetal sex determination test based on the chromosomal pattern in the amniotic fluid surrounding the developing embryo for determination of abnormalities in the foetus.

The statutory ban on amniocentesis is because of illegal sex determination that increases female foeticides, massive child immunisation. **(3 Marks)**

12. A test cross is a cross between the F1 progeny and its homozygous recessive parents. Test cross is used for the determination of dominant character which is coming from the homozygous dominant genotype or heterozygous genotype. For example: TT and Tt for tallness.

Representation of genetic cross:

Parents: Tt (tall) X tt (dwarf)

Gametes: Tt tt

F_1 generation : Tt Tt Tt Tt

Result: All the progeny obtained are tall.

When Heterozygous tall (Tt) plant is crossed with homozygous dwarf (tt) plant:

Parents: Tt (tall) X tt (dwarf)

Gametes: Tt tt

F_2 generation : Tt Tt tt tt

Result: 50% tall and 50% dwarf progenies are obtained in F_2 generation. **(3 Marks)**

Test cross is used for the determination of the heterozygosity of the plant.

13. (a) B in BAC stands for Bacterial artificial chromosomes and Y in YAC stands for yeast artificial chromosomes.

BAC and YAC are commonly used host cells for cloning of DNA fragments using specialised vectors.

(b) Less than 2 percent of the genome codes for proteins and the function of over 50 percent of the discovered genes are unknown.

(c) **SNPs** are Single nucleotide polymorphism. Scientists have identified about 1.4 million locations where single base DNA differences occur in humans.

This information helps to revolutionise the processes of finding chromosomal locations for disease – associated sequences and also tracing the human history. **(3 Marks)**

14. Difference between homology and analogy:

Homology	Analogy
(i) Homologous organs are those organs that are anatomically similar but perform different functions.	**(i)** Analogous organs are those that are anatomically not similar but perform same function.
(ii) This type of evolution is called divergent evolution.	**(ii)** This type of evolution is called convergent evolution.
(iii) Homology indicates common ancestry.	**(iii)** Analogy do not share common ancestry.
For example: Thorn and tendrils of *Bougainvillea* and *Cucurbita.*	**For example:** Flippers of penguins and Dolphins.

(3 Marks)

15. (a) Children who had suffered from chicken pox in their childhood may not contract the same disease in their adulthood because they have developed antibody against chicken pox virus. The active memory intiates highly intense response during the second encounter. This kind of immunity is called active immunity which provides protection against the same disease as immune cells already produced antibodies against the disease causing antigens.

(b) Viral infected cells secrete proteins called **interferons** that protect non-infected cells from further viral infection. **(3 Marks)**

16. (a) The limitations related to traditional breeding techniques are as follows:

It is difficult to maintain the purity of the offsprings that are produced by traditional breeding techniques.

It also took a long time and not able to produce many offsprings in one time.

The method of producing thousands of plants through tissue culture from a single explants is called ***micropropagation.***

(b) The advantages of micropropagation are as follows:

(i) Micropropagation is used for the production of many plants in a shorter time.

(ii) Disease free plants can be produced by this method.

(c) Micropropagation is commercially adopted for the production of banana and sugarcane. **(3 Marks)**

17. (a) The organic farmers control pests by developing pest resistant in genetically modified plants. The desired gene of interest are introduced into the plant to make it resistant for pest. For example:

- **Bt cotton:** The cotton plants were incorporated with Bt toxin gene of the bacterium *Bacillus thuringenesis.* The gene which codes for toxic insecticidal proteins are called *cry* gene. Hence, *crylAc* and *cryIIAb* control the cotton bollworm whereas *crylAb* controls corn borer.
- A nematode *Meloidegyne incognitia* infects the roots of tobacco plant and causes reduction in yield. RNA interference (RNAi) involves silencing of a specific RNA. By using *Agrobacterium* vectors, nematode specific gene is introduced into host plant and the introduction of DNA produces both sense and antisense RNA into the host cells. The two RNAs are complementary to each other results in the formation of double-stranded RNA which initiates RNA interference mechanisms and provide protection against the pest.

(b) In conventional pest control method, pesticides are used for killing pest that causes harm to the crop. Pesticides are the toxic chemicals that causes harm to soil, crop as well as humans and animals. This results in reduction in crop yield and soil erosion.

Whereas organic farming does not involve the use of pesticides, hence causes less harm to nature. **(3 Marks)**

18. (a) Selectable markers are used for the identification and elimination of non-transformants that selectively permits the growth of the transformants. The genes encoding resistance to antibiotics such as ampicillin, chloramphenicol, tetracycline and kanamycin are commonly used selectable markers.

Note

Transformation is a procedure through which a piece of DNA is introduced in a host bacterium.

(b) The selectable markers are developed to differentiate recombinants from non-recombinants on the basis of their ability to produce colour in the presence of chromogenic substrate.

In this, a recombinant DNA is inserted within the coding sequence of an enzyme, which is referred as **insertional inactivation**. The presence of a chromogenic substrate gives blue coloured colonies if the plasmid in the bacteria does not have insert.

The presence of insert results in **insertional inactivation** of the beta-galactosidase enzyme and the colonies does not produce any colour and are identified as recombinant colonies. **(3 Marks)**

19. (a) It is necessary to make a cell competent in order to enhance the efficiency of the cell to take up the foreign DNA easily. As DNA being hydrophilic in nature, it cannot pass through the cell membranes. The cell can be made competent by treating it with a specific concentration of a divalent cation such as calcium which increases the efficiency with which DNA enters the bacterium through pores in its cell wall.

(b) **Biolistics** or gene gun is suitable for plants, and in this method the cells are bombarded with high velocity micro-particles of gold or tungsten coated with DNA. **(3 Marks)**

20. ADA (Adenosine deaminase deficiency) can be treated by enzyme replacement therapy in which functional ADA is given to the patient by injection. In this process:

- Lymphocytes from the blood of the patients are grown in a culture outside the body.
- A functional ADA cDNA (using a retroviral vector) is then introduced into these lymphocytes which are subsequently returned to the patient.

Disadvantages associated with enzyme-replacement therapy are:

- This method is not completely curative
- The cells are immortal as the patients require periodic infusion of such genetically engineered lymphocytes.

(3 Marks)

Note

ADA deficiency is caused because of the deletion of the gene that codes for adenosine deaminase enzyme. Severe combined Immunodeficiency disorder (SCID) is caused because of the defect in gene which codes for adenosine deaminase enzyme.

21. *Mycorrhizae* are association between fungi and the root nodules of higher plants. This type of population interaction is called **mutualism.** In this, the fungi help the plant in the absorption of essential nutrients from the soil whereas the plant in turn provides the fungi with energy-yielding carbohydrates.

The interaction between cattle egret and grazing cattle is **commensalism.** In this type of population interaction, the egrets always forage close to where the cattle are grazing because the cattle, as they move stir up and flush out from the vegetation insects which is difficult for the egrets to find and catch. **(3 Marks)**

Note

Commensalism *is a type of population interaction in which one species benefits and the other is neither harmed nor benefited.* ***Mutualism*** *is a type of population interaction in which both the interacting species are benefited from each other.*

22. Difference between Primary and Secondary succession:

Primary Succession	Secondary succession
Primary succession occurs in an area where no living organisms ever existed.	Secondary succession occurs in a area where all the living organisms are lost that are existed there.
For example: Bare rock, ponds and deserts.	For example: The area affected by natural calamities, covered under deforestation.

(3 Marks)

Note

***Ecological succession** refers to the gradual and fairly predictable change in the species composition of a given area.*

SECTION - D

23. (a) Lack of proper education and unawareness about infertility are the main cause for blaming females in India.

People should be given knowledge and awareness about several medical techniques that are available to overcome the infertility problems in both male and female. Educate people that not only females are suffering from infertility as males are also suffering from infertility.

(b) Infertility is caused because of physical, congenital, diseases, drugs, immunological problems or even psychological problems.

(c) When infertility is caused because of inability of the male partner to inseminate the female or because of very sperm count in the ejaculates is corrected by **artificial insemination**.

In this technique, the semen collected either from the husband or a healthy donor is artificially introduced either into the vagina or into the uterus (IUI-Intra-uterine insemination) of the female. **(4 Marks)**

Note

Infertility refers to the inability or failure of a couples to produce children in spite of unprotected sexual co-habitation.

SECTION - E

24. (a) The menstrual phase of the menstruation cycle is starts when the menstrual flow occurs and it lasts for 3-5 days. The menstrual flow results because of the breakdown of endometrial lining of the uterus and its blood vessels which forms liquid that comes out through vagina. Menstruation occurs if the released ovum is not fertilised. **(1 Mark)**

Note

*In human females, menstruation is repeated at an average interval of about 28/29 days and the cycle of events starting one menstruation till the next one is called the **menstrual cycle.***

(b) During the follicular phase, the primary follicles in the ovary grow to become a fully mature Graafian follicle. The endometrium of uterus regenerates through proliferation. This is reason that follicular phase is also called as proliferative phase.

The changes in the ovary and the uterus are induced by changes in the levels of pituitary and ovarian hormones. The secretion of gonadotropins (LH and FSH) increases gradually during this phase and also stimulates follicular development as well as secretion of estrogens by growing follicles. **(2 Marks)**

(c) The level of both LH and FSH increases and attain a peak level in the middle of cycle (about 14th day). Rapid secretion of LH leads to its maximum level during the mid-cycle called LH surge induces rupture of Graafian follicle and thereby release of ovum (ovulation). The ovulatory phase or ovulation is followed by the luteal phase during which the remaining parts of the Graafian follicle transform as the **corpus luteum.**

The corpus luteum secretes a large amount of progesterone which is essential for maintenance of the endometrium. Endometrium is necessary for implantation of the fertilized ovum and other events of pregnancy. During pregnancy all events of the menstrual cycle stop and there is no menstruation. In the absence of fertilisation, the corpus luteum degenerates and this causes disintegration of the endometrium results in menstruation. **(1 Mark)**

(d) **Diagrammatic representation of Graafian follicle:**

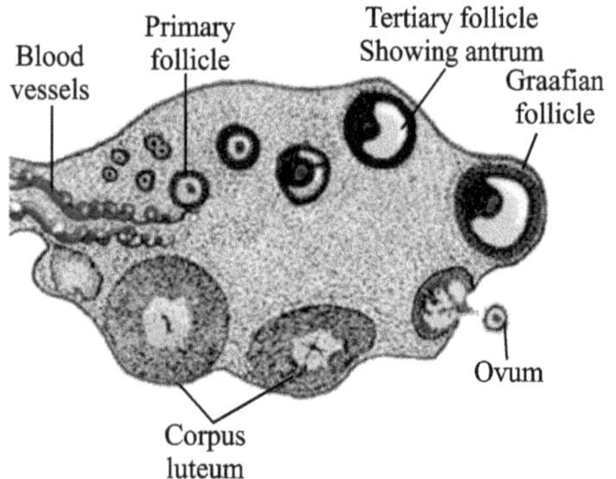

(1 Mark)

OR

(a) The procedure used to ensure cross-pollination in hermaphrodite flower are as follows:

- **Emasculation:** If the female parent bears bisexual flowers, removal of anthers from the flower bud before the anther dehisces by using a pair of forceps is called emasculation.
- **Bagging:** Emasculated flower is covered with a bag of suitable size generally made up of butter paper to prevent contamination of its stigma with unwanted pollen and this process is called bagging.

When the stigma of bagged flower attains receptivity, mature pollen grains collected from anthers of the male parent are dusted on the stigma and the flowers are rebagged and the fruits allowed to develop.

(3 Marks)

The process of transfer of pollen grains to the stigma of a pistil is termed as ***pollination.*** *The pollination can be divided into three types such as autogamy and geitonogamy are the type of self-pollination whereas xenogamy is a type of cross-pollination.*

(b) **Diagrammatic representation of megasporangium of an angiosperm:**

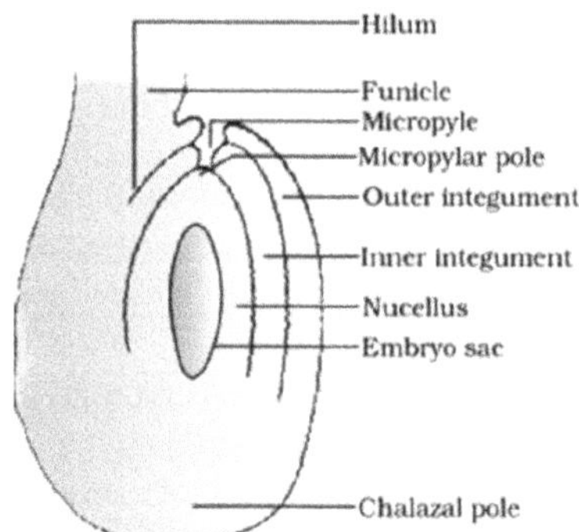

(2 Marks)

25. Matthew Meselson and Franklin Stahl performed the following experiment in 1958 to prove that DNA replicates semiconservatively:

(i) They grwo *E.coli* in medium containing $^{15}NH_4Cl$ (^{15}N is the heavy isotope of nitrogen) as the only nitrogen source for many generations. This result was that ^{15}N was incorporated into newly synthesised DNA.

(ii) This heavy DNA molecule could be distinguished from the normal DNA by centrifugation in a cesium chloride (CsCl) density gradient.

(iii) Then they transferred the cells into a medium with normal $^{14}NH_4Cl$ and took samples at different time intervals as the cells multiplied and extracted the DNA that remained as double-stranded helices. The different samples were separated independently on CsCl gradients to measure the densities of DNA.

(iv) Thus, the DNA that was extracted from the culture one generation after the transfer from ^{15}N to ^{14}N medium had a hybrid or intermediate density. DNA extracted from the culture after another generation was composed of equal amounts of this hybrid DNA and of 'light' DNA. **(5 Marks)**

Taylor and colleagues in 1958 performed experiment by using radioactive thymidine to detect distribution of newly synthesised DNA in the chromosomes was performed on Vicia faba (faba beans). This experiment proved that the DNA in chromosomes also replicate semiconservatively.

OR

(a) (i) In bacteria, there are three major types of RNAs such as mRNA, tRNA and rRNA.

(ii) A single DNA-dependent RNA polymerase synthesises all three types of RNA in prokaryotes.

(iii) **Initiation:** RNA polymerase binds to promoter and initiates the process of transcription. It uses nucleoside triphosphate as substrate and polymerises in a template depended manner.

(iv) **Elongation:** This is the second step involved in bacterial transcription that facilitates the opening of the helix and continues elongation of DNA duplex.

(v) **Termination:** Once the RNA polymerase reaches the terminator region, the nascent RNA and RNA polymerase enzyme falls off, results in the termination of transcription.

The bacterial RNA polymerase requires initiation factor (sigma factor) to initiate the process of transcription and termination factor (Rho factor) to terminate the process of transcription.

Diagrammatic representation of transcription in bacteria:

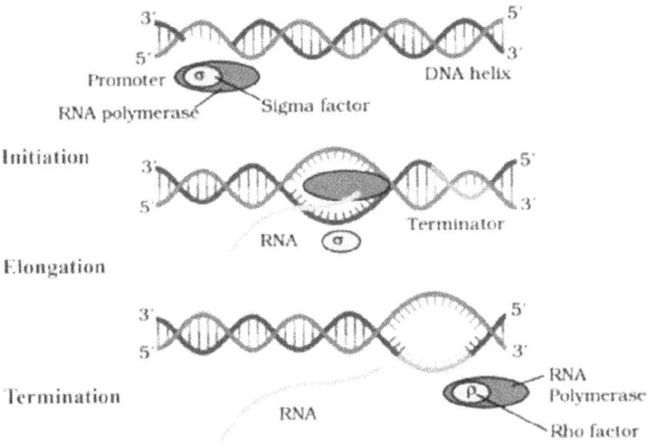

(3 Marks)

(b) The hnRNA or heterogeneous nuclear RNA (hnRNA) is a precursor of mRNA transcribed by RNA polymerase II enzyme in eukaryotes.

The hnRNA is also called primary transcript and it contains both the exons and the introns. It is non-funtional.

So, the process of removal of introns from the exons in a hnRNA is called **splicing** and the exons are joined together by DNA ligase enzyme.

The process of **capping** involves addition of unusual nucleotide (methyl guanosine triphosphate) to the 5'-end of the hnRNA.

The process of **tailing** involves the addition of adenylate residues (200-300) are added at 3'-end in a template independent manner.

The fully processed hnRNA is called mRNA which is transported out of the nucleus for translation.

(2 Marks)

In prokaryotes, the process of transcription and translation occurs simultaneously in the cytoplasm of the cell. Whereas in eukaryotes, the process of transcription takes place in the nucleus and translation takes place in the cytoplasm.

26. (a) The two growth curves are exponential growth curves and logistic growth curves.

Diagrammatic representation of Growth curves:

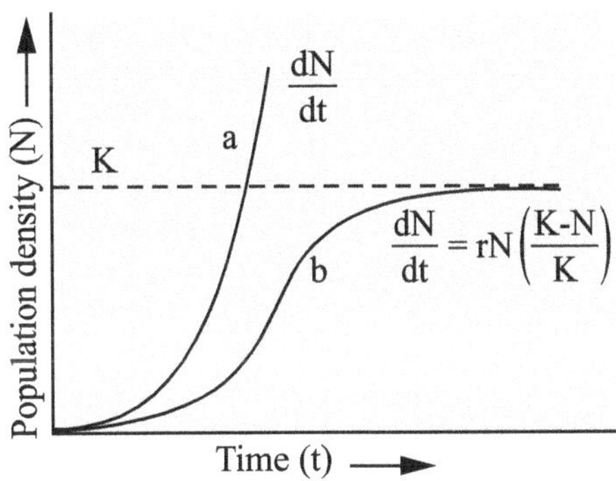

A represents exponential growth curve whereas b represents logistic growth curve. **(2 Marks)**

(b) The exponential growth curve is formed when the availability of resources in the habitat are unlimited. A J-shaped curve is formed in exponential growth curve.

The exponential growth equation is $N_t = N_0 e^{rt}$

where

N_t = Population density after time t

N_0 = Population density at time zero

r = intrinsic rate of natural increase

e = the base of natural logarithms

Logistic growth occurs when the available resources are limited results in competition between individuals for limited resources. So, the fittest individual will survive and reproduce.

A S-shaped or sigmoid growth curve is formed. The logistic growth equation is

$$\frac{dN}{dt} = rN\left[\frac{K-N}{K}\right]$$

where,

N = Population density at time t

r = Intrinsic rate of natural increase

K = Carrying capacity **(2 Marks)**

(c) The human population at present is represented by the logistic growth. No, the growth is not sustainable because with the growing population and the depleting natural resources, it would be difficult in the future to fulfil the demands of growing population. **(1 Mark)**

Note

***Carrying capacity (K)** is defined as in a given habitat that has enough resources to support a maximum possible number, beyond which no further growth is possible.*

OR

(a) The four function functions of an ecosystem are as follows:

- **Productivity:** The productivity is defined as the rate of biomass production. Productivity is represented by the autotrophic phytoplanktons, algae, floating abd submerged plants.
- **Decomposition:** Decomposers such as fungi, bacteria, flagellates. The decomposers break down complex organic matter into inorganic substances such as carbon dioxide, water and nutrients.
- **Energy flow:** There is a unidirectional flow of energy from the sun to producers and then to consumers.
- **Nutrient cycling:** The movement of nutrient elements through the various components of an ecosystem. The pond ecosystem involves the process of conversion of inorganic substances into organic material with the help of solar energy.

(4 Marks)

(b) In the pond ecosystem, the Grazing Food chain is the major food chain for the energy flow:

Producer → Primary consumer → Secondary consumer → Tertiary consumer

(Phytoplankton) (Zooplanktn) (small fishes) (Large fishes)

(1 Mark)

Delhi 2016

CBSE Board Solved Paper

Time Allowed : 3 Hours — ***Maximum Marks : 70***

General Instructions:

(i) There are a total of **26** questions and **five** sections in the question paper. All questions are compulsory.

(ii) Section **A** contains question number **1** to **5**, Very Short Answer type questions of **1** mark each.

(iii) Section **B** contains question number **6** to **10**, Short Answer type–**I** questions of **2** marks each.

(iv) Section **C** contains question number **11** to **22**, Short Answer type–**II** questions of **3** marks each.

(v) Section **D** contains question number **23**, Value Based Question of **4** marks.

(vi) Section **E** contains question number **24** to **26**, Long Answer type questions of **5** marks each.

(vii) There is no overall choice in the question paper, however, an internal choice is provided in **one** question of **2** marks, **one** question of **3** marks and all the **three** questions of **5** marks. In these questions, an examinee is to attempt any **one** of the **two** given alternatives.

SECTION - A

1. According to de-Vries what is saltation ?

2. Excessive nutrients in a fresh water body cause fish mortality. Give two reasons.

3. Suggest the breeding method most suitable for animals that are below average in milk productivity.

4. State a difference between a gene and an allele.

5. Suggest a technique to a researcher who needs to separate fragments of DNA.

SECTION - B

6. Explain the significance of meiocytes in a diploid organism.

7. Mention the kind of biodiversity of more than a thousand varieties of mangoes in India represent. How is it possible?

8. List the events that reduce the Biological Oxygen Demand (BOD) of a primary effluent during sewage treatment.

9. Discuss the role the enzyme DNA ligase plays during DNA replication.

10. Name the causative organism of the disease amoebiasis. List three symptoms of the disease.

OR

Identify 'A', 'B', 'C' and 'D' in the given table.

Crop	Variety	Resistance to disease
A	Himgiri	Leaf rust
Cauliflower	Pusa Shubhra	B
Brassica	Pusa Swarnim	C
Cowpea	B	Bacterial blight

SECTION - C

11. Why is breast-feeding recommended during the initial period of an infant's growth ? Give reasons.

12. Give an example of an autosomal recessive trait in humans. Explain its pattern of inheritance with the help of a cross.

13. Describe the experiment that helped Louis Pasteur to dismiss the theory of spontaneous generation of life.

14. Plant breeding technique has helped sugar industry in North India. Explain how.

15. Suggest and describe a technique to obtain multiple copies of a gene of interest *in vitro*.

16. What is a GMO ? List any five possible advantages of a GMO to a farmer.

17. During a school trip to 'Rohtang Pass', one of your classmate suddenly developed 'altitude sickness'. But, she recovered after sometime.

(a) Mention one symptom to diagnose the sickness.

(b) What caused the sickness ?

(c) How could she recover by herself after sometime ?

18. How has RNAi technique helped to prevent the infestation of roots in tobacco plants by a nematode *Meloidegyne incognitia ?*

19. "In a food-chain, a trophic level represents a functional level, not a species." Explain.

OR

(a) Name any two places where it is essential to install electrostatic precipitators. Why it is required to do so?

(b) Mention one limitation of the electrostatic precipitator.

20. Prior to a sports event blood & urine samples of sportspersons are collected for drug tests.

(a) Why is there a need to conduct such tests ?

(b) Name the drugs the authorities usually look for.

(c) Write the generic names of two plants from which these drugs are obtained.

21. Describe the experiment that helped demonstrate the semi-conservative mode of DNA replication.

22. Given below is a list of six micro-organisms. State their usefulness to humans.

(a) *Nucleopolyhedrovirus*

(b) *Saccharomyces cerevisiae*

(c) *Monascus purpureus*

(d) *Trichoderma polysporum*

(e) *Penicillium notatum*

(f) *Propionibacterium sharmanii*

SECTION - D

23. Reproductive and Child Healthcare (RCH) programmes are currently in operation. One of the major tasks of these programmes is to create awareness amongst people about the wide range of reproduction related aspects. As this is important and essential for building a reproductively healthy society.

(a) "Providing sex education in schools is one of the ways to meet this goal." Give four points in support of your opinion regarding this statement.

(b) List any two 'indicators' that indicate a reproductively healthy society.

SECTION - E

24. (a) Explain the post-pollination events leading to seed production in angiosperms.

(b) List the different types of pollination depending upon the source of pollen grain.

OR

(a) Briefly explain the events of fertilization and implantation in an adult human female.

(b) Comment on the role of placenta as an endocrine gland.

25. (a) How are the following formed and involved in DNA packaging in a nucleus of a cell ?

(i) Histone octomer

(ii) Nucleosome

(iii) Chromatin

(b) Differentiate between Euchromatin and Heterochromatin.

OR

Explain the role of lactose as an inducer in a *lac* operon.

26. (a) Why should we conserve biodiversity ? How can we do it ?

(b) Explain the importance of biodiversity hot-spots and sacred groves.

OR

(a) Represent diagrammatically three kinds of age-pyramids for human populations.

(b) How does an age pyramid for human population at given point of time helps the policy-makers in planning for future.

Solutions

SECTION - A

1. According to Hugo de Varies saltation is a single step large mutation. He said that speciation is caused due to mutation. Saltation is responsible for speciation. **(1 Mark)**

Mutation is defined as the sudden and permanant alteration in the nucleotide sequence of DNA.

2. Fish mortality rate increases due **to algal bloom** that is caused due to the presence of large amount of nutrients in the water bodies. Excessive nutrients support the growth of algae in the water bodies that deteriorate the quality of water by depleting the dissolved oxygen in water. **(1 Mark)**

3. Outcrossing is the best known breeding method for animals that are below average in milk productivity. This method involves the mating of animals within the same breed that have no common ancestors on both side of their pedigree for 4-6 generations. **(1 Mark)**

4. The difference between gene and allele are as follows:

Gene	Allele
(i) Gene is a segment of DNA that controls a specific trait.	(i) Allele is defined as specific form of a gene.
(ii) They are responsible for the expression of specific traits.	(ii) Alleles are responsible for variation as a specific trait can be expressed.
(iii) They are not found in pairs.	(iii) They are always found in pairs.

5. DNA fragments are separated by using molecular biology technique called gel electrophoresis. In this technique, DNA molecules are separated on the basis of their size in an electric field. DNA is negatively charge so it moves towards a positively charged anode in an agarose gel matrix. **(1 Mark)**

As, DNA fragments are separated according to their size through the pores of agarose gel so, ***smaller the size of fragment farther it moves.***

SECTION - B

6. Meiocytes are specialised cells that are found in sexually reproductive organisms. Meiocytes undergo the process of meiosis in order to produce male and female gametes that carry one set of chromosomes. Thus, they help in maintaining the chromosome number in organisms. **(2 Marks)**

7. In India, there are around 1000 different varieties of mangoes produced due to genetic diversity. Genetic diversity is produced due to difference in soil found in different regions. It also occur due to different agricultural practices as well as use of various horticulture techniques that are used in India. **(2 Marks)**

Genetic diversity is defined as the type of diversity in which the number and types of genes as well as chromosomes that are found in different species. It leads to variation in the genes and their alleles in the same species. It leads to speciation as well as evolution of new species.

8. The primary effluent is passed into large aeration tanks just after the primary treatment. In the large aeration tanks, the primary effluent is constantly agitated mechanically and air is also pumped into it. This process supports the vigorous growth of useful microbes that consists of flocs of bacteria and fungi. Such microbes consume large portion of organic matter to the effluent also reduce the biochemical oxygen demand of the primary effluent. **(2 Marks)**

9. During DNA replication, the lagging strand of template DNA is discontinuous (5'→ 3'). The formed segments are short segments of replicated DNA (3'→ 5') are called **OKAZAKI** fragments. The OKAZAKI fragments of DNA **are joined together by DNA ligase enzyme.** **(2 Marks)**

10. Amoebiasis or amoebic dysentery is caused by ***Entamoeba histolytica***. **(2 Marks)**

Symptoms of Amoebiasis:

- Appearance of blood in the stool.
- Pain in the abdomen.
- Fever
- Diarrhoea

OR

Crop	Variety	Resistance To disease
Wheat	*Himgiri*	Leaf rust
Cauliflower	*Pusa Shubhra*	**Black rot and curl blight**
Brassica	*Pusa Swarnim*	**White rust**
Cowpea	***Pusa komal***	Bacterial blight

(2 Marks)

SECTION - C

11. Doctors recommend breast feeding during the initial period of infant's growth to maintain the health of baby. The first yellow milk that comes out from the mammary gland of the mother just after parturition is called colostrum. It is rich in protein such as lactalbumin and lactoprotein. It also contains antibody IgA that provide innate immunity to the infant. **(3 Marks)**

12. **Sickle cell anaemia** is an example of autosomal recessive hereditary disorder. In this disorder, the erythrocytes become sickle shaped due to deficiency of oxygen. This disorder is caused due to the formation of abnormal haemoglobin-S. Genes for sickle cell erythrocytes is represented by **HbS** whereas normal genes are represented by **HbA**.

Representation of cross of sickle cell anaemia:

Parents Carrier man Carrier women

Gametes $Hb^A\ Hb^S$ X $Hb^A\ Hb^S$

$(Hb^A)\ (Hb^S)$ $(Hb^A)\ (Hb^S)$

Offspring Hb^AHb^A Hb^AHb^S Hb^AHb^S $Hb^S\ Hb^S$

ratio 1 : 2 : 1 **(3 Marks)**

Note

In case of sickle cell anaemia, abnormal haemoglobin HbS is differ from normal haemoglobin HbA only by one amino acid at 6th amino acid of beta-globin chain of haemoglobin. The glutamic acid is replaced by valine due to substitution mutation of Thymine (T) by Adenine (A) at the second position of triplet codon such as CTC into CAC. The substitution mutation occurs at 11th chromosome. Codon CTC is transcribed into GAG that codes for amino acid glutamic acid. Whereas CAC is transcribed into GUG that codes amino acid valine.

13. Louis Pasteur conducted the Swan-necked flask experiment to dismiss the theory of spontaneous generation of life which is as follows:

(a) Two swan-necked flasks are used that contains nutrient broth.

(b) The nutrient broths were made sterile by boiling in order to kill existing microbes present in the broth.

(c) One of the swan necked flask was broken just after sterilisation and kept open for some time.

(d) The dust particles contain bacteria through air entered into the broken neck of flask.

(e) The broth present in broken flask became cloudy whereas broth of unbroken flask remained clear.

(f) The appearance of cloudiness of nutrient broth indicates the presence of microbial growth in the broken flask.

(g) This experiment concluded that, appearance of microbial life in the broken flask after sterilisation indicates that pre-existing life form. **(3 Marks)**

14. In North India, a variety of sugarcane such as *Saccharum barberi* was grown that had poor sugar content and low yield. Whereas another sugarcane variety *Saccharum officinarum* that had high sugar content and thicker stems. This variety of sugarcane does not grown in North India. So these two different varieties of sugarcane were crossed in order to obtain the desired qualities of sugarcane such as higher yield, high sugar content, thick stems and ability to grow in the belt of North India. **(3 Marks)**

15. With the help of recombinant DNA technology called Polymerase Chain Reaction (PCR) technique multiple copies of gene of interest are obtained in *Vitro.* A single PCR amplification cycle involves three steps which are as follows:

(a) **Denaturation:** This is the first step of PCR, in which the target DNA is heated at high temperature such 94-96°C. It facilitates the separation of two strands of DNA. Each separated strand of DNA acts as a template for synthesis of DNA.

(b) **Annealing:** This is the second step of PCR, in which two oligonucleotide primers are used to hybridize each single stranded template DNA. The sequence of primers is complementary to 3' end of the template DNA strand.

This step of PCR occurs at low temperature 40-60°C than denaturation. The annealing temperature depends upon the length and sequence of the primers.

(c) **Extension:** This is third and last step of PCR, in which enzyme *Taq*DNA polymerase synthesizes the DNA between the primers. This step also requires dNTPS and Mg^{2++}. The optimum temperature for extension is 72°C. **(3 Marks)**

Note

Enzyme used in PCR is a DNA polymerase such as Taq DNA polymerase. This enzyme is stable at high temperature as it is isolated from thermostable bacteria Thermus aquaticus.

16. **GMOs are Genetically modified organisms**. They are defined as a living organisms whose genes are manipulated or altered by using recombinant DNA technology.

The advantages of GMOs are as follows:

(i) GMOs are resistant to diseases, pest and insects. So it reduces the use of harmful pesticides and other chemical fertilisers that harm the crops.

(ii) GMOs crops are more tolerant to abiotic stress such as cold, drought, heat and salt stress.

(iii) Such crops have high crop yield and nutritional value.

(iv) GMOs reduce post-harvest loss of crops.

(v) GMOs increase the efficiency of mineral usage by plants and also prevents exhaustion of soil. **(3 Marks)**

Note

Golden rice is genetically modified crop which is obtained by recombinant DNA technology. It contains good quantities of beta-carotene which is a principal source of vitamin A. Due to the presence of beta-carotene, the rice grain appear golden in colour.

17. (a) Altitude sickness is also called **mountain sickness.** It is caused due to the presence of low oxygen pressure at higher altitude. Nausea and fatigue are the symptoms of altitude sickness. **(1 Mark)**

(b) Altitude sickness in person is caused when the body is not able to get sufficient oxygen due to atmospheric pressure. **(1 Mark)**

(c) After some time her body is able to adapt the changing atmosphere. Her body is ready to compensate low oxygen pressure by producing more red blood cells. It also tends to decrease the bind affinity for haemoglobin by increasing breathing rate. **(1 Mark)**

18. *Meloidogyne incognitia* is a nematode that causes infections in the root of tobacco plants. This reduces the yield of tobacco plants. In order to protect the tobacco plants from infection, a process called **RNA interference** occurs in all eukaryotic organisms as a method of cellular defense. The process of RNA interference involves **mRNA silencing** because of complementary dsRNA molecule that get binds to and prevents the translation of mRNA.

The complementary RNA is obtained due to the infection by viruses that contain a RNA genome or mobile genetic elements (transposons). It replicate via a RNA intermediate.

By using *Agrobacterium* vectors, nematode-specific gene were used to introduced into the host plant. After the introduction of DNA into the host, it produces both sense and anti-sense RNA in the host cells.

The two RNA's are complementary to each other formed a double strand (dsRNA) that initiates the process of RNAi and silenced the specific mRNA of the nematode. After that, the nematode is not able to survive in a transgenic host expressing specific interfering RNA.

In this way, the transgenic plant got itself to be protected from the parasite. **(3 Marks)**

19. In a trophic level, the position of species is determined by their function as well as mode of nutrition in a specific food chain. The species may occupy more than one trophic level within the same ecosystem. If the mode of nutrition of species changes results in the change in trophic level of species. One species can become primary level of consumer in one food chain and also become secondary level of consumer in another food chain. **(3 Marks)**

Note

In ecology, food chain is defined as the sequence of transfer of energy and matter in the form of food from one organism to other. Food chain is divided into four levels such as producers (plants), primary consumers (herbivores), secondary consumers (carnivores) and tertiary consumers (carnivore).

OR

(a) Electrostatic precipitator is installed in automobiles and thermal power plants because a large amount of harmful gases are released from automobiles and thermal power plants. Electrostatic precipitators are used to remove particulate matter from their exhaust.

(b) One drawback of using electrostatic precipitators is that it cannot remove particulate matter having size less than 2.5 micrometer in diameter. Such particulate matters are harmful for health. **(3 Marks)**

20. (a) There is a need to conduct blood and urine test for sports persons because some sports persons take narcotics analgesics, anabolic steroids, diuretics and several hormones in order to increase their muscle strength and performance. These tests help to determine whether a sports person has taken any drugs and it also ensures a fair play. **(1 Mark)**

(b) The sports authorities are usually looking for narcotic drugs such as analgesics, diuretics and hormones such as gonadotropins and steroids, opiates such as oxy contin and cannabinoids. **(1 Mark)**

(c) The generic names of two plants are given below:

- Smack or heroin is obtained from the *Papaver somniferum.* **(½ Mark)**
- Ganja and marijuana is obtained from the *Cannabis sativa.* **(½ Mark)**

21. The semiconservative nature of DNA replication was experimentally proved by Matthew Meselson and Franklin stahl in 1958 by using heavy nitrogen (^{15}N) in *E.coli*. It involves following steps such as:

(1) They grow *E.coli* in a medium containing $^{15}NH_4Cl$. As nitrogen serves as the only source for many generations. ^{15}N is the heavy isotope of nitrogen. So, the ^{15}N was incorporated into newly synthesized DNA.

(2) This heavy DNA molecule is distinguished from normal DNA molecule by cesium chloride (CsCl) density gradient centrifugation. Then they transfer the cells into another medium containing normal $^{14}NH_4Cl$. They took the samples at different time interval as the cells multiplied and then DNA was extracted from the cells. In this ways, different samples were separated independently on CsCl gradients in order to measure the densities of DNA.

(3) The DNA was extracted from the culture medium one generation after the transfer from ^{15}N to ^{14}N medium had a hybrid or intermediate densities. The DNA extracted from the culture medium after another generation was composed of equal amounts of this hybrid and of light DNA. **(3 Marks)**

Diagrammatic representation of semiconservative DNA replication:

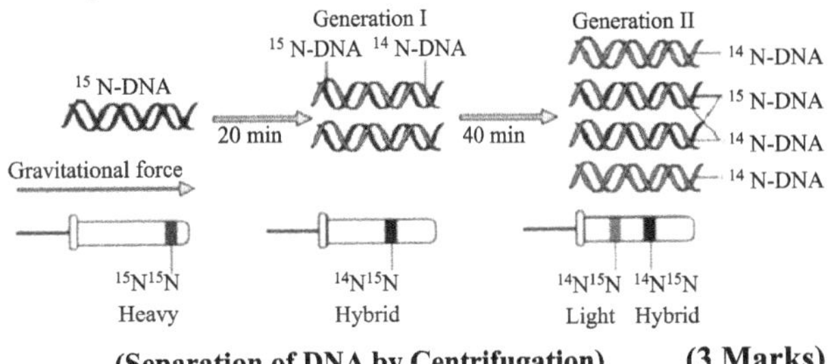

(Separation of DNA by Centrifugation) **(3 Marks)**

An experiment was performed by Taylor and his colleagues in 1958 to experimentally proved that the DNA in chromosomes also replicate semiconservatively. This experiment involves radioactive thymidine in order to detect the distribution of newly synthesised DNA in the chromosomes. This experiment was performed on Vicia faba (faba beans).

22. (i) ***Nucleopolyhedovirus*** **:** *Nucleopolyhedovirus* is a biological control agent that is used as a species-specific insecticide. **(½ Mark)**

(ii) ***Saccharomyces cerevisiae*** **:** *Saccharomyces cerevisiae* is also called baker's yeast. It is used in baking and beverage industry. It is used for making breads, south Indian cuisine, cakes and in beverages it is used for making alcohol. **(½ Mark)**

(iii) ***Monscus perpureus*** **:** It is yeast that is used for the production of a blood-cholesterol lowering agents called as **statins.** **(½ Mark)**

(iv) ***Trichoderma polysporum:*** It is fungus used for the formation of bioactive molecule called **cyclosporine A.** It is used as an immuno suppressive agent in organ-transplant patients. **(½ Mark)**

(v) ***Penicillium notatum:*** It is a bacteria used for the production of antibiotics. **(½ Mark)**

(vi) ***Propionibacterium sharmanii:*** It is a bacterium used for the production of "Swiss cheese". The appearance of large holes in the 'Swiss cheese" is because of the production of carbon dioxide by bacteria. **(½ Mark)**

SECTION - D

23. (a) Sex education is one of the best ways in order to create a reproductively healthy society. It also helps people in following ways: **(2 Marks)**

- Sex education helps to proper knowledge to curious adolescents. It helps them to prevent from being them misguided and also prevents them from believing them about sex-related aspects.
- It helps to create awareness about sexually transmitted disease and its prevention ways.
- Sex education provides proper knowledge about reproductive organs and other changes related to puberty to the adolescents.

(b) The indicators that represent a reproductively healthy society are as follows: **(2 Marks)**

- Increase medical facilities for all sex related problems.
- On time detection and better cure of sexually transmitted diseases.

SECTION - E

24. (a) **Pollination is a defined as the process of transfer of pollen grains from anthers to stigma.** It involves followings steps such as: **(3 Marks)**

- When the pollen grains fall on the stigma, pollen tube is formed and it enters one of the synergids and also releases two male gametes.
- One of the male gametes moves towards the egg and fuse to form a zygote.
- While the other male gamete fuses with polar nuclei and forms a primary endosperm nucleus. This process is termed as **triple fusion.**
- The central cell becomes the primary endosperm cell after the process of triple endosperm. The primary endosperm nucleus forms endosperm whereas zygote is further developed into the embryo.
- A seed refers to the fertilized ovules that are further inside a fruit.
- The integuments of the ovules are hardened to form the seed coat whereas the micropyle facilitates the entry of oxygen and water into the seeds.

(b) There are three different types of pollinations such as: **(2 Marks)**

(i) **Autogamy:** This type of pollination requires transfer of pollen grains from anther to stigma of same flower. In this, the anther and stigma lie close to each other so that self-pollination can occur. Some plants such as *Oxalis, Commeline* and *Viola* produces two types of flowers such as **Chasmogamous flowers:** Such flowers are similar to the flowers of other species with exposed anthers and stigma.

Cleistogamous flowers: Such flowers do not open at all. The anthers and stigma lie close to each other.

(ii) **Geitonogamy:** In this type of pollination, the transfer of pollen grain from anther to the stigma of another flower of same plant. It involves cross-pollination through pollinating agents. But genetically it is similar to autogamy as the pollen grains come from the same plant.

(iii) **Xenogamy:** This type of pollination involves transfer of pollen grains from anther to stigma of a different plant. In this, pollination brings genetically different types of pollen grains to the stigma.

Plants uses one biotic agent such as animals and two abiotic agent such as wind and water for pollination.

OR

(a) **Fertilization:** The process of fertilization is defined as the process of fusion of a sperm with an ovum.

- Fertilization occurs only if the ovum and sperms are transported simultaneously to the ampullary-isthmic junction.
- During the process of fertilization, a sperm comes in contact with the *zona pellucida* layer of the ovum and also induces the changes in the membrane in order to block the entry of additional sperms.
- Sperm secretion help it to enter into the cytoplasm of the ovum through the zona pellucida and the plasma membrane.
- It induces the completion of the meiotic division of the secondary oocyte.
- The second meiotic division is unequal results in the formation of a second polar body and a haploid ovum.
- Zygote is formed by the fusion of haploid nucleus of the sperms and the ovum.

Implantation:

- The mitotic division starts when the zygote moves through the isthmus of the oviduct called cleavage towards the uterus. It forms 2, 4, 8, 16 daughter cells called blastomeres.
- Then, the embryo with 8 to 16 blastomeres stages is called morula.
- It continues to divide and then transforms into blastocyst as it moves further into the uterus.
- The blastomeres present in the blastocyst are arranged into an outer layer called trophoblast whereas the inner groups of cells are attached to the trophoblast called inner cell mass.
- After this, the trophoblast layer gets attached to the endometrium whereas the inner cell mass gets differentiated into the embryo.
- After attachment, the uterine cells rapidly and covers the blastocyst.
- Now the blastocyst becomes embedded in the endometrium of the uterus and this process is called **Implantation** that results in pregnancy. **(3 Marks)**

(b) Placenta plays an essential role during pregnancy as it facilitates the supply of oxygen and nutrients to the embryo. It also helps in the removal of carbon dioxide and other metabolic waster produced by the embryo. It also acts as an endocrine tissue and produces hormones such as human chorionic gonadotropin (hCG), human placental lactogen(hPL), estrogens, and progestrogens. Relaxin hormone is also secreted by the ovary during the later phase of pregnancy. **(2 Marks)**

25. (a) (i) Histone octomer: The histones are positively charged basic proteins. They are rich in basic amino acid such as lysine and arginines. They are organised to form a unit of eight molecules called a histone octomer.

(ii) Nucleosome: The negatively charged DNA molecule is wrapped around the positively charged histone octomer in order to form a structure called nucleosome. In a typical nucleosome, 200 bp of DNA helix are present.

(iii) Chromatin: The nucleosomes are unit together to form a chromatin. The nucleosome appears like beads-on-strings on the chromatin. It is packed to form chromatin fibres that further coil and condense at the metaphasic stage of cell division in order to form chromosome. It involves non-histone proteins for packaging called non-histone chromosomal protein (NHC). **(3 Marks)**

(b) The difference between euchromatin and hetero chromatin are as follows:

Euchromatin	Heterochromatin
(i) It is region of chromatin that is loosely packed.	(i) It is region of chromatin that is densely packed.
(ii) It stains light.	(ii) It stains dark
(iii) Euchromatins are transcriptionally active	(iii) Heterochromatin are transcriptionally inactive.

(2 Marks)

OR

Lactose acts as the substrate for enzyme beta-galactosidase. This enzyme regulates the switching on and off the operon because of this it is termed as inducer. So, in the absence of glucose (carbon source), if lactose is added in the growth medium of the bacteria. The lactose is transported into the cells by the action of permease enzyme that increases permeability of the cell to beta-galactosides.

Lactose induces the operon in following manner:

- In a *lac* operon, the repressor protein is synthesised from the *i* gene.
- This repressor protein gets bind with the operator region of the operon and prevents RNA polymerase enzyme from transcribing the operon.
- In the presence of lactose as an inducer, the repressor protein is inactivated. It allows RNA polymerase enzyme to activate the promoter and initiates the process of transcription. **(5 Marks)**

26. (a) There is need to conserve biodiversity because of the following reasons:

- Commercially important products such as food, timber and other essential industrial products are obtained from nature.
- Oxygen production and pollination is totally dependent on nature.
- There is need to conserve the endangered species and protect the biodiversity for our future generations.

Biodiversity can be conserved in two ways:

(i) **In situ conservation:** It involves the conservation of plants and animals species in their natural habitat. For this, biodiversity hotspots are being identified and protected. It involves wildlife sanctuaries, national parks and biosphere reserves.

(ii) Ex-situ conservation: The threatened and endangered species are taken out of their natural habitats and kept in special setting like zoological gardens and wildlife parks.

(iii) Cryopreservation: The gametes of endangered plants and animals are kept viable by preserving them at a very low temperature (-196°C) in a liquid nitrogen. **(3 Marks)**

(b) Importance of biodiversity hotspots:

Biodiversity hotspots are regions that contain high level of species richness and higher degree of endemism. Such areas are very important because the total number of biodiversity hotspots in the world is 34 and hotspots can reduce the mass extinction by approximately 30%. It involves biodiversity regions such as Western Ghats and Sri-Lanka, Indo-Burma and Himalaya covers high biodiversity regions.

Importance of scared grooves:

Scared grooves are the forest regions that involve all trees and wildlife species. It provide protection all plants and wildlife species.

In India, the scared grooves involve:

- Western Ghats regions of Karnataka and Maharashtra
- Khasi and Jaintia Hills in Meghalaya
- Aravalli Hills in Rajasthan
- Sarguja, Chanda and Baster areas of Madhya Pradesh. **(2 Marks)**

OR

(a) Age pyramid is defined as a way for representing the age-sex structure of a population. There are three types of age distribution pyramids such as expanding, stable and declining. A population is composed of individuals of different age groups.

Diagrammatic representation of age pyramids for human population:

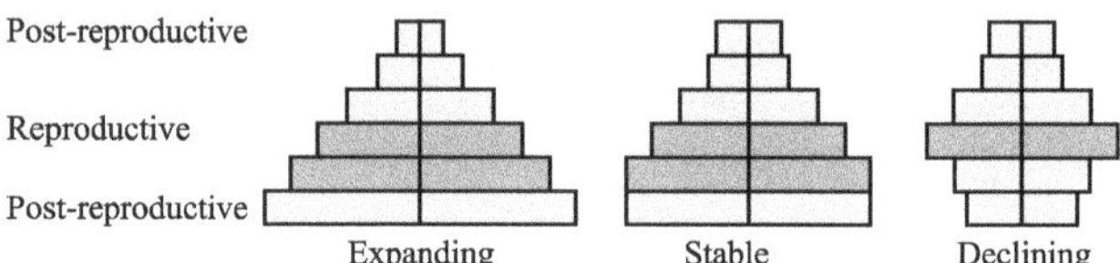

(3 Marks)

(b) The structure of age pyramid helps in the determination of growth status of the population. It involves three types of structure that represents that whether the population is expanding, stable or declining. The structure of age pyramids for human population emphasis on providing food to population, development of proper health care facilities and so on.

For example: If the human population is growing then, the policy makers will make the policies to increase the food resources for **(2 Marks)**

All India 2015

CBSE Board Solved Paper

Time Allowed : 3 Hours | *Maximum Marks : 70*

General Instructions:

(i) There are a total of **26** questions and **five** sections in the question paper. **All** questions are compulsory.

(ii) Section **A** contains question number **1** to **5**, Very Short Answer **type** questions of **one** mark each.

(iii) Section **B** contains question number **6** to **10**, Short Answer type **I** questions of **two** marks each.

(iv) Section **C** contains question number **11** to **22**, Short Answer type **II** questions of **three** marks each.

(v) Section **D** contains question number **23**, Value Based Question of **four** marks.

(vi) Section **E** contains question number **24** to **26**, Long Answer type questions of **five** marks each.

(vii) There is no overall choice in the question paper, however, an internal choice is provided in **one** question of **two** marks, **one** question of **three** marks and **all three** questions of **five** marks. An examinee is to attempt any **one** of the questions out of the **two** given in the question paper with the same question number.

SECTION - A

1. How many chromosomes do drones of honeybee possess? Name the type of cell division involved in the production of sperms by them.

2. What is a cistron?

3. Retroviruses have no DNA. However, the DNA of the infected host cell does possess viral DNA. How is it possible?

4. Why do children cured by enzyme-replacement therapy for adenosine deaminase deficiency need periodic treatment?

5. List two advantages of the use of unleaded petrol in automobiles as fuel.

SECTION - B

6. Why do moss plants produce very large number of male gametes? Provide one reason. What are these gametes called?

7. Select the homologous structures from the combinations given below:

(i) Forelimbs of whales and bats

(ii) Tuber of potato and sweet potato

(iii) Eyes of octopus and mammals

(iv) Thorns of *Bougainvillea* and tendrils of *Cucurbita*

(b) State the kind of evolution they represent.

8. (a) Why are the plants raised through micro propagation termed as somaclones?

(b) Mention two advantages of this technique.

9. Explain the different steps involved during primary treatment phase of sewage.

10. What is mutualism? Mention any two examples where the organisms involved are commercially exploited in agriculture.

OR

List any four techniques where the principle of ex-situ conservation of biodiversity has been employed.

SECTION - C

11. State what is apomixis. Comment on its significance. How can it be commercially used?

12. During a monohybrid cross involving at all pea plant with a dwarf pea plant, the off spring populations were tall and dwarf in equal ratio. Work out a cross to show how it is possible.

13. Explain the significance of satellite DNA in DNA fingerprinting technique.

14. What does the following equation represent? Explain $p^2 + 2pq + q^2 = 1$

15. A heavily bleeding and bruised road accident victim was brought to a nursing home. The doctor immediately gave him an injection to protect him against a deadly disease.

(a) Write what did the doctor inject into the patient's body.

(b) How do you think this injection would protect the patient against the disease?

(c) Name the disease against which this injection was given and the kind of immunity it provides.

16. Enumerate any six essentials of good, effective Dairy Farm Management Practices.

17. State the medicinal value and the bioactive molecules produced by *Streptococcus*, *Monascus* and *Trichoderma*.

OR

What are methanogens? How do they help to generate biogas?

18. Rearrange the following in the current sequences to accomplish an important biotechnological reaction:
    (a) In vitro synthesis of region of DNA of interest
    (b) Chemically synthesised oligonucleotides
    (c) Enzyme DNA-polymerase
    (d) Complementary region of DNA
    (e) Genomic DNA template
    (f) Nucleotides provided
    (g) Primers
    (h) Thermostable DNA-polymerase (from *Thermusaquaticus*)
    (i) Denaturation of ds-DNA

19. Describe any three potential applications of genetically modified plants.

20. How did an American Company, Eli Lilly use the knowledge of r-DNA technology to produce human insulin?

21. How do snails, seeds, bears, zooplanktons, fungi and bacteria adapt to condition sun favourable for their survival?

22. With the help of a flow chart, show the phenomenon of biomagnification of DDT in an aquatic food chain.

SECTION - D

23. Your school has been selected by the Department of Education to organize and host an interschool seminar on "Reproductive Health-Problems and Practices". However, many parents are reluctant to permit their wards to attend it. Their argument is that the topic is "too embarrassing."

Put forth four arguments with appropriate reasons and explanation to justify the topic to be very essential and timely.

SECTION - E

24. (a) Plan an experiment and prepare a flow chart of the steps that you would follow to ensure that the seeds are formed only from the desired sets of pollen grains. Name the type of experiment that you carried out.
    (b) Write the importance of such experiments.

OR

Describe the roles of pituitary and ovarian hormones during the menstrual cycle in a human female.

25. (a) Why are thalassemia and haemophilia categorized as Mendelian disorders? Write the symptoms of these diseases. Explain their pattern of inheritance in humans.
    (b) Write the genotypes of the normal parents producing a haemophilic son.

OR

How do m-RNA, t-RNA and ribosomes help in the process of translation?

26. (a) List the different attributes that a population has and not an individual organism.
    (b) What is population density? Explain any three different ways the population density can be measured, with the help of an example each.

OR

"It is often said that the pyramid of energy is always upright. On the other hand, the pyramid of biomass can be both upright and inverted." Explain with the help of examples and sketches.

Solutions

SECTION - A

1. In honeybees, the females are diploid and males are haploid as they have total 16 chromosomes.

   The males are developed from unfertilized eggs and these eggs chromosome are multiply mitotically to produce more haploid cells. **(1 Mark)**

2. Cistron is that segment of DNA which specifies synthesis of a polypeptide. **(1 Mark)**

Note

ADA deficiency is caused because of the deletion of the gene that codes far adenosine deaminase enzyme. SCID (Severe Combined Immunodificiency disorder) is caused because of the defect in gene which codes for adenosine deaminase enzyme.

3. After attacking the host cell, retrovirus enters into macrophages (as in case of HIV) where RNA genome of the virus replicates to form viral DNA with the help of enzyme reverse transcriptase. This viral DNA gets incorporated into the host cell's DNA and directs the infected cells to produce more viruses. The macrophages continue to produce virus and works as a HIV factory. Hence, the infected host cell possesses viral DNA. **(1 Mark)**

4. The introduction of genetically engineered lymphocytes into an ADA deficiency patient is not a permanent cure because, the genetically engineered lymphocytes die after somedays. Hence, the patient requires periodic infusion of genetically engineered lymphocytes, so the cure is not permanent. **(1 Mark)**

5. Following are the two advantages of using unleaded petrol as fuel in automobiles:
   - The use of unleaded petrol in vehicles fitted with catalytic converters help in reducing emission of poisonous gases.
   - As unleaded petrol does not emit harmful compounds, it helps in preventing health diseases like bronchitis, asthma and lung diseases. **(1 Mark)**

SECTION - B

6. Mosses are bryophytes and they need water for fertilisation. They lay their flagella tedmale gametes that swim across the water to reach the female gamete. During this process, many of the male gametes are destroyed or lost. Thus, moss plants produce very large number of male gametes so that even if some of the gametes get destroyed, the remaining can fertilise the female gamete. These male gametes are called antherozoids. **(2 Marks)**

7. (a) Homologous organs are the organs having similar structure and origin but performing different functions.

   From the given options, following are homologous structures:

   Forelimbs of whales and bats are similar in structure but perform different functions of swimming and flying, respectively.

   Thorns of *Bougainvillea* and tendrils of *Cucurbita are* both modifications of a stem arising from axillary bud but perform different functions of protection and climbing, respectively. **(1 Mark)**

Note

Homology indicates common anastory and is based on divergent evolution.

   (b) The evolution represented by homologous organs or structures is divergent evolution as they have common origin but have diverged (became dissimilar) with evolution due to adaptations to different needs.

   (1 Mark)

8. (a) The plants obtained by micropropagation are called somaclones because they are genetically identical plants developed from any part of a plant by tissue culture. **(1 Mark)**

   (b) The advantages of micropropagation are as follows:

   (i) It helps in the propagation of a large number of plants in a short span of time.

   (ii) Healthy plant can be recovered from diseased plant by meristem culture because meristem are free of viruses in diseased plant. **(1 Mark)**

9. The steps involved in the primary treatment of sewage involves:
   - This involves the physical removal of large and small particles from the sewage through filtration and sedimentation.
   - Floating debris are removed by sequential filteration.
   - Then the girt (soil and small pebbles) are removed by sedimentation.
   - All solids that settle form the primary sludge, and the supernatant forms the effluents.
   - The effluent from the primary settling tank is taken for secondary treatment. **(2 Marks)**

10. Mutualism is a type of population interaction between the organisms of two species in which both organisms are benefited from each other.

Examples of the organisms involved that are commercially exploited in agriculture are as follows:

(i) **Commercial exploitation of *Rhizobium* in agriculture:** Continuous growth of crops leads to the nutrient deficiency in soil. Farmers, then grow leguminous crops containing *Rhizobium* in its roots to replenish the lost nutrients (especially nitrogen) in the soil.

(ii) **Commercial exploitation of Mycorrhiza in agriculture:** Mycorrhiza is an association of the soil fungus with the roots of higher plants. Farmers use Mycorrhiza commercially in agriculture as it improves the soil quality and reduces soil erosion by improving plant rooting capacity. The fungal hyphae spread into the root tissues and help the plants to optimally use the soil's water and minerals.

Thus, to increase the yield of plants and to replenish the soil nutrients. Mycorrhiza is commercially exploited in agriculture. **(2 Marks)**

OR

Four techniques where the principle of ex-situ conservation of biodiversity has been employed are as follows:

- Botanical gardens, zoological parks and wildlife safari are the conventional methods of ex-situ conservation.
- Gametes of threatened species can be preserved in viable and fertile condition for long periods at a low temperature (–196°C) using cryopreservation techniques.
- Eggs can be fertilised Invitro, and plants can be propagated using tissue culture methods (micropropagation).
- Seeds of many different genetic strains of commercially important plants are kept viable for long periods in seed banks. **(2 Marks)**

Ex-situ conservation is a conservation approach in which threatened plants and animals are taken out from their natural habitat and placed in special setting where this can be protected and given special care.

SECTION - C

11. **Apomixis:** It is a form of asexual reproduction that mimics sexual reproduction, and seeds are produced without fertilisation. It is called apomix is or agamospermy, *e.g.*, Grasses.

Significance: Diploid egg cell is formed without reduction division and develops into embryo without fertilisation, e.g., *Asteraceae* and Grasses.

Commercial applications of apomixis :

(i) By apomixis, hybrid varieties of seeds can be produced, which will provide higher and better yield.

(ii) Apomixis prevents the loss of specific characteristics in the hybrid plants.

(iii) Apomixis is a cost-effective method of producing seeds. **(3 Marks)**

12. When a cross is made between tall pea plant which is heterozygous and dwarf (small) pea plant which is homozygous. This cross can be represented as follows :

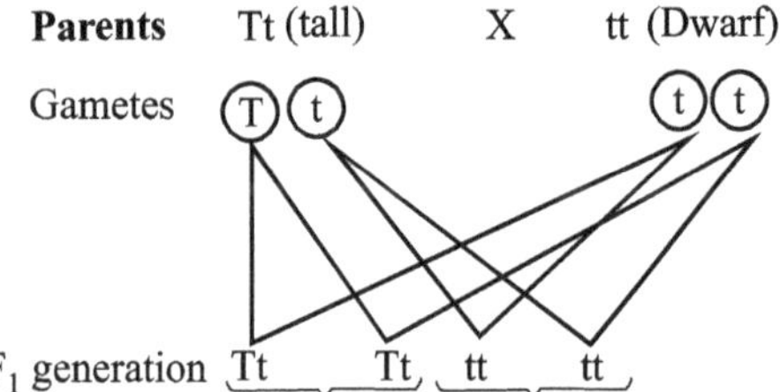

The ratio will be 50% dominant and 50% recessive incase of hybrid or heterozygous individual. **(3 Marks)**

13. Short nucleotide repeats in the DNA are very specific in each individual and vary in number from person to person but are inherited. These are called the **'Variable Number Tandem Repeats' (VNTRs)**. These are also called **"minisatellites"**.

Role of VNTR in DNA fingerprinting: DNA fingerprinting technique for identifying individuals generally using repeated sequences in the human genome that produces a pattern of bands that is unique for every individuals. Each individual inherits these repeats from his/her parents which are used as genetic markers in a personal identity test. For example, a child might inherit a chromosome with six tandem repeats from the mother and the same tandem repeats four times in the homologous chromosome inherited from the father. The half of VNTR alleles of the child resemble that of the mother and half that of the father. **(3 Marks)**

14. Hardy weinberg's principle states that allele frequencies are stable and is constant from generation to generation. The gene pool remains constant called **genetic equilibrium**. Sum total of all the allele frequencies is one. Suppose there are two alleles 'A' and 'a' in a population. Their frequencies are p and q, respectively. The frequency of AA individual in a population is P^2. It can be explained that the probability that an allele A with a frequency of p appear on both the chromosomes of a diploid individual is simply the product of the probabilities, *i.e.*, p^2. In the same way, the frequency *aa* is q^2 and for *Aa* is *pq*.

$p^2 + 2pq + q^2 = 1$

where, p^2 represents frequency of homozygous dominant genotype,

$2pq$ represents the frequency of the heterozygous geno type and represents the frequency of homozygous recessive. **(3 Marks)**

Note

VNTRs (Variable Number Tandem Repeats) are repetitive units of 10-60bp and show a higher degree of polymorphism as these base pairs sequences are different in different individuals.

15. (a) In the patient's body, the doctor has injected antiserum containing preformed antibodies against the causative organism or toxin produced by it.

(b) The solution injected by the doctor had antibodies; hence, the injection would protect the patient against the disease and provide him humoral immunity.

(c) The disease against which this injection was given is tetanus caused by *Clostridium tetani*, which usually exists in environment as spores and may again access to the body through wound.

The kind of immunity that the injection containing antiserum provides is passive immunity as preformed antibodies are used because fast action is required in this emergency case. **(3 Marks)**

16. Six important ways of good and effective dairy farm management practices are as follows:

(a) Identification of improved cattle breeds is an important condition of cattle management. Hybrid cattle breeds are essential for the improved productivity. Therefore, it is necessary that hybrid cattle breeds should have a mixture of various desirable genes such as high milk yield and resistance to disease.

(b) Cattle should be fed in scientific manner with healthy and nutritious food consisting of roughage, fibre concentrates and high levels of proteins and other nutrients.

(c) They should be housed-well and kept in ventilated roofs to prevent them from heat, cold and rain.

(d) Animals should be kept in disease-free conditions. Regular bath and brushing should be ensured to control disease. Visit of a veterinary doctor is necessary on regular basis.

(e) The procedure of milking should be hygienic; emphasis should be given to storage and transportation of milk, so that the quality of milk is not affected.

(f) Regular inspection of dairy farms should be done by appointed officials to ensure that all the instructions are being strictly followed. **(3 Marks)**

17. *Streptococcus* : The genetically modified Streptococcus produce the enzyme streptokinase which is used as clot-buster for removing clots from blood vessels of patients who have undergone myocardial infraction leading to heart attack.

Monascus Perpureus : It produces statins that help in lowering blood cholesterol levels.

Trichoderma Polysporum : It produces cyclosporin A that is used as an immuno suppressive agent in organ transplantation. **(3 Marks)**

OR

Methanogens are anaerobic bacteria growing on cellulosic material and produce large amount of methane alongwith CO_2 and H_2 gas.

These bacteria are commonly found in the anaerobic sludge during sewage treatment. Examples are: *methana bacterium, Methanococcus*.

Methanogens are the bacteria found in cattle dung (gobar) and in anaerobic sludge during sewage treatment. They grow anaerobically on cellulosic material and produce a large amount of methane (main constituent of biogas) alongwith CO_2 and H_2. Thus, methanogens are used in biogas production. **(3 Marks)**

18. The given steps refer to the steps involved in the polymerase chain reaction:

(b) Chemically synthesised oligonucleotides

(f) Nucleotides provided

(h) Thermostable DNA-polymerase (from Thermus aquaticus)

(i) Denaturation of ds DNA

(g) Primers

(e) Genomic DNA template

(c) Enzyme DNA-polymerase

(d) Complementary region of DNA

(a) In *vitro* synthesis of region of DNA of interest

(3 Marks)

Note

Polymerase chain reaction is a molecular biology technique used for the formation of large number of copies of samples produced in small quantities. PCR amplification is commonly used by medical and forensic application.

19. Three potential applications of genetically modified (GM) plants are as follows:

(i) **Pest resistance:** Crop losses from insects pests can be incredible, resulting in financial loss for farmers and starvation in developing countries. Growing GM foods such as BT corn, Bt cotton etc. can help eliminate the application of chemical pesticides & reduce the cost of bringing a crop to market.

(ii) **Disease resistance:** There are many viruses, fungi & bacteria which cause plant diseases. Plant biologists are working to create plants with genetically engineered resistance to these diseases.

(iii) **Cold tolerance:** Unexpected frost can destroy sensitive seedlings. An antifreeze gene from cold water fish has been introduced into plants such as tobacco and potato.

(3 Marks)

Genetic modification has enhanced nutritional value of food e.g., vitamin 'A' enriched rice.

20. Insulin hormone is released as a pro-hormone, which consists of three peptide chains; A, B and C. This pro-hormone insulin is converted to mature insulin by removal of C peptide. The American company, Eli Lilly, used the knowledge of rDNA technology as follows:

(i) DNA sequences corresponding to the two polypeptide, A and B of insulin are synthesised *invitro.*

(ii) They are introduced into plasmid DNA of *E.coli.*

(iii) This bacterium is cloned under suitable conditions.

(iv) The transgenes expressed in the form of polypeptides-A and B, secreted into the medium.

(v) They are extracted and combined by creating disulphide bridge to form human insulin. **(3 Marks)**

21. **Snails** adapt to unfavourable conditions by producing **epiphragm** during aestivation that covers the opening of its shell and thus prevent desiccation.

Seeds adapt to unfavourable conditions by getting into the state of dormancy.

Bears adapt to unfavourable conditions by hibernation and reducing their body metabolic activities by 75%.

Zooplanktons adapt to unfavourable conditions by entering into diapause (stage of suspended development).

Fungi adapt to unfavourable conditions by reducing their metabolic rate and forming thick-walled spores.

Bacteria adapt to unfavourable conditions by forming endospores. **(3 Marks)**

Adaptation refers to the any attribute of the organism (morphological, physiological and behavioural) that enables the organisms to survive and reproduce in its habitat.

22. Biomagnification refers to increase in concentration of the toxicant at successive trophic levels. Biomagnification takes place because a toxic substance is accumulated by an organism cannot be metabolised or exerted and passed on to the next higher trophic level.

This phenomenon is well-known for DDT and mercury the concentration of DDT is increased at successive trophic levels and can ultimately reach 25 ppm in fish-eating birds. It becomes accumulated in birds and cannot be metabolised or excreted out. This high level of DDT disturbs calcium metabolism in birds causing thinning of egg shells and their premature breaking eventually causing decline in bird population.

Fish eating birds (DDT 5ppm)

↓

Large fish (DDT 2ppm)

↓

Small fish (DDT 0.5 ppm)

↓

Zooplankton (DDT 0.04 ppm)

↓

Water (DDT 0.003ppb) **(3 Marks)**

SECTION - D

23. Reproductive health is the total well-being in all aspects of reproduction. It includes the physical, emotional, behavioural and social well-being of an individual. Therefore, there is an urgent need to educate and discuss topics related to the reproductive health.

Following are the topics about reproductive health that should be discussed with the students:

Sexually transmitted diseases, such as AIDS and Gonorrhoea, are transmitted from one individual to another through sexual contact. Therefore, making the students aware about these diseases will help to prevent their spread. Lack of knowledge about there productive status may lead to unwanted pregnancies. Hence, it is necessary to create awareness among people, especially the youth.

Learning about one's sexuality at a proper age may help the students to know about the different changes happening in their body; thereby, leading to a better mental and physical state of health.

Counselling and creating awareness about reproductive health also help to solve the problem related to infertility, birth control, mortality, etc. **(4 Marks)**

Infertility refers to the inability or failure of a couples to produce children inspite of unprotected sexual co-habitation.

SECTION - E

24. (a) To obtain seeds formed only from the desired sets of pollen grains one can opt for artificial hybridisation. Following are the steps involved:

A bisexual flower is taken.

↓

Anthers are removed from the flower bud before the anther dehisces (emasculation).

↓

Emasculated flower is covered with butter paper, to prevent contamination of its stigma with unwanted pollen

↓

When the bagged stigma attains receptivity, the desired set of mature pollen grains is dusted (pollination).

↓

Rebagging is done.

↓

Fruits are allowed to develop.

↓

Desired seeds are obtained.

(3 Marks)

(b) Artificial hybridisation is important for the following reasons:

- It helps to improve the crop yield.
- It ensures that the crops produced have the desired characteristics.
- It helps to yield commercially superior varieties.

(2 Marks)

OR

The rhythmic series of changes that occur in the reproductive organs of female primates (monkeys, apes and human beings) is called **menstrual cycle**.

- It is repeated at an average interval of about 28/29 days.
- The first appearance of menstruation at puberty is called **menarche**.
- The menstrual cycle has four phases. These are:

(i) Menstrual Phase

- The soft tissue of endometrial lining of the uterus disintegrates causing bleeding.
- The unfertilized egg and soft tissues are discharged.
- It lasts for 3-5days.

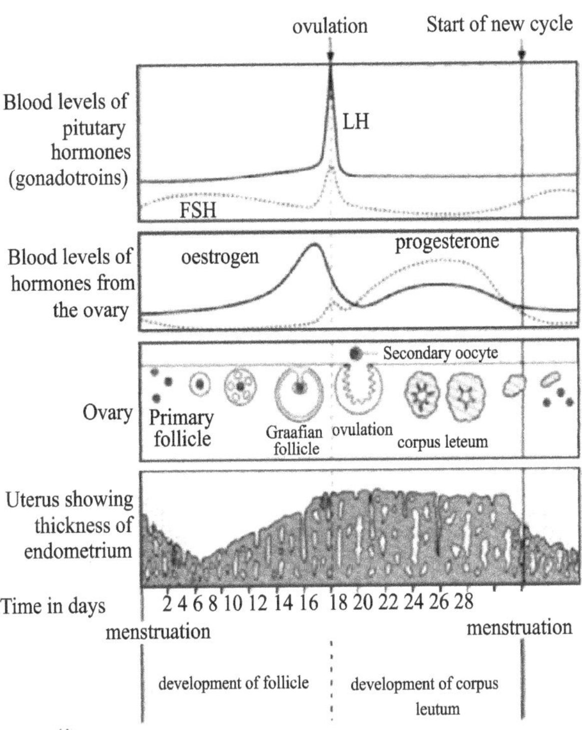

(ii) Follicular Phase/Proliferative Phase

- The primary/follicles in the ovary grow and become a fully mature Graafian follicle.
- The endometrium of the uterus is regenerated due to the secretion of LH and FSH from anterior pituitary and ovarian hormone, estrogen.
- It lasts for about 10 to 14 days.

(iii) Ovulatory Phase

- Rapid secretion of LH (LH surge) induced rupture of Graafian follicle, thereby leading to ovulation (released of ovum).
- It lasts for only about 48 hours.

(iv) Luteal Phase/Secretory Phase

- In this phase the ruptured follicle changes into corpus luteum in the ovary and it secrete the hormone progesterone.
- The endometrium thickens further and their glands secrete a fluid into the uterus.
- If ovum is not fertilised, the corpus luteum undergoes degeneration and this causes disintegration of the endometrium leading to menstruation.
- Estrogen and progesterone levels rise during this phase.
- It lasts for only 1day.
- During pregnancy all events of the menstrual cycle stop and there is no menstruation. The menstrual cycle permanently stops in females at the age of around 50 years. This is called **menopause**.

(5 Marks)

25. (a) Thalassaemia and haemophilia are categorised as Mendelian disorders because they occur by mutation in a single gene.Their mode of inheritance follows the principles of Mendelian genetics. Mendelian disorders can be autosomal dominant (muscular dystrophy) autosomal recessive (thalassaemia), sex linked (haemophilia)

Symptoms of Thalassaemia:

Thalassaemia minor results only in mild anaemia, characterised by low haemoglobin level.

Thalassaemia major is also known as Cooley's anaemia. In this disease, affected infants are normal but as they reach 6 to 9 months of age, they develop severe anaemia, skeletal deformities, jaundice, fatigue, etc.

Symptoms of Hemophilia:

Person suffering from this disease does not develop a proper blood clotting mechanism.

A haemophilic patient suffers from non-stop bleeding even on a simple cut, which may lead to death.

Pattern of Inheritance of Thalassaemia:

Pair of alleles Hb^A and Hb^T controls the expression of this disease.

Conditions for thalassemia :

Hb^A and Hb^A : Normal

Hb^A and Hb^T : Carrier

Hb^T and Hb^T : Diseased

Let us assume that both father and mother are the carriers (Hb^AHb^T) of beta thalassaemia.

Parents	Hb^AHb^T		Hb^AHb^T	
	(Father)	×	(Mother)	
Offsprings	Hb^AHb^A	Hb^AHb^T	Hb^AHb^T	Hb^THb^T
	Normal	Carrierchild	Carrierchild	Child with

Pattern of Inheritance of Haemophilia:

Haemophilia is an X-linked genetic disorder. Compared to females, males have higher chances of getting affected because females have two XX chromosomes while males have only one X and Y chromosome. Thus, for a female to get affected by one haemophilia, she have the mutant allele on both the X chromosomes while males can be affected if they carry it on the single X chromosome.

Conditions for haemophilia:

XY; XX: Normal

X^hY:

HaemophilicX^hX:

Carrier

X^hX^h :Haemophilic

Let us assume that a carrier female (X^hX) is married to a normal male.

Parents		XY		X^hX
		(Male)	×	(Female)
	X^hX	XX	X^hX	XX
Offsprings	Carrier	Normal	Haemophilic	Normal
Figenuation	female	female	male	male

(3 Marks)

Hemophilia is caused because of the absence of blood clotting factor VIII (Hemophilia-A) and IX (hemophilia-B)

(b) When a normal male marries a carrier female (she is considered normal as she contains the mutant gene on one of her X chromosomes), they can produce a haemophilic son. So, the genotype of the parents would be XY and X^hX. **(2 Marks)**

Parents		XY	×	X^hX
		(Male)		(Female)
	X^hX	XX	X^hY	XY
Offsprings	Carrier	Normal	Haemophilic	Normal
	daughter	daughter	son	son

OR

Translation is the process of polymerising amino acid to form a polypeptide chain.

The triplet sequence of base pairs in mRNA defines the order and sequence of amino acids in a polypeptide chain.

The process of translation involves the following three steps:

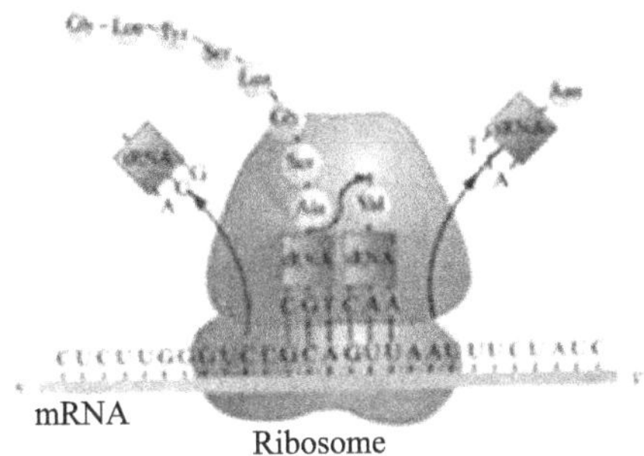

(i) Initiation

(ii) Elongation

(iii) Termination

During the initiation of the translation, tRNA gets charged when the amino acid binds to it using ATP.

The start (initiation) codon (AUG) present on mRNA is recognised only by the charged tRNA.

The ribosome acts as an actual site for the process of translation and contains two separate sites in a large subunit for the attachment of subsequent aminoacids.

The small subunit of ribosome binds to mRNA at start codon (AUG) followed by the large subunit. Then, it initiates the process of translation.

During the elongation process, the ribosome moves one codon downstream along with mRNA so as to leave the space for binding of another charged tRNA.

The amino acid brought by tRNA gets linked with the previous amino acid through a peptide bond and this process continues result in the formation of a polypeptide chain.

When the ribosome reaches one or more stop codon (VAA, UAG and UGA), the process of translation gets terminated. The polypeptide chain is released and the ribosomes get detached from mRNA. **(5 Marks)**

Codon AUG codes for amino acid Methionine that serves as an initiation codon in eukaryotes. Whereas GUG codes for aminoacid valine and acts as initiation codon in prokaryotes.

26. A population certain characteristics that an individual organisms does not have are as follows:

(i) Natality refers to the number of birth during a given period in the population that are added to the initial density.

(ii) Mortality refers to the number of deaths in the population during a given period.

(iii) Percentage revers to the sex-ratio of male and female.

(b) Population density means number of individuals present per unit area. Population density can be measured by determining the population size. The different methods to study population size are as follows:

(1) **Quadrat method:** It is a method that involves the use of square of particular dimensions to measure the number of organisms.

Example: The number of *Parthenium* plants in a given area can be measured using the quadrat method.

(2) **Direct observation:** It involves the counting of organisms in the given area.

Example: In order to determine the number of bacteria growing in a petridish, their colonies are counted.

(3) **Indirect method:** In this method, there is no need to count the organisms individually.

Example: The number of fishes caught per trap gives the measure of their total density in a given water body.

OR

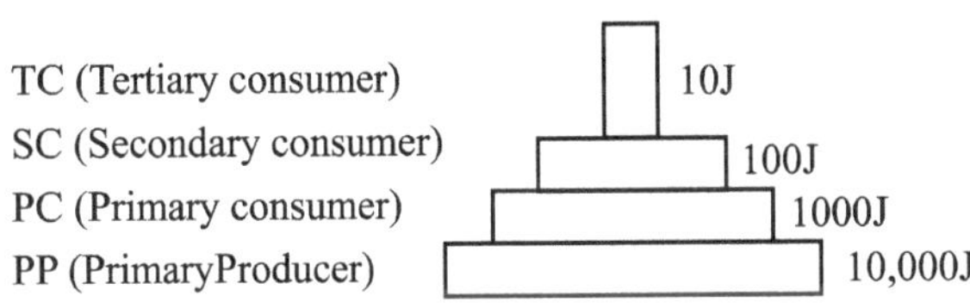

1,000,000 J of Sunlight

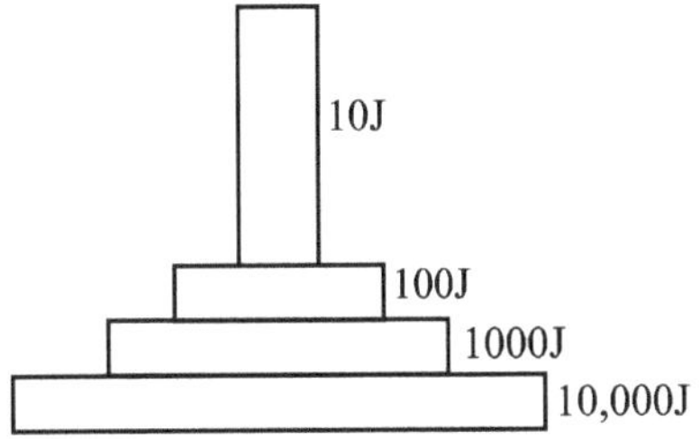

Pyramid of energy is always upright because when energy flows from a particular trophic level to the next trophic level, some energy is always lost as heat as well as for performing various activities at each step. Maximum energy is present at the producers level and minimum at level of top carnivores (top consumers). Thus, pyramid of energy is always upright.

(a) The pyramid of biomass in a sea ecosystem is inverted. Because, the sum total of the weight of phytoplankton (producer) is far less than a few fishes feeding at higher trophic levels.

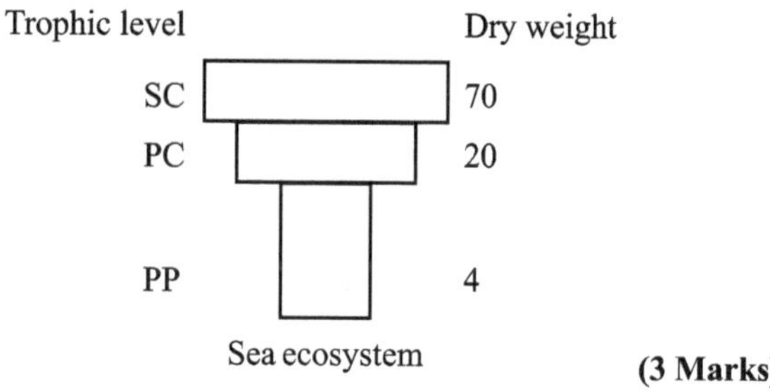

Sea ecosystem

(3 Marks)

(b) Pyramid of biomass in a forest ecosystem is upright because producers are more in biomass than primary consumers. Primary consumers are more than secondary consumers and secondary consumers are more than tertiary consumers (top). **(2 Marks)**

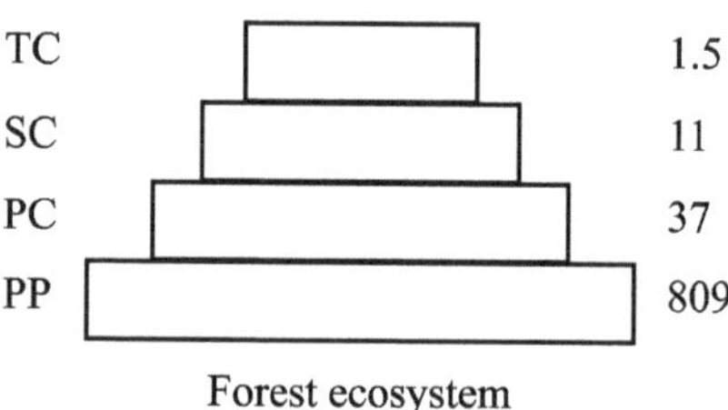

Forest ecosystem

Delhi 2015

CBSE Board Solved Paper

Time Allowed : 3 Hours ***Maximum Marks : 70***

General Instructions:

(i) There are a total of **26** questions and **five** sections in the question paper. **All** questions are compulsory.

(ii) Section **A** contains question number **1** to **5**, Very Short Answer **type** questions of **one** mark each.

(iii) Section **B** contains question number **6** to **10**, Short Answer type **I** questions of **two** marks each.

(iv) Section **C** contains question number **11** to **22**, Short Answer type **II** questions of **three** marks each.

(v) Section **D** contains question number **23**, Value Based Question of **four** marks.

(vi) Section **E** contains question number **24** to **26**, Long Answer type questions of **five** marks each.

(vii) There is no overall choice in the question paper, however, an internal choice is provided in **one** question of **two** marks, **one** question of **three** marks and **all three** questions of **five** marks. An examinee is to attempt any **one** of the questions out of the **two** given in the question paper with the same question number.

SECTION - A

1. A geneticist interested in studying variations and patterns of inheritance in living beings prefers to choose organisms for experiments with shorter life cycle. Provide a reason.

2 Name the transcriptionally active region of chromatin in a nucleus.

3. State a reason for the increased population of dark coloured moths coinciding with the loss of lichens (on tree barks) during industrialization period in England.

4. Indiscrimate diagnostic practices using X-rays etc., should be avoided. Give one reason.

5. What is Biopiracy?

SECTION - B

6. After a brief medical examination a healthy couple came to know that both of them are unable to produce functional gametes and should look for an 'ART' (Assisted Reproductive Technique). Name the 'ART' and the procedure involved that you can suggest to them to help them bear a child.

7. Differentiate between male and female heterogamety.

8. How has mutation breeding helped in improving the production of mung bean crop ?

9. Mention a product of human welfare obtained with the help of each one of the following microbes :

(a) LAB

(b) Saccharomyces cerevisiae

(c) Propionibacterium sharmanii

(d) Aspergillus niger

10. Many fresh water animals can not survive in marine environment. Explain.

OR

How are productivity, gross productivity, net primary productivity and secondary productivity interrelated ?

SECTION - C

11. Double fertilization is reported in plants of both, castor and groundnut. However, the mature seeds of groundnut are non-albuminous and castor are albuminous. Explain the post fertilization events that are responsible for it.

12. Describe the process of Parturition in humans.

13. A teacher wants his/her students to find the genotype of pea plants bearing purple coloured flowers in their school garden. Name and explain the cross that will make it possible.

14. (a) A DNA segment has a total of 1000 nucleotides, out of which 240 of them are adenine containing nucleotides. How many pyrimidine bases this DNA segment possesses ?

(b) Draw a diagrammatic sketch of a portion of DNA segment to support your answer.

15. Explain adaptive radiation with the help of a suitable example.

16. A team of students are preparing to participate in the interschool sports meet. During a practice session you find some vials with labels of certain cannabionoids.

(a) Will you report to the authorities ? Why ?

(b) Name a plant from which such chemicals are obtained.

(c) Write the effect of these chemicals on human body.

17. Enlist the steps involved in inbreeding of cattle. Suggest two disadvantages of this practice.

18. Choose any three microbes, from the following which are suited for organic farming which is in great demand these days for various reasons. Mention one application of each one chosen. Mycorrhiza; Monascus; Anabaena; Rhizobium; Methanobacterium; Trichoderma.

19. Recombinant DNA-technology is of great importance in the field of medicine. With the help of a flow chart, show how this technology has been used in preparing genetically engineered human insulins.

20. Draw a labelled sketch of sparged-stirred-tank bioreactor. Write its application.

21. Following the collision of two trains a large number of passengers are killed. A majority of them are beyond recognition. Authorities want to hand over the dead to their relatives. Name a modern scientific method and write the procedure that would help in the identification of kinship.

22. Many plant and animal species are on the verge of their extinction because of loss of forest land by indiscriminate use by the humans. As a biology student what method would you suggest along with its advantages that can protect such threatened species from getting extinct ?

OR

"Determination of Biological Oxygen Demand (BOD) can help in suggesting the quality of a water body." Explain.

SECTION - D

23. Since October 02, 2014 "Swachh Bharat Abhiyan" has been launched in our country.

(a) Write your views on this initiative giving justification.

(b) As a biologist name TWO problems that you may face while implementing the programme in your locality.

(c) Suggest TWO remedial methods to overcome these problems.

SECTION - E

24. A flower of tomato plant following the process of sexual reproduction produces 240 viable seeds.

Answer the following questions giving reasons :

(a) What is the minimum number of pollen grains that must have been involved in the pollination of its pistil?

(b) What would have been the minimum number of ovules present in the ovary ?

(c) How many megaspore mother cells were involved ?

(d) What is the minimum number of microspore mother cells involved in the above case ?

(e) How many male gametes were involved in this case ?

OR

During the reproductive cycle of a human female, when, where and how does a placenta develop ? What is the function of placenta during pregnancy and embryo development?

25. Explain the genetic basis of blood grouping in human population.

OR

How did Hershey and Chase established that DNA is transferred from virus to bacteria ?

26. "Analysis of age-pyramids for human population can provide important inputs for longterm planning strategies." Explain.

OR

Describe the advantages for keeping the ecosystems healthy.

Solutions

SECTION - A

1. A geneticist prefers to choose organisms for experiments with shorter life cycle because it helps the geneticist to study many generations in the shorter life spans of those organisms. **(1 Mark)**

2. Euchromatin is the transcriptionally active region of chromatin in a nucleus. **(1 Mark)**

Nucleosomes constitute the repeating unit of a structure in nucleus called chromatin that appears as a thread-like structure. Some region of chromatin are loosely packed (and stains light) and are called euchromatin and the chromatin that is more densely packed and stains dark are called as Heterochromatin.

3. Before industrialization, it was observed that there were more white-winged moths or melanised moths were found on the trees than dark-winged moths. But after industrialization in 1920s, it was observed that there were more dark-winged moths were found in the same area. It occurs because during post-industrialisation period, the tree trunks became dark due to industrial smoke and soots. In this condition, the white-winged moth did not survive because of predators. Hence dark-winged or melanised moth survived. **(1 Mark)**

Before industrialisation, the tree trunks are covered by white-coloured lichen and in the background the white winged moth survived.

4. Indiscrimate diagnostic practices using X-rays should be avoided because excessive use of X-rays leads to cause mutation and cancer. **(1 Mark)**

X-rays are ionizing radiation that can affect the atoms in living things. Cells on exposure to ionizing radiation lead to cause tissue and DNA damage.

5. The term biopiracy is defined as the use of bio-resources by multinational companies and other organisations without proper authorisation from the countries as well as people concerned without compensatory payment. **(1 Mark)**

SECTION - B

6. The doctor suggests **ZIFT (Zygote intra fallopian transfer)** to those couples who are not able to bear a child. In this procedure, the sperm is collected either from the husband or donor and an ovum is collected from wife or donor. Then sperm and ova are induced to form zygote under controlled conditions in the laboratory. Then the zygote or early embryos upto 8 blastomeres stages are then transferred into the fallopian tube of the female for further development. **(2 Marks)**

ART (Assisted reproductive technology) *involves the treatments and procedures for those couples that are not able to bear child.*

7. The difference between male and female heterogamety are as follows:

Male heterogamety	Female heterogamety
(i) In male heterogamety, male produces two different types of gametes.	(i) In female heterogamety, female (human) produces two similar types of gametes or in case of insects, two types of gametes.
(ii) Gametes produced are XY and XO.	(ii) ZW is the only one type of heterogamete produced by female.
(iii) Examples: Grasshoppers, bugs	(iii) Example: Birds, reptiles, fishes.

(2 Marks)

The term heterogamety refers to the sex of a species in which the chromosomes are not same.

8. Mutation breeding is a process in which mutation is induced artificially by the use of chemicals or radiations such as gamma radiations. Then selection and use of such plants that contains desirable character as a source in breeding. In case of mung beans, mutation breeding is used to induce resistance against yellow mosaic virus and powdery mildew. **(2 Marks)**

9. (a) **LAB (Lactic acid bacteria):** LAB are commonly grow in milk and helps in the conversion of milk into curd. It produces acid that helps in coagulation and partial digestion of milk proteins. LAB also plays essential role in checking disease causing microbes.

(b) ***Saccharomyces cerevisiae***: It is also called baker's yeast. It is used for making bread and also used in beverage industry.

(c) ***Propionibacterium sharmanii:*** It is used for the production of large holes in 'Swiss cheese'. Large holes are produced in the cheese because of the production of large amount of carbon dioxide by bacteria.

(d) ***Aspergillus niger:*** It is a fungus used for the production of citric acid. **(2 Marks)**

10. Many fresh water fishes cannot survive in the marine environment because their bodies are not adapted to the marine environment. As freshwater fishes lose body water because the surrounding water has higher salt concentration (hypertonic solution) and this makes the survival of fresh water fishes difficult in marine water. **(2 Marks)**

OR

Productivity: Productivity is defined as the rate of biomass production.

Gross primary productivity: Gross primary productivity is defined as the rate of organic matter production during photosynthesis.

Net primary productivity: Net primary productivity involves the gross-productivity minus respiratory losses (R).

So, NPP = GPP-R

Secondary productivity: Secondary productivity is defined as the rate of formation of new organic matter by consumers.

As per their definitions, all the terms are interrelated to each other. **(2 Marks)**

SECTION - C

11. The post fertilization events that are responsible for the formation of non-albuminous mature seeds of groundnut and albuminous seeds of castor are as follows:

The primary endosperm nucleus divides repeatedly to give rise to free nuclei and this stage is called free nuclear endosperm. The cell wall is formed after the formation of cellular endosperm.

Hence, if the endosperm is consumed fully by the developing embryo before seed maturation results in the formation of non-albuminous seeds such as in groundnut. Whereas if the endosperm is persist in the mature seed and can be used up during seed germination then is called as albuminous such as in castor. **(3 Marks)**

*The process of double fertilisation involves the fusion of one gamete with nucleus of egg cell results in the formation of zygote whereas other male gamete move towards the two polar nuclei that is located in the central cell and fuses with polar nuclei to give rise to **primary endosperm nucleus (PEN)**. It is also called triple fusion as it involves the fusion of three haploid nuclei.*

12. The process of parturition involves following events:

- The average duration of human pregnancy is about 9 months and this period is called gestation period.
- The process of parturition involves vigorous contraction of the uterus at the end of pregnancy results in the expulsion or delivery of the foetus. So, parturition is defined as the process of delivery of the foetus and is also called childbirth.
- It is induced by a complex neuroendocrine mechanism. As the signals for parturition are originate from the fully developed foetus and the placenta results in induction of mild uterine contractions and this process is called foetal ejection reflex.
- Foetal ejection reflex triggers the release of oxytocin from the maternal pituitary.
- Oxytocin hormone acts on the uterine muscle and causes stronger uterine contraction that stimulates the secretion of oxytocin.
- The stimulatory reflex between the uterine contraction and oxytocin secretion that leads to cause stronger and stronger contractions.
- It leads to cause expulsion of the baby out of the uterus through the birth canal. **(3 Marks)**

13. Purple colour is a dominant phenotype in pea plant and the genotype of the pea plant with purple flowers can be determined by test cross.

In test cross, the pea plant whose genotype is to be determined is crossed with a homozygous recessive parent (ww) having white flowers. It helps the students to determine whether the genotype of the plant is heterozygous dominant (Ww) or homozygous dominant (WW).

Diagrammatic representation of a test cross is as follows:

Parents:	WW (purple)		X	ww (white)
Gametes:	W W			w w
F_1 generation :	Ww	Ww	Ww	Ww
Result:	All flower are voilet			

Interpretation: Unknown flower is homozygous dominant

Parents:	Ww (Purple) (Dominant phenotype)	X	ww (white) (Homozygous recessive)	
Gametes :	Ww	ww		
F_2 generation :	Ww	Ww	ww	ww

Result: 50% flowers are violet and 50% flowers are white.

Interpretation: Unknown flower is heterozygous

(3 Marks)

14. (a) According to chargaff's rule, the ratio of purine (adenine and guanine) and pyrimidine is equal.

As, the ratio of adenine + thymine and guanine + cytosine = 1

If a DNA contains 1000 nucleotides and out of this, 240 are adenine.

Then, the ratio of adenine and thymine are same = 240

So, number of pyrimidine bases = 1000-240

= 520

Ratio of cytosine= $\frac{520}{2}$ =260

Ratio of guanine = $\frac{520}{2}$ =260

Hence, the number of pyrimidine nitrogenous bases = Cytosine + Thymine

= 260 + 240 = 500 **(2 Marks)**

(b) **Diagrammatic representation of structure of DNA:**

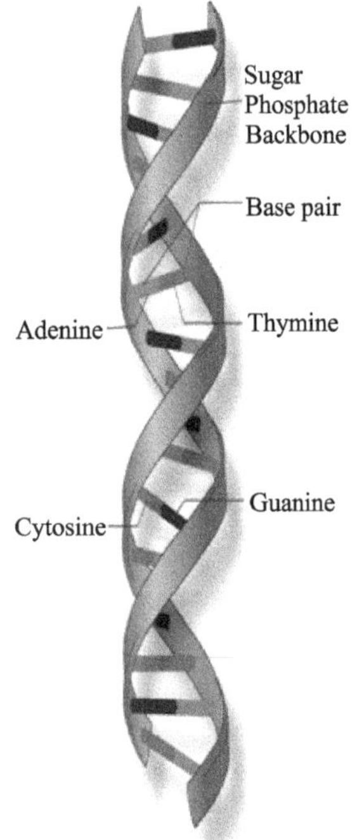

(1 Mark)

15. Adaptive radiation is defined as the process of evolution of different species in a specific geographical area starting from a point and literally radiating to another areas of geography or habitat. Darwin finches and Australian marsupials are examples of adaptive radiation. **(2 Marks)**

16. (a) Yes, I would like to report the matter to the higher sports authorities because cannabinoids are classified under drugs and its abuse is considered as an illegal practice. **(1 Mark)**

(b) Natural cannabinoids are obtained from the inflorescences of the plant *Cannabis sativa.* **(1 Mark)**

(c) Cannabinoids are the group of chemicals that interact with the cannabinoids receptors present in the brain. It affects the cardiovascular system of the body.

(1 Mark)

17. Inbreeding refers to the mating of more closely related individuals within the same breed for 4-6 generations. It involves the mating of superior males and superior females of the same breed that are identified in pairs. The progeny obtained after mating are evaluated and superior males and females are identified for further mating. The animals having high yielding capacity of the same breed are mated.

Disadvantages of inbreeding:

- Inbreeding increases homozygosity.
- It also increases inbreeding depression as continued inbreeding reduces fertility and productivity. **(3 Marks)**

18. (a) ***Mycorrhiza:*** It is an fungi that plays an essential role in the symbiotic association with plants and involves in nitrogen fixation in plants. It is also involved in the absorption of phosphorus from soil and passes it to the plants.

(b) ***Monascus purpureus:*** It is yeast that is used for the commercial production statins used as a blood-cholesterol lowering agents.

(c) ***Anabaena:*** It is a cyanobacteria that is involved in nitrogen fixation. They are autotrophic and free-living. They are also used as a good source of biofertiliser

(d) ***Rhizobium:*** It forms symbiotic association with the root nodules of the leguminous plant. They fix atmospheric nitrogen into organic and absorbable forms for plants that can be used as a source of nutrient.

(e) ***Methanobacterium:*** It is an bacteria used for the biological generation of methane by anaerobic processes.

(f) ***Trichoderma polysporum:*** It is a fungus used for the production of bioactive molecule called cyclosporine A that is used as an immunosuppressive agent in organ-transplant patients. **(3 Marks)**

19. Representation of flow chart for the production of recombinant insulin:

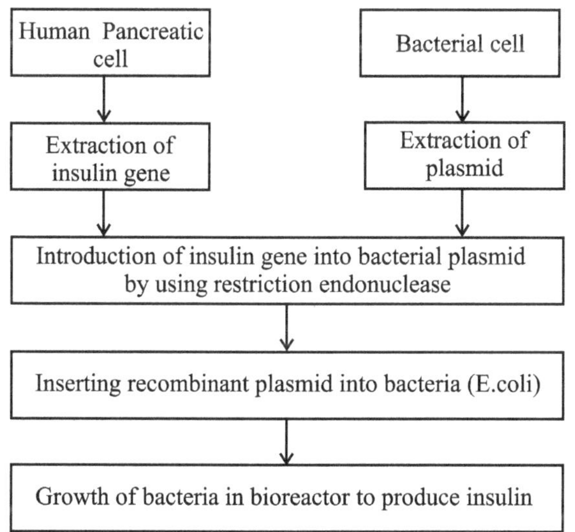

Diagrammatic representation of recombinant insulin:

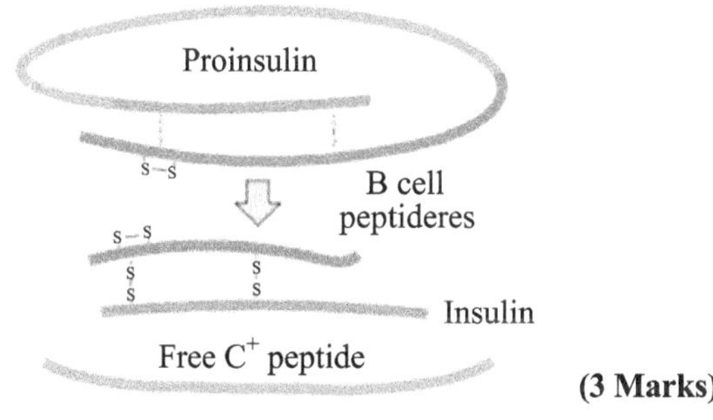

(3 Marks)

20. Diagrammatic representation of sparged-stirred-tank bioreactors:

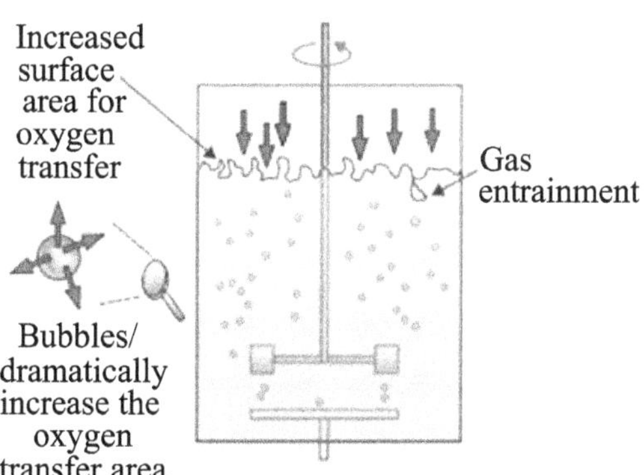

Bioreactors refers to an apparatus in which a biological reaction is carried out.

Application of sparged-stirred-tank bioreactor:

- Sparged-stirred tank bioreactors are used for the production of large amount of proteins.
- It is also used for the large-scale production of alcohol.

(3 Marks)

21. DNA fingerprinting is the molecular biology technique and a modern scientific method which is used for the kinship analysis.

Procedure used in DNA fingerprinting:

- Variable Number Tandem Repeats (VNTRs) are satellite DNAs that shows higher degree of polymorphism.
- In DNA fingerprinting, VNTRs probes are used.
- DNA from an individual is collected from every tissue such as blood, hair-follicle, skin, bone and so on.
- Isolated DNA sample from an individual is then cut with the help of restriction endonucleases.
- Then, the fragments are separated through gel electrophoresis on the basis of their size.
- Then, the separated DNA fragments are immobilised on a synthetic nylon or nitrocellulose membrane.
- Immobilised DNA fragments are hybridised with the help of VNTRs probe.
- The hybridised DNA fragments can be detected by autoradiography.
- VNTRs probes vary in sizes from 0.1-20kb.
- So, in the autoradiogram, a band of different sizes will be obtained.
- Such bands are serves as the characteristics of an individual.
- VNTRs are different in every individual. **(3 Marks)**

Note

DNA fingerprinting technique was developed by Alec Jeffreys and he used satellite DNA as probe that represents very higher degree of polymorphism called VNTRs (Variable Number Tandem Repeats). VNTRs are repetitive units of 10-60pb and show a higher degree of polymorphism as these base pair sequences are different in different individuals.

22. As a biology student, following method would be suggested in order to protect the threatened species from getting extinct are:

- Ex-situ conservation: In this, the threatened species of plants and animals are taken out of their habitats. Such species of both plants and animals are kept in special habitat such as zoological parks, botanical gardens and wildlife parks to provide natural environment for their survival.
- Gametes of several endangered plants and animal species can be preserved by methods involves cryopreservation. It can be fertilized in vitro followed by propagation through tissue culture methods.
- Seeds are preserved in seed banks and this method is called **off-site conservation method.** **(3 Marks)**

OR

BOD (Biological oxygen demand) refers to the amount of oxygen consumed if all the organic matter in one litre of water were oxidised by bacteria.

BOD of the water body helps in the determination of quality of water body. Presence of more organic waste increases the BOD that consumes a large amount of oxygen from water. Greater the BOD of waste water indicates that water is more polluting by microorganisms. **(3 Marks)**

BOD test helps in the measurement of oxygen uptake by micro-organisms in a sample of water.

SECTION - D

23. "Swachh Bharat Abhiyan" was started by India's current Prime Minister Narendra Modi on October 02, 2014.

(a) I am completely in support for the movement of "Swachh Bharat Abhiyan". It is our primary duty to clean our nation because waste materials cause biggest disaster as it make difficulty in the progress and development of a country. The waste material results in unclean surroundings that lead to cause health hazards. Wastes support the growth of mosquitoes and flies that are responsible for spread of various infectious diseases. Waste material also pollutes air and water results in pollution. It effects the development and economic growth of the country.

(b) Two problems arises while implementing the programme in my locality such as:

- Improper sanitation management.
- Failure in the separation of biodegradable and non-biodegradable wastes.

(c) The methods used to overcome these problems are as follows:

- Maintain proper awareness regarding sanitation among people and also encourage them to maintain proper sanitation in their locality in order to overcome sanitation problem.
- Separate dustbins are placed everywhere for degradable and biodegradable wastes so that those wastes can be used and recycled accordingly.

(4 Marks)

Placenta acts as an endocrine tissue and produces several hormones like human charionic gonadotropin (hCG) human placental lactogen (hPL), estrogens, progestogens during pregnancy, a hormone called relaxin is also secreted by the ovary hCG, hPL and relaxin are produced in women only during pregnancy.

SECTION - E

24. The number of viable seeds that are produced by the tomato plant by sexual reproduction is 240.

(a) The minimum number of pollen grains that is involved in the pollination of its pistil is 240 because each pollen grains contains two male gametes. One male gamete fuses with polar nuclei and forms endosperm whereas the other male gamete fuses with the egg cell to form zygote and it is further developed into seeds. So, 240 pollen grains are required to obtain 240 seeds.

(1 Mark)

(b) 240 ovules present in the ovary and are involved in the process of fertilisation as the 240 seeds are viable. After fertilisation, the ovary develops into fruit and ovules are developed into seeds. So, the numbers of ovules are further developed into seeds. **(1 Mark)**

(c) 240 megaspore mother cells are involved in the process of gametogenesis. As, in this process only one megaspore of the tetrad becomes functional and further developed. Whereas the other three megaspores are degenerated. **(1 Mark)**

(d) 60 microspore mother cells are involved in the process of gametogenesis. They have undergone meiotic division prior to dehiscence of anther. As each microspore mother cell gives rise to 4 microspores and 1 microspores mother cell would produce 4 microspores. So, 60 microspore mother cells are required to obtain 240 microspores. **(1 Mark)**

(e) 240 male gametes are required for the process of seed formation as each male gamete will fuse with one egg to form zygote that will be further developed into the seed. **(1 Mark)**

OR

The placenta develops after the implantation of zygote in the uterus during the reproductive phase of human female.

After implantation, numerous finger-like projections called chorionic villi are formed on the trophoblast. The chorionic villi are surrounded by uterine tissues and maternal blood. Placenta is surrounded by uterine tissues.

- Placenta plays an essential role during embryonic development as it facilitates the supply of oxygen and nutrients to the embryo.
- It is also involved in the removal of carbon dioxide and other excretory waste materials by the embryo.
- The placenta is connected to the embryo through an umbilical cord that helps in the transportation of substances in and out from the embryo. **(5 Marks)**

25. The inheritance of human blood group is an example of codominance and multiple alleles. ABO blood grouping in human beings are controlled by *I* gene. The plasma membrane of the red blood cells has sugar polymers that are found on the surface of RBCs and is controlled by this gene.

The *I* gene has three alleles I^A, I^B and *i*. The gene I^A and I^B are dominant over *i* and both I^A and I^B express their own types of sugars. This phenomenon is called **co-dominance.** Hence, red blood cells have both A and B types of sugars. There are three different alleles and there are six different genotypes of the human ABO blood types.

Tabular representation of genetic basis of Blood Groups in Human population:

Allele from Parent 1	Allele from Parent 2	Genotype of offspring	Blood types of offspring
I^A	I^A	I^AI^A	A
I^A	I^B	I^AI^B	AB
I^A	i	I^Ai	A
I^B	I^A	I^AI^B	AB
I^B	I^B	I^BI^B	B
I^B	i	I^Bi	B
i	i	$i\,i$	O

(5 Marks)

OR

To proof that DNA is the genetic material an experiment was performed by Alfred Hershey and Martha Chase in 1952. They worked with viruses that infect bacteria called bacteriophage.

Following steps are involved in Hershey and Chase experiment:

- They grow viruses on a different medium containing radioactive phosphorus and radioactive sulphur.
- Viruses grown in the presence of radioactive phosphorus contained radioactive DNA but not protein because DNA contains phosphorus but is absent in protein.
- Whereas virus grown in a medium containing radioactive sulphur contained radioactive protein but not radioactive DNA because sulphur is absent is DNA.
- Radioactive phages were allowed to attach to *E.coli* bacteria.
- As the infection proceeded, the viral coats were removed from the bacteria by agitating them in a blender.
- Then the virus particles were separated from the bacteria by spinning them in a centrifuge.
- So the bacteria that infected with viruses that contain radioactive DNA were radioactive.
- This indicates that DNA was the material that can be passed from the virus to bacteria.

- Bacteria that were infected with viruses that contain radioactive proteins were not radioactive.
- This indicates that proteins did not enter the bacteria from the viruses.
- Hence, it is proved that DNA is the genetic material that is passed from virus to bacteria.

Diagrammatic representation of Hershey and Chase experiment:

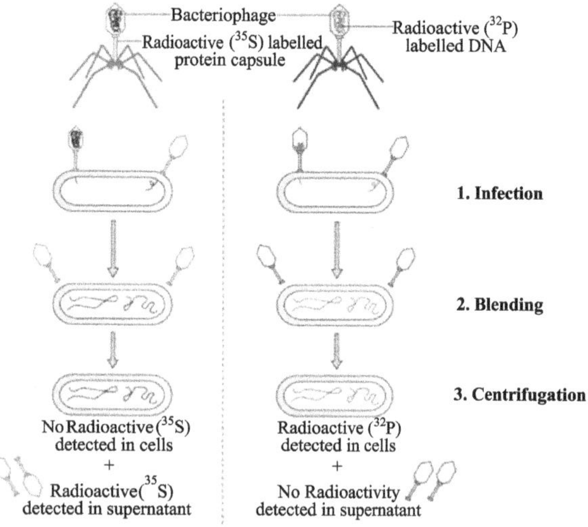

(5 **Marks**)

26. Age pyramid is defined as a way for representing the age-sex structure of a population. There are three types of age distribution pyramids such as expanding, stable and declining. A population is composed of individuals of different age groups.

The analysis of age pyramid helps in the determination of growth status of the population. It involves three types of structure that represents that whether the population is expanding, stable or declining. The structure of age pyramids for human population emphasis on providing food to population, development of proper health care facilities and so on.

Diagrammatic representation of age pyramids for human population:

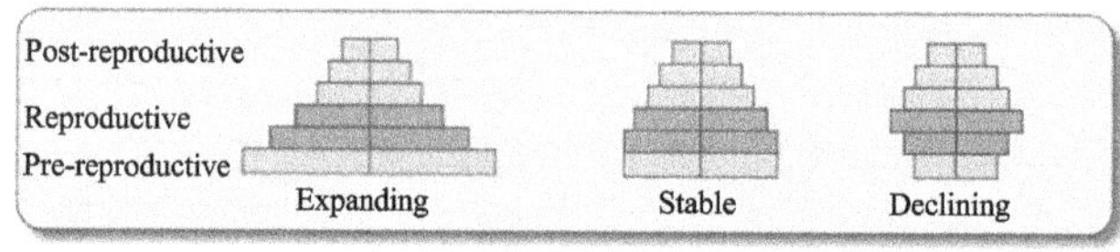

(5 Marks)

OR

The advantages of maintaining an ecosystem healthy are as follows:

- Healthy forest ecosystem helps in purification of air and water.
- It is important to maintain the biodiversity for the maintenance of a healthy ecosystem.
- Healthy ecosystem controls drought and flood conditions and also maintains nutrient cycle.
- Healthy ecosystem provides aesthetic, spiritual and cultural values.
- It is also responsible for generation of fertile soil and also provide safe habitat for wildlife. (5 **Marks**)

All India 2014

CBSE Board Solved Paper

Time Allowed : 3 Hours | *Maximum Marks : 70*

General Instructions:

(i) All questions are compulsory.

(ii) This question paper consists of four Sections **A, B, C** and **D**. Section **A** contains **8** questions of **one** mark each, Section **B** is of **10** questions of **two** marks each, Section **C** is of **9** questions of **three** marks each and Section **D** is of **3** questions of **five** marks each.

(iii) There is no overall choice. However, an internal choice has been provided in **one** question of **2** marks, **one** question of **3** marks and all the questions of **5** marks weightage. A student has to attempt only **one** of the alternatives in such questions.

(iv) Wherever necessary, the diagrams drawn should be neat and properly labelled.

SECTION - A

1. Name the parts of the flower which the tassels of the corn-cob represent.
2. Mention any two contrasting traits with respect to seeds in pea plant that were studied by Mendel.
3. Why is secondary immune response more intense than the primary immune response in humans?
4. Why is it not possible for an alien DNA to become part of a chromosome anywhere along its length and replicate normally?
5. State the role of C-peptide in human insulin.
6. Name the enzymes that are used for the isolation of DNA from bacterial and fungal cells for recombinant DNA technology.
7. State Gause's Competitive Exclusion Principle.
8. Name the type of association that the genus *Glomus* exhibits with higher plants.

SECTION - B

9. Why are the human testes located outside the abdominal cavity? Name the pouch in which they are present.
10. In **Snapdragon**, A cross between true-breeding red flower (RR) plants and true-breeding white flowered (rr) plants showed a progeny of plants with all pink flowers.

    (a) The appearance of pink flowers is not known as blending. Why?

    (b) What is the phenomenon known as ?
11. With the help of one example, explain the phenomena of co-dominance and multiple allelism in human population.
12. Write the scientific name of the fruit-fly. Why did Morgan prefer to work with fruit-flies for his experiments? State any three reasons.

    OR

    Linkage or crossing-over of genes are alternatives of each other. Justify with the help of an example.
13. List the symptoms of *Ascariasis*. How does a healthy person acquire this infection?
14. Explain the significant role of the genus *Nucleopolyhedrovirus* in an ecological sensitive area.
15. How does a restriction nuclease function? Explain.
16. How have transgenic animals proved to be beneficial in:

    (a) Production of biological products

    (b) Chemical safety testing
17. Describe the mutual relationship between Fig. tree and wasp and comment on the phenomenon that operates in their relationship.
18. Construct an age pyramid which reflect an expanding growth status of human population.

SECTION - C

19. Make a list of any three outbreeding devices that flowering plants have developed and explain how they help to encourage cross-pollination.

OR

Why are angiosperm anthers called dithecous? Describe the structure of its microsporangium.

20. If implementation of better techniques and new strategies are required to provide more efficient care and assistance to people, then why is there a statutory ban on amniocentesis? Write the use of this technique and give reason to justify the ban.

21. Why is pedigree analysis done in the study of human genetics? State the conclusions that can be drawn from it.

22. Identify 'a', 'b', 'c', 'd', 'e' and 'f' in the table given below :

No.	Syndrome	Cause	Characteristics of affected individuals	Sex Male/Female/Both
1.	Down's	Trisomy of 21	'a' (i), (ii)	'b'
2.	'c'	XXY	Overall masculine development	'd'
3.	Turner's	45 with OX	'e' (i), (ii)	'f'

23. Community Service department of your school plans a visit to a slum area near the school with an objective to educate the slum dwellers with respect to health and hygiene.

(a) Why is there a need to organize such visits?

(b) Write the steps you will highlight, as a member of this department, in your interaction with them to enable them to lead a healthy life.

24. The following graph shows the species – area relationship. Answer the following questions as directed.

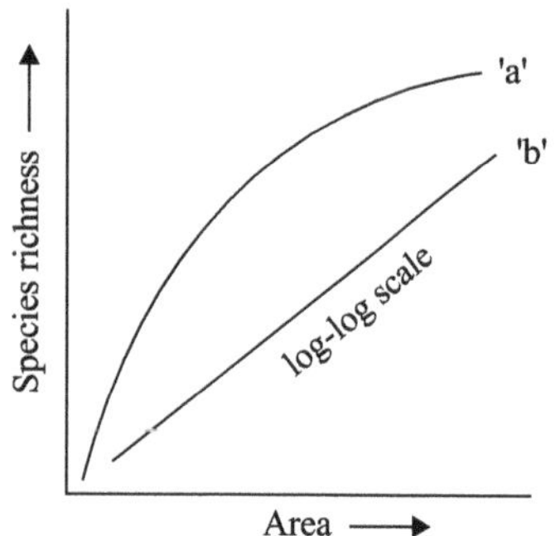

(a) Name the naturalist who studied the kind of relationship shown in the graph. Write the observation made by him.

(b) Write the situations as discovered by the ecologists when the value of 'Z' (slope of the line) lies between

(i) 0.1 and 0.2

(ii) 0.6 and 1.2

What does 'Z' stand for ?

(c) When would the slope of the line 'b' become steeper?

25. Name and describe the technique that helps in separating the DNA fragments formed by the use of restriction endonuclease.

26. State the function of a reservoir in a nutrient cycle. Explain the simplified model of carbon cycle in nature.

27. Since the origin of life on earth, there were five episodes of mass extinction of species.

(i) How is the 'Sixth Extinction', presently in progress, different from the previous episodes ?

(ii) Who is mainly responsible for the 'Sixth Extinction'?

(iii) List any four points that can help to overcome this disaster.

SECTION - D

28. (a) Where does fertilization occur in humans? Explain the events that occur during this process.

(b) A couple where both husband and wife are producing functional gametes, but the wife is still unable to conceive, is seeking medical aid. Describe any one method that you can suggest to this couple to become happy parents.

OR

(a) Explain the different ways apomictic seeds can develop. Give an example of each.

(b) Mention one advantage of apomictic seeds to farmers.

(c) Draw a labelled mature stage of a dicotyledonous embryo.

29. (a) Describe the various steps of Griffith's experiment that led to the conclusion of the 'Transforming Principle'.

(b) How did the chemical nature of the 'Transforming Principle' get established?

OR

Describe how the *lac* operates, both in the presence and absence of an inducer in *E.coli*.

30. With advancement in genetics, molecular biology and tissue culture, new traits have been incorporated into crop plants.

Explain the main steps in breeding a new genetic variety of crop.

OR

(a) State the objective of animal breeding.

(b) List the importance and limitation of inbreeding. How can the limitations can be overcome.

(c) Give an example of new breed of cattle and poultry.

Solutions

SECTION - A

1. The tassels of the corn-cob represent stigma and style of the flower. **(1 Mark)**

2. The two contrasting traits related to the seeds of pea plant that were studied by Mendel are as follows: **(1 Mark)**

   Seed shape- Round seeds and Wrinkled seeds

   Seed colour- Yellow and Green

3. The secondary immune response is more intense than primary immune response because the secondary immune response is based on the memory of the first encounter. The secondary immune response takes place when our body encounters the same antigen for second time. Our body have memory of the first encounter that recognize the pathogen quickly on subsequent exposure and initiates the production of antibodies. **(1 Mark)**

The secondary immune response is pathogen specific and is characterised by memory.

4. It is not possible for an alien DNA to become part of a chromosome anywhere along its length and replicate normally because the process of replication does not initiate randomly at any place in the DNA as it only initiates at the origin of replication. **(1 Mark)**

5. The C-peptide in human insulin is a short stretch of amino acids that is present in proinsulin and during the process of maturation of insulin this C-peptide is removed. So, it is involved in the synthesis of mature insulin. **(1 Mark)**

An American company Eli lily in 1983 prepared two DNA sequence corresponding to A and B chains of human insulin and introduced them in plasmids of E.coil to produce insulin chains. Chain A & chain B were separately produced & joined together by disulphide bond.

6. Enzymes that can be used for the isolation of DNA from bacterial cell is lysozyme and for fungal cell is chitinase for recombinant DNA technology. **(1 Mark)**

7. Gause's *Competitive Exclusion Principle'* states that two closely related species competing for the same resources cannot co-exist indefinitely and the competitively inferior one will be eventually eliminated. **(1 Mark)**

8. Fungi are able to form symbiotic association with the root nodules of plants and are called mycorrhiza. So many members of the genus *Glomus* form mycorrhiza. The fungal symbiont in this association absorbs phosphorus from soil and passes it to the plant. Plants having such associations show other benefits such as these are resistance to root-borne pathogens, tolerance against salinity and drought. It also promotes the overall growth and development of plant. **(1 Mark)**

SECTION - B

9. The testes are located outside the abdominal cavity in a pouch like structure called scrotum because the process of spermatogenesis or sperm production requires lower temperature (2-2.5°C) than the normal body temperature (37°C). The scrotum helps in maintaining the low temperature of the testes. **(2 Marks)**

10. (a) The appearance of pink colour in a Snapdrgon flower or *Antirrhinum sp.* is not considered as blending because the process of blending involves intermixing of two characters but in Snapdragon flower, the alleles do not mix with each other. So, they tends to maintain their originality and reappear in F2 generation. The development of pink colour is because the dominant allele is not completely dominant over the recessive allele. **(1 Mark)**

    (b) This phenomena is called incomplete dominance. **(1 Mark)**

11. The phenomena of multiple allelism and co-dominance are represented by ABO blood group in human beings. The gene *i* for the blood group contains three alleles such as I^A, I^B and *i*. These alleles represent the phenomena of multiple allelism as it contain more than two alleles that controls the same characters. The alleles I^A and I^B are co-dominant and express themselves independently in a next generation. The presence of both the blood group I^A and I^B produces blood group AB and this is an example of co-dominance. **(2 Marks)**

Co-dominance is a form of inheritance in which the alleles of a gene pair in a heterozygote are independently expressed themselves in a hybrid.

12. The scientific name of the fruit fly is called *Drosophilla melanogaster.* Morgan prefers to work with fruit-flies for his experiment because of the following reasons such as: **(2 Marks)**

- They are easily grown on a simple synthetic medium in a laboratory.
- They complete their life cycle in about two weeks and a single mating could produce a large number of offsprings.
- There was a clear differentiation of sexes as male and female flies are easily distinguishable.

OR

Linkage is defined as the tendency of two or more non-allelic genes to be inherited together because they are located more or less closely on the same chromosome. Whereas crossing over is defined as the process by which two homologous chromosome paired and exchange chromosomal segments of the coiled DNA. **(1 Mark)**

So, if the linkage is high then the crossing over will be low whereas if linkage is less than the crossing over will be more.

For example, in drosophila, a yellow bodied and white eyed female was crossed with brown bodies and red eyed male, F1 progeny is produced and then they are inter-crossed. The F2 phenotypic ratio of drosophila deviated significantly from Mendel's 9:3:3:1, the genes for eye colour and body colour are closely located on the 'X' chromosome indicates high linkage. So, they are inherited together and the recombinants were formed due to crossing over but at low percentage **(1 Mark)**

13. The symptoms of Ascariasis are as follows:

- Constipation
- Abdominal pain and cramps
- Stools with excess mucous and blood clots

Houseflies act as mechanical carriers and serves to transmit the parasite from faeces of infected person to food and food products. Drinking water and food contaminated by the faecal matter are the main source of infection. **(2 Marks)**

14. The genus *Nucleopolyhedrovirus* are baculoviruses that are used as a biological control agents. These viruses are excellent source for species-specific, narrow spectrum insecticidal applications. There will be negative impact on plants, mammals, birds, and fish or even on non-target insects. Such viruses are used for integrated pest management programme (IPM). **(2 Marks)**

15. Restriction enzymes belong to a larger class of enzymes called nucleases. They are of two types such as endonuclease and exanucleases. Restriction endonuclease is the most widely used enzyme in recombinant DNA technology and molecular biology. This enzyme is involved in the process of gene modification. It recognizes specific sequences of nucleotides that is known as recognition site and produces a double strand nick in the desired DNA. The action of restriction endonuclease can be on palindromic sequences. For example, *EcoRI*cuts the DNA at the following palindromic sequence:

5' GAATTC 3'

3'CTTAAG 5'

Exonucleases remove nucleotides from the ends of the DNA. **(2 Marks)**

Pallindromes are groups of letters that form the same words when read both forward and backward. For example "MALAYALAM"

16. (a) The first transgenic cow called Rosie was made in 1997 that produces human-protein-enriched milk. The milk of that cow contains human alpha-lactalbumin and was nutritionally a more balanced diet for human babies than normal natural- cow. **(1 Mark)**

(b) Transgenic animals carry genes that make them more sensitive to toxic substances and the results obtained in less time. **(1 Mark)**

17. The relationship between the fig tree and wasp shows mutualism, the wasp lays its egg and also pollinates the fig's. On the other hand, the fig not only provides shelter (fruit) for oviposition to wasp but also allows its larva to feed on seeds. **(2 Marks)**

Mutualism is a type of population interaction that confers benefits on both the interacting species.

18. Diagrammatic Representation of Expanding age pyramid:

Post-reproductive

Reproductive

Post-reproductive

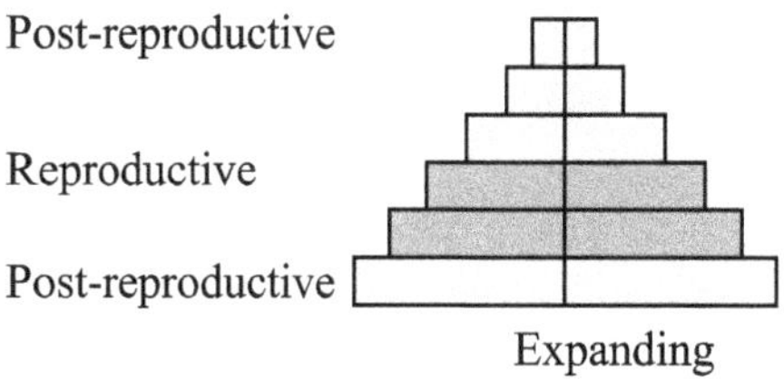

Expanding

Expanding age pyramid indicates that the population is growing. **(2 Marks)**

Age pyramids represent age distribution of males and females in a combined diagram. As, the shape of the pyramid reflects the growth status of the population.

SECTION - C

19. The outbreeding devices developed by plants are as follows:

- Some species of plants, pollen release an receptivity of stigma are not synchronised. Either the pollen is released before the stigma becomes receptive or stigma becomes receptive much before the release of pollen. **(1 Mark)**
- Some species of plants, the anther and stigma are placed at different positions so that the pollen cannot come in contact with the stigma of the same flower. Both these devices prevent autogamy. **(1 Mark)**
- The third device helps to prevent inbreeding is self-incompatibility. It is genetic mechanism that prevents self-pollen (from the same flower or other flowers of the same flower) from fertilising the ovules by inhibiting pollen germination or pollen tube growth in the pistil. **(1 Mark)**

OR

An angiosperm anther is bilobed with each lobe having two theca and because of this is called dithecous.

Structure of microsporangium:

A microsporangium is surrounded by four wall layers such as epidermis, endothecium, middle layer and tapetum. The outer three wall layers provide protection to the microsporangium and also help in dehiscence of anther to release the pollen. The innermost wall layer is the tapetum. It provide nourishment to the developing pollen grains. Cells of the tapetum possess dense cytoplasm and contain more than one nucleus. **(3 Marks)**

*The outer hard layer called the exine is made up of **spocropollenin** which is one of the most resistant organic material. It can tolerate high temperature as well as all biochemical and enzymatic degeradation.*

20. Aminocentesis is a foetal-sex determination test based on the chromosomal pattern in the amniotic fluid surrounding the developing embryo. This technique is used for the determination of sex and other metabolic disorders of the developing embryo. It is also used for the determination of genetic disorders in the developing foetus. Their will statutory ban on amniocentesis for sex-determination of developing foetus that increases female foeticides, and massive child immunisation. **(3 Marks)**

21. Pedigree analysis is done to study the human genetics because it provides all essential information that can be utilised to trace the inheritance of a specific trait such as abnormality or disease. Several disorders are inheritable and depend on the genetics of the families. They inherit the genes from such families. So pedigree analysis is done to trace such inheritance patterns. **(3 Marks)**

The conclusions that can be drawn from the pedigree analysis are:

- The pattern of inheritance and tracing of Mendelian disorders.
- The trait in question is dominant or recessive.
- The trait is linked to the sex chromosomes or autosomes.

In the pedigree analysis the inheritance of a specific terait is represented in the family tree over generations.

22.

S. No	Syndrome	Cause	Characteristics of affected individuals	Sex Male/ Female/ Both
1.	**Down's**	**Trisomy of 21**	(i) The affected individual is short statured with small round head. (ii) They have furrowed tongue and partially open mouth.	Commonly occurs in males.
2.	Klinefelter's syndrome	**XXY**	**Overall masculine development**	This disorder occurs in males.
3.	**Turner's**	**45 with XO**	(i) Such females are sterile as there ovaries are rudimentary (ii) They also lacks secondary sexual characters.	Commonly occurs in females.

(3 Marks)

The chromosomal disorders are caused due to absence or excessive or abnormal arrangement of one or more chromosomes.

23. (a) There is need to Organize Community Service Department to visit a slum area is to create awareness about disease and their effects on the body and health and hygiene.

(b) The steps we will highlight, as a member of this department in our interaction with them to enable them to lead a healthy life will be:

- Explain them the importance of healthy life and healthy people more efficient at work.
- Health also increases productivity, economy, longevity and also reduces infants as well as maternal mortality.
- To make them aware of the various diseases and their effect.
- Teach people about the proper disposal of waste, control of vectors like mosquitoes, importance of hygienic food and drinking, balanced diet.
- Maintenance of hygienic environment, proper disposal of waste, and control of vector. **(3 Marks)**

24. (a) Alexander Von Humboldt was the naturalist who studied the relationship shown in the graph. He observed that within a region the species richness increases with the increase in explored area it only upto a limit. **(1 Mark)**

(b) When the value of z lies between **(1 Mark)**

(i) z = 0.1 to 0.2 for small or average area.

(ii) z = 0.6 to 1.2 for large area for example continent.

Z stands for slope of line.

(c) The slope of the line 'b' becomes steeper when very large areas such as continents are considered for species-area relationship. **(1 Mark)**

25. The technique that is used for separating DNA fragments in the lab is called gel electrophoresis. In this technique, restriction endonuclease is used for cutting DNA fragments. **(3 Marks)**

- The DNA fragments are negatively charged molecules so they can be separated by forcing them to move towards the anode under an electric field through a medium or matix.
- The most commonly used matrix is called agarose that is a natural polymer extracted from sea weeds.
- The DNA fragments separate according to their size through sieving effect provided by the agarose gel
- So, the smaller the fragment size, farther, it moves.
- The separated DNA fragments can be visualised only after staining the DNA with a compound known as ethidium bromide followed by exposure to UV radiation.
- A DNA marker with fragments of known lengths is usually run through the gel at the same time as the samples.
- By comparing the bands of the DNA samples with those from the DNA marker one can work out at the approximate length of the DNA fragments in the samples.

26. The movement of nutrient elements through the various components of an ecosystem is called nutrient cycling. It is also called biogeochemical cycles. It is of two types such as gaseous and sedimentary. The reservoir for gaseous type of nutrient cycle such as nitrogen and carbon cycle exists in the atmosphere and for the sedimentary cycle such as sulphur and phosphorus cycle. This reservoir is located in Earth's crust.

Environmental factors such as soil, moisture, pH, temperature and so on tends to release the nutrients in the atmosphere.

The main function of the reservoir is to meet with the deficit that occurs due to imbalance in the rate of influx and efflux. **(3 Marks)**

27. (i) The sixth extinction is different from previous extinctions in several ways:

The sixth extinction occurs rapidly such as the reduction in a number of species per unit area per unit time. It is accelerated by human activities such as deforestation, industrialization and so on. **(1 Mark)**

(ii) Human activities that lead to global warming and disruption of environmental as well as ecological balance are responsible for the sixth extinction. **(1 Mark)**

(iii) The disaster can be overcome by following ways: **(1 Mark)**

- Afforestation
- Reduction in over-exploitation of natural resources
- Conservation of species and their natural habitats in order to minimize the losses.
- Create awareness among people regarding global warming and their consequences.

SECTION - D

28. (a) The process of fertilization takes place at only if the ovum and sperms are transported simultaneously to the ampullary-isthmic junction. The process of fusion of a sperm with an ovum at this junction is ampullary-isthmic junction of fallopian tube.

The events involved in the process of fertilisation are as follows:

- During the process of fertilization, a sperm comes in contact with the *zona pellucida* layer of the ovum and also induces changes in the membrane that block the entry of additional sperms.
- It ensures that only one sperm can fertilise an ovum.
- The secretions of the acrosome help the sperm enter into the cytoplasm of the ovum through the zona pellucida and the plasma membrane.
- This induces the completion of the meiotic division of the secondary oocyte.
- The second meiotic division is also unequal and results in the formation of second polar body and a haploid ovum.
- The haploid nucleus of the sperms and that of the ovum fuse together to form a diploid zygote.

(3 Marks)

The acrosome of the sperm secretes hylauronidase enzyme to peneterate the corona radiata layer of the ovum.

(b) The technique suggested to the couples who are not able to conceive is IVF (In vitro fertilisation). This method involves embryo transfer. In this method, ova from the wife or donor female and sperms from the husband or donor male are collected. The ova and sperm are induced to form zygote under stimulated conditions in the laboratory. **(2 Marks)**

IVF is the method of fertilization that takes place outside the body in almost the conditions similar to that of body. This technique is also called test tube programme.

OR

(a) There are two ways by which the apomitic seeds are produced:

Agamospermy: In this method, the seeds are produced from diploid cells without meiosis and fertilization. For example: Apple.

Adentive embryony: In this method, the nucellus and integuments extends into the embryo sac and develops into embryo. It involves the formation of more than one embryo. For example: citrus fruit. **(3 Marks)**

(b) The main advantage of apomictic seeds is that there is no segregation of characters in the hybrid progeny. The apomictic seeds are cost effective and high yielding. **(1 Mark)**

(c) **Diagrammatic Representation of mature stage of dicotyledonous embryo:** **(1 Mark)**

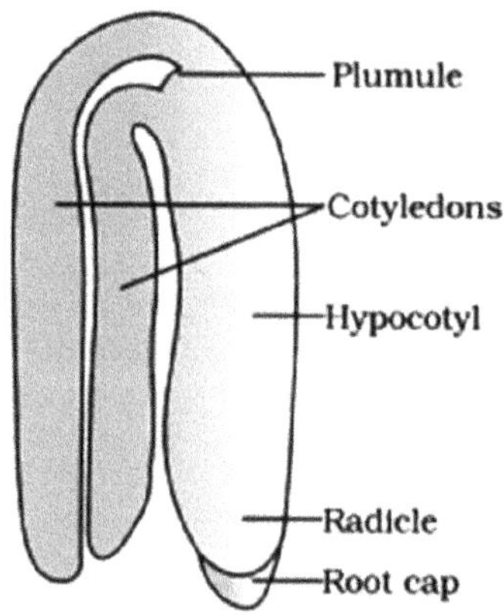

29. (a) The transforming principle was proposed by Frederick Griffith in 1928. He performed his experiment with *Streptococcus pneumonia* a bacteria which is responsible for causing pneumonia. **(3 Marks)**

The following steps are involved in his experiment:

- When *Streptococcus pneumonia* bacteria are grown on a culture plate, some bacteria produces smooth shiny colonies (s) whereas other produce rough colonies (R).
- It is because the S strain bacteria have a mucous polysaccharide coating whereas the R strain bacteria lack this coating.
- When the mice infected with the S strain or virulent strain, the mice die because of pneumonia infection.
- When the mice infected with the R strain do not develop pneumonia.
- Then, Griffith was able to kill bacteria by heating. He observed that heat-killed S strain bacteria injected into mice did not kill them.
- When he injected a mixture of heat-killed S and live R bacteria, the mice died. He recovered living S bacteria from the dead mice.

After this experiment, he concluded that the R strain bacterium has been transformed by the heat-killed S strain bacteria. As some 'transforming principle' was transferred from the heat-killed S strain and enabled the R strain to synthesise a smooth polysaccharide coating and become virulent. This is because of the transfer of the genetic material.

(b) The biochemical characterisation of Transforming principle was determined by Oswald Avery, Colin Macleod and Maclyn McCarty. Prior it was thought that the genetic material was protein.

The following steps are involved in his experiment:

- They purified biochemicals such as proteins, DNA and RNA from the heat-killed S cells to determine which one could transform live R cells into S cells.
- They discovered that DNA alone from S bacteria caused R bacteria to become transformed.
- They also discovered that protein-digesting enzymes such as proteases and RNA-digesting enzymes such as RNases did not affect the transformation.
- Hence, it was proved that the transforming substance was not protein and RNA.
- Digestion with DNase did inhibit transformation and the DNA caused the transformation.
- So, they concluded that DNA is the hereditary material. **(2 Marks)**

OR

Lac operon was proposed by Jacob and Monad in 1961. It contains following components such as: **(5 Marks)**

(i) **Structural gene:** There are three types of structural genes that codes for different enzymes and facilitates the process of transcription in the presence of inducer (lactose).

- The **z gene** codes for enzyme beta-galactosidase that regulates the switching on and is responsible for the hydrolysis of disaccharide, lactose into its monomeric unit's glucose.
- **Y gene** codes for enzyme permease that increases the permeability of the cell to beta-galactosides.
- **a gene** codes for enzyme transacetylase.

(ii) **Promoter:** It is the sequence of DNA at which the RNA polymerase enzyme get binds and initiates the process of transcription.

(iii) **Operator:** It is sequence of DNA that is adjacent to promoter.

(iv) **Regulator gene:** A gene that codes for repressor protein and binds with the operator and because of it operon is switched "off".

(v) **Inducer:** Lactose is inducer that helps in switching "on" of operon.

Lactose acts as the substrate for enzyme beta-galactosidase. This enzyme regulates the switching on and off the operon because of this it is termed as inducer. So, in the absence of glucose (carbon source), if lactose is added in the growth medium of the bacteria. The lactose is transported into the cells by the action of permease enzyme that increases permeability of the cell to beta-galactosides.

Lactose induces the operon in following manner:

- In a *lac* operon, the repressor protein is synthesised from the *i* gene.
- This repressor protein gets bind with the operator region of the operon and prevents RNA polymerase enzyme from transcribing the operon.
- In the absence of lactose, the repressor gene produces repressor protein and get binds with the operator gene. It prevents the RNA polymerase enzyme to get binds with the operon.

Diagrammatic Representation of *lac* operon in the absence of lactose:

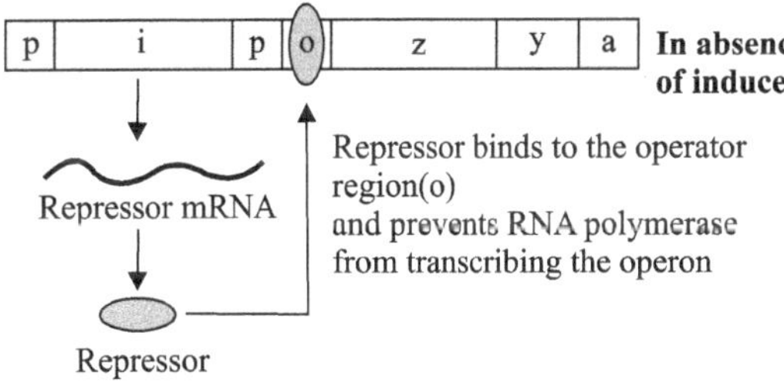

- In the presence of lactose as an inducer, the repressor protein is inactivated. It allows RNA polymerase enzyme to activate the promoter and initiates the process of transcription by structural genes.

Diagrammatic Representation of *lac* operon in the presence of inducer:

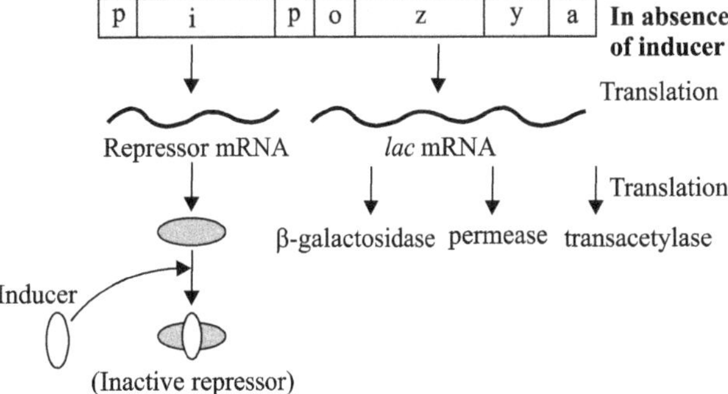

30. Plant breeding refers to a technique that involves the manipulation of plant species in order to produce desired genotypes and phenotypes. The main steps that involves in plant breeding for the production of genetic variety of crop are as follows:

(i) **Collection of variability:** The genetic variability is the root of any crop breeding programme. In many crops, the pre-existing genetic variability is available from the wild relatives of the crop. It involves the collection and preservation of all the different wild varieties, species and relatives of the cultivated species. The entire collection of plants or seeds that contains all the diverse alleles for all genes in a given crop is called **germplasm collection.**

(ii) **Evaluation and selection of parents:** The germplasm is evaluated to identify the plants with desirable combination of characters. The selected plants are multiplied and used in the process of hybridisation. Purelines are created wherever the desirable and possible.

(iii) **Cross hybridisation among the selected parents:** The desired characters are formed by the combination of two different plants. For example high protein quality of one parent may need to be combined with disease resistance from another parent. It can be achieved by cross hybridising the two parents to produce hybrids that genetically combine the desired characters in one plant.

(iv) **Selection and testing of superior recombinants:** This step involves the selection of the progeny of the hybrids. The plants that have the desired character combination. The selection process involves the success of the breeding objective and requires careful scientific evaluation of the progeny. This step yields plants that are superior to both of the parents.

(v) **Testing, release and commercialisation of new cultivars:** The newly selected lines are evaluated for their yield and other agronomic traits of quality, disease resistance and so on. This evaluation is done by growing these in the research field and recording their performance under ideal fertiliser application irrigation and other crop management practices. The evaluation in research fields is followed by testing the materials in farmer's field for atleast three growing seasons at several locations in the country. Then the material is evaluated in comparison to the best available local crop cultivar to check or reference cultivar. **(5 Marks)**

OR

(a) Animal breeding aims to increase the yield of animals and also improving the desirable qualities of the animals. **(1 Mark)**

(b) Inbreeding refers to the mating of more closely related individuals within the same breed for 4-6 generations.

Importance of inbreeding:

- Inbreeding increases homozygosity.
- It helps in accumulation of superior genes
- It helps in the elimination of desirable genes.

Limitations of inbreeding:

- Inbreeding leads to inbreeding depression.
- It reduces fertility and productivity.

The limitations of inbreeding can be overcome by techniques such as outbreeding, outcrossing, cross breeding and interspecific hybridisation. All these techniques involve the breeding of selected animals with unrelated superior animals of the same breed. **(3 Marks)**

(c) **Example of new breed of cattle is** *Hisardale* and **Example of new breed of poultry is** *Hampshire.* **(1 Mark)**

Delhi 2014

CBSE Board Solved Paper

Time Allowed : 3 Hours | *Maximum Marks : 70*

General Instructions:

(i) All questions are compulsory.

(ii) This question paper consists of four Sections **A, B, C** and **D**. Section **A** contains **8** questions of **one** mark each, Section **B** is of **10** questions of **two** marks each, Section **C** is of **9** questions of **three** marks each and Section **D** is of **3** questions of **five** marks each.

(iii) There is no overall choice. However, an internal choice has been provided in **one** question of **2** marks, **one** question of **3** marks and **all** the questions of **5** marks weightage. A student has to attempt only **one** of the altematives in such questions.

(iv) Wherever necessary, the diagrams drawn should be neat and properly labelled.

SECTION - A

1. Write the name of the organism that is referred to as the 'Terror of Bengal'

2. What are 'true breeding lines' that are used to study inheritance pattern of traits in plants ?

3. Name any two types of cells which act as 'Cellular barriers' to provide Innate Immunity in humans.

4. Mention the type of host cells suitable for the gene guns to introduce an alien DNA.

5. How is 'stratification' represented in a forest ecosystem ?

6. Give an example of an organism that enters 'diapause' and why.

7. Identify 'a' and 'b' in the figure given below representing proportionate number of major vertebrate taxa.

Vertebrates

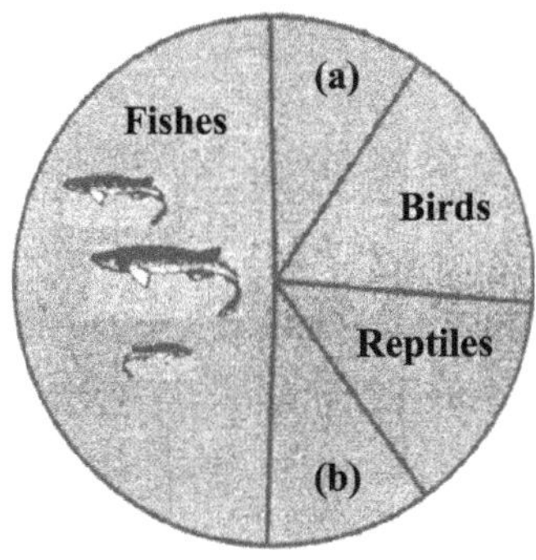

8. State the cause of Accelerated Eutrophication.

SECTION - B

9. Why do algae and fungi shift to sexual mode of reproduction just before the onset of adverse conditions ?

10. A cross was carried out between two pea plants showing the contrasting traits of height of the plant. The result of the cross showed 50% of parental characters.

(i) Work out the cross with the help of a punnett square.

(ii) Name the type of the cross carried out.

11. How does the gene 'I' control ABO blood groups in humans? write the effect the gene has on the structure of red blood cells.

OR

Write the types of sex-determination mechanisms the following crosses show. Give an example of each type.

(i) Female XX with Male XO

(ii) Female ZW with Male ZZ

12. (i) Name the scientist who suggested that the genetic code should be made of a combination of three nucleotides.

(ii) Explain the basis on which he arrived at this conclusion.

13. State the disadvantage of inbreeding among cattle. How it can be overcome ?

14. Explain with the help of a suitable example the naming of a restriction endonuclease.

15. State how has *Agrobacterium tumifuciens* been made a useful cloning vector to transfer DNA to plant cells.

16. Construct an age pyramid which reflects a stable growth status of human population.

17. Apart from being part of the food chain, predators play other important roles. Mention any two such roles supported by examples.

18. How are 'sticky ends' formed on a DNA strand ? Why are they so called ?

SECTION - C

19. Explain any three advantages the seeds offer to angiosperms.

20. Name and explain the role of inner and middle walls of the human uterus.

21. A colourblind child is born to a normal couple. Work out a cross to show how it is possible. Mention the sex of this child.

OR

Mendel published his work on inheritance of characters in 1865, but it remained unrecognized till 1900. Give three reasons for the delay in accepting his work.

22. Women are often blamed for producing female children. Consequently, they are ill-treated and ostracized. How will you address this issue scientifically if you were to conduct an awareness programme to highlight the values involved?

23. (a) Name the tropical sugar cane variety grown in South India. How has it helped in improving the sugar cane quality grown in North India ?

(b) Identify 'a', 'b' and 'c' in the following table :

No.	Crop	Variety	Insect Pests
1.	Brassica	Pusa Gaurav	(a)
2.	Flat bean	Pusa Sem 2	(b)
3.	(c)	Pusa Sawani Pusa A-4	Shoot and fruit borer

24. Why are beehives kept in crop field during flowering period? Name any two crop fields where this is practiced.

25. How did the process of RNA interference help to control the nematode from infecting roots of tobacco plants ? Explain.

26. Study the graph given below and answr the questions that follow :

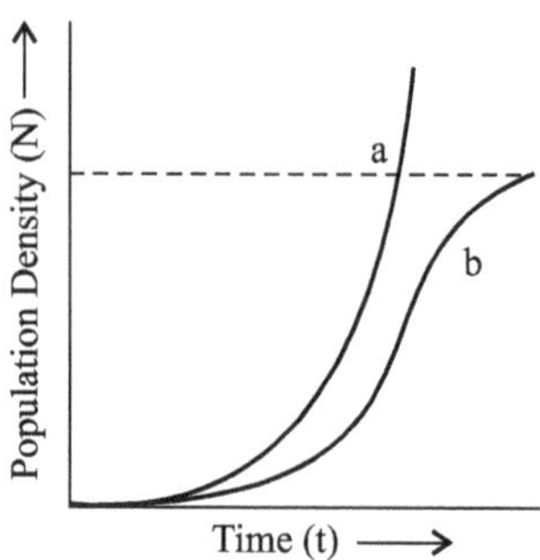

(i) Write the status of food and space in the curves (a) and (b).

(ii) In the absence of predators, which one of the two curves would appropriately depict the prey population?

(iii) Time has been shown on X-axis and there is a parallel dotted line above it. Give the significance of this dotted line.

27. (i) What is primary productivity? Why does it vary in different types of eco-systems?

(ii) State the relation between gross and net primary productivity.

SECTION - D

28. (a) Coconut palm is monoecious, while date palm is dioecious. Why are they so called?

(b) Draw a labelled diagram of sectional view of a mature embryo sac of an angiosperm.

OR

(a) How 'oogenesis' markedly different from 'spermatogenesis' with respect to the growth till puberty in the humans?

(b) Draw a sectional view of human ovary and label the different follicular stages, ovum and Corpus luteum.

29. (a) Explain the process of DNA replication with the help of a schematic diagram.

(b) In which phase of the cell cycle does replication occur in Eukaryotes ? What would happen if cell-division is not followed after DNA replication ?

OR

(a) Explain Darwinian theory of evolution with the help of one suitable example. State the two key concepts of the theory.

(b) Mention any three characteristics of Neanderthal man that lived in near east and central Asia.

30. (a) Name the technology that has helped the scientists to propagate on large scale the desired crops in short duration. List the steps carried out to propagate the crops by the said technique.

(b) How are somatic hybrids obtained ?

OR

(a) Cancer is one of the most dreaded diseases of humans. Explain 'Contact inhibition' and 'Metastasis' with respect to the disease.

(b) Name the group of genes which have been identified in normal cells that could lead to cancer and how they do so ?

(c) Name any two techniques which are useful to detect cancers of internal organs.

(d) Why are cancer patients often given α-interferon as part of the treatment ?

Solutions

SECTION - A

1. An organism that is referred to as 'Terror of Bengal' is called water hyacinth or *Eicchornia crassipes.* **(1 Mark)**

Water hyacinth is called 'terror of Bengal' because it is an alien species which were introduced in India for their lovely flowers and it causes havoc by their excessive growth. They grow abundantly in eutrophic water bodies and leads to an imbalance in the ecosystem dynamics of the water body.

2. True breeding lines are those plants that have been generated through repeated self-pollination and have become homozygous for particular traits. This trait is then passed onto the future generations if bred with another true breeding plant. **(1 Mark)**

3. certain types of leukocytes (WBCs) such as Polymorpho-Nuclear Leukocytes (PMNL-neutrophils), monocytes and natural killer cells in the blood as well as macrophages in the tissues that can phagocytise and destroy microbes. These cells act as cellular barriers and provide innate immunity in humans. **(1 Mark)**

Innate immunity is non-specific type of defence which is present at the time of birth.

4. An undifferentiated plant cells are the most suitable host cells for the gene guns or biolistics gun. Plant cells are used because they have rigid cell wall that can be broken easily by bombarding them with high velocity micro-particles of gold or tungsten coated with DNA in a gene gun.**(1 Mark)**

5. Stratification refers to the vertical distribution of different species occupying different levels. It involves trees occupy top vertical strata or layer of a forest, shrubs the second and herbs and grasses occupy the bottom layers. **(1 Mark)**

6. Under unfavourable conditions several zooplankton species in lakes and ponds are enter into a *diapause,* a stage of suspended development. **(1 Mark)**

Diapause takes place in adverse conditions such as drought, extreme temperature, and reduced food availability. The physiological and metabolic activities are inhibited during this phase.

7. In the given figure, **a** represents amphibians and **b** represents mammals. **(1 Mark)**

8. Accelerated eutrophication is the ageing of a water body because of nutrient enrichment of water. This phenomenon can either be natural or artificial.

Causes of accelerated eutrophication:

- Fertilizers runoff from the field to the water body results in algal bloom that leads to cause eutrophication.
- Industrial and sewage effluent also leads to increase the temperature and Biochemical oxygen demand of the water body. It results in increased biological activity leads to cause algal blooms. **(1 Mark)**

SECTION - B

9. Organisms such as fungi and algae that switch to sexual mode of reproduction during adverse conditions because sexual reproduction brings variation into the individuals. It helps individuals to adapt the changing environmental conditions and promotes survival in unfavourable conditions. This process helps in the continuity of the species. **(2 Marks)**

*When two parents (male and female) participate in the reproductive process and the fusion of male and female gametes is called **sexual reproduction**.*

10. (i) **Diagrammatic Representation of Cross:**

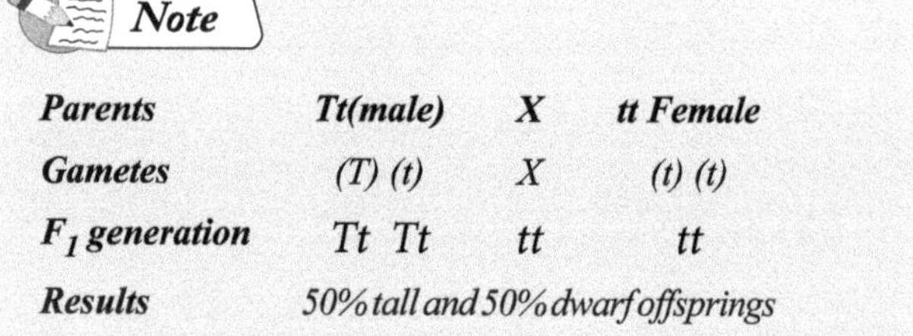

Parents	Tt(male)	X	tt Female
Gametes	(T) (t)	X	(t) (t)
F_1 generation	Tt Tt	tt	tt
Results	50% tall and 50% dwarf offsprings		

In the above cross, 50% progeny is tall (dominant) and 50% progeny is dwarf (recessive). **(1 Mark)**

(ii) The type of cross carried out is called test cross. In test cross, an unknown dominant phenotype is crossed with an individual homozygous recessive for that specific trait. **(1 Mark)**

11. The inheritance of human blood group is an example of codominance and multiple alleles. ABO blood grouping in human beings are controlled by *I* gene. The plasma membrane of the red blood cells has sugar polymers that are found on the surface of RBCs and is controlled by this gene.

The I gene has three alleles I^A, I^B and i. The gene I^A and I^B are dominant over i and both I^A and I^B express their own types of sugars. This phenomenon is called co-dominance. Hence, red blood cells have both A and B types of sugars. While i allele do not produce any sugar. There are three different alleles and there are six different genotypes of the human ABO blood types.

Tabular representation of genetic basis of Blood Groups in Human population:

Allele from	Allele from Parent 2	Genotype of offspring	Blood types of offspring
I^A	I^A	I^AI^A	*A*
I^A	I^B	I^AI^B	*AB*
I^A	i	I^Ai	*A*
I^B	I^A	I^AI^B	*AB*
I^B	I^B	I^BI^B	*B*
I^B	i	I^Bi	*B*
i	i	ii	*O*

OR

(i) The type of sex determination mechanism shown in female XX with male XO is male heterogamety such as in Humans.

(ii) The type of sex determination mechanism shown in female ZW with male ZZ is female heterogamety such as in Birds. **(2 Marks)**

12. (i) George Gamow was scientist who suggested that the genetic code should be made of a combination of three nucleotides.

(ii) According to George Gamow, there are only 4 nitrogenous bases and if they have to code for 20 amino acids, the code should constitute a combination of bases. He also suggested that in order to code for all the 20 amino acids, the code should be made up of three nucleotides. This was a very bold proposition, because a permutation combination of 4^3 (4×4×4) that would generate 64 codons. He provide an evidence that the codon was triplet in nature. **(2 Marks)**

A codon is a sequence of three DNA or RNA nucleotides. There are 64 codon out which 61 codes for 20 aminoacides and 3 codons are stop codon that terminates the process of translation.

13. Disadvantage of inbreeding is inbreeding depression. Inbreeding reduces fertility and productivity of an animal. It can be overcome by using different techniques such as:

Outbreeding in which breeding of the unrelated animals that may be between individuals of the same breed but no common ancestors.

Out crossing is a technique in which mating of animals within the same but having no common ancestors on either side of their pedigree upto 4-6 generations.

Cross-breeding is a technique in which superior males of one breed are mated with superior females of another breed.

Interspecific hybridisation involves the mating of male and female animals of two different species. **(2 Marks)**

Inbreeding refers to the mating of more closely related individuals within the same breed for 4-6 generations.

14. The convention for naming enzyme restriction endonucleases such as ECoRI contains the first letter of the name that comes from the genes and the second two letters comes from the species of the prokaryotic cell from which they were isolated.

For example: in case of ECoRI comes from *Escherichia coli* RY 13. In this, the letter 'R' is derived from the name of strain. Roman numbers following the names indicate the order in which the enzymes were isolated from that strain of bacteria. **(2 Marks)**

15. *Agrobacterium tumifaciens,* is a pathogen of several dicot plants is able to deliver a piece of DNA known as 'T-DNA' to transform normal plant cells into tumor.

- To direct these tumor cells to produce the chemical required by the pathogen.
- Retroviruses in animals have ability to transform normal cells into cancerous cells.
- The tumor inducing (Ti) plasmid of *Agrobacterium tumifaciens* has modified into a cloning vector and is no more pathogenic to the plants and is used to deliver genes of interest into a variety of plants.
- The Ti plasmid contains genes that codes for the synthesis of auxin and cytokinin hormone and its introduction in a plant helps to produce its own nutrient machinery. **(2 Marks)**

16. Diagrammatic Representation of Stable Age pyramid:

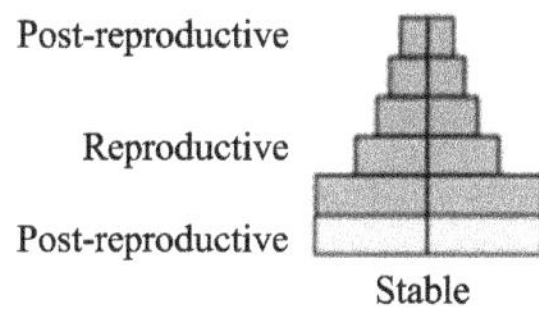

Stable age pyramid indicates equal proportion of population in each age group. **(2 Marks)**

Age pyramids represent age distribution of males and females in a combined diagram. As, the shape of the pyramid reflects the growth status to the population.

17. Important roles played by predators apart from being a part of the food chain:
    - Predators check the prey-population.
    - They prevent the over-population of prey and
    - Predators also help in maintaining the biodiversity in an ecosystem. **(2 Marks)**
18. The sticky ends are produced by the restriction enzymes. The restriction enzymes cut the strand of the DNA a little away from the centre of the palindromic sites, but between the same two bases on the opposite strands. This leaves single stranded portions at the ends. There are overhanging stretches called sticky ends on each strand.

    They are called sticky ends because they form hydrogen bonds with their complementary cuts. This stickiness of the ends facilitates the action of the enzyme DNA ligase.

    Diagrammatic Representation of action of Restriction Enzymes:

The enzyme cuts both DNA strands at the same site
EcoRI cuts the DNA between bases G and A only when the sequence GAATTC is present in the DNA
Vector DNA
Foreign DNA
EcoRI
Sticky end
Sticky end
DNA fragments join at sticky ends
Recombinant DNA

(2 Marks)

SECTION - C

19. The three advantages that seeds offer to angiosperms are as follows:
    - The seeds of angiosperms provide protection to the embryo from harsh environmental conditions.
    - It provides nourishment and parental care to the developing embryo.
    - The dispersal of the seeds to far-off places prevents competition among the members of the same species and prevents their extinction. **(3 Marks)**

In angiosperms, there are two types of seeds albuminous and non-albuminous. Non-albuminous seeds have no residual endosperm as it is completely consumed during embryo development e.g. pea and groundnut where as albuminous seeds retain a part of endosperm e.g. wheat, maize and castor.

20. The middle wall of the uterus is called myometrium. It consists of smooth muscles that bring about contraction of uterine muscles during delivery of the baby.

    The inner wall of the uterus is the inner glandular layer called endometrium and it plays an essential role during menstrual cycle. As it undergoes cyclic changes during menstrual cycle. Endometrium is necessary for implantation of the fertilised ovum and other events of pregnancy. **(3 Marks)**
21. Colour blindness is a sex-linked disease. The gene for this disorder is present on X chromosome. As males have only one X chromosome while females have two X chromosomes. If a colour blind child is born from a normal couple then in this case, the mother will be carrier for colour blindness and colour blind child will be male.

    Diagrammatic Representation Cross of Colourblindness:

Parents	***X^CX (Mother)***	***X***	***XY (Father)***
Gametes	*X^C X*	*X*	*X Y*
F_1 generation	*X^C X*	*X^C Y*	*XX XY*
Results	*Carrier female*	*Colour blind male*	*Normal child male and female*

(3 Marks)

OR

Three reasons that are responsible for the delay in accepting Mendel's work:
- Lack of communication and publicity.
- His concept of factors or gene as discrete units that did not blend with each other was not accepted in the terms of variations that occur naturally in nature.
- Mendel's approach to explain biological phenomena with the help of mathematics was also not accepted.

(3 Marks)

22. The sex of the child is determined by father as the type gametes child receives from the father. As, the father contains two types of chromosomes such as XY whereas the mothers contains only XX chromosomes. When X chromosome from father fuses with the X chromosome from mother then the child will be girl while if the Y chromosome from father fuses with X chromosome of mother then the

child will be boy. So, the female or mother is not responsible for the sex determination of child. Women should not be ill-treated for giving birth to a girl child, as both males and females are equally important for the balance of nature and continuity of species. **(3 Marks)**

23. (a) *Saccharum officinarum* is the tropical variety of sugar cane grown in South India that had higher stems and higher sugar contents. *Saccharum barberi* was grown in North India and had poor sugar content and yield. So these two species were successfully crossed to get sugar varieties that combining the desirable qualities of high yield, thick stems, high sugar content and ability to grow in the sugar cane areas of North India. **(2 Marks)**

(b)

S.No	Crop	*Variety*	Insect pests
1.	**Brassica**	*Pusa Gaurav*	Aphids
2.	**Flat beans**	*Pusa Sem 2* *Pusa Sem 3*	Jassids, aphids and fruit borer
3.	Okra (Bhindi)	*Pusa Sawani* *Pusa A-4*	**Shoot and fruit borer**

(1 Mark)

24. Beehives are kept in the crop fields during the flowering period to increase efficiency of pollination and also improves yield. Bees collect huge amount of nectar and produces more honey and in return they pollinate the flowers from which they collect nectar. This technique is practiced in the crop fields such as sunflower and apple. **(3 Marks)**

*Bee-keeping or **apiculture** is the maintenance of hives of honeybees for the production of honey.*

25. *Meloidogyne incognitia* is a nematode that causes infections in the root of tobacco plants. This reduces the yield of tobacco plants. In order to protect the tobacco plants from infection, a process called **RNA interference** occurs in all eukaryotic organisms as a method of cellular defense. The process of RNA interference involves **mRNA silencing** because of complementary dsRNA molecule that get binds to and prevents the translation of mRNA.

The complementary RNA is obtained due to the infection by viruses that contain an RNA genome or mobile genetic elements (transposons). It replicate via an RNA intermediate.

By using *Agrobacterium* vectors, nematode-specific gene were used to introduced into the host plant. After the introduction of DNA into the host, it produces both sense and anti-sense RNA in the host cells.

The two RNA's are complementary to each other formed a double strand (dsRNA) that initiates the process of RNAi and silenced the specific mRNA of the nematode. After that, the nematode is not able to survive in a transgenic host expressing specific interfering RNA.

In this way, the transgenic plant got itself to be protected from the parasite. **(3 Marks)**

26. (i) The curve (a) represents exponential growth of the population when the responses are not limiting the growth. Whereas curve (b) represents logistic growth of the population when responses are limiting the growth. **(1 Mark)**

(ii) In the absence of predator, the curve (a) is increasing as the responses are not limiting the growth. So in the absence of predator, prey population continuously increases. **(1 Mark)**

(iii) The parallel dotted line represents K (carrying capacity). **Carrying capacity** is defined as in nature; a given habitat has enough resources to support a maximum possible number beyond which no further growth is possible. **(1 Mark)**

27. (i) Primary productivity is defined as the amount of biomass or organic matter produced per unit area over a time period by plants during photosynthesis. The primary productivity depends on different plant species present in a given ecosystem and each of their photosynthetic efficiency. The environmental factors, availability of various nutrients vary in different ecosystems results in variations in primary productivity.

(ii) Gross primary productivity of an ecosystem is the rate of production of organic matter during photosynthesis. A considerable amount of Gross primary productivity is utilized by the plants in respiration. Net primary productivity or NPP is the Gross primary productivity minus the respiratory losses (R).

NPP = GPP-R **(3 Marks)**

*The rate of biomass production is called **Productivity** and it is expressed in terms of $g^{-2}\ yr^{-1}$ or $(kcal\ m^{-2})\ yr^{-1}$.*

SECTION - D

28. (a) Coconut palm is monoecious because both male and female gametes are borne on the same plant. Whereas in case of date palm, it is dioecious because both male and female flowers are borne on different plants. A single plant has either male flower or female flower. **(2 Marks)**

(b) **Diagrammatic Representation of Mature Embryo Sac of an Angiosperm:**

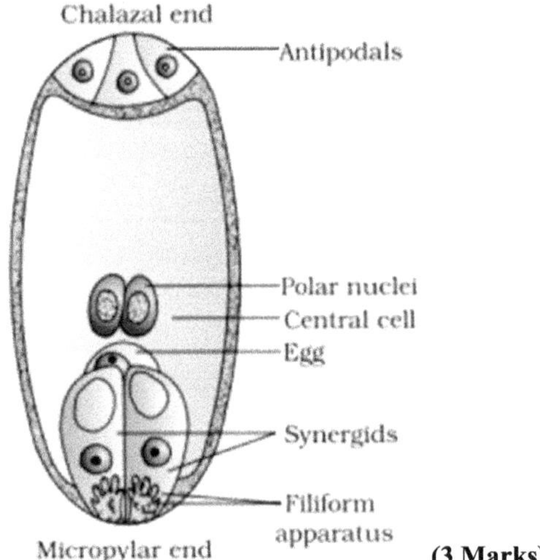

(3 Marks)

OR

(a) The process of formation of a mature female gamete is called oogenesis and is different from spermatogenesis. Oogenesis is initiated during the embryonic development stage when a couple of millions of oogonia or gamete mother cells are formed within each fetal ovary. These cells start division and enter into prophase-I of the meiotic division and get temporarily arrested at that stage called primary oocytes.

Each primary oocyte then gets surrounded by a layer of granulosa cells and then called the primary follicle. A large number of these follicles degenerate during the phase from birth to puberty. So, at puberty only 60,000-80,000 primary follicles are left in each ovary. The primary follicles get surrounded by more layers of granulosa cells and a new theca and this is called secondary follicles. Then secondary follicles transforms into a tertiary follicle that is characterised by a fluid filled cavity called antrum. The theca layer is organised into an inner theca interna and an outer theca externa.

The primary oocyte within the tertiary follicle grows in size and completes its first meiotic division. It is an unequal division that results in the formation of a large haploid secondary oocyte and a tiny first polar body. The secondary oocyte retains bulk of the nutrient rich cytoplasm of the primary oocyte. The tertiary follicle further changes into the mature follicle or Graafian follicle. The secondary oocyte forms a new membrane called zonapellucida surrounding it. Then the Graafian follicle ruptures to release the secondary oocyte from the ovary by the process called ovulation.

Whereas in the process of spermatogenesis, the immature male germ cells or spermatogonia produce sperms in the testis that begins at the puberty.

(3 Marks)

Spermatogenesis starts at the age of puberty due to significant intrease in the secretion of gonadotropin releasing hormone (GnRH).

(b) **Diagrammatic Representation of sectional view of ovary and follicular stages of ovum as well as corpus luteum:**

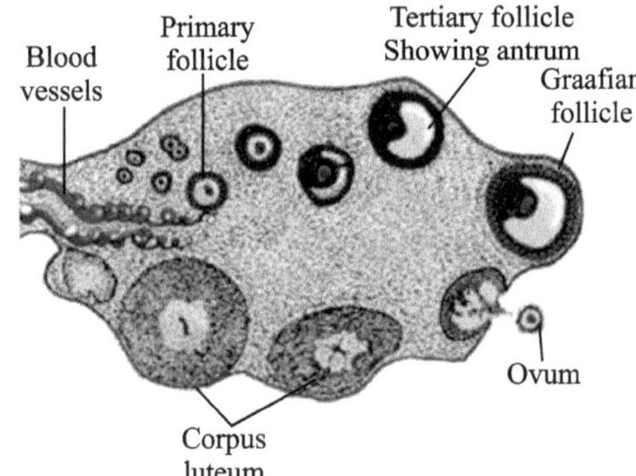

(2 Marks)

29. (a) DNA replication is the biological phenomenon in which a duplicate copy of DNA is synthesised. It involves following steps:

- The process of DNA replication takes place in the S-phase of the cell cycle.
- DNA dependent DNA polymerase enzyme is required for the process of replication.
- Deoxyribonucleoside triphosphate (DNTPs) plays dual role such as it acts as substrate as well as provides energy for polymerisation reaction.
- It originates at specific regions in DNA called the origin of replication because of the requirement of the origin of replication that a piece of DNA if needed to be propagated during recombinant DNA that requires a vector.
- DNA polymerase enzyme polymerises a large number if nucleotides in a very short time.
- For long DNA molecules, since the two strands of DNA cannot be separated in its entire length because of very high energy requirement.

- So the replication takes place within a small opening of the DNA helix called replication fork. The DNA-dependent DNA polymerase catalyse the polymerisation only in one direction such as 5'→3'.
- One strand called as template strand having polarity 3'→5', so the replication is continuous while the other strand having polarity 5' →3', so the replication is discontinuous.
- The discontinuously synthesised fragments are called okazaki fragment are later joined by the DNA ligase enzyme.

Diagrammatic Representation of replication fork during replication:

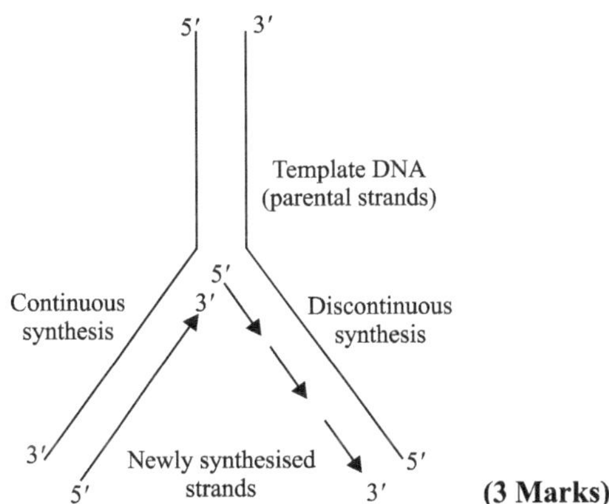

(3 Marks)

(b) In eukaryotes, the replication of DNA takes place at S-phase of the cell-cycle. The replication of DNA and cell division cycle should be highly coordinated. If cell division is not followed after DNA replication then the replicated chromosome would not be distributed to daughter nuclei. A repeated replication of DNA without any cell division results in the accumulation of DNA inside the cell. This would increase the volume of the cell nucleus causes cell expansion. **(2 Marks)**

OR

(a) Branching descent and natural selection are the two key concepts of Darwinian theory of Evolution.

According to the concept of Branching descent, various species have come into existence from a common ancestor.

In Natural selection, the nature selects the individuals that are most fit to adapt to their environment. It occurs because of availability of limited natural resources, variations in the characters of the members of population and inheritance of variations to next generation.

According to the Darwin theory of evolution:

- New forms keep on gradually evolving with time in the history.
- Those organisms that adapt themselves better to the surrounding survive and reproduce whereas other die and promotes the survival of the fittest one.
- There is always variation in characteristics of populations that help them to adapt better to the surroundings.

Example of natural selection is industrial melanism in which before industrialization, it was observed that there were more white-winged moths or melanised moths were found on the trees than dark-winged moths. But after industrialization in 1920s, it was observed that there were more dark-winged moths were found in the same area. It occurs because during post-industrialisation period, the tree trunks became dark due to industrial smoke and soots. In this condition, the white-winged moth did not survive because of predators. Hence dark-winged or melanised moth survived. **(3 Marks)**

Evolution is defined as the change in the characteristics of a species over several generations and is responsible for natural selection.

(b) The three characteristics of Neanderthal man are as follows:

- They have brain capacity 1400cc and lived near east and central Asia between 1,00,000-40,000 years back.
- They used hides to protect their body.
- They buried their dead. **(2 Marks)**

30. (a) Tissue culture refers to the technique that helps scientists to propagate the desired crops on a large scale in a short duration. Hence, a large number of plants are propagated through this culture and this process is also referred to as micropropagation.

The following steps are carried out to propagate crops by tissue culture:

- Explants are derived from any part of the plant to be propagated.
- The explants are grown in sterile conditions in special nutrient media to regenerate complete plants.
- The nutrient medium must contain a carbon source such as sucrose, organic salts, vitamins, amino acids and phytohormones such as auxin and cytokinin.

- All the plants obtained by tissue culture technique are called somaclones as they are genetically identical to each other as well as to the parent plant. Many important food plants such as tomato, banana, apple and so on have been produced on commercial scale by using plant tissue culture technique. **(3 Marks)**

(b) Somatic hybrids are hybrids produced by somatic hybridisation technique. In this technique, isolated single cells from plants are digested by scientists. Further they have digesting the cell walls to isolate naked protoplasts. Isolated protoplasts from two different varieties of plants having a desirable character that can be fused to get hybrid protoplasts that can be further grown to form a new plant. **(2 Marks)**

OR

(a) Normal cells show a property called contact inhibition by virtue of which contact with other cells that inhibits their uncontrolled growth. Cancer cells lack the property of contact inhibition because of thus the cancerous cells divides continuously and give rise to masses of cells called tumors.

There are two types of tumors such as benign and malignant. Benign tumors normally remains at their original location and do not spread to the other parts of the body results in little damage. Whereas the malignant tumors are a mass of proliferating cells called neoplastic or tumor cells. Such cells grow rapidly, invading and also damaging the surrounding normal tissue. All the tumor cells divide actively and grow. These cells also starve the normal cells by competing for vital nutrients. The cells sloughed from such tumors reach distant sites through blood and they get lodged in the body. Then they start a new tumor at new location and this property is called **metastasis** which is the most feared property of malignant tumors. **(2 Marks)**

(b) **Cause of cancer:** The transformation of normal cells into cancerous neoplastic cells is induced by physical, chemical or biological agents. These agents are called carcinogens. Ionising radiations such as X-rays and gamma rays while non-ionizing radiation involves UV cause DNA damage results in neoplastic transformation. **(1 Mark)**

(c) The chemical carcinogens present in tobacco smoke causes lung cancer. Cancer causing viruses called oncogenic viruses that have genes called viral oncogene. Certain genes called cellular oncogene or proto oncogene that have been identified in normal cells that are activated under several conditions that leads to cause oncogenic transformation of the cells.

Techniques such as techniques as radiotherapy, CT (Computer Tomography) and MRI (Magnetic Resonance Imaging) are useful for the detection of cancers in the internal organ.

Cancer patients are treated with substances called biological response modifiers called **alpha-interferon**. It activates their immune system and help in destroying the tumor. **(2 Marks)**

All India **2013**

CBSE Board Solved Paper

Time Allowed : 3 Hours *Maximum Marks : 70*

General Instructions:

(i) All questions are compulsory.

(ii) This question paper consist of **four** Sections **A, B, C** and **D.** Section **A** contains **8** questions of **one** mark each, Section **B** is of **10** questions of **two** marks each, Section **C** is of **9** questions of **three** marks each and Section **D** is of **3** questions of **five** marks each.

(iii) There is no overall choice. However, internal choice has been provided in one question of **2** marks, one question of **3** marks and two questions of **5** marks weightage. A student has to attempt only one of the alternatives in such questions.

(iv) Wherever necessary, the diagrams drawn should be neat and properly labelled.

SECTION - A

1. Name an organism where cell division in itself is a mode of reproduction.

2. When does a human body elicit an anamnestic response?

3. Name any two diseases the 'Himgiri' variety of wheat is resistant to.

4. State the role of transposons in silencing of mRNA in eukaryotic cells.

5. Why are green algae not likely to be found in the deepest strata of the ocean?

6. State what does 'standing crop' of a trophic level represent.

7. Why is the use of unleaded petrol recommended for motor vehicles equipped with catalytic converters?

8. Name the type of biodiversity represented by the following:

(i) 1000 varieties of mangoes of India.

(ii) Variations in terms of potency and concentration of reserpine in *Rauwolfia vomitoria* growing in different regions of Himalayas.

SECTION - B

9. In angiosperms, zygote is diploid while primary endosperm cell is triploid. Explain.

10. A cross between a red flower bearing plant and a white flower bearing plant of Antirrhinum produced all plants having pink flowers. Work out a cross to explain how this is possible.

11. List the two main propositions of Oparin and Haldane.

12. Write the events that take place when a vaccine for any disease is introduced into the human body.

OR

Why is a person with cuts and bruises following an accident administered tetanus antitoxin? Give reasons.

13. Name the bacterium response for the large holes seen in "Swiss Cheese". What are these holes due to?

14. Name the source of the DNA polymerase used in PCR technique. Mention why it is used.

15. Write any four ways used to introduce a desired DNA segment into a bacterial cell in recombinant technology experiments.

16. Why is proinsulin so called? How is inuslin different from it?

17. Where would you expect more species biodiversity – in tropics or in polar regions? Give reasons in support of your answer.

18. "It is possible that a species may occupy more than one trophic level in the same ecosystem at the same time." Explain with the help of one example.

SECTION - C

19. Explain the steps in the formation of an ovum from an oogonium in humans.

OR

Suggest and explain any three Assisted Reproducive Technologies (ART) to an infertile couple.

20. Why are human females rarely haemophilic?

Explain. How do haemophilic patients suffer?

21. In a maternity clinic, for some reasons the authorities are not able to hand over the two new-borns to their respective real parents. Name and describe the technique that you would suggest to sort out the matter.

22. Explain the increase in the numbers of melanic (dark winged) moths in the urban areas of post-industrialization period in England.

23. Describe how biogas is generated from activated sludge. List the components of biogas.

24. Name the pest that destroys the cotton bolls.

Explain the role of *Bacillus thuringiensis* in protecting the cotton crop against the pest to increase the yield.

25. (a) Write the importance of measuring the size of a population in a habitat or an ecosystem.

(b) Explain with the help of an example how the percentage cover is a more meaningful measure of population size than more numbers.

26. Differentiate between two different types of pyramids of biomass with the help of one example of each.

27. (a) Describe the endosperm development in coconut.

(b) Why is tender coconut considered a healthy source of nutrition?

(c) How are pea seeds different from castor seeds with respect to endosperm?

SECTION - D

28. (a) Draw a L.S. of a pistil showing pollen tube entering the embryo-sac in an angiosperm and label any six parts other than stigma, style and ovary.

(b) Write the changes a fertilized ovule undergoes within the ovary in an angiosperm plant.

OR

(a) Draw a diagrammatic sectional view of a human seminiferous tubule, and label Sertoli cells, primary spermatocyte, spermatogonium and spermatozoa in it.

(b) Explain the hormonal regulation of the process of spermatogenesis in humans.

29. (a) Write the conclusion drawn by Griffith at the end of his experiment with *Streptococcus pneumoniae.*

(b) How did O. Avery, C MacLeod and M. McCarty prove that DNA was the genetic material? Explain.

OR

(a) Explain the mechanism of sex-determination in humans.

(b) Differentiate between male heterogamety and female heterogamety with the help of an example of each.

30. A person in your colony has recently been diagnosed with AIDS. People/residents in the colony want him to leave the colony for the fear of spread of AIDS.

(a) Write your view on the situation, giving reasons.

(b) List the possible preventive measures that you would suggest to the residents of your locality in a meeting organised by you so that they understand the situation.

(c) Write the symptoms and the causative agent of AIDS.

Solutions

SECTION - A

1. The cell is itself is a mode of reproduction in Monera and Prostista. For example: bacteria and amoeba. **(1 Mark)**

2. Anamnestic response is the secondary immune response which is produced when the body encounters the same antigen which is entered previously in the body. As the body recognises the pathogen, immune system starts producing antibodies against the foreign antigens for subsequent encounter and this response is very intense. **(1 Mark)**

3. The *Himgiri* variety of wheat is resistance to *leaf* and *stripe rust, hill bunt* diseases. **(1 Mark)**

4. Transposons are also called as mobile genetic elements and the process of mRNA silencing is used for the prevention of mRNA translation. In mRNA silencing, transposons are acts as a complementary RNA in order to stop the process of mRNA translation. **(1 Mark)**

Transposons are repetitive DNA sequences that have capability to move from one genome location to another genome location.

5. The green algae acts as producer and they synthesise their own food by the process of photosynthesis. In the deepest strata such as in the benthic zone sunlight is not available. The green algae are not likely found in the deepest strata of the ocean because of the non-availability of sunlight for the process of photosynthesis. **(1 Mark)**

6. Standing crop at a trophic level is referred to the amount of biomass or mass of living material at a successive trophic level at a given time. **(1 Mark)**

7. Motor vehicles equipped with catalytic converter should use unleaded petrol because lead in the petrol inactivates the catalyst. Catalytic converters may reduce the emission of harmful gasses from the automobiles. **(1 Mark)**

8. (i) Genetic diversity refer to the total number of genetic characteristics in the genetic makeup of a species. 1000 varieties of mangoes in India is an example of genetic diversity. The vast genetic diversity in India is observed as it lies within tropical latitudes that provide a constant and predictable environment as well as availability of more solar energy results in higher productivity. **(½ Mark)**

   (ii) The genetic variation represented by the medicinal plant *Rouwolfia vomitoria* which is growing in different Himalayan ranges is because of the potency and concentration of the active chemical (reserpine) produced by this plant. It is an example of genetic diversity. **(½ Mark)**

SECTION - B

9. The fusion of one haploid male gamete with haploid female gamete (egg cells) results in the formation of a diploid zygote and this process is called sexual reproduction. Whereas endosperm is formed when other male gamete move towards the two polar nuclei which is located in the central cell and its fusion with the two polar nuclei results in the formation of triploid primary endosperm nucleus (PEN). This process is called triple fusion. The central cell after triple fusion becomes the **primary endosperm cell (PEC)** and develops into the **endosperm** whereas the zygote develops into an **embryo.** **(2 Marks)**

The process of double fertilisation involves two types of fusions such as syngamy and triple fusion that takes place in the embryo sac of the flowering plants.

10. A cross between a red flower bearing plant and white flower bearing plant of *Antirrhinum* produces all plants having pink flowers is an example of incomplete dominance. **(2 Marks)**

P generation:	RR (red)	X	rr (white)	
	↓		↓	
Gametes:	R		r	
F_1 generation:		Rr (all pink)		
Gametes:	Rr (male)	X	Rr (female)	
F2 generation:	RR (Red)	Rr (pink)	Rr (pink)	rr(white)
	1	1	1	1

The phenotypic and genotypic ratio obtained in incomplete dominance is 1:2:1

Incomplete dominance states that a form of gene interaction in which two alleles that controls a trait is dominant over each other and the progeny obtained is the intermediate of the two alleles.

11. Oparin of Russia and Haldane of England proposed the following:

   (i) The first form of life could come from pre-existing non-living organic molecules such as RNA, proteins, etc. and the formation of life was preceded by chemical evolution such as formation of diverse organic molecules from inorganic constituents. **(1 Mark)**

(ii) The conditions on Earth were - high temperature, volcanic storms, reducing atmosphere containing CH_4, NH_3, and so on. **(1 Mark)**

12. The principle of immunisation or vaccination is based on the property of 'memory' of the immune system. In vaccination, a preparation of antigenic proteins of pathogen or inactivated/ weakened pathogens (vaccine) is introduced into the body. The antibodies that are produced in the body against these antigens would neutralise the pathogenic agents during actual infection and vaccines also generate memory B and T-cells that recognise the pathogen quickly on subsequent exposure and encounters the foreign antigen with a massive production of antibodies. **(2 Marks)**

Immunization refers to the process in which a person is made immune or resistant to an infectious disease by the administration of a vaccine.

OR

Person with cuts and bruises following an accident is administered with tetanus antitoxin provides protection from the infection by bacteria *Clostridium tetani*. This bacterium is responsible for causing tetanus infection which can be fatal if left untreated. The bacterium enters into the body through cuts or wounds and is usually found in soil and manure. So, at the time of accidents there is a higher risk of entering bacteria in the skin and hence tetanus antitoxin is administered in order to reduce the chances of infection by providing passive immunity to the bacterial toxin.

(2 Marks)

The overall ability of a body to fight against disease - causing mircoorganisms by the immune system is called immunity.

13. The production of large holes in 'Swiss cheese' is because of the production of a large amount of carbon dioxide by a bacterium named *Propionibacterium sharmanii*. **(2Marks)**

14. DNA polymerase used in PCR is *Taq* DNA polymerase which is isolated from a bacterium *Thermus aquaticus*. This bacterium is found in hot springs and hydrothermal vents. The *Taq* polymerase remains active at high temperature during denaturation process of PCR. **(2 Marks)**

PCR stands for Polymerase Chain Reaction is a molecular biology technique used for the formation of large number of copies of samples produced in small quantities. PCR amplification is commonly used by medical and forensic applications.

15. The four ways used for the introduction of a desired DNA segment into bacterial cell in the recombinant DNA technology are as follows: **(½ × 4 = 2 Marks)**

(i) **Chemical method:** In this process, the bacterial cells must be first made 'competent' to take up DNA. It is done by treating the bacterial cell with a specific concentration of a divalent cation such as calcium that increases the efficiency with which DNA enters the bacterium through pores in its cell wall. Recombinant DNA can then be forced into such cells by incubating the cells with recombinant DNA on ice, followed by placing them briefly at 42°C (heat shock). Then, putting them back on ice. So, this enables the bacteria to take up the recombinant DNA.

(ii) **Microinjection:** In this method, recombinant DNA is directly injected into the nucleus of an animal cell.

(iii) **Biolistics or gene gun:** This method is suitable for plants, as cells are bombarded with high velocity micro-particles of gold or tungsten coated with DNA.

(iv) **Disarmed pathogen:** In this method, vector is allowed to infect the cell results in the transfer of the recombinant DNA into the host.

16. In humans, insulin is synthesised as a prohormone that contains an extra stretch called the **C peptide** and it is not present in the mature insulin. As a mature insulin contains two short polypeptide chains such as Chain A and Chain B that are linked together by a disulphide bond. The prohormone is non-functional whereas mature insulin is functional. **(2 Marks)**

17. Tropics has more species diversity than polar regions because of the availability of sufficient sunlight that promotes higher productivity. Less seasonal variations are observed in tropic regions than Polar Regions and tropics remains undisturbed form many years so they have a long evolutionary time for diversification of species. **(2Marks)**

18. Yes, it is possible that a species may occupy more than one trophic level in the same ecosystem at the same time. For example, man is an omnivore as he can consume plants so they are called as a primary consumer and when man consumes animals such as goat and chicken which consume plants and become secondary consumer. In this way, a species occupying more than one trophic level in the same ecosystem at the same time. **(2 Marks)**

SECTION - C

19. The process of formation of a mature female gamete is called **oogenesis.** This process is initiated during the embryonic development stage when a couple of million gamete mother cells or oogonia are formed within each fetal ovary as no more oogonia are formed and added after birth.

Such cells start division and enter into prophase-I of the meiotic division. The cells get temporarily arrested at that stage called **Primary oocytes.**

Each primary oocyte then gets surrounded by a layer of granulosa cells and then called **Primary follicle** and the primary follicles get surrounded by more layers of granulosa cells and a new theca. This is called **secondary follicle.**

Then the secondary follicle transform into a tertiary follicle which is characterised by a fluid filled cavity called **Antrum.**

The theca layer is organised into an inner theca internal and an outer theca externa. The primary oocyte within the tertiary follicle grows in size and completes its first meiotic division.

It is an unequal division results in the formation of a large haploid **secondary oocyte** and a tiny first polar body. The tertiary follicle changes into the mature follicle or **Graafian follicle.** The secondary oocyte forms a new membrane called **Zona pellucida**.

The Graafian follicle then ruptures to release the secondary oocyte (ovum) from the ovary by the process called **Ovulation.** **(2 Marks)**

Diagrammatic representation of steps involved in the process of oogenesis: **(1 Mark)**

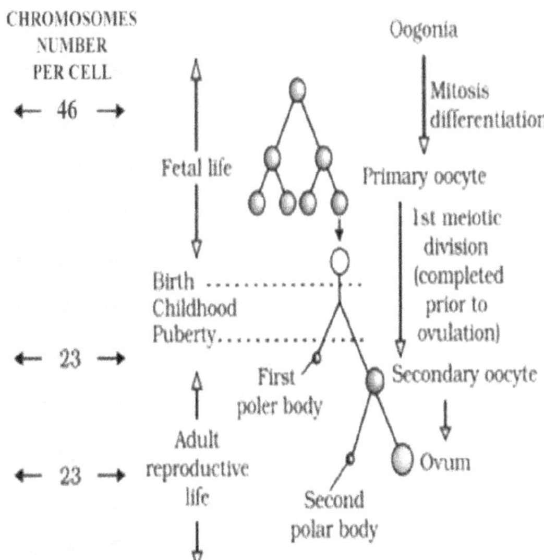

OR

The ARTs suggested to infertile couples are as follows:

(i) **In *vitro* fertilisation (IVF)** technique involves collection of ova from the wife/donor (female) and sperms from the husband/donor (male) are collected and are induced to form zygote under stimulated conditions in the laboratory.

(ii) **Zygote intra fallopian transfer (ZIFT)** involves the transfer of zygote or early embryos upto 8 blastomeres into the fallopian tube of the female.

(iii) **Gameter intra fallopian transfer (GIFT)** involves the transfer of an ovum which is collected from a donor into the fallopian tube of another female who cannot produce egg but can provide suitable environment for fertilisation and its further development. **(3 Marks)**

***ARTs (Assisted reproductive technology)** is used for treatment of infertility in couples who are unable to produce offsprings. This method involves fusion of male gamete (sperm) and female gamete (egg) outside the body.*

20. Haemophilia is a sex linked recessive disorder which is transmitted from unaffected carrier female to male progeny. This disorder is more common among males than females. Humans have 22 pairs of autosomal chromosomes and one pair of sex chromosome. There are 46 chromosomes in humans. Females have XX chromosome while males have X and Y chromosome. So, male offspring inherit X-chromosome from their mother and Y-chromosome from their father. Males only have one X-chromosome if the X-chromosome carries mutation and this is the case of reason that males are suffering from haemophilia, While in females, as they have two X chromosomes, and this is a recessive disorder so females are only the carrier of this disease and can pass this disorder to male offsprings. **(3 Marks)**

Genetic cross for haemophilia:

Parents:	**XX^h (female)**		**X**	**X^hY (male)**
Gamtes:	**X X^h**			**X^hY**
F_1 generation:	**X X^h**	**XY**	**$X^h X^h$**	**X^hY**
	(Carrier female)	(normal male)	(haemophilic female)	(haemophilic male)

Hemophilia is caused because of the absence of blood clotting factor VIII (Hemophilia-A) and IX (haemophilia B) and impairs the ability of the body to control blood clotting and coagulation even by a simple cut.

21. DNA fingerprinting technique is used to describe the parental identification of two newborns in a maternity clinic.

The steps involved in the process of DNA fingerprinting are as follows:

- Isolation of DNA from the new borns and parents.
- DNA digestion by restriction endonucleases
- DNA fragments are separated by electrophoresis technique.
- Separated DNA fragments are transferred (blotting) to synthetic membranes such as nitrocellulose or nylon membrane.
- Hybridisation using labelled VNTR probe and,
- Hybridised DNA fragments are detected by using autoradiography. **(3 Marks)**

*The DNA fingerprinting technique was developed by Alec Jeffreys and he used a satellite DNA as probe that represents a very high degree of polymorphism called **VNTR (Variable Number of Tandem Repeats). VNTRs** are repetitive units of 10-60 bp and show a higher degree of polymorphism as these base pair sequences are different in different individuals.*

22. During post-industrialisation period, the tree trunks became dark due to industrial smoke and soots. So under this condition, the white winged moth did not survive due to predators, dark-winged or melanised moth survived. Whereas before industrialisation, thick growth of almost white-coloured lichen covered the trees-in that background the white winged moth survived but the dark-coloured moth were picked out by predators. **(3 Marks)**

23. Cow dung and other organic wastes are converted into slurry with 90% of water. A small quantity of activated sludge is pumped back into aeration tanks in order to serve as the inoculums. The remaining part of the sludge is pumped into large tanks called anaerobic sludge digesters. During the digestion, mixture of gases is produced called biogas by bacteria. This mixture involves methane, carbon dioxide and hydrogen gas. **(3 Marks)**

The bacteria that produce methane are called methanogens and one commonly known bacterium is Methanobacterium. These bacteria are found in the rumen of cattles and help in the breakdown of cellulose and provide essential nutrition to the cattle.

24. Cotton bollworms destroy the cotton bolls. The strains of *Bacillus thuringiensis* produce proteins that kill several insects such as lepidopterans, coleopterans and dipterans. *Bacillus thuringiensis* forms protein crystals contain a toxic called insecticidal protein. This toxin protein exists in an inactive form protoxins but once an insect ingest the inactive toxin, then it is converted into an active form of toxin due to the alkaline pH of the gut which solubilise the crystals.

The activated toxin binds to the surface of the midgut epithelial cells and creates pores that cause cell swelling and lysis results in death of the insect. The toxin is coded by a gene name **cry.** So, the protein encoded by the genes cryIAB controls corn borer. **(3 Marks)**

25. (i) Measurement of population in a habitat help in the determination of relative abundance of a particular species and their effect of the species on the available resources of habitat.

(ii) In some cases it is very difficult to count the number of organisms for determination of population of an area. For example, in a laboratory culture of bacteria or counting number of trees in a dense forest is impossible as well as consumes lots of time. In such cases, calculation of percentage of the area which is covered by a particular organism than to sit or by counting them by number for the determination of population. **(3 Marks)**

26. The two types of pyramid of biomass are as follows: **(3 Marks)**

(i)

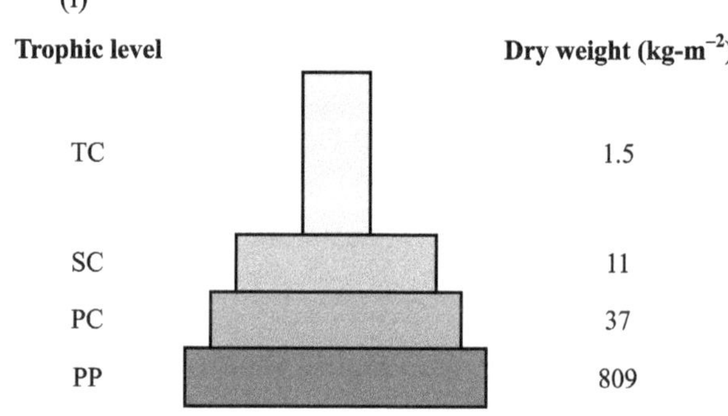

Pyramid of biomass is upright and it occurs in grasslands where the biomass of the producers is much higher than that of primary consumer. This indicates that there is sharp decrease in biomass at higher trophic level.

(ii)

Pyramid of biomass is inverted and it occurs in aquatic ecosystems and the biomass of producers is much lower than that of primary consumers. This inverted pyramid indicates that a small standing crop of phytoplankton supports large standing crop of zooplankton.

27. **(a)** The process of triple fusion involves fusion of other male gamete with two polar nuclei which is located in the central cell results in the formation of a triploid **primary endosperm nucleus (PEN).** The central cell after triple fusion becomes the **primary endosperm cell (PEC)** and develops into the **endosperm.**

Endosperm provides nourishment to the developing embryo in angiosperms.

(b) The water of tender coconut is healthy source of nutrition because it is rich in nutrients such as proteins, carbohydrates, minerals, vitamins and fibre. It can also effectively replenish lost electrolytes in the body.

(c) Mature seeds are of two types such as non-albuminous and albuminous. Pea is a type of non-albuminous seeds that have no residual endosperm as it is completely consumed during embryo development. Whereas castor is a type of albuminous seeds that retain a part of endosperm as it is not completely used during embryo development. **(3 Marks)**

SECTION - D

28. (a) Diagrammatic representation of L.S of flower showing growth of a pollen tube:

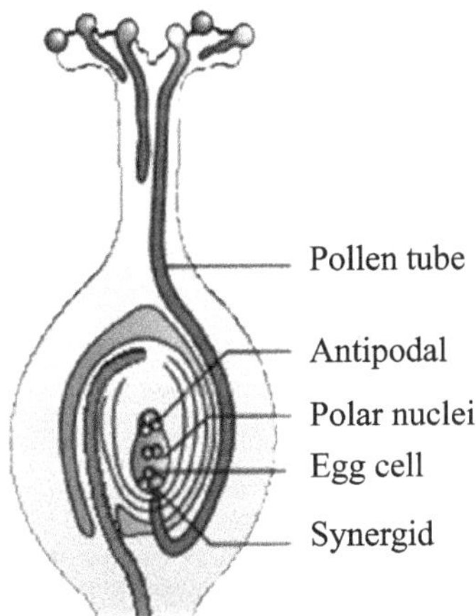

(2 Marks)

(b) When the unfertilized ovule passes through double fertilization and then fertilised ovule is formed which further develops into seed. In this process, the hilum and funiculus are present. Outer integument is developed into texta whereas inner integument is developed into tegman. The chalaza and micropyle are also present while nucellus is absent. In embryo sac, synergids and antipodal cell are degenerate. The central cell then develops into endosperm and egg is developed into the zygote and then into the embryo. **(3 Marks)**

Hilum is the region where the body of the ovule fuses with funicle thus, hilum represents the junction between ovule and funicle.

OR

(a) Diagrammatic representation of sectional view of a seminiferous tubule (2 Marks)

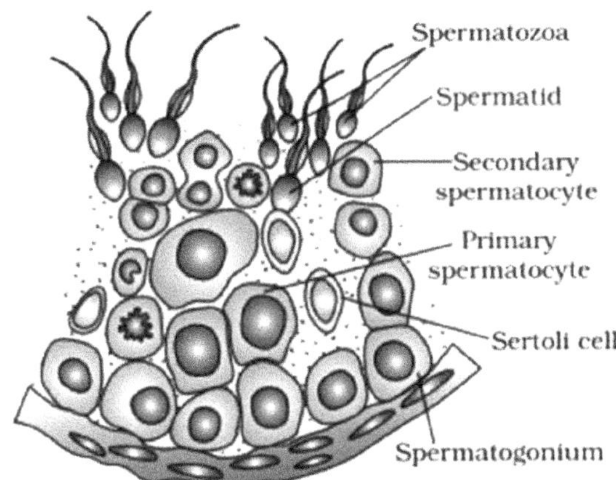

(b) The hormonal regulation of the process of spermatogenesis in humans are as follows: (3 Marks)

- The process of spermatogenesis starts at the age of puberty due to significant increase in the secretion of gonadotrophin releasing hormone (GnRH).
- The increase in the level of GnRH acts at the anterior pituitary gland and also stimulates the secretion of two gonadotropins such as luteinising hormone (LH) and follicle stimulating hormone (FSH).
- LH acts at the Leydig cells and also stimulates the synthesis and secretion of androgens. Androgen then stimulates the process of spermatogenesis.
- FSH acts on the Sertoli cells and also stimulates the secretion of some factors that help in the process of spermiogenesis.

29. (a) Griffith concluded that the R-strain bacteria had somehow been transformed by the heat-killed S strain bacteria. Some 'transforming principle,' transferred from the heat killed S-strain that had enabled the R strain to synthesise a smooth polysaccharide coat and become virulent. This is because of the transfer of the genetic material. **(2 Marks)**

(b) The biochemical characterisation of Transforming principle was determined by Oswald Avery, Colin Macleod and Maclyn McCarty. Prior it was thought that the genetic material was protein.

The following steps are involved in his experiment:

- They purified biochemicals such as proteins, DNA and RNA from the heat-killed S cells to determine which one could transform live R cells into S cells.
- They discovered that DNA alone from S bacteria caused R bacteria to become transformed.

- They also discovered that protein-digesting enzymes such as proteases and RNA-digesting enzymes such as RNases did not affect the transformation.
- Hence, it was proved that the transforming substance was not protein and RNA.
- Digestion with DNase did inhibit transformation and the DNA caused the transformation.

So, they concluded that DNA is the hereditary material. **(3 Marks)**

OR

(a) The chromosome pattern in the human female is XX and that in the male is XY. So, all the haploid gametes produced by the female (ova) have the sex chromosome X while in the male gametes (sperms) the sex chromosome could be either X or Y. Hence, 50 % of the sperms carry the X chromosome whereas the other 50 % carry the Y. After the fusion of the male and female gametes the zygote carries either XX or XY depends on whether the sperm carrying X or Y chromosome fertilized the ovum.

Zygote carrying XX would develop into a female baby and XY would become male baby. It is concluded that the sex of a child is dependent on father not on mother. **(3 Marks)**

(b) The difference between male and female heterogamety are as follows:

Male heterogamety: Male heterogamety in human males is XY while males of insects such as grasshopper and bugs are XO.

Female heterogamety: Female heterogamety is observed in some species of birds, fishes and insects. Females of butterfly and moth consists of ZO sex chromosomes and females of fish, reptiles and birds consist of ZW sex chromosome. **(2 Marks)**

30. (a) Recently AIDS is diagnosed in our area and it is a life-threatening disease. So it is our prime responsibility to create awareness among the people in order to combat the situation. There is no need to isolate the person who is suffering from AIDS from the society. The infected person needs help and sympathy instead of being shunned by society. We must have educated people about AIDS. **(1 Mark)**

(b) In a society meeting, we must have to educate people about the mode of infection of AIDS as it cannot be spread through direct contact with the infected person. It can be spread by following reasons:

- Sexual intercourse with multiple partners
- Transfusion of contaminated blood and blood products
- By sharing of infected needle as in case of intravenous drug abusers
- From infected mother to her foetus through placenta.

Preventive measures involves:

- Use of condom during sexual intercourse with the infected person.
- Proper disposal of needles after use
- Use clean needle
- Pregnant women take medical care immediately
- Avoid sharing of sharp objects or needles **(2 Marks)**

(c) **AIDS** is Acquired Immunodeficiency Syndrome and is caused by the Human Immuno deficiency Virus (HIV), which is a group of viruses called retrovirus. This virus has an envelope that encloses the RNA genome.

Symptoms: The infected person is suffering from a bouts of fever, diarrhoea and weight loss. Due to decrease in the number of helper T lymphocytes, T person starts suffering from infections caused by *Mycobacterium,* viruses, fungi and even parasites like *Toxoplasma.*

The infected person becomes immune deficient as the patient is unable to protect themselves from such infections. **(2 Marks)**

*AIDS can be diagnosed by **Enzyme Linked Immuno-sorbent assay (ELISA)**. It can be treated by using anti-retroviral drugs which is partially effective and such drugs only prolong the life of the patient but cannot prevent death and is inevitable.*

Delhi 2013

CBSE Board Solved Paper

Time Allowed : 3 Hours *Maximum Marks : 70*

General Instructions:

(i) All questions are compulsory.

(ii) This question paper consist of **four** Sections **A, B, C** and **D.** Section **A** contains **8** questions of **one** mark each, Section **B** is of **10** questions of **two** marks each, Section **C** is of **9** questions of **three** marks each and Section **D** is of **3** questions of **five** marks each.

(iii) There is no overall choice. However, internal choice has been provided in **one** question of **2** marks, **one** question of **3** marks and **two** questions of **5** marks weightage. A student has to attempt only **one** of the alternatives in such questions.

(iv) Wherever necessary, the diagrams drawn should be neat and properly labelled.

SECTION - A

1. An anther with malfunctioning tapetum often fails to produce viable male gametophytes. Give any one reason.

2. Why sharing of injection needles between two individuals is not recommended?

3. Name the enzyme and state its property that is responsible for continuous and discontinuous replication of the two strands of a DNA molecule.

4. Identify the examples of convergent evolution from the following:

(i) Flippers of penguins and dolphins

(ii) Eyes of octopus and mammals

(iii) Vertebrate brains

5. Write the importance of MOET.

6. Why is the enzyme cellulase needed for isolating genetic material from plant cells and not from the animal cells?

7. Name the type of biodiversity represented by the following:

(a) 50,000 different strains of rice in India

(b) Estuaries and alpine meadows in India.

8. Write the equation that helps in deriving the net primary productivity of an ecosystem.

SECTION - B

9. Geitonogamous flowering plants are genetically autogamous but functionally crosspollinated. Justify.

10. When and where do chorionic villi appear in humans? State their function.

11. In a cross bet:-veen two tall pea plants some of the offsprings produced were dwarf. Show with the help of Punett square how this is possible.

12. A student on a school trip started sneezing and wheezing soon after reaching the hill station for no explained reasons. But, on return to the plains, the symptoms disappeared. What is such a response called? How does the body produce it ?

13. Name two commonly used bioreactors. State the importance of using a bioreactor.

14. Write the function of adenosine deaminase enzyme. State the cause of ADA deficiency in humans. Mention a possible permanent cure for a ADA deficiency patient

15. Expand the following and mention one application of each:

(i) PCR

(ii) ELISA

OR

(a) Mention the difference in the mode of action of exonuclease and endonuclease.

(b) How does restriction endonuclease function ?

16. Name any two sources of e-Wastes and write two different ways for their disposal.

17. Why the pyramid of energy is always upright ? Explain.

18. Explain why very small animals are rarely found in polar region.

SECTION - C

19. Draw a diagram of the microscopic structure of human sperm. Label the following parts in it and write their functions.

(a) Acrosome

(b) Nucleus

(c) Middle piece

20. With the help of any two suitable examples explain the effect of anthropogenic actions on organic evolution.

21. (a) Why is human ABO blood group gene considered a good example of multiple alleles ?

(b) Work out a cross up to FI generation only. between a mother with blood group A (Homozygous) and the father with blood group B (Homozygous). Explain the pattern of inheritance exhibited.

22. Describe the structure of a RNA polynucleotide chain having four different types of nucleotides.

23. Differentiate between inbreeding and outbreeding in cattle. State one advantage and one disadvantage for each one of them.

24. (a) Why are the fruit juices bought from market clearer as compared to those made at home?

(b) Name the bioactive molecules produced by Trichoderma oolysoorurn and Monaseus purpureus.

25. (a) Why are transgenic animals so called ?

(b) Explain the role of transgenic animals in (i) Vaccine safety and (ii) Biological products with the help of an example each.

26. How have human activities caused desertification ? Explain.

OR

How does algal bloom destroy the quality of a fresh water body ? Explain.

27. Explain mutualism with the help of any two examples. How is it different from commensalism ?

SECTION - D

28. (a) Draw a diagrammatic sectional view of a mature anatropous ovule and label the following parts in it :

(i) that develops into seed coat.

(ii) that develops into an embryo after fertilization.

(iii) that develops into an endosperm in an albuminous seed.

(iv) through which the pollen tube gains entry into the embryo sac.

(v) that attaches the ovule to the placenta.

(b) Describe the characteristic features of wind pollinated flowers.

OR

(a) Draw a diagrammatic sectional view of the female reproductive system of human and label the parts

(i) where the secondary oocytes develop

(ii) which helps in collection of ovum after ovulation

(iii) where fertilization occurs

(iv) where implantation of embryo occurs.

(b) Explain the role of pituitary and the ovarian hormones in menstrual cycle in human females.

29. (a) Write the conclusion drawn by Griffith at the end of his experiment with *Streptococcus pneumoniae.*

(b) How did O. Avery, C MacLeod and M. McCarty prove that DNA was the genetic material? Explain.

OR

(a) Explain the mechanism of sex-determination in humans.

(b) Differentiate between male heterogamety and female heterogamety with the help of an example of each.

30. A child suffering from Thalassemia is born to a normal couple. But the mother is being blamed by the family for delivering a sick baby.

(a) What is Thalassemia?

(b) How would you counsel the family not to blame the mother for delivering a child suffering from this disease? Explain.

(c) List the values your counselling can propagate in the families.

Solutions

SECTION - A

1. Tapetum provides nourishment to the developing pollen grain and a malfunctioned tapetum fails to produce viable male gametes as they lack nourishment. **(1 Mark)**

Tapetum is the innermost layer of microsporangium and cells of the tapetum possess dense cytoplasm and generally have more than one nucleus.

2. Sharing of injection needles is not recommended between two individuals because it leads to the transmission of fatal and incurable diseases such as hepatitis B and AIDS that can be transmitted from one person to another on coming in contact with the body fluid of an infected person. **(1 Mark)**

3. An enzyme DNA-dependent DNA polymerase is responsible for the continuous and discontinuous replication of the DNA strand. DNA-dependent DNA polymerase enzyme catalyses the polymerisation of DNA in only direction such as from 5'→3' and is called coding strand and is discontinuous. Whereas the complementary strand having polarity 3'→5' is called antisense strand and is continuous. **(1 Mark)**

The discontinuously synthesised fragments are joined together by an enzyme DNA ligase.

4. (i) Flippers of penguins and Dolphin is an example of convergent evolution and are analogous structures.
   (ii) Eyes of octopus and mammals are also an example of convergent evolution as the structures are analogous structures.

Analogous structures are those that are not anatomically similar structures but perform similar functions.

   (iii) Vertebrate brain is an example of divergent evolution and is homologous organ. **(1 Mark)**

5. MOET stands for Multiple Ovulation Embryo Transfer. It is animal breeding programme for herd improvement. This technology has been demonstrated for cattle, sheep, rabbits, buffaloes, mares and so on in order to increase the high milk yielding breeds of females. It also helps in the formation of high quality (lean meat with less lipid) meat-yielding bulls that have been bred successfully in order to increase the herd size in a shorter time. **(1 Mark)**

6. Plants cells have cellulose in their cell wall that can be degraded by cellulase enzyme in order to isolate DNA. While in case of animal cell, cell wall is absent and due to this, cellulase enzyme is not required for isolation of DNA **(1 Mark)**

Lysozyme enzyme is used for breaking bacterial cell whereas chitinase enzyme is used for breaking fungal cells.

7. (a) The availability of 50,000 genetically different strains of rice is an example of genetic diversity. Genetic diversity is produced due to difference in soil found in different regions. It is also occurs due to different agricultural practices as well as use of various horticulture techniques that are used in India.

Genetic diversity is defined as the type of diversity in which the number and types of genes as well as chromosomes that are found in different species. It leads to variation in the genes and their alleles in the same species. It leads to speciation as well as evolution of new species.

   (b) The availability of estuaries and alpine meadows in India is an example of ecological diversity. India has a greater ecosystem diversity than a Scandinavian country like Norway. **(1 Mark)**

Ecological diversity is defined as the type of biodiversity which involves the variation in the ecosystems that are found in a region or the variation in ecosystems over the whole planet.

8. Net primary productivity is defined as the Gross primary productivity (GPP) minus respiration losses (R).

   NPP = GPP – R

   Where Gross primary productivity of an ecosystem is defined as the rate of production of organic matter during photosynthesis. **(1 Mark)**

Productivity refers to the rate of biomass production whereas primary productivity refers to the amount of biomass or organic matter produced per unit area over a time period by plants during photosynthesis.

SECTION - B

9. Geitonogamy involves the transfer of pollen grains from the anther to the stigma of another flower of the same plant. Geitonogamy is functionally cross-pollination that involves pollinating agent but genetically is similar to autogamy since the pollen grains come from the same plant. **(2 Marks)**

Autogamy is a type of self-pollination in which pollination is achieved within the same flower. In this, transfer of pollen grains from the anther to the stigma of the same flower.

10. After implantation, finger-like projections appear on the trophoblast called chorionic villi. It is surrounded by the uterine tissue and maternal blood. The chorionic villi and uterine tissue become interdigitated with each other and jointly form a structural and functional unit between the developing embryo or foetus and maternal body called placenta. **(2 Marks)**

The placenta is connected with the embryo through umbilical cord which helps in the transportation of substances to and from the embryo.

11. The given cross represents in a form of Punett square are as follows:

Parents:	Tt	X	Tt	
Gametes:	Tt	Tt		
F_1 generation:	Tt	Tt	Tt	tt
	(Tall plant)	(Tall plant)	(Tall plant)	(Dwarf)

When two heterozygous tall parents are crossed, three heterozygous tall and one dwarf plant is obtained. **(2 Marks)**

Punett square was developed by a British geneticist, Reginald C.Punnett and is defined as a graphical representation for calculation of probability of all the possible genotypes of offsprings in a genetic cross.

12. The student is suffering from allergy and the substances to which such as immune response is produced are called allergens. Allergy is because of the release of chemicals such as histamine and serotonin from the mast cells. **(2 Marks)**

The antibodies produced to allergic response are of IgE type.

13. The two commonly used bioreactors are stirred-tank bioreactor and sparged stirred-tank bioreactor.

A stirred-tank bioreactor is cylindrical or with a curved base in order to facilitate the mixing of reactor contents and stirrer facilitates the mixing and availability of oxygen throughout the bioreactor. Alternatively air can be bubbled through the reactor. Whereas in a sparged stirred-tank bioreactor, a sparge which is a ring made of metal or glass that facilitates the mixing and oxygen availability throughout the bioreactor.

Bioreactors are important as large volume (100-1000 litres) of culture can be processed. Bioreactor provides optimal conditions for growth such as temperature, pH, substrate, salts, vitamins and oxygen for production of desired product. **(2 Marks)**

Bioreactors are the large vessels in which raw materials are biologically converted into specific products such as enzymes, proteins by using animal cells, plant cells or microbes.

14. ADA deficiency is caused because of the deletion of the gene that code for adenosine deaminase enzyme. Severe combined Immunodeficiency disorder (SCID) is caused because of the defect in gene which codes for adenosine deaminase enzyme. The enzyme plays crucial role in the proper functioning of immune system.

ADA (Adenosine deaminase deficiency) can be treated by enzyme replacement therapy in which functional ADA is given to the patient by injection. In this process:

- Lymphocytes from the blood of the patients are grown in a culture outside the body.
- A functional ADA cDNA (using a retroviral vector) is then introduced into these lymphocytes which are subsequently returned to the patient.

Disadvantages associated with enzyme-replacement therapy are:

- This method is not completely curative
- The cells are immortal as the patients require periodic infusion of such genetically engineered lymphocytes.

ADA deficiency can be permanently cured if gene isolates from marrow cells produces ADA is introduced into cells at early embryonic stages. **(2 Marks)**

The first clinical gene therapy was given in 1990 to a 4-year old girl suffering from adenosine deaminase (ADA) deaminase.

15. (i) PCR stand for Polymerase Chain Reaction. It is a molecular biology for the synthesis of many copies of a specific DNA in vitro. It is used for the diagnosis of infectious diseases even if the small is present in minute quantities.

PCR requires sets of primers (small chemically synthesised oligonucleotides that are complementary to the regions of DNA) and Enzyme Taq DNA polymerase.

The enzyme Taq DNA polymerase is a thermostable enzyme as it can tolerate higher temperature (upto 96 °C) as it is extracted from a bacterium Thermus aquaticus.

(ii) ELISA stands for Enzyme Linked Immunosorbent Assay is a molecular biology and immunological technique used for the diagnosis of AIDS. It is used for the measurement of antibodies in the blood and the test can be used for the determination of antibodies in the blood during infection. **(2 Marks)**

The enzyme used in ELISA is horseradish peroxidise.

OR

(a) Restriction enzymes are larger class of enzymes called nucleases and they are of two types exonucleases and endonucleases.

Exonucleases remove nucleotides from the ends of the DNA whereas endonucleases make cuts at specific positions within the DNA.

(b) Restriction endonuclease functions by 'inspecting' the length of a DNA Sequence and one it recognise the sequence, it will get bind with the DNA and cut each of the two strands of the double helix at specific points in their sugar-phosphate backbones.

Each restriction endonuclease recognises a specific nucleotide sequences the DNA. Restriction enzymes cut the strand of DNA away from the centre of the palindrome sites but between the same two bases on the opposite strands.

This leaves single stranded portions at the ends and there are overhanging stretches called **sticky ends** on each strand. These are named so because they form hydrogen bonds with their complementary cut. This stickiness of the ends facilitates the action of the enzyme DNA ligase.

Restriction endonucleases are used in genetic engineering for formation of 'recombinant' molecules of DNA, which are composed of DNA from different sources or genomes. **(2 Marks)**

Diagrammatic representation of steps involved in the formation of recombinant DNA by action of restriction endonuclease:

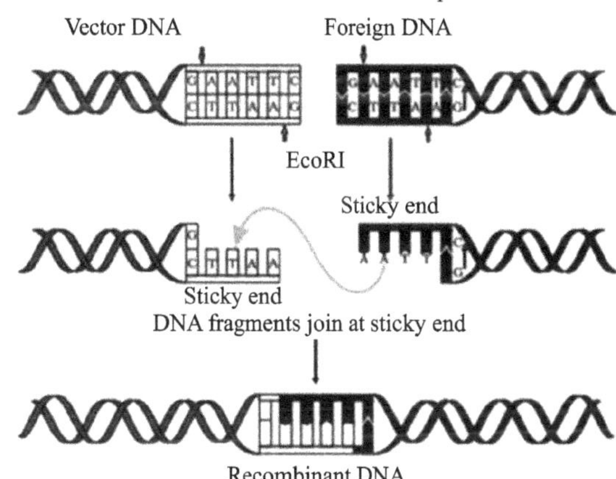

Palindrome is group of letters that form the same words when read both forward and backward, e.g., 'MALAYAM'.

16. Irreparable computers and other electronic goods such as mobile phones are two sources of electronic wastes (e-wastes).

The e-wastes are buried in landfills or incinerated. **(2 Marks)**

17. The pyramid of energy is always upright because the energy flow in a food chain is always unidirectional and also with every increasing trophic level, some amount of energy is lost into the environment and never goes back to the sun.

Diagrammatic Representation of Pyramid of energy:

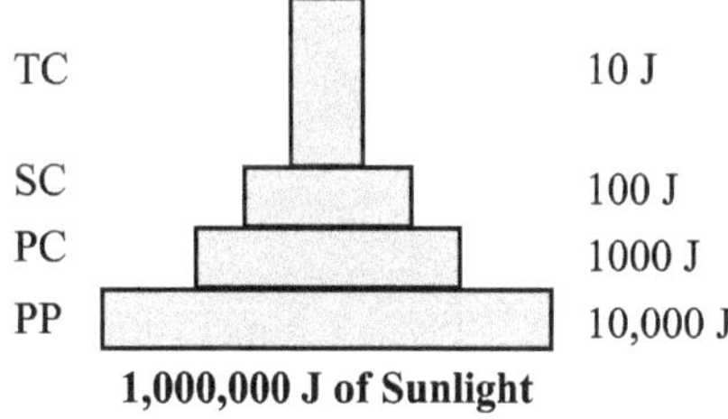

(2 Marks)

The pyramid of energy represents that primary producers converts only 1% of the energy in the sunlight available to them into NPP.

18. Small animals have a larger surface area relative their volume and they tends to lose body heat fast when it is cold outside. They have to expand much energy for generation of body heat through metabolism and this is reason that small animals are rarely found in the polar regions. **(2 Marks)**

SECTION - D

19. Diagrammatic representation of human sperm:

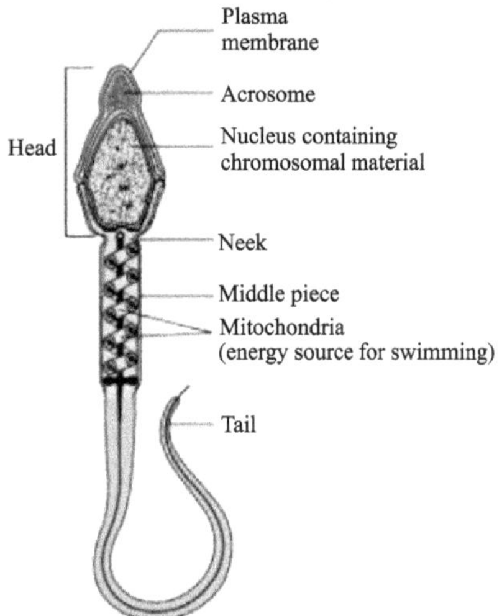

(a) **Acrosome:** The anterior portion of sperm head contains an elongated haploid nucleus and is covered by a cap-like structure called acrosome. It is filled with enzymes that help in fertilisation of the ovum. **(1 Mark)**

The acrosome contains hyaluronidase enzyme that breaks the outer membrane called zona pellucida layer of the ovum and allows the haploid nucleus of the sperm to fuse with the haploid nucleus in the ovum.

(b) **Nucleus:** The nucleus of the sperm cell contains the genetic material such as DNA and during the process of fertilisation; the haploid nucleus of the sperm tends to fuse with haploid nucleus of the egg to form a diploid zygote. **(1 Mark)**

(c) **Middle piece:** The middle piece possesses numerous mitochondria, which produces energy for the movement of tail that facilitates sperm motility which is essential for fertilisation. **(1 Mark)**

20. The effect of anthropogenic actions on organic evolution:

(i) **Industrial melanism:** Before industrialization, it was observed that there were more white-winged moths or melanised moths were found on the trees than dark-winged moths. But after industrialization in 1920s, it was observed that there were more dark-winged moths were found in the same area. It occurs because during post-industrialisation period, the tree trunks became dark due to industrial smoke and soots. In this condition, the white-winged moth did not survive because of predators. Hence dark-winged or melanised moth survived.

(ii) Use of herbicides and pesticides results in the selection of resistant varieties in very short time scale. It also leads to the development of microbes resistant to several antibiotics in a shorter time period because of anthropogenic actions. **(3 Marks)**

21. (a) The inheritance of human blood group is an example of codominance and multiple alleles. ABO blood grouping in human beings are controlled by I gene. The plasma membrane of the red blood cells has sugar polymers that are found on the surface of RBCs and is controlled by this gene.

The *I* gene has three alleles I^A, I^B and *i*. The gene I^A and I^B are dominant over *i* and both I^A and I^B express their own types of sugars. This phenomenon is called **Codominance.** Hence, red blood cells have both A and B types of sugars. While i allele do not produce any sugar. There are three different alleles and there are six different genotypes of the human ABO blood types. **(2 Marks)**

Tabular representation of genetic basis of Blood Groups in Human population:

Allele from Parent 1	Allele from Parent 2	Genotype of offspring	Blood types of offspring
I^A	I^A	$I^A I^A$	A
I^A	I^B	$I^A I^B$	AB
I^A	i	$I^A i$	A
I^B	I^A	$I^A I^B$	AB
I^B	I^B	$I^B I^B$	B
I^B	i	$I^B i$	B
i	i	$i\,i$	O

(b) **Genetic Cross:**

Parents: $I^A I^A$ (Mother) X $I^B I^B$ (Father)

Gametes: I^A I^A X I^B I^B

F_1 generation: $I^A I^B$ $I^A I^B$ $I^A I^B$ $I^A I^B$

The above cross indicates that, if the mother has A blood group (homozygous) and father has B blood group (homozygous) conditions, then, all the offsprings will have AB blood group. **(1 Mark)**

22. RNA (Ribonucleic acid) is a single stranded nucleic acid. It is a polymer of ribonucleotides that contains four nitrogenous bases such as adenine, guanine, uracil and cytosine.

Nucleoside = Nitrogenous base + Pentose sugar –ribose sugar (linked by N-glycosidic bond)

Nucleotide = Nucleoside + phosphate group (linked by phosphodiester bond)

Nucleotides are linked together by 3'-5' phosphodiester bond for the formation of polynucleotide chain of RNA.

In a polynucleotide chain, a phosphate moiety remains free at 5' end of ribose sugar (5' end of polymer chain) and one –OH group remains free at 3' end of ribose (3' end of polymer chain). **(3 Marks)**

Diagrammatic representation of RNA polynucleotide:

5' phosphate
3' hydroxyl
OH
A U G C

Note

RNA is unstable because of the presence of 2'-OH group at second position in ribonucleotide as well as the presence of uracil in place of thymine.

23. **Inbreeding:** Inbreeding refers to the mating of more closely related individuals within the same breed for 4-6 generations.

Reduced fertility and productivity in a herd of cattle is because of inbreeding depression. Inbreeding depression occurs because of inbreeding. This problem can be overcome by mating of selected animals with the unrelated superior animals of the same breed. This helps to restore the fertility and productivity.

Disadvantage of inbreeding is inbreeding depression. Inbreeding reduces fertility and productivity of an animal.

Advantage of inbreeding is it increases homozygosity as inbreeding helps in the development of pureline in any animal.

It can be overcome by using different technique such as:

Outbreeding in which breeding of the unrelated animals that may be between individuals of the same breed but no common ancestors or between different breeds (cross-breeding) or different species (inter-specific hybridisation).

Advantages of outbreeding is that it produces hybrids with desirable characters such as better lactation period, high milk productions and high-quality meat.

Disadvantage of outbreeding: It causes outbreeding depression because of this there is decline in reproductive fitness. **(3 Marks)**

24. (a) The bottled juices that we have brought from the market are clearer as compared to those made at home because the bottled juices are clarified by the use of pectinases and proteases enzymes.

(b) Trichoderma polysporum is fungus that produces an bioactive molecule called cyclosporin A that is used as an immunosuppressive agents in organ-transplant patients.

Monascus purpureus is an yeast that produces statin which is used as a blood-cholesterol lowering agent. **(3 Marks)**

Statin acts by competitively inhibiting the enzyme responsible for synthesis of cholesterol.

25. (a) Animals that have had their DNA manipulated to possess and express a foreign of interest are known as transgenic animals. Transgenic animals such as rats, rabbits, pigs, sheep, cows and fish have been produced.

(b) (i) Vaccine safety: Transgenic mice are being developed for use in testing the safety of vaccines before they are used on humans. Transgenic mice are being used for testing the safety of the polio vaccine.

(ii) Biological products: Medicines required for treatment of certain human diseases that contains biological products but are expensive to make.

So, transgenic animals that produce useful biological products can be created by the introduction of the portion of DNA (or genes) that codes for a particular product such as human protein called alpha-1-antitrypsin) which is used for the treatment of emphysema.

Similarly, transgenic animals are used for the treatment of phenylketonuria (PKU) and cystic fibrosis. In 1997, the first transgenic cow, Rosie, produced human protein-enriched milk (2.4 grams per litre). The milk contained the human alpha-lactalbumin and was nutritionally a more balanced product for human babies than natural cow-milk. **(3 Marks)**

26. Human activities such as over-cultivation, unrestricted grazing, deforestation and poor irrigation practices results in arid patches of land. The open lands without any cover of vegetation are prone to soil erosion.

The soil erodes are unable to provide nutrition to the plants. The land becomes barren over the years and such large barren patches extend and also meet over time in order to form a desert. Rapid urbanisation is also responsible for desertification. **(3 Marks)**

Desertification is a type of land degradation in which biological productivity is lost due to natural processes or induced by human activities whereas fertile areas become increasingly more arid.

OR

Presence of large amount of nutrients in water promotes the excessive growth of planktonic or free-floating algae called algal bloom. It imparts a distinct colour to the water bodies and algal blood leads to cause deterioration of the water quality and fish mortality. Some bloom-forming algae are extremely toxic to human beings and animals.

(3 Marks)

27. Mutualism is a type of population interaction that confers benefits on both the interacting species. For example: lichens represent an intimate mutualistic relationship between a fungus and photosynthesising algae or cyanobacteria.

The Mycorrihzae are associations between fungi and the roots of higher plants. The fungi help the plant in the absorption of essential nutrients from the soil while the plant in turn provides the fungi with energy-yielding carbohydrates.

Commensalism is a type of population interaction in which one species benefits and other is neither harmed nor benefitted.

For example: an orchid growing as an epiphyte on a mango branch and barnacles growing on the back of a whale benefit while neither the mango tree not the whale derives any apparent benefit. **(3 Marks)**

SECTION - E

28. (a) **Diagrammatic representation of a typical anatropous ovule:**

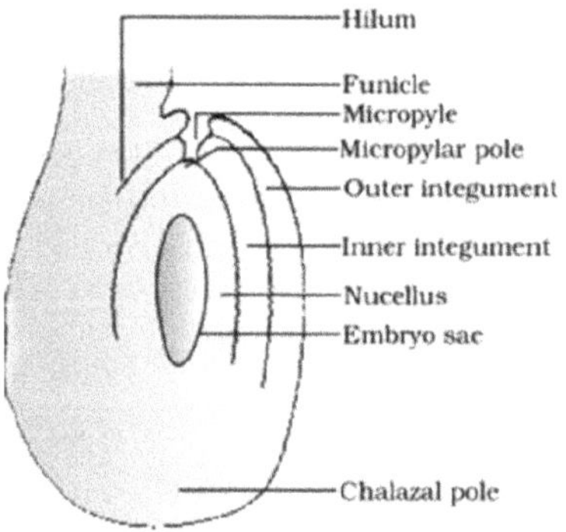

(i) Integument
(ii) Embryo sac
(iii) Nucellus
(iv) Micropyle
(v) Funicle **(2 Marks)**

(b) The characteristic features of wind-pollinated flowers are as follows:

- Pollen grains are light, dry and non-sticky
- Flower produces a large number of pollen grains.
- Open flowers with well-exposed stamen so that pollen can easily be dispersed
- Flowers have a large and feathery stigma.

(3 Marks)

OR

(a) **Diagrammatic representation of section view of female reproductive system:**

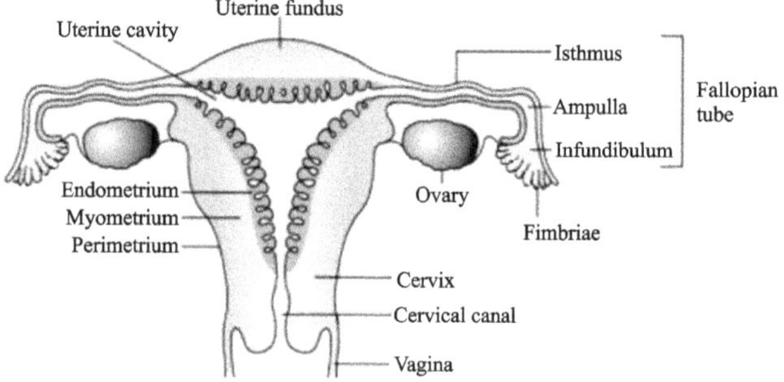

(i) Ovary
(ii) Fimbriae
(iii) Isthmus and ampulla junction
(iv) Endometrium **(2 Marks)**

(b) Changes that takes place in the ovary and uterus during menstrual cycle are caused because of the change in the levels of pituitary and ovarian hormones. After menstrual phase gonadrotropin hormone such as LH (luteinising hormone) and follicular stimulating hormone (FSH) are released from pituitary. Their level gradually increases during follicular phase and it stimulates the development of follicles and secretion of estrogen hormone by growing follicles. So, both LH and FSH attain peak on 13th and 14th day. Rapid secretion of LH causes ovulation on day 14.

During luteal phases, Graafian follicle changes into corpus luteum which secretes progesterone which plays an important role in the maintenance of endometrium that is necessary for implantation. **(3 Marks)**

29. Malaria is caused by *Plasmodium* which is a tiny protozoan. Different species of *Plasmodium* such as *P. vivax, P. malaria,* and *P. falciparum* are responsible for different types of malaria.

Plasmodium enters the human body as sporozoites (infectious form) through the bite of infected female Anopheles mosquito. The parasites initially multiply within the liver cells and then attack the red blood cells (RBCs) results in their rupture.

The rupture of RBCs is associated with release of a toxic substance, haemozoin, which is responsible for the chill and high fever recurring every three to four days. Such parasites enter the mosquito's body and undergo further development. The parasites multiply within them in order to form sporozoites that are stored in their salivary glands.

When these mosquitoes bite a human, the sporozoites are introduced into the human body and initiate the events.

(5 Marks)

Diagrammatic representation of stages of the life cycle of Plasmodium:

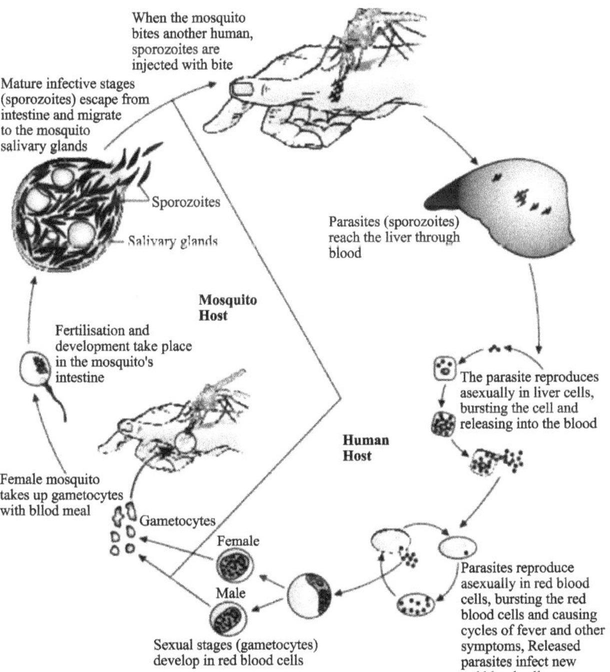

Note

Malignant malaria is caused by the infection of Plasmodium falciparum which is the most serious one and can even be fatal. The malarial parasite requires two hosts such as human and mosquitoes –to complete its life cycle and the female Anopheles mosquito is the vector.

OR

(a) Plant breeding is the purposeful manipulation of plant species in order to create desired plant type that are better suited for cultivation, give better yields and are disease resistant.

Classical plant breeding involves two processes such as:

(i) Hybridisation of pure lines

(ii) Artificial selection for producing plant with desired characters of higher yield or resistance to diseases.

(2 Marks)

(b) The process of artificial induction of chemicals through the use of chemicals or radiations such as gamma radiations and selection as well as use of plant that have desirable character as a source in breeding is called mutation breeding.

For example: In mung bean, resistance to yellow mosaic virus and powdery mildew were induced by mutations.

(1 Mark)

Note

Mutation is the process by which genetic variations are created through changes in the base sequence within the genes results in the creation of a new character or trait which is not found in the parental type.

(c) Biofortification is a type of breeding programme in which the breeding crops with high levels of vitamins and minerals or higher protein and healthier fats is the most practical means for improvement of public health.

Breeding for improved nutritional quality is undertaken with the objectives of improving:

(i) Protein content and quality

(ii) Oil content and quality

(iii) Vitamin content and

(iv) Micronutrient and mineral content.

Biofortification is a boon for crops such as maize, wheat and rice. As the maize hybrids contains twice the amount of the amino acids lysine and tryptophan as compared to existing maize hybrid.

Wheat variety such as Atlas 66, contains a high protein content and it has been used as a donor for improving cultivated wheat. Iron-fortified rice variety is also developed that contains five times iron than commonly used varieties of rice.

Several vegetables are also rich in Vitamins and minerals for example carrot enriched in vitamin A, spinach, pumpkin, vitamin C enriched bitter gourd, bathua, mustard, tomato. Iron and calcium enriched spinach and bathua, protein enriched beans such as broad, lablab, French and garden peas. **(2 Marks)**

All the biofortified vegetables are developed by Indian Agricultural Research Institute.

30. (a) Thalassemia is an autosomal recessive disorder. It is caused due to the mutation or deletion of gene that controls the formation of globin chain of haemoglobin. This results in anaemia. **(1 Mark)**

(b) Thalassemia is an autosomal recessive disorder as in this disorder the mutation is carried on one of the autosomes, so the carrier can be any one of the two parents and has an equal probability for coming from both mother and father. So, to just blame the mother for the child's abnormality is unjustified. **(2 Marks)**

(c) The following values can be given to the families such as:

- provide a healthy diet to the children
- accepting their child with all the positives and negatives
- neither of the parents are responsible for giving birth to a sick child
- the defect is caused because of a random change in the genes of the child
- provide emotional support to child to overcome his/her anxiety, depression and fear about the disorder. **(2 Marks)**

Thalassemia is a type of Mendelian disorder.

www.ingramcontent.com/pod-product-compliance
Ingram Content Group UK Ltd.
Pitfield, Milton Keynes, MK11 3LW, UK
UKHW061133310726
14090UKWH00037B/1282

9 789355 642707